... k wears me wherever I go **Does no...**
-broke mine Suit. Degree. Still afraid...
point of it all? Power *Git y'all's f...*
d for Barack Obama Colors run together. Why can't people? *I he...*
ay no attention to my packaging *I am STILL not fro...*
Whites also impress you?! Diversity don't count, if it's Whi...
What if classrooms can't change racism? Not Chines...
...u mean, "you" people? I am not like the rest *Easy...*
g you Hardest jails to escape are gateless Pride or crute...
...? Am I failing my Latino son? *I am not like my paren...*
k guy I'm a girl. Not a fantasy *To you, always th...*
Chinese on the phone Really, but you don't look Mexica...
nan Every now and then, I remember Grandparen...
ong Angry Black men are so scary *Embarrassed that I'...*
...uilt trip *Stop seeing my son as predator* I was taugh...
...ays putting other people at ease *You don't have to whisp...*
...aightening my hair *My natural hair isn't a statemen...*
...ck is harder Red hair gets the most stares *Black kid...*
...Just stop making everything about race *Repeating prope...*
...y name? Try harder Born in America. I am American Yo...
...e 100-years ago *So much depends on so little* So...
be wrong? This old wound will never heal No, i did no...
...chicken in public *Underneath we all taste like chicke...*
...'re so similar? Not "illegal" human and deservin...
Hispanic is not a race *You're White and you can dance...*
...uCajun You feel superior but you're not *Since whe...*
...der why I'm mad Worry *I will say the wrong thin...*

100
YEARS

SIMON &
SCHUSTER

ALSO BY MICHELE NORRIS

The Grace of Silence: A Family Memoir

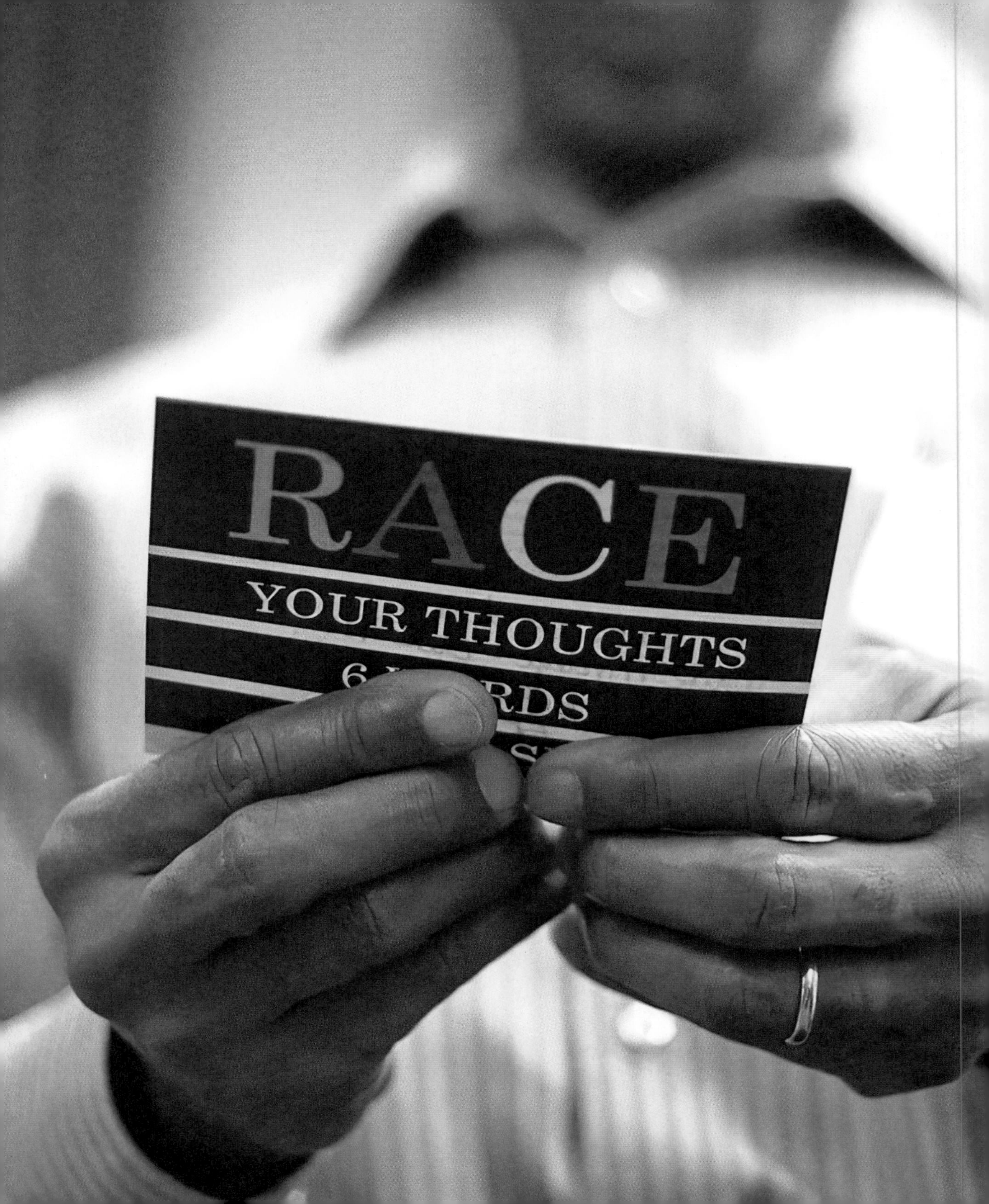
RACE
YOUR THOUGHTS

Our Hidden Conversations

WHAT AMERICANS REALLY THINK ABOUT RACE AND IDENTITY

. . .

Michele Norris

SIMON & SCHUSTER
New York London Toronto Sydney New Delhi

OVERLEAF

*A group of riders on the 325-mile Dakota 38+2 Memorial Ride to Mankato,
Minnesota, site of the largest mass execution in U.S. history. President
Abraham Lincoln approved the hanging of thirty-eight Dakota Indians and,
later, two chiefs following their uprising against the U.S. government.*

1230 Avenue of the Americas
New York, NY 10020

Copyright © 2024 by Michele Norris

Lucille Clifton, "why some people be mad at me sometimes" from *How to Carry Water: Selected Poems.*
Copyright © 1987 by Lucille Clifton. Reprinted with the permission of The Permissions Company, LLC
on behalf of BOA Editions Ltd, boaeditions.org.

Select writings reprinted with permission of the *Washington Post,
National Geographic,* and The Race Card Project™.

First Simon & Schuster hardcover edition January 2024

SIMON & SCHUSTER and colophon are registered trademarks of Simon & Schuster, Inc.

Simon & Schuster: Celebrating 100 Years of Publishing in 2024

For information about special discounts for bulk purchases, please contact
Simon & Schuster Special Sales at 1-866-506-1949 or business@simonandschuster.com.

For a variety of teaching tools and community resources for educators, librarians,
and others please visit www.simonandschuster.com. These resources and information
about partnerships and events can also be found at www.theracecardproject.com.

The Simon & Schuster Speakers Bureau can bring authors to your live event.
For more information or to book an event, contact the Simon & Schuster Speakers Bureau
at 1-866-248-3049 or visit our website at www.simonspeakers.com.

Interior design by Jason Snyder
Cover design by Kadir Nelson
Editorial coordination by Melissa Bear

Manufactured in China

10 9 8 7 6 5 4 3 2 1

Library of Congress Cataloging-in-Publication Data is available on file.
ISBN 978-1-9821-5439-4
ISBN 978-1-9821-5441-7 (ebook)

For Betty and Belvin Norris. They gave me the gift of curiosity.
Forever grateful.

• • •

For Broderick and our kids, who cheered me up
and cheered me on during this journey.
Love you all so very much. I am blessed to have a partner
who understands that love is the best part of any story.

• • •

For Carter, and the world I hope you will inherit.

they ask me to remember
but they want me to remember
their memories
and I keep on remembering
mine.

—*Lucille Clifton*

CONTENTS

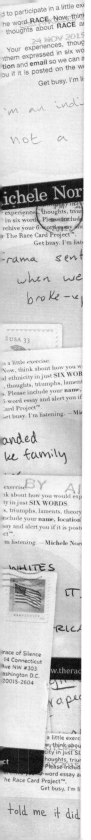
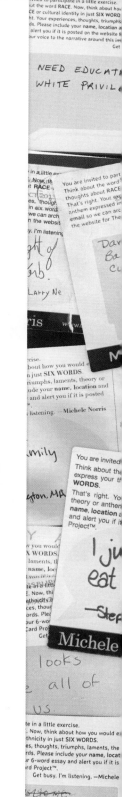

WE NEED EDUCATION ON WHITE PRIVILEGE!

— Richard Flügel

Michele Norris   www.theracecardproject.com

Pink Baby

ENGLAND

Madison, WI

_norris   theracecardproject@gmail.com   #theracecardproject

I'm am not

You are invited to participate in a little exercise. Think about the word RACE. Now, think about how you would express your thoughts about RACE and ethnicity in just SIX WORDS. That's right. Your experiences, thoughts, triumphs, laments, theory or anthem expressed in six words. Please include your name, location and email so we can archive your 6-word essay and alert you if it is posted on the website for The Race Card Project™.

Get busy. I'm listening. —Michele Norris

AIDS K
more
com
Emily St

I Want Now

MOM WAS A DEMOCRAT UNTIL 2008

CHERYL GEERHEORD
SHEFFIELD, MA

Grace of Silence
5614 Connecticut
Ave NW #303
Washington D.C.
20015-2604

Grama sent
$100 when we
broke-up.

Michele Nor

Michele Norris   @michele_norris   #theracecardproject

Michele Norris   www.theracecardproject.co

I grew up scared of myself.

— madeleine
Northampton, MA

Grace of Silence
5505 Connecticut
Ave NW #303
Washington D.C.
20015

Asian g
get r
or
Arranc

God looks
like all of
us.

June Landis, Ephrata

Michele Norris   @michele   #therace

778 Bullets fired at
514 students

IT'S TIME
TALKED A

I'm the cool
white guy. ANON

ANNA, GHANA, w

Strutters
ught:

Michele Norr

.COM
IL.COM

nd James
"Sis"

Thank you, Michele

The internet has helped
fuel racism.

they told me

JAPANESE-
AMERICAN
CAUCASIAN
BLACK-
OUR
FAMILY

Race. Your Thoughts. 6 Words. Please Send.

PROLOGUE
A Magnificent Detour

THIS BOOK IS THE RESULT of a magnificent detour.

More than a decade ago, I set out to write a book about how Americans talk and think about race. The rise of Barack Obama's political fortunes at that time was beginning to shift how the nation saw itself. The changes were both intense and highly nuanced. Tea Party followers in Uncle Sam costumes began taking to the streets and screaming, "I want my country back!" Latino voters met anger with anticipation, marching for immigration reform with signs in the air and hope in their hearts. Black voters quite literally wore pride on their shoulders: "Barack to the Future" T-shirts were on back order.

People long consigned to America's margins were holding themselves taller, feeling a swell of pride stoked by a political victory that many had once considered unimaginable. Even some of the political operatives who fought the Obama campaign with every fiber of their beings conceded that the occasion of the first Black first family moving into the White House was an undeniable milestone. And to many, that mark felt like a thunderclap signaling upending change.

America's demographics were shifting. A nation built on a foundation of White supremacy was heading toward majority-minority status.

In popular media, this was heralded as progress. But in private spaces and quiet conversations, this shift was also met with dread and anxiety. After all, if you've paid any attention to how minorities have been treated in this country over centuries, you might reasonably be concerned about becoming one.

And demographic change was just one jolt amid a ripple of seismic shocks because it was happening alongside so many other cultural shifts—economic tumult, technological upheaval, global conflict, the normalization of gay marriage and the widening embrace and celebration of LGBTQ+ life, the centering of Latino language and culture, a warming climate, unapologetic White nationalism, growing diversity in advertising and entertainment, and of course that constant stream of videos capturing the killings of Black Americans by police or would-be vigilantes. All of it was amplified, exaggerated, or ingested through social media platforms that seemed to fertilize the most fetid of human emotions—anger, umbrage, envy, shame, or fear. All of it added up to vertigo.

I wanted to hear the crackle and pop coming from society's structural alterations.

I wanted to chronicle the visible changes in the United States, but more than that, I wanted to somehow capture the subtler subterranean shifts. I grew up with old folks who used to say that if you listened to the little noises an old house made—the hiss of the boiler, the strain of pipes snaking through the walls, the crackle and pop of wood adjusting to weather or weathering from too many people occupying too small a space—it would reveal a narrative emerging on the horizon. I wanted to hear the crackle and pop coming from society's structural alterations. I wanted to put my ear to the private conversations spurred on by new realities and changing demographics. I had a plan. I landed a book contract . . . and then I took a left turn.

After listening to the changing conversation among the elder African Americans in my family, I wound up writing a completely different book: a family memoir called *The Grace of Silence*. The election of Barack Obama ushered in a whoosh of candor from the older folks who'd raised me. Proud as they were of a moment that felt like touching America's summit, they couldn't help but think about their own long climbs up the rough side of the mountain. The elders began unburdening themselves by shedding stories they had long kept to themselves.

I learned that my father had been shot in the leg by a police officer in Birmingham, Alabama, in 1946 while entering a building to join fellow Black World War II veterans. The men were studying the US Constitution so they could answer questions used in poll tests that were meant to limit "Negro" access to the ballot. Those tests often included questions about obscure aspects of the US Constitution or Alabama state government. As a sailor in the navy, my father was part of the battle to defend democracy overseas, but he returned to a country—and more specifically a Southern state—where democracy was too narrowly defined to embrace Black people. After he left Alabama and migrated north, he never talked about getting wounded during that encounter with the police in downtown Birmingham. He never even told my mother in all their years of marriage.

It turned out my mother was also holding tight to a hidden story. I learned that my maternal grandmother worked for Quaker Oats as an itinerant Aunt Jemima in the 1940s and '50s, doing pancake demonstrations at county fairs and chamber of commerce events, traveling across a six-state region in the Midwest with a hoopskirt and headscarf in her suitcase.

My grandma Ione wore the costume, but she refused to speak in the presumed lingo of the enslaved that was part of a preapproved script. Instead, she used her itinerant perch to conduct herself as an ambassador for her people. She served up pancakes using the crisp elocution I always remembered from my childhood.

I uncovered news accounts covering her visits to some of those small towns, and in those articles, she told reporters about her work and how she saw her role. She knew she was standing before White audiences, and especially White children, who had never encountered a Black woman before, and instead of reinforcing a denigrating stereotype, she used that moment to show small-town audiences something that would blow their minds.

Both stories were almost lost in the cavern of locked-away family secrets, buried under shame, angst, and the fierce desire to just keep moving forward. Instead of the book I had intended to write exploring changing racial attitudes across America, I wound up authoring a memoir exploring how my own family carefully avoided certain conversations, hoping to submerge their pain and set the next generation on a path toward something better.

I embarked on a thirty-six-city book tour that kept me hopscotching across the country for weeks. In places like Seattle, Sacramento, Louisville, Des Moines, and Detroit, I spoke in bookstores, churches, auditoriums, and at book festivals. I had hoped my book—and the tour—would jump-start candid conversations about race, but I feared that audiences would cross their arms and go silent if I forced the issue. In my experience, people would rather eat their toenails than participate in a no-holds-barred conversation about race.

I needed something to draw audiences in, and I found it by asking people to participate in a 6-word exercise through something I called The Race Card Project. I have always cringed when the accusations fly about someone allegedly "playing the race card." It's usually a proxy for "you're making me uncomfortable so please stop talking." Or it's a diversionary tactic used to avoid having to speak about race with any kind of precision or specificity. A shorthand for "just shut up." So, I flipped the script, turning that accusatory phrase into a prompt to spark conversation. I printed two hundred little black postcards at my local FedEx Kinko's asking people to condense their thoughts on race or cultural identity into one sentence of six words. The front of the cards simply read:

Race. Your Thoughts. 6 words. Please send.

I left the cards everywhere I traveled: in bookstores, in restaurants, at the information kiosks in airports, on the writing desks at all my hotels. Sometimes I snuck them inside airline in-flight magazines or left them at the sugar station at Starbucks. I hoped a few of those postcards would come back, thinking it would be worth the trouble if even a dozen people responded.

Much to my surprise, strangers who stumbled on those little black cards would follow the instructions and use postage stamps to mail their 6-word stories back to me in Washington, DC. Since my parents were both postal workers, this gave me an extra thrill. Here I was, doing my part to support the Postal Service. Who says snail mail is dead?

Half a dozen cards arrived within a week, then twelve, then twenty. Over time, that trickle became a tide.

Though limited to just six words, the stories are often shocking in their candor and intimacy. They reveal fear, disappointment, regret, and resentment. Some are kissed by grace or triumph. A surprising number arrive in the form of a question, which suggests that many people hunger not just for answers but for permission to speak their truths. It was amazing what people could pack into such a small package:

Reason I ended a sweet relationship
Too Black for Black men's love
Urban living has made me racist
Took 21 years to be Latina
I suspect Grandpa was a Jew
Was considered White until after 9/11
I tend to scare White people
Gay, but at least I'm White
I'm only Asian when it's convenient

Taken together, these stories revealed an obscured truth. People weren't running away from talking about race; a lot of them were desperate to discuss it through the prism of personal experience. To keep the conversation going, I created a complementary website for The Race Card Project, where people could submit their 6-word stories online instead of having to mail them in. The stories poured into the site, my email inbox, and eventually on social media sites. They came first from all over America, then from more distant ports of call, with submissions from Tokyo, Sydney, Glasgow, and Abu Dhabi. Eventually we'd log Race Card Project stories from more than one hundred countries.

Over time we added two words to the submission form: "Anything Else?" That changed everything. People sent in poems, essays, memos, and historical documents to explain why they chose their six words. The archive came alive. It became an international forum where people could share their own stories but also learn much about life as lived by someone else.

Over time we added two words to the submission form: "Anything Else?" That changed everything.

In the beginning, most of the submissions were anonymous. So many cards came in signed "Anon" that I thought it was some new biblical-sounding hipster name I'd never heard of. Eventually, my kids explained it was shorthand for anonymous. With time, and much to my surprise, many contributors began signing their names, knowing their stories could be placed on a website for the world to see. They included their contact information and uploaded photos. They explained how they found the project and offered context about their lives. And despite the alleged toxicity of the subject matter, the tone of most stories was relaxed and intimate, written as if approaching an old friend. Their courage and comfort seemed bolstered by knowing they were adding their voice to a great big chorus: Everyone was singing in their own octave, humming their own tune, speaking their own dialect—but doing it together. Sometimes harmonious. Often discordant. Silent no more.

Taken together, this unique archive provides a window into America's beating heart during a period bookended by the presidencies of Barack Obama and Donald Trump, and then punctuated by a global pandemic, a flash of protests after the police murder of George Floyd, the siege of the capitol on January 6, and the reversal of *Roe v. Wade*—certainly one of the most interesting and tumultuous eras of modern American history.

So, here's the thing: if you take enough left turns in life, you wind up right where you started. I wanted to write a book about how Americans talk and think about race, and I had planned to go out into the nation to hunt down those conversations. Instead, those stories now come to me. I have received more than 500,000 of these stories. They continue to arrive every day in my mailbox and my email inbox. They come from people who linger after my lectures to share something they've never said out loud before.

Sure, there is also a lot of pain and anger and angst and anxiety reflected in the collection. That cannot be avoided. The topic, after all, is race. But there is also humor and uplift and, for me, the satisfaction that comes with knowing that I have provided a space for people to share their truths. I've learned much from the stories people have shared and the way those stories are absorbed or interpreted. Readers often have diametrically different reactions or interpretations. Stories familiar to one person are foreign or offensive to someone else. The six words that elicit laughter in some quarters can bring someone else to tears.

It's a more powerful narrative thread than anything I've experienced in more than three decades in journalism. I am constantly awed by the honesty and the enthusiasm and, yes, even the grace contained in the responses. People who disagree nonetheless connect with one another at the website. They spar and argue, and their words are sometimes like poison darts. But they are engaging with one another—often across a chasm of some kind, colliding with another point of view. This is something that is increasingly rare at a time when most of us consume a media diet that affirms or confirms what we already believe.

The people who spend time with The Race Card Project might not find common ground, but they are exposed to new ideas and worlds beyond their realms.

Over the years, I have often dipped into the inbox to interview people who have shared their stories, and as we close our conversations, there's almost always a gush of relief, joy, or profound thanks—even if the story or the memory they shared was steeped in pain or humiliation. Even if the conversation began with someone berating me for constantly poking the bear by talking about race. People who share their stories feel seen, heard. They don't necessarily get validation or empathy or understanding. I have found that few are looking for that. What they want is an on-ramp to discuss topics that are often portrayed as toxic or taboo. What they also get is an opportunity to learn about someone else's journey. These stories are powerful in their simplicity. Even if you are offended, surprised, saddened, or unmoved, you have glimpsed inside someone else's vulnerability. That is a potent thing.

I am not naive enough to believe that this automatically leads to enlightenment or changed minds, but I do put stock in Oliver Wendell Holmes Sr.'s assertion that a mind stretched by a new idea or sensation never fully shrinks back to its former dimension.

My beautiful Black boys deserve HOPE!

Maria Roach • Bowie, MD

My children are too young to understand racism. They
see people in three categories: family, friends, neighbors.
But I see the moms who fearfully pull their children off the
playground when my family arrives. There are good people
and bad. Judge by actions, not by skin color!

Pay no attention to my packaging
Michael Taylor • Nashville, TN

I am more than my wrapping
Sandra • Westtown, NY

Ignore the cover. Read the book.
Nancy Ellen Farley • Sacramento, CA

You are unique like EVERYONE else
Colonel Patterson • Gingellville, MI

Race, is someone expected to win?
Anonymous • USA

Hispanic since I came to USA
Amaia Diaz • USA

No, not mixed... Just albino Black
Brandi Green • Chicago, IL

I constantly am asked, "What are you?" or, "Are you mixed?" Nope. I'm Black and albino. It's a fascinating existence.

Yellow: Neither White nor Black enough

Yuri Yamamoto • Raleigh, NC

I am a Japanese immigrant. I sometimes feel lost in this society where race is all about Black and White. I often feel that I am neither White nor Black enough to contribute significantly to a diversity conversation, most of which seems to be about reconciliation and healing from slavery. While growing up in Japan, I learned that we were yellow. I don't understand why there is no yellow mentioned in this country, even though there are histories of East Asian immigrants in the US. Also, it is frustrating that being an Asian does not seem to count as "minority" when it comes to higher education and jobs even though we are a racial minority.

Are you what they call "White"?

Anne Corley • Mercer Island, WA

I was born in North Carolina, 1937, so grew up during segregation. In 1968 I went to a Black elementary school in eastern Virginia and asked if I could volunteer to help in a classroom, and I took my little blond boys (three and five) with me. We ate lunch with all the children, and those were the words a little six-year-old girl came up and asked me. When I answered yes, she smiled a big smile and skipped off as if she had made a big discovery. I continue to do volunteer work—now with a group in south Seattle that helps the families of prisoners, and those innocent words and sweet little face come back to me very often.

We won't make it like this

Brad • Downingtown, PA

It's OK to take up space

Reese Marcosa • Tustin, CA

Black Boy. White World. Perpetually Exhausted.

Esayas Mehretab • Richmond, VA

I grew up in the West End of Richmond, Virginia, in a predominantly affluent, White community. I was not White, and I was not affluent. I had no space for myself to go to and talk about my experiences, my struggles, and what life was like for me as a Black boy. Opportunities to discuss my shared experiences were rare. It was exhausting to conform to others' perceptions of you, hold in uncomfortable emotions because it made others feel uneasy to be around you, to feel isolated even though I was surrounded by "friends." As I grew older and began seeing the world for what it was, especially the injustices of being Black in America, I learned that there were two justice systems, one for the privileged and one for the underprivileged. I learned that 95 percent of African American history wasn't taught in schools. I learned that my skin color started conversations and ended them, as well. I experienced being pulled over immediately after getting in my car with some friends because my friend and I (the only two Black men) fit the descriptions of bank robbers. There were an inconceivable number of police officers pointing guns at us, yelling at us, threatening us, and then giving us absolutely no apology besides, "We didn't mean to; we thought you were someone else, and you fit the description." That was six to eight months before Black Lives Matter started.

My friends and I still have not spoken about that traumatizing night on our first night out in downtown Richmond, Virginia. I was eighteen and had just moved in to my first apartment and was attending my first year at Virginia Commonwealth University. That's how I was introduced to the city. My parents don't know about this story. I always think how differently that night could have ended up. I could have been a statistic and become an unwanted catalyst to the Black Lives Matter movement. From that point on, I have seen countless Black lives taken by police and stand your ground laws. It has made me exhausted. All of it. It's draining, but this time I have hope, and a fire has awoken in me that was on the cusp of going out. Thank you for letting me share my story.

I am not a criminal, statistic, failure

James McCray • Hemet, CA

I am not what society has labeled me. I am not a criminal because I am so-called African American. I am not a statistic because I grew up in a single-parent household. Studies suggest that when a young Black boy grows up without a father in the home, chances are he will get in trouble with the law at an early age, drop out of school, and be defiant toward his mother; by the way, I did not do any of these. I am not a failure.

Be twice as good as everyone

Brandon Hopson • Portsmouth, VA

Sometimes as an African American, I feel as if I have to work twice as hard to top White people in order to achieve success.

My world told me I'm Black.

Robert Franklin • Denver, CO

When will race not matter anymore

Bob Kenyon • San Jose, CA

Old men die, we move forward

Nathan Poe • Birmingham, AL

This apartment is no longer available

Susan Alvarez • Los Angeles, CA

From love to fear— foreigner's view

David Chen • New York, NY

I grew up in China listening to artists like 50 Cent, 2Pac, Snoop Dogg, and Jay-Z. I have every one of Jay-Z's songs memorized, and for a Chinese kid, that wasn't easy. For as long as I can remember, I was fascinated by African American (is this the politically correct term?) culture. As I started high school, I transitioned into R&B with Ne-Yo, Chris Brown, and Jason Derulo. Back then, I dreamed of being Black. In my head, Blacks were talented at music, sports, and being cool.

Fast-forward a few years; my parents decided to send me to college in the US. I found myself in Michigan, and my first roommate was an African American. He was one of the kindest and most loving people I'd ever met. He treated me like a brother, and I thought of him as my brother. He'd always ask me why I was trying to sound like him. It wasn't intentional. I had learned most of my English from rap songs. After spending two years with my roommate, I became more and more involved with the African American community. I loved it—everyone I met was as kind as him.

Later I moved to New York, and during my two years here, my perception was somewhat crushed. I was robbed twice and chased with a knife. The perpetrators were all African American. I started to develop a fear of the Blacks in New York; I would walk away from Blacks at night and would almost always speed up my pace. Subconsciously I felt horrible. I felt guilt; I felt shame because I was slowly becoming the person I did not want to be. I felt like I was racist.

Recently my old roommate got married, and I was reminded of the wonderful times we spent together. I wish I could be that guy again, but I still cannot control the fear that I feel.

Sag your pants, lose your chance

Paul • Houston, TX

Whether right or wrong, the impressions we make
on others play a big part in how others treat us.

There is some truth in stereotypes

G.B. • Charlottesville, VA

Black leaders feign sorrow; celebrate payday

R.M. • Philadelphia, PA

White males often feel left out

Sheridan Saint-Michel •
Lewisville, TX

Grandparents immigrated from Sweden; no fence

Richard Lindberg • Milwaukee, WI

No White woman cooks like that

Meredith Christensen • Katy, TX

White guilt when I check Hispanic

Ethan • West Jordan, UT

I'm not apologizing for being White

Debi Gerbert •
Ponte Vedra Beach, FL

1950 school registration, Joji becomes George

George Joji Hamamoto •
Colorado Springs, CO

Who decides when you're over it?

Shani Blackwell • Chicago, IL

Who decides when people who have experienced
inequality should get over those experiences?

Black good Samaritans, or would-be robbers?

Samuel C. Johnson • Keezletown, VA

I am a White man, now sixty-seven years of age. In May 1968 (a month after the assassination of Dr. Martin Luther King Jr.), I had just completed basic training in the army in North Carolina and was on my way to my home area near Philadelphia. I got off the train in Philadelphia at 30th Street Station around midnight and walked to the entrance ramp of the Schuylkill Expressway to hitch a ride home. I was in my dress khaki uniform, and soon a car stopped to give me a ride. They were four or five young Black men who gave me a friendly invitation to get in, which I did. After I got in, I was very conscious of the situation I was in—late at night, one White guy and four or five Black guys—but I did not feel threatened. I told them my destination—King of Prussia, a White suburb of Philadelphia— and they immediately offered to take me where I was going. I was struck by their generosity, and we had friendly conversation on the ride to my destination.

My destination was a friend's house, where I knew I was as welcome as one of the family. I had decided to spend the night at my White friends' home, but I had not contacted them in advance about my plans, and so they were not expecting me. When we pulled up at my friends' house, the driver of the car

White girls should marry White boys!

Janet Little • Dayton, OH

From a rural small town—I hadn't seen any couples that were of different races. During the 1994 O. J. Simpson trial, at age six, I ignorantly asked my mother, "Was that Black boy married to that White girl that died?" Her only response was "Yes, but White girls should only marry White boys, and Black girls should marry Black boys." When I asked why, she said because that's how it is. To this day, it still makes me cringe. My husband and I will be having children within the next few years. She doesn't know that we've thought and prayed about adopting children, with a particular heart for Ethiopia.

told me he needed to get some water in the house for the leaky radiator of his car. Responding to my knock, a teenage daughter opened the door. Explaining the situation, I invited my Black companions into the house to get some water. As they came in and passed through the living room, all the commotion woke up my friend's parents. When the father saw several Black men, strangers, in his living room he started yelling and went to get his gun. I was filling their jug with water, and when I heard that, I got them out of the house as fast as I could, bringing my time with them to a rude and unceremonious end. My friend's parents, the father especially, chastised me for being so gullible and stupid for risking my own safety and theirs with these "n*****s." They believed that because these young men were Black, they had criminal intent to rob the house.

I was young and inexperienced and thought that maybe my White friends were right. I didn't know what to think. In the decades since, I have often thought about that experience and how dangerous it was for these Black Good Samaritans, who gave me a ride and almost got shot by my White friend. And I have become aware of how common it is for White people to assume that Black men are dangerous or criminal, and to respond inappropriately with "preemptive" violence. I often wish that I could somehow connect today with those young Black men who gave me a ride then and nearly got shot. I wish that we could talk together about that experience and their perspective on it. If they have not been shot and are still alive.

You need to leave, White boy

Neo Wolf • Lewisburg, TN

First, I'm Native American, but being a lighter skin color in a predominantly Black neighborhood meant I was White, no matter what. I was always told I had no business there and that I "need to leave," "get out," "find somewhere else to live," "you don't belong here," all the while knowing I had nowhere else to go and no means to go anywhere else. I was constantly outnumbered on the streets, cursed, beaten, and almost killed on one occasion simply for looking White. Racism is a problem for people of all colors. Those who say minorities can't be racist are absolutely wrong.

You don't look like a Mexican

Macella Lopez • Phoenix, AZ

In high school (1986), a few girls at lunch told me these exact words. I was shocked, and I angrily replied, "Well, what the hell does a Mexican look like to you?" My family had just moved to Phoenix from Denver, so I could only imagine their only image of a Mexican was a landscaper or food worker, and if you spoke Spanish, you were a Mexican (no matter what your country of origin).

What's Good? I'm a Nuyorican, baby!

Christina Labrador • Copiague, NY

"Are you Indian?" the man behind the 7-Eleven counter asks me. "Are you Egyptian?" the parking attendant asks. "You look Israeli," the bouncer at Cafe Wha? says. "Girl, you Black," my Israeli friends say. "I know what restaurant you'll like," as the man handing out flyers on the street gives me a menu of an Indian eatery. "You're Boricua!" the dapper gentleman with a sharp suit, black sunglasses, and fedora proudly guesses. "You sound like a Brooklyn Puerto Rican," the hipster girl says with a curious head tilt, after she and her partner ask where I'm from. "I thought you were White. I had no concept of Latino," says the boyfriend. "I thought Latinos weren't Black," says the racist with pores glowing neon red once I reveal my Black, Indigenous culture. I get mistaken for Italian, Brazilian, Iranian, Mediterranean, Middle Eastern, Indian. . . . It's rare when people guess Puerto Rican. But when they do . . . there's a little dance I do inside my head. I maybe might express it outside, too.

People often fear what is unfamiliar

Joyce Hansen • Seattle, WA

I still cry 51 years later

Dana • Cincinnati, OH

My name is Jamaal; I'm white.

Jamaal Allen • Des Moines, IA

When people have seen my name before they've seen my face, I get "Oh, *you're* Jamaal." Yes, I am, and the African American behind me is Chris.

It is not uncommon for people to follow up with, "I expected you to be—"and then there's a pause, a sudden realization they are on the verge of sounding racist. There's a look—not quite deer in the headlights, but it is a definite freeze. What to say next? I've heard several: taller, older, different (usually accompanied by an uncomfortable chuckle). Very few people have the courage to say *darker*. Several people have told me that Jamaal is a Black name. It's not. It's an Arabic name. Arabic is a language, not a color.

Halfway through my first year teaching, the principal who had hired me confided that I was lucky to have gotten the job. I agreed. I had watched many of my classmates from grad school go from job fair to job fair and interview to interview, whereas I had been able to parlay my student teaching directly into a job at the same school with only one interview.

That wasn't what he meant. They had not been planning to take another student teacher when my application showed up. But, in his words, as he scanned through it and saw a Jamaal who plays basketball and counts Muhammad Ali among his heroes, he thought, "We could use a little diversity." Sorry to disappoint you.

So, no, as a White man, a majority of majorities, from a small rural town in southern Oregon with a high school of around four hundred students and two Black and two Hispanic families, I don't know a lot about race. I do, however, know a little about stereotyping.

Yes, *I have my green card*

Melanie • Las Vegas, NV

I'm a redneck, not a racist.

Anonymous • Spokane, WA

Indo-Pak American. Sounds like Camping Gear

Talia Karim • Boulder, CO

Why can't they pick normal names?

Nathan Arrowsmith • Tempe, AZ

Separate only your laundry by color

Amber Martin • Shamokin, PA

There will always be a "they"

Geoff Kincade • Glendale, CA

Should be "Black lives matter, TOO!"

Eve Holton • Hollandale, MN

Bullies grow up. Black boys die.

Mandolin • Oakland, CA

I'm mixed Black and White, and I often feel like I don't belong.
Both sides have shown me beauty and ugliness.

Anti-racist is a code for anti-White.

Ryan McKee • Coweta, OK

Pro-Black doesn't mean anti-White

Bobby Brown • Baltimore, MD

xxx

Andes shadows follow me, no Quechua

Carmen Mendoza Tintaya • Arlington, VA

My parents are from a remote village in Arequipa, Peru, where accessible roads were built only in 2006. Now with both my parents gone, I find myself looking for my identity and looking toward that little village. I haven't made the trip yet. I moved to the US when I was young with no appreciation for my heritage. I wish I could have asked my parents to teach me Quechua—their first language. Now I feel that I don't have a past. I need to find my history.

INTRODUCTION
Post-Racial?

IT'S HARD TO EVEN SAY that word today without a smirk or an eye roll. But in the lead-up to the 2008 election of Barack Obama, that word was everywhere. And yet, its ubiquitous presence seemed to come from nowhere. It had been used only about a dozen times in print before 2006, and most of the citations were linked either to the now deceased Harvard professor Derrick Bell or to the Studio Museum director Thelma Golden's early discourse on post-Black art from the early 1900s, where she explained why artists of African descent were rejecting the White art world's attempt to define their work or their mission. Neither of these iconic figures were using the term *post-racial* to move past or reject the complexities of race. Indeed, quite the opposite.

So, what did that magical word *post-racial* mean when applied to America's political landscape? It was a prayer, a wish, an aspired-to state where race no longer mattered and racial hierarchies were a thing of the past. It was a rhetorical paean asserting through gauzy language that we had arrived at new cultural terrain. If America, with its tortured history of slavery, internment camps, Native genocide, and institutionalized segregation, had sent a Black man to the White House through popular vote, could it mean that this country had transcended race? Had we finally found the right ointment to heal our deepest national wound?

The answers now are obvious, and the question in hindsight was ridiculously naive.

The election of Barack Obama marked not the end of racial anxiety but rather the beginning of a thorny new chapter in American history, where the subject of race would be ever more complex. Race is still a tender bruise on our body politic, and if anything, the rise of a Black president and the tanning of America through rapid demographic shifts only intensified the throb. And then, the election of a president who reveled in division and was—and still is—embraced as a personal hero by even the most ardent White nationalists has further infected a wound that will not heal.

I have spent the past decade examining that wound. Its causes. Its symptoms. Things that aggravate the pain and the things that over time could lessen the ache. In 2010, when I began collecting 6-word stories on race and cultural identity, those literary microbursts allowed me to roam America's most intimate corridors and listen to people of all races, creeds, and backgrounds unburden themselves.

People have come to The Race Card Project by the thousands, often to express things they would never say out loud among their family, classmates, coworkers, or closest friends. They take the time to share their thoughts even if they don't agree with my politics or accuse me of being a race-baiter. They come by accident when they are roaming an online search engine looking for information about some aspect of race or identity and stumble upon the website.

The stories they share are not in news archives or history books because they emanate from deeply personal spaces. Stories that have been buried or stayed unspoken because they were deemed unremarkable when compared to the monumental narratives of those who marched or died or shook this nation's conscience through public action. The stories of Freedom Riders overshadow small acts of courage witnessed and recalled by only a few. And the bellow and howl of cross burners and potbellied Southern sheriffs fighting to maintain White supremacy drown out the rustle of millions of Americans who either relaxed or tightened their grip on a foundational system that granted White privilege in almost all matters.

These smaller stories make up the big, broad canvas that sits behind those bold strokes of history. And when you look closely at that wide-embrace, multihued vision of America, you also see how the binary tensions between Black and White America have obscured other important cultural tendrils. In the grand discussion of race in America, Asians, Latinos, mixed-race Americans, Indigenous Americans, and Arabs—indeed people of all colors and creeds—often find themselves sidelined, asking, "What about me?"

And many of these stories in The Race Card Project archive have nothing to do with traditional notions of race in America. Instead, they reveal how race intersects or crashes into other aspects of identity and community. People share stories about living with physical and mental disabilities. They write about their military service or phobias or memories of abuse. They write about families who arrived as immigrants from Italy, Latvia, Uruguay, India, or Greece and struggled mightily to figure out how to become "fully American."

As cards have poured in from more than one hundred countries, I learned that people the world over figure out how to divide themselves over dialect, religion, geography, hair texture, access to water, class, caste, and skin color. Always skin color and its light to dark gradations. People in every corner of the world, from sub-Saharan Africa to the northernmost Nordic countries, are hung up about hue.

The essays have served as invitations into worlds previously unavailable to me—or perhaps to any of us—because many people who submit their stories say they've never shared them with anyone before. They are heartfelt and frank, and they underscore that while America may be far more integrated than it was half a century ago—certainly cause for celebration—our experiences around race and identity are nonetheless more complicated as a result.

> **The stories people share leap from a place of vulnerability.**

The stories people share leap from a place of vulnerability. And in truth, that can sometimes give writers more than they bargained for. After a White woman in Atlanta wrote, "Educated. Black strangers scare me still," visitors to the website chastised, applauded, or even threatened her. But a few invited her to visit one of several historically Black universities in the area to meet Black people who might chase away her notion that dark skin was inherently dangerous.

A man who tweeted "Purses are clutched when I approach" prompted responses from several women who admitted that they do exactly that. Some, upon reading about the assault on his dignity, pledged to think more about their implicit actions. The comment stream and the traffic patterns on the website showed that people remained engaged with the content even when they were pushed well outside their comfort zones.

After lecturing about The Race Card Project in Los Angeles, I was pulled aside by a nattily dressed Korean businessman, who leaned in close to confess that he hates the Asian gangs that occasionally show up on the nightly news in Southern California. He also confided that he secretly respects the young toughs. Deep down, he finds himself quietly rooting for hoodlums who look like they could be distant members of his family. And, yes, he understands the paradox since he's stood before cameras next to city lawmakers to denounce those Asian gangs as a scourge on society. But here's what he had never been able to say out loud: those gang members represent an image of Asian manhood rarely seen in popular culture, where, to his mind, Korean, Chinese, Japanese, and South Asian men are too often portrayed as smart—but soft.

When he shared his story, he shook his shoulders and his head in the way one does after downing a brisk drink. "God, that felt good," he said. "I have been wanting to say that for years." That whoosh of relief was later echoed by Celeste Green, née Brown, who was cruising through her timeline on Twitter one Sunday afternoon in 2012 when she noticed a hashtag conversation around The Race Card Project. Impulsively she typed, "We aren't all strong black women."

Impulsively she typed, "We aren't all strong black women."

It was like throwing new kindling on the fire. The timeline lit up with responses from a diaspora of women and even a few men from Los Angeles to Boston and even as far away as Dublin.

"Isn't Strong Black Woman a compliment?"

"No! It's strong like oxen. Less than human."

"Like saying it doesn't matter how we treat them because they will survive."

"Time to stop putting up walls and be vulnerable."

"Wasn't the whole feminist movement about being strong? What gives?"

"I feel like I'm forced to be strong."

"It makes me sound like a weed, not a flower."

Celeste Green said she wrote the first thing that came to mind, with no idea it would ignite such strong debate. She'd never uttered those six words out loud before, but she realized they had been forming in her consciousness for quite some time. They came from the fear of being stereotyped as too aggressive, and from the tension between the need to be independent and the desire to find a life partner who celebrates her strength and empathizes with her vulnerabilities.

Green, now a thirty-five-year-old ob-gyn, said the experience changed her approach to talking about race. "When I saw all those comments, I was terrified at first," she told me. "It felt like some people were attacking me or questioning my values. In the end, I felt validated. I felt empowered. I realized that there was value in participating in that dialogue even though we are told it is supposed to be the third rail."

When it was time to write an admission essay for her second attempt at applying for medical school, she crafted her personal statement around the 6-word story she sent to The Race Card Project and the debate it sparked.

Now practicing medicine in Texas, Green said the strong-Black-woman trope is both a laurel and a weapon. It's a trap for women who feel like they must always strive to fulfill that expectation. And it's a cage when Black women are made to feel like they can handle almost anything in life without comfort or respite. In her own profession, a raft of studies has shown that Black patients are systematically undertreated for pain and discomfort. A survey of White medical students found that more than half of medical students and residents subscribed to the false stereotype that Black patients feel less pain than White patients. Similar studies have found that Black children are less likely to get pain medication when undergoing surgery and Black veterans were less likely to be offered opioids or other medications for very high levels of pain.

•   •   •

The Race Card Project was meant to serve as a conversation starter. It has become so much more. Though it's not possible to explain every facet of racial experience, the selection of 6-word stories from The Race Card Project form a vibrant mosaic that illustrates the American experience in a brand-new way, one that will serve as an illuminating archive well into the future as we try to understand the years when America was steaming toward majority-minority status. You will notice that the stories have drifted in from all over America. The 6-word stories mainly appear as people submitted them, with minor edits in the backstories to trim for length or fix typos. Some people signed their names, others provided just a first name or initial, and some preferred to remain anonymous. The variety in their approach or comfort level is understandable given this subject matter. Some of the cards have pictures or illustrations. In some cases, the race of the writer is clear. In some cases, that's not quite clear, and the ambiguity creates a potent undertone. However they entered this space, I am so very grateful for people's time, candor, perspective, and trust.

The idea of a "post-racial" America has been thoroughly debunked, though that phrase is still in circulation, mostly as a punch line. But one truth is clearer than ever: if we want to understand how to build a society that celebrates difference—or at least doesn't hold back individuals or communities because of it—we must examine or interrogate the idea that people don't want to talk about race or identity. More than not, I have found that people are desperate for a safe and brave space where they won't face rebuke or embarrassment for tiptoeing toward a toxic subject. The Race Card Project has provided that space for hundreds of thousands of those conversations. It is my hope that many more will join that dialogue on their own terms upon reading these stories.

This book is like a scrapbook of the fourteen-year journey collecting these stories.

I will share my thoughts, observations, essays, indexes, headlines, and interviews on the following pages. But what I really want to do is share the stories of people who have opened up their lives in The Race Card Project archives. Throughout these pages you will find a continuing river of their stories and photos surrounding my writing. You can read this book from start to finish, or you can open to almost any page and you will encounter a person, a place, a story, a perspective that might linger in your mind, long after you've set this book aside. Some of the 6-word stories are presented in groupings to convey the repetition or connection among some of the themes. But overall, a reader will encounter an avalanche of issues raining down from all directions. That is what we see in the inbox each day. Sometimes the stories seem to be in direct conversation with one another. But on most days, it feels like people are speaking all at once from different spaces and perspectives.

As you read these pages, I want you to experience what I see, feel, and imagine when I go to the inbox online or when I roll by the mailbox to pick up black-and-white-striped postcards that people still send to us after fourteen years.

In some ways, doing this work reminds me of roaming the streets and the alleys of my childhood during warm summer months, when working-class people would throw their windows wide open to keep their electricity bills from soaring along with the temperature. I learned an awful lot about our community during those long, hot summers.

Whether I was in Minnesota, where I was raised, or Birmingham, where my grandparents lived, summers were the months when kitchen-table intimacies and family business floated out through window screens like the scent of peach cobbler cooling on the counter.

The man up the street who was always so quiet and seemed to let his wife do all the talking yelled with a thick accent at the sportscaster on TV. I couldn't understand a word he said but, even as a kid, assumed he was cussing someone out. The lady who lived in a big house by herself and was always shooing away the ever-growing collection of Black children from our newly integrated neighborhood. We just wanted to play kickball, and the four corners of the quiet intersection where her house sat were part of the makeshift diamond we used to run the bases. She didn't want us anywhere near her property—even on the sidewalk—and that left us with the impression that she didn't much like Black folks. But boy, did she like Black music. When we raced our Sting-Ray bikes up and down the alley behind her house, you could hear her warbling along with Nat King Cole and the 5th Dimension, singing as if she was in the front row at a concert.

You just don't know what goes on behind closed doors.

You just don't know what goes on inside someone's head . . . or in their soul.

But you get a better idea of someone's anthems and aspirations, their anxieties and their triumphs, when you're able to hear their stories.

The word *eavesdropping* has a bit of a taint to it, but that's what these stories allow. Eavesdropping with permission. It's like walking through America's neighborhoods at a moment when all the windows are open and the drapes are pulled wide. When people have let their guards down and are speaking their truths out loud—revealing something about themselves, about their families, their communities, their country, our shared planet.

Does her Black baby doll offend?

Michele Martini • USA

When it came time to choose my daughter's first baby doll, there were only dark-skinned dolls left in the specific brand/style I wanted. Thinking it didn't matter, I bought it. She has since chosen her own doll—also dark-skinned. I've gotten a few comments. Most people seem to think we're making some kind of political statement. I'm wondering if it is offensive to others—seeing this naked Caucasian child lugging around a naked African American baby (because both she and her baby are usually naked). Her love for her baby is obvious in the photo, which is why I included it.

My son needed a "White" name

Lisa Dumelow • USA

My children are multicultural (their father was a refugee from Cuba). When our only son was born, his father wanted to name him after himself and his father—Remberto. But I knew that although the girls may not be affected by Latina names, my son would be judged, and negative assumptions would be made (he was born in 1992, and the Mariel boatlift was in the recent past—not to mention *Scarface*, which made people assume all Cubans were drug dealers).

Even though his last name was Hispanic, we gave him an Anglo-Saxon first name, Christopher, to "counteract" the assumptions that would be made if both his first and last names indicated his Latin ethnicity. He ended up being much lighter skinned than his three sisters, and in the end, no one believed he was anything other than "White." But it always made me sad to have to worry about how he would be perceived in life just because of a name.

I'm relieved my son looks White

Michelle Welsh • Severna Park, MD

I'm biracial White and Pakistani. I look Pakistani. My husband is White. My son is a big, blond, fair-skinned, blue-eyed toddler. We live in an affluent [largely White] town.

I'm grateful he will never be asked his nationality, be the "diversity hire," or live with an identity crisis. Is that wrong? To want life to be easier for your children, even if it seems like a step backward?

Strange fruit in a plum tree

Ronnie Dunn • Cleveland, OH

My family was the third African American family to move on my street, Gay Avenue, on Cleveland's Eastside in 1964. I was three years old and the youngest of three children. My siblings, a sister and brother, and four years older than I, had already started school.

The grandchildren, a boy and girl, of our kind, elderly White neighbors to the left of us became my first playmates outside of the home. Their parents, as well as their uncle and his wife, lived in the home with their grandparents.

One spring day in 1965 as my mom did laundry in our basement, and [me] and my White playmates were playing and climbing in the plum tree in their backyard, their aunt raised a window in the back of the house and called for them to "come in the house and don't ever let me catch you playing with that N-word again!" They climbed down from the tree confused and went into the house.

I stayed there sitting in the tree for what must have been several minutes, not grasping what happened and that they were not coming back out to play. I climbed down from the tree, crossing to my backyard, and rang the side doorbell. I could see my mother at the bottom of the basement steps as she looked up through the screen door and saw me standing there.

As she came up the stairs and unlocked the door, she asked, "Why are you coming in the house?" I fumbled over the words as I tried to explain to her what had occurred and what my playmates' aunt had said. A somber expression came over my mother as she bent down to pick me up and carried me into our living room and sat me in her lap as we sat in my dad's favorite recliner.

She reached down next to the chair and picked up a volume of children's Bible stories that was placed next to the chair in a small wood bookcase. On the cover of this book was a picture of the typical European image of Jesus sitting on a large rock surrounded by multiracial children of various nationalities, and my mother used this to teach me about race and to explain to me how some people think they are better than others based on the color of their skin. She told me that no one was any better than I am.

That was my introduction to the concept of race and racism, a lesson that I was forced to learn before I even started kindergarten. I never played with my playmates again, and seemingly in a relatively short time, the family moved from the neighborhood. I started school the next year, and my kindergarten class was probably 60 percent White. But by the time I was in the third grade, my school was more than 95 percent Black.

Why is your baby so brown?

Gina Rodriguez • Hollywood, FL

As a White Cuban (who looks very White) born in Miami, I felt very comfortable in this city, as I was in the majority with all the Hispanics. Moving to Jacksonville, Florida, and having a Brown baby with my Brown Dominican husband, I was stopped everywhere and asked, "Why is your baby so Brown?" The teachers would give my daughter books about Black girls.

Everywhere we go now, people do not think that I am with my husband and daughter: "Ma'am, you are going to have to wait your turn."

"But I am with them" is a common refrain at the grocery store, the airport, the mall. I know people look at my family and think I am the stepmom.

My husband uses me for my supposed "White privilege": "You go return at the store; they would never question a White lady." I don't feel I have White privilege as I am a fluent Spanish speaker, but do I?

His grandma was so happy he was marrying me. "You are going to Whiten up this family." Yet as the only brown-eyed girl in my entire family of blue-eyed people, they were sorry for me that I didn't have blue eyes. Why should I feel bad about not having blue eyes? I am bringing up my daughter to be proud of her brown skin and curly hair. Not enough discussion about Hispanics and discrimination.

White guy. Black church. Met wife

Randy Nelson • Gilbert, AZ

At the end of a failed marriage, I explained my love of gospel music (my first record purchase was Bobby "Blue" Bland when I was seven years old) to our marriage counselor. She "made" me go to a Black church as part of my recovery. That led me to be open to the possibility of dating a Black woman. I met Rose on Match.com, and we have been gloriously married for twelve years!

Dude, you look like a terrorist

Spencer Scranton •
Los Angeles, CA

Good morning, but there's no response

Clyde Jasper • Oakland, CA

I'm a tall Black man with dreadlocks. I'm a husband and a father. I'm a property owner and a taxpayer. I'm a veteran. I vote. I graduated Phi Beta Kappa from a world-class university in Berkeley, California. In passing, I many times acknowledge a White person's presence and humanity with a "good morning," and they look at me but don't respond.

I'm "lucky." I don't "look Jewish"

Alice Swenson •
Milwaukee, WI

Now that I am incognito as a Jew (having the last name Swenson), when people do find out, they do say this from time to time. It bums me out every time. What does a Jew look like? Like me! This is such a backhanded compliment. I never know what to say. Thank you? How dare you?

If you were Black, you'd know

Frank K. Norris • Knoxville, TN

I have a good fishing buddy friend. I'm White, and he is Black. One day I was driving on the interstate through the center of town, and he said to me, "The speed limit on this stretch of the interstate is fifty-five miles per hour."

I was driving sixty-five miles per hour and was completely surprised. I said that I had lived here all my life and did not know that.

He said: "If you were Black, you'd know."

Tonight, I am ashamed of myself

Maria Santos • San Diego, CA

It's 8:00 p.m. on the highway. Wife in the back of shiny new family car with crying five-month-old for thirteen miles. Still far from destination. Need to breastfeed, need to pull over.

Next exit: Inglewood.

What I know about Inglewood. Black neighborhood. "Inglewood is always up to no good." A reputation for violent crime, backed up by statistics. Racism is real. Crime is real. At the gas station. One young Black man on a bicycle. Could be twenty. Could be thirty. Not older. Baby still crying. Wife tells me not to make eye contact. Can't help it. Young man walks toward the car. I freak out. Don't be racist. Baby in the back seat. Don't be racist. Wife is telling me to leave. Don't be racist. Inglewood is violent. Don't be racist, don't be racist, don't be racist.

I got racist.

White van peels out of the gas station. Young man yells. I tell myself, if I was alone, I would have talked to him. Acknowledged his humanity, which transcends melanin.

I tell myself a lot of things to evade guilt.

I put myself in his shoes. Well, the best I can. How insulting and dehumanizing it must feel to be needy, approach a stranger with friendly eyes, and watch them shun you. This is the stuff even he must sometimes think is over the top. It's just too blatant. If he screamed the ugliest things in the world to me, he deserved to.

Worst of all, I'm not sure this ever unfolds differently. The truth is the chances of the young man trying to attack me were low. Not sure how low. 30 percent? 1 percent? .01 percent? I would never take a .01 percent chance with my daughter. Yet it's my cruelty that's keeping me up tonight.

Much progress: much more to do

Robert Markel • Charlestown, MA

Raised in a very White town in Chester County, Pennsylvania, I had little consciousness of race issues until high school. We had one Black student in my class, and he was the salutatorian. At the end of our senior year at Archmere Academy, several members of the class went to lunch together at the Charcoal Pit in Wilmington, Delaware. Shortly after we sat down, the manager, whom I knew very well, came up and asked me to step away for a talk. He informed me that the restaurant, which I had patronized dozens of times, did not serve "Negroes."

We were shocked. As it happened, President Joe Biden, who was one of our classmates, was with us at the restaurant. I relayed the message to the group; we sat there embarrassed, looking at one another, and Joe said, "Let's get out of here." We left. I did not return for many years.

In the summer of 1963, I had a summer job at DuPont's Chestnut Run plant outside Wilmington. I worked as a laborer in shipping and receiving, brooming floors and breaking down packages. The Black man who worked with me had two years of college and was a minister in Wilmington. I wondered why he was working as a laborer when he seemed educated and qualified for a better job. One day he told me that DuPont had a policy of not allowing Blacks to take the exam for a White collar desk job. I was astonished. That summer, DuPont changed its policies and liberalized employment practices. My friend was allowed to take the test, and he moved up to a better job in the main offices. In August, DuPont excused any employee who wanted to attend the March on Washington. I called my friend Pete McLaughlin, and we decided to go.

We made our way to the steps of the Lincoln Memorial and sat there to hear Dr. King and other speakers. There is a film that I saw at the JFK Library in Boston that shows a sea of Black people on the steps and two White boys sitting on the steps. Pete and I did not pay much attention to most of the speakers, but when Dr. King began to speak, we were transfixed by his words and his magnificent speaking style.

Unforgettable experience.

Grandmother ate in kitchen with housekeeper

Alice J. Walker • Gay, GA

This concerns a story told to me about my grandmother, who died in 1960 when I was five years old. In the midfifties, she lived with my aunt and uncle and their boys in Rome, Georgia. On one rare occasion, she was home alone when Carrie May, the housekeeper, came to clean. Grandmother fixed lunch for both of them; when it was ready, she sat down in the kitchen, and Carrie went out on the back porch to eat.

It was a cold, rainy day. Grandmother said, "Carrie, come into the kitchen and eat; you shouldn't be out there." Carrie didn't want to, but Grandmother assured her that no one else would know. She came into the kitchen, and the two women ate together.

My aunt boiled the girl's utensils

Michael Vines • New York, NY

Just want to make sure that you understand "the girl" was how many people in the 1950s and '60s referred to their maid.

Saw the hurt in his eyes

Ed Karesky • Escondido, CA

When I was in fourth grade, a new family moved into our lower-middle-class apartment complex. They were African American. I was out riding my bicycle with a friend when the six-year-old of that family rode his bike up to us and asked if he could ride with us. We said no, and I saw the look of hurt in his eyes before we rode away. Later, I thought about it and wondered if he thought it was because he was Black. It wasn't. My best friend in school named Bobby was Black. It was because we thought he was too young and wouldn't be able to keep up. I never saw that young boy again, but fifty-five years later, at the age of sixty-five, I still remember his face and regret we didn't let him join us.

Lives were destroyed because we're different

Jordan Mix • Versailles, KY

I have a strong background of German in my family because it is on my dad's side and mom's side.

In 1855, my great-great-great-great-great-great-grandparents immigrated from Switzerland and Germany to Louisville, Kentucky. As soon as they got to Louisville, Bloody Monday happened. It was an election day, and a lot of Germans had moved to this area (they were now one-third of the population).

The issue grew out of a bitter rivalry between the Democrats and the Know-Nothings. The Know-Nothings, who were anti-Catholic and nativist, did not like the fact that the Germans' vote had such power over the election, so on election day they had armed guards at the poll. Then after the polls closed, they went and destroyed homes in the German community and the Irish Catholic churches. Also, they fired at and attacked people, dragging them out into the street. After it was all said and done, twenty-two people were killed.

My family had just moved to Jefferson (a neighborhood in Louisville, Kentucky) and had to suffer this. This event made a lot of the immigrants pack up and leave, but not my family. Some of them still live there today.

I chose these six words because these people persecuted the Germans just because they were different. What if I had lived in that time? I would've been the one scared after just moving there and being attacked just because of my culture. My family had to deal with a lot of difficulties just moving to the US, let alone being attacked and having their lives ruined just because they were German.

Leave identity issues to other people

Phyllis W. Allen • Fort Worth, TX

I am a sixty-year-old woman who has lived through segregation, integration, Colored, Negro, Black, African American, segregation marches, integration, Pan-Africanism, opulent consumption, financial catastrophe, and now I'm just me.

Why is the pool filled up?

Alonzo Peeke • Morris, MN

When I was in fourth grade, we moved from Overland Park, Kansas, to Lynchburg, Virginia. My dad and I would shoot hoops and take walks at Riverside Park, a beautiful, forested park right off the James River. We were walking home, and we came across a strange structure like a ruined monument, old stone with grass growing over the side like it had overflowed somehow.

We followed a sort of retaining wall, but the wall had numbers along the edge like a pool. I asked Dad, "Why anyone would fill in a pool?" Dad didn't know but said he'd ask around.

I forgot about it until we passed by the pool again much later and I asked Dad if he'd found out what had happened. In the summer of 1961, rather than allow Black people to swim in the pools in Lynchburg with Whites, the city chose to drain all three and fill them with dirt. I remember standing on the wall looking down at the nine-foot mark and the grass growing around it in silence, with my father. I suppose it was a monument, after all.

He can't swim, Dad saves him

Jim Michonski • Virginia Beach, VA

I grew up in a military family. The March on Washington happened when I was two years old. We mostly lived outside of the US until I was nine. I don't have memories of and was not exposed to the racial turmoil of the 1960s.

One of the strongest experiences that gave me insight into what it meant to be Black happened a couple years after moving back to the States. The community I lived in had no public pools. The only pool available for the civilian community was part of a social club. The club was for the most part segregated. At that time there was no explicit discriminatory racial policy, but it seemed implied. Membership dues kept most people from joining.

My father coached and played sports. One year at the end of the baseball season, he had a pool party for the baseball all-stars on the military base where he worked. The social club pool was not available, in part, I believe, because there would be Black boys attending the party.

One Black boy, a very athletic and talented ballplayer who was also very polite and well-liked, decided he would dive off the board in the deep end of the pool. He did this once or twice. We didn't notice that as he jumped his momentum carried him to the shallow end where he could touch bottom. He couldn't swim, but we didn't notice.

A little later, he dove again. This time he took too steep an angle and didn't make it to the shallow end. He started flailing in the water. Several adults, including my father, jumped in to save him. In the aftermath, I learned why he couldn't swim. The reason was segregation and discrimination concerning public pools. We almost lost a great kid because there was no place for him to learn how to swim.

I was introduced to racial discrimination in a deeply personal and scary way. A peer almost drowned because of it. I also learned there are many of all races that found ways to get around the ingrained racial culture of the community.

Lady, I don't want your purse
Sherry LeGare-Underwood • Montgomery, AL

If I only had one dollar for every time I shouted this in my head to a White woman in the movie theater or restaurant or grocery store that grabs her purse from wherever she has it sitting and pulls it to her side when she sees me approaching, pushing my shopping cart full of kale and tofu or whatever (as I watch the White people pass her without provoking any concern for the safety of her handbag).

I'm the blond on the bus
Peggy Magnusson • San Pedro, CA

In exchange for the stress of freeway traffic, I have begun taking the bus to and from work. For most of my life, I have lived in largely White, upper-middle-class communities. Now I sit shoulder to shoulder with people of color. Sometimes I am uncomfortable.

My struggle, you have no idea
Kyle Conway • USA

Navigating through corporate America as a Black man has been a struggle. Always has. Will it get better? You have no idea. I come to work, put on the show of happiness all while struggling. Can I truly provide ideas in this meeting, or will I be labeled? As a Black man in corporate America, I don't get the luxury of being a straight shooter, or straight to the point. I . . . get labeled. There are moments of laughter on the inside when I enter the elevator and watch the White ladies grab their purses, only to see them again in a meeting and magically become accepted. It's like something clicks and magically there's an understanding . . . he's not a threat.

Clutching your purse, locking your doors...

Council Clarkson • Gainesville, FL

You don't have to do this when I pass by, White lady. Don't worry, the big, bad Black man is not going to hurt you. I'm hurt every time this happens—which is too often—because I really am not out to hurt anyone. I was hurt the most when it happened at my own church. A group of visitors were at my church, and when I came up, the White lady saw me and proceeded to lock herself inside the gym. "Look, lady, don't come to my church and be afraid of me."

After seeing the movie *The Butler*, I noticed how this idea of double consciousness—being who I am naturally, as well as putting on "a face" for White folks—plays out in my own life. When I'm in public and I pass a Black person and I'm in a smiling mood, I smile. Cool. But if I have something on my mind and I don't feel like smiling, oh well, no smile.

Now for White people, it's different. If I'm smiling, cool. But if I'm contemplative and a White person approaches—I've just recently noticed—I put on the smiley face. Well, maybe not always smiley but the pleasant I-am-your-friend face. As unintentional as it may be, I know why I do it—because I don't want to be perceived as threatening—but my question to you is: Should I have to? You see, if I walk past a Black person and I have wrinkles in my forehead because my mind is on something else, I'm comfortable with the fact that they don't see me as a threat.

I will not steal your purse

Henderson Smith III • Saint Louis, MO

I told this [to a] lady in Cincinnati, Ohio, after she grabbed her purse when she saw me walking down the supermarket aisle. I explained to her that I was a logistics engineer at GE Aircraft Engines and a captain in the Air National Guard.

Do they have the same father?

Lisa Hatcher • Richmond, VA

When my children were about eight, five, and two years old, an elderly woman with a heavy Southern drawl spoke to me in the grocery store. "You have three beautiful children." A pause, then she added, "Do they have the same father?" I was taken aback. Their father is Jamaican, with a background of English, Portuguese, and African. Throughout their childhood, people have a hard time seeing that the three of them are siblings.

No, I did not swim here

Jordan Corona • Lakeland, FL

I'm Cuban and Arabic, and any time I tell someone that, they ask me if I'm a terrorist and if I swam here, especially since I live in Florida.

White privilege, enjoy it, earned it

Douglas Thomas • FL

I am not apologizing for something I have no control over. Every major contribution to mankind was done by people of my race. Society owes White people a debt of gratitude, not scorn.

I don't know Inez's last name

Rosemary Brinson • Kalama, WA

Reflecting on growing up in Duplin County, North Carolina, my grandma Cora was the matriarch of a large family. Inez was her helper, confidant, friend, and nurse for decades. My sister and I loved her, and we played with her grandchildren. Over fifty years later, I think about Inez, and I realize I don't know her last name. Why is that? I hope her beautiful family is carrying on sharing her caring spirit with their lives. Inez meant the world to Grandma and to me, too.

My grandparents met in the KKK

Alisa Rose • Ann Arbor, MI

I didn't know that until recently. My aunt found my grandfather's robes in a trunk when he died. My grandmother was a little embarrassed. The times have changed in my hometown—the KKK is not active anymore that I know of. But the town is still less than 2 percent African American.

ARE YOU BLACK, ASIAN, OR NORMAL?

Jenna Overton • Langhorne, PA

I'm a half-Black college student. My friends and I were discussing race one day, and a few of the White males in the group (my boyfriend among them) reasoned that they probably couldn't think about race in the same way minorities do because to be White is to be "normal."

I think grandma had a secret.

Freya • United Kingdom

1

Bread Crumbs

THINK OF A VISIT WITH A GRANDPARENT. Few things are as comforting. Their loving hands and overflowing wisdom. The smell of baked goods in the oven and a whiff of Old Spice. The candy dish is always full. There's always a place at the table, always a warm embrace, and even when they fuss, the admonition is always steeped in adoration.

Anyone who has lived long enough to reach their seventies, eighties, nineties, and beyond has witnessed incredible change: Cellular phones. Flat-screen televisions. Self-driving cars. Personal computers . . . a man on the moon . . . the fall of the Berlin Wall . . . the growing acceptance of marriage equality for the LGBTQ+ community . . . GPS that spits out directions . . . ATMs that spit out money . . . six women appearing on a debate stage on live television during the 2020 Democratic primary as they competed to serve as president of the United States.

The America those senior citizens grew up in was very different. Laws, customs, and social norms around race, sexuality, and gender were rigid and enforced. The idea of a Black president . . . a gay CEO . . . four women justices on the US Supreme Court . . . all of it unthinkable.

In truth, today's elders came of age during a time when a White person playing with, dancing with, even speaking to a person of color was in many cases a revolutionary act. The color line was deep and wide and seemingly impenetrable. The confines for women, the disabled, and queer or brown-skinned people of all kinds were often uncompromising. A lot of Americans—to be specific, a lot of those who are senior citizens today—were invested in making sure that certain people knew their place and kept their place.

The racialized social order was so rigid that, to change their "ranking" in the cultural hierarchy, some resorted to tweaking a few words on a government document or slipping silently past a cultural barrier to pass as someone of another race, another religion, another persona entirely.

For years, they kept those stories to themselves—the ones about enforcing the social order, the ones about subverting it, and the ones that unleashed a hidden ache that throbbed for a lifetime. How do they explain a past that is so out of sorts with the world their children and their children's children embrace? How do you say you enforced segregation . . . or fought against women's rights . . . or marched with forces that are morally on the wrong side of history?

How do you say that you anglicized the family name and stopped identifying as Jewish or Italian or Native American or Melungeon? How do you relay the horrors of driving down a country road and seeing a body hanging limp from a tree, a body you recognized as a member of your community? A body that looked like your husband or son? A body that made you think of the gentle folds in your own chestnut-colored skin and the scars—both physical and emotional—that never really heal? How do you introduce the memory of the little sign that once hung in the window at your family's restaurant that read, "No Dogs, Negroes, Mexicans"?

How do you tell *that* story?

Do you tell that story?

Or do you leave a trail of clues so your loved ones will figure it out over time? Do you scatter coded hints of your history in conversation or surface artifacts that you hope clueless loved ones might stumble upon?

Our inbox at The Race Card Project suggests an awful lot of people have chosen that last option, leaving a trail of clues for the next generation without telling those stories outright: A New Yorker is given the ledger used by her Southern great-great-great-grandfather who owned "buckets of land and pages of people." An adult now understands why in childhood her parents were always so worried when they went into town with Grandma—if locals figured out that Grandma was actually American Indian, they might have sent her away to live on the reservation. A Saint Louis man who remembers when his parents inherited a fancy sideboard with ornate woodwork carved by the enslaved people his ancestors once "owned" in Mississippi. Peter Seay said that piece of furniture had a ghostly presence in his home.

"It stood as [a] gravestone in my childhood home, constantly [reminding] me of my grandparents' death, the lives my ancestors came from, and the deep pains caused by my last name," Seay said. "It is to be left to me next. I do not look forward to this day nor the circumstances that will bring it again into my home."

When asked to share their six words on race, a lot of people find their minds going straight to their parents, grandparents, or some other branch of the family tree.

My great-grandfather changed his name
Mother's warnings at four, instilled racism
Grandma feared Blacks. Grandson IS Black.
Grandfather's funeral. Only one Caucasian attended!
Grandma didn't let Dad speak Spanish
We lost our culture to survive

In retrospect, we should have expected that people trying to make sense of their racial identities today would compare or contextualize their current views of self with the older folks in their orbit who lived by a different set of rules. The distance between an eighteen-year-old and an eighty-year-old may not seem that great when they're sitting across from each other at the holiday table, but the chasm is quite vast when measured against their norms and expectations around race. The eighteen-year-old and the octogenarian could rightfully view each other as people who are the products of alien worlds.

In many cases, the older people have not just stories, but secrets. The younger people have questions or judgments or an inkling that the kindly elders who hold such a treasured place in their hearts were once people they would barely recognize when young themselves. People with harder edges or hardened attitudes. People who could barely dream of the things we take for granted today. People whose anthems clash with the accepted ethos of this moment.

Mom's racism took my love away
Dad said date your own race
My grandfather would hate my children
My Dad's prejudices live in me
I hear my grandfather's hateful words.
Grandma you can't say that anymore

3

The deep well of stories in our fourteen-year collection that revolve around parents, caregivers, or elders should not be surprising. After all, this country—indeed, this world—has shifted significantly in four generations.

America's evolution in the past one hundred years is cause for pride and some degree of celebration. However, there is too often an impulse to think of things like slavery or suffrage or the Civil War in terms of ancient history. Our history of bondage and forced segregation, of color codes and gender strictures, of broken treaties and internment camps, is rendered as chapters in an old, dusty book, so far removed that it's like a fossilized relic.

But consider this: The last known survivor of the last known US slave ship died in 1940. 1940! Matilda McCrear, who arrived in Mobile, Alabama, in 1860 on a ship called *Clotilda*, lived long enough to see the Civil War, World War I, and the early stage of the Second World War before she died at age eighty-two. (McCrear had to approximate her age throughout her life because her exact birth date was not recorded.)

When television writer Norman Lear was born in New Haven, Connecticut, more than one hundred years ago, the longest-living Confederate generals were still alive. General Felix Huston Robertson was a retired lawyer in Waco, Texas, and Brigadier General John McCausland was still operating a family farm in West Virginia. McCausland was infamous for commanding his forces to burn Chambersburg, Pennsylvania, to the ground when locals refused his ransom demand of $500,000 in US currency or $100,000 in gold. After the Civil War, McCausland was arrested and faced arson charges for his crimes at Chambersburg, but he was pardoned by President Ulysses S. Grant. He died in January 1927. To put this in context, that's the same winter that actors Sidney Poitier and Harry Belafonte were born (in February and March) and the same year that actress Betty White would have been old enough to enter kindergarten.

With all the battles over Confederate statues and the questions of how slavery or the Civil War should be taught, the debate is too often framed as if we're looking through some kind of long-focus telescopic lens. But it's really like that faint message stenciled on your car's side-view mirrors: "Objects in mirror are closer than they appear." We should always remember that Harriet Tubman and Ronald Reagan walked this earth at the same time. We should remember that former Confederate soldiers were still alive into the early 1950s, when *I Love Lucy* was first airing on TV and American children were clamoring for new toys making their debut on the market like Matchbox cars and Mr. Potato Head.

And we should understand that when it comes to race, the events of the past are as tethered to the lives we live today as they are to our older relatives, who witnessed the dizzying evolution of this country.

Today, young people are inheriting a world where racial tensions are still present, but integration is now the norm—in the workplace and at the mall, in the classroom and in the military, in sports stadiums and in the entertainment beamed into American homes. A generation that lives and learns together, dates and marries freely, and fully expects that those who commit offensive racial transgressions will face a fierce wall of opprobrium could easily stand in judgment of older loved ones who enforced or enjoyed segregation or disdained gay rights.

How do elders who lived in that very different world tell their children or grandchildren who they were—or what they endured or accepted, celebrated, or upheld? From my own experience, I learned that sometimes they don't. And after more than a decade of collecting stories about race and identity, I know that my family is not unique.

The stories that go unspoken still loom large, and even though they're never fully articulated, they can shape individual lives with the impact of a jackhammer against concrete. Through the stories that have landed in The Race Card Project's inbox, I've learned that sometimes people can't tell you who they are or what they've seen for all kinds of reasons. Shame. Fear. Guilt. A focus on getting to someplace better. A worry about dragging their kids into the muck. A brand of denial that calcifies and corrodes, the way salty seaside air can turn a padlock to rust. Some doors are best left unopened. But sometimes people do figure out how to leave a faint stream of specks, snippets, and scraps . . . revealing tiny bits of themselves . . . like a trail of bread crumbs.

The three stories that follow fall into what I call that bread-crumbs category: stories that surfaced only after a key clue was revealed.

A phone call.

A birth certificate.

A decades-old petition for child support.

Three individual stories. Three lives changed forever when three women, each in her own way, tried to figure out where those bread crumbs led.

BIRTHDAY PRESENT:
YOU ARE BLACK. SORTA?

Arlene Lee • Chestertown, MD

ARLENE LEE OF CHESTERTOWN, MARYLAND, sat at her computer in January 2011 and sent these six words to The Race Card Project website: "Birthday Present: You are Black. Sorta?"

Arlene was surprised she found the gumption to share the story with someone she'd never met and surprised at the burden that seemed to physically lift from her shoulders when she started to type out her story.

On the night before she turned fifty back in 2011, Arlene was feeling nostalgic, so she decided to rifle through the papers left behind by her then recently deceased mother, an immigrant who had moved to America from Peru. Along with the bank statements and childhood report cards, Lee discovered something she had never seen before. Her mother had two birth certificates in her files. When Lee's mother moved to the US from Peru in 1958, she obtained a new birth certificate and a new profile that would form the basis of a new life in America. As Arlene Lee compared the two documents, she saw that her mother had erased the fact that she had been born out of wedlock. The original birth certificate revealed that Arlene's grandparents had never been married. While comparing the two documents, Lee spotted something in the numbers. The birth years did not align. In obtaining a new birth certificate in adulthood, Arlene's mother had moved the clock forward, shaving nearly eight years off her age. With that new piece of paper, the twenty-five-year-old Dora Lores became eighteen again. That demographic sleight of hand made Arlene chuckle at the memory of her mother's vainglorious beauty rituals: night creams and rollers and pearls at the dinner table. She worked as a nurse and wore a simple uniform to work each day, but at home she carried herself like an heiress.

But there was something else in those two birth certificates. To this day, Arlene struggles to describe the exact emotion upon spotting the discrepancy. Scanning her eyes back and forth between the original birth certificate and the replacement issued years later, Arlene noticed that her mother had changed her race from Black to White. The word *negro* was right there in black and white on the Peruvian document that had been issued after her mother's birth.

All her life, Arlene's mother told her that she never knew her father. "He loved my mother, but he left us," she'd said. That wasn't true. Her father was neither absent nor invisible. He was Black and originally from the island of Dominica. And if he was Black, that meant Arlene had to rethink all the boxes she had checked in her life, blithely labeling herself as White because that was the way she was raised by a fair-skinned Latina woman who worked hard to erase her accent, married a White man from rural West Virginia, and raised their daughter in a house with only hints of her Peruvian roots. The White label was a badge of honor for Dora Lores, and she proudly passed it on to her daughter. But was it really, fully Arlene's to claim?

"My mother raised me to be White, and I am, at least by self-identification, I guess," Arlene said.

But is she? When she told her husband, she remembered why she fell in love with him in the first place. He was solid. He understood her tears weren't about the word *negro* but the fact that her mother kept a lifelong secret from her only daughter. "Doesn't matter," he said. He loved her no matter what. "Explains the hair," he added, and they had a good laugh. Arlene had spent a lifetime and a fortune in beauty products trying to tame hair that reached for the sky. Her sons reacted with humor, too, but she didn't find that funny. When she sat down to tell her two boys about the discovery, they broke into Ebonics, calling each other *dawg* and *bro*. They recited rap lyrics. She was grateful she could tell them together—they were both home for their grandmother's funeral—but she found their response bizarre. "For me, it was not a light moment," Arlene said. "The levity was not working."

Her mother's relationship with the grandkids was a conundrum and, as it turned out, a clue to her inner life. When they were born, she was uncharacteristically panicky about their health in the hospital. As a nurse, she had worked in an ER and in burn units. Dora Lores was typically unflappable, but the birth of both boys fried her circuitry. She was fluttering and perspiring, and Arlene remembers muttering under her breath to her husband, "You'd think she is the one about to give birth."

She sees it through a different lens now. All that nervous energy reached back to Peru . . . reached back to the river port city of Iquitos, which sits 2,300 miles inside the Amazon Basin.

It's a place so remote that it is designated as the world's largest city that cannot be reached by road that isn't on an island. The only way to get there is by boat or plane. A place made famous by Klaus Kinski in the 1982 West German film *Fitzcarraldo*, directed by Werner Herzog. A place where Dora Lores grew up in the jungle with her very dark-skinned father, who was originally from Dominica. Jose Lores, whose original name was Joseph Labadie, was one of thousands of workers brought to Peru from the Caribbean as the country capitalized on the global demand for rubber. After Dora's mother died, Jose Lores was a single parent and traded his work on ships for handyman jobs on dry land.

He managed to send Dora's older sister to Lima, the capital of Peru, with church missionaries. Dora was too young, so she stayed behind. The woman who loved doilies and pearls and deviled eggs served on gleaming silver platters grew up in the ruins of a house perched in the hills above the Amazon, Nanay, and Itaya Rivers. Two walls, a blue tarp, and mosquito netting when they could find it. That was the home, where dinner was prepared over an open fire. No plumbing or electricity. A hard life in thick jungle until she too was old enough to leave with the missionaries from the Seventh-day Adventist Church.

Arlene has learned through her aunts and her cousins that Dora was very close to her father. When she left, he told her, "This is the last time I will see you." And it was. Arlene now believes that her mother's constant fidgety nerves, her constant pacing in the hospital room, her outsize paranoia were the manifestations of a deep-seated worry that her father's ethnic roots would resurface, and the long arm of ancestry might reach out and grace her grandson with cappuccino skin or coiled hair or features that would conflict with the story of Whiteness Dora had wrapped around herself like a protective netting back in the jungles of Peru.

Arlene now thinks her mother was terrified that her sons would look Black. Dora loved those boys, and while she rarely talked about her life in Peru, she developed culinary nostalgia in her sixties, spending hours preparing the boys dishes from her childhood. Lomo saltado—stir-fried beef—and papa a la huancaína—potatoes with a spicy cheese sauce, carefully garnished with olives and slices of boiled eggs. All Arlene tasted was envy. "I understand that my life experience was crafted very carefully for me to be White," Arlene said. "Mom was generally very, very private.

"I was fascinated about the country. The only way I could discover what her life was like was to write papers about Peru as a student. Deviant behavior project in college—cocaine in Peru! Water project—infrastructure in Peru! That is how I would learn things, and even under those circumstances—reluctantly—if I asked about her [about them], she would shut that story down."

So, when Dora started to go down memory lane in her kitchen? "I was horribly jealous," said Arlene. "I mean, wow—you are going to do that with them, but you would not teach me?"

Grandparents often have a different relationship with their grandchildren than with the children they raised. It's more relaxed. More forgiving. More open. That was certainly true for Dora. She was a political conservative. Her grandsons were progressives, and their cross-generational arguments would last for hours, especially when the subject turned to a political newcomer named Barack Hussein Obama. Arlene was in the Hillary Clinton camp before the 2008 election, but like so many other voters, she was cajoled by her kids to move toward Obama and his message of hope. It was a much longer journey of the soul for Dora Lores. She could not imagine what the world would think of a country that would elect a Black man as president. "Who would respect America after that?" she would say. "We will lose our standing in the world. It would be a disaster."

Arlene sees all of this through new eyes. Her mother was having a debate with herself. Her secret self. All that bombast about America was likely an exercise in self-censure—maybe even self-hatred.

That stings.

Of course that stings. Dora Lores lived long enough to see Barack Obama's inauguration. Though she thought he was handsome and classy, his Blackness trumped all of that. "She was horrified by his presidency. Horrified that this was the face of the United States." And she also wondered why he identified only as Black when his mother was White. "Isn't he both? Why does he say he is only Black? Why would he do that?"

Her grandsons' retort came down to three words: it's his choice. Arlene never had a choice. Her mother chose Whiteness and served it up to her daughter as part of her birthright. She has now spent more than a decade unwrapping what that gift means, retracing her mother's life, traveling to the places where she did missionary work, back to Iquitos—back to the mountain where Dora lived in the jungle, back to the docks where the Amazon is clogged by so many boats and ships and barges and rafts that it looks like an interstate highway during rush hour. Back to the little courthouse in the square where a gaggle of cousins helped Dora obtain her bogus birth certificate. As luck would have it, Dora's half sister from her mother's first marriage worked in the clerk's office where the documents were issued.

Arlene is still searching for anything she can find about her grandfather's itinerant life.

Arlene's grandfather is still an enigma. He kept to himself. It was like he was almost invisible. That is not unusual. In a country that celebrates its Spanish and Incan heritage, Afro-Peruvians (also called afrodescendiente Peruvians) have long been marginalized. Brought to the country as slaves and later domestics, construction workers, rubber collectors, miners, blacksmiths, and field hands on the sugarcane plantations, Afro-Peruvians make up around 5 percent of the country's 33 million people. Until a few years ago, the country didn't even know how many Afro-Peruvians were living within its borders.

The 2017 census was the first census since 1940 where the country collected this kind of race data. Academic studies indicate that a large percentage of Afro-Peruvian children, especially girls, don't attend school. Many Black Peruvians don't participate in government health or social-aid programs because of discrimination or problems with access, and a World Bank study found that 70 percent of Afro-Peruvians surveyed did not seek medical care for illnesses because of limited access or perceived discrimination. They are most visible as waiters, doormen, field hands, and water taxi drivers. Even those who gain an education have a hard time finding work in hospitals, schools, or professional offices or as clerks. The coded language frequently used to deny entry is that employers are seeking someone with "good presence," a euphemism for light skin or a White-looking appearance. To be Black, and especially dark-skinned, in Peru today is much like living in 1920s America. Several international studies exploring life for Peru's Black minority population have found that discrimination is rampant and often without recourse.

Arlene is still searching for anything she can find about her grandfather's itinerant life. One of the last times a cousin saw him was several decades ago. By her cousin's math, he would have been close to one hundred years old. He was on a wooden raft paddling down the Amazon. More recently, another cousin she met in her quest to learn more about her Peruvian roots told Arlene that her grandfather had spent his final years living with a distant relative in Colombia.

After all that she has learned, is her identity different? In the first years after discovering her mother's secret she would still check "White" when she filled out forms. That has changed. She now checks "other." "I finally felt like I could tell my own truth," Arlene said. "So, when I checked 'other,' I felt like I was finally saying, 'This is who I am. And it's not who you think I am.'"

Is her viewpoint also different? Absolutely, and it has changed in the decade that I have chatted with Arlene. "Other than the fact that I have curly hair, I am very White," Arlene said in 2015. "For me, I am very aware of the unseen. I approach everything with more openness and more humility, and I realize there is so much you just don't know. I try not to assume that I can know someone based on just what I see and the little bit we share with each other."

As with many things, timing is everything. Arlene discovered her Black lineage at an interesting moment. Her mother arrived in the US and chose to be White in the 1950s, an era where being Black carried a high cost. Laws and hardened attitudes dictated where Black people could live, eat, work, and prosper. Arlene discovered that her mother was part Black when US voters had sent a Black family to the White House and Black culture—from Beyoncé to LeBron to Oprah, Ava, Serena, and Wakanda—had become America's greatest cultural export. Her decision to claim otherness and increasingly embrace what it means to be part Black was happening at a moment when demographic change was ushering in an era where Whiteness was no longer the presumed cultural default, and racial tensions seemed to stay on a high simmer. It happened at a moment when another occupant in the White House was purposely divisive. Someone who coddled White nationalists. Someone, in all honesty, her mother would have probably supported.

"It breaks my heart that we never had a chance to talk about it, that she didn't feel she could trust her only child to understand, and that she didn't feel she could ever come out of hiding," Arlene says. "Both of those things make me sad, the lack of trust and the apparent belief that the world hasn't changed so much since 1958 that her race would be a nonissue. It clearly is an issue. And now, I have a new prism through which to see things."

Arlene devotes a good deal of her time to working on programs aimed at undoing racism. It's work that started before her discovery. It's work that has deepened significantly since then.

She increasingly introduces herself as biracial. Longtime friends marvel at her story and suggest she should write a screenplay. Black colleagues wonder if she is trying to now claim something that she has not yet earned. When people split into affinity groups during her anti-racism work, colleagues wonder where she will go. Or more specifically, where she *should* go.

Arlene has had a full decade to think about her mother's decision and the motives behind it. "I think she was trying to live in this country without the kind of oppression that she had experienced and take advantage of the colorism and take advantage of the privileges that come with being light-skinned," Arlene said. "And I think she was also trying to make my life easier."

I asked Arlene what might have happened if her father had made the discovery in his lifetime. He was a White man who had long assumed that he had married a White Peruvian. "I honestly believe that his racism would have overcome whatever love he had for her." I wondered if I had heard that sentence correctly, and Arlene must have sensed that because she pressed on to underscore an assertion that she was certain her mother held. Her father's racism, she said, was a more powerful force than the love he felt for his beloved wife. "He was very open about his racism," she said. "He was one of these typical redneck racists who used racially derogatory terms on a regular basis without thinking about it." At the same time, though, he had friendly relationships with men he knew from the military who were Black.

"He was one of those people who would single someone out and say, 'Oh well, they're one of the good ones,'" Arlene said. "That was the only way he was able to sort of maintain what I think was this weird cognitive dissonance of being so racist and having Black people in his life that he was comfortable with." Would that cognitive dissonance have been extended to his wife, Dora? "I think that would have been too close, too much," Arlene said. "I don't think he would have been able to overcome it. He had a strong sense that being Black was being less than. . . . As a group, Black people were not equals in his mind. So, I think he would've had a really hard time discovering that he had married a Black woman."

As Arlene is talking about her dad's potential rejection of her mother, the obvious question is what that would have done to their father-daughter bond. She'll never know. He died before Dora's secret was unveiled.

A trail of clues led Arlene Lee to her cultural heritage. Dora Lores never came out of hiding in life, but she made sure her daughter would find the truth after she died. She could have easily destroyed the birth certificates; instead, on her deathbed, she repeatedly implored her daughter, Arlene, to visit the safe in the attic where the two birth certificates were kept. By the time Arlene retrieved the documents, her mother had slipped away.

Arlene's story stretches from an Amazonian village in Peru to Central California to Washington, DC, and the Eastern Shore of Maryland, where she now lives. In every one of those places, the history of race and the current facets of racial identity are extremely different and would not necessarily be yoked together if not for that simple 6-word yarn. That story submitted by Arlene Lee explores the notion of Whiteness from the perspective of those who can claim it by birthright and the growing number of Hispanics who choose to check "White" when they fill out census forms. It also explores the generational tension when a parent or grandparent embraced a world or worldview that is out of step with today's accepted norms.

About five years after she made the discovery, Arlene was walking into a grocery store. As she was about to take a cart, one of the men who collect the carts from the parking lot said, "Excuse me, ma'am? You have the most beautiful hair." At this point she had let her curls roam free, setting aside the blow-dryers and flat irons that used to dominate her mornings. The compliment felt good. Really good. "For the first time in my life, I told that young man my grandfather was Black and Caribbean and that is probably where my hair came from," Arlene said. She spoke louder than she usually does. Louder than was needed for the man to hear clearly. Loud enough for several people in the entrance portico to take notice.

"My mother would have never wanted me to say that. It just happened spontaneously. I don't even understand it. I just know in that moment it felt right."

Epilogue

Arlene and I have had many conversations over the past decade. She has changed jobs and moved to new locations. She has visited Iquitos and made deeper connections to her Peruvian family. And recently, Arlene became a grandmother. Her son decided that his daughter's name should honor the great-grandfather he never met. Labadie, Jose Lores's original last name before he moved from Dominica to Peru, is her middle name.

White mother afraid for her children

Sally • Poughquag, NY

I was afraid of speaking up.

Audrey Cao • New York, NY

So afraid of late night walks?

Eliza Buchanan • Davis, CA

Suit. Degree. Still afraid of ME!

C. N. Hart • Los Angeles, CA

Why are we afraid of TRUTH?

Denise Johnson • Pittsburgh, PA

I am afraid of offending you...

Ellyn Ebersole • Martinsburg, WV

Don't be afraid to teach me.

Eleanor Chalstrom • Sioux City, IA

White male. Wear hoodie. Not afraid.

Chris • Santa Barbara, CA

Asian and afraid to go out

Maddie Hsia • Minneapolis, MN

Afraid of not being "Asian" enough

Gwyn • Chicago, IL

What is everyone so afraid of?

Amalia • Long Beach, CA

Afraid of Blacks, wish I wasn't

Royce Wood • USA

MOM'S SECRET CHILDREN, MY MIXED-RACE SIBLINGS.

Diana Stasko • San Francisco, CA

DIANA STASKO GREW UP in the San Francisco Bay Area, and while she had cousins and lots of friends, she always kind of marveled at the kids who came from big, loud households with lots of seats at the dinner table and a gaggle of toys all over the place. Her family circle was more compact. She grew up as an only child. But actually, the correct thing to say is that she grew up thinking she was an only child. The six words she sent to The Race Card Project in October 2013 tell a different story. I spend a lot of time talking to people who send in their stories. The conversations are often rich and complex, full of undulating emotions. I thought it best to tell Diana's story in her own words.

"Mom's secret children, my mixed-race siblings."

When Diana Stasko was thirty-five years old, she received an early-morning phone call that would change her life. It's a story of secrets and heartbreak, but also a story of compassion and grace. She's now fifty-two, and she has had time to process that phone call and all that followed.

DIANA: It was 7:30 in the morning, on a workday. I was kind of in a hurry and the phone rang and I picked it up and this woman asked for my mother by her birth name, something that my mom didn't use regularly. Her first name is Winifred. . . . I was thinking, is this someone trying to get some information or trying to pull some scam on me or my mom? And I said, "Well, she's not here." And they said, "Well, where is she?"

I said, "She doesn't live here"—because I didn't live with my mom. . . . The conversation progressed to the person saying, "I'm looking for Winifred because my friend Ed Mitchell thinks Winifred might be his birth mother."

I didn't understand what she was saying. I could not make sense of that sentence. I was pretty dumbfounded, and it was like she was speaking a foreign language to me.

She went on to tell me that my mom's name was on [the] birth certificate and that [Ed Mitchell] was born on a certain street in San Francisco, which Mom had told me that she used to live on. I, too, had lived on that street in the nineties, so that opened the door just slightly. I think she told me the year that he was born, which obviously would have been before I was born.

She asked if he could call me, and I said no.

I thought, "This is just too [much]; this can't be real." I was not going to talk to a stranger when I was still not convinced this wasn't some sort of social-security-number-stealing scam.

She said, "Well, would you like to call him?" And I said, "OK, maybe." I think she gave me his phone number and we hung up and I finished getting ready for work. My head is just spinning. I'm trying to just put pieces together in my head what I knew about my mom's life before I was born. Mom is a very good storyteller and had a very adventure-filled life before I was born. She lived in San Francisco in the 1950s. She knew a lot of the beatnik characters of the time.

So, I'm trying to just make sense of all this on my way to work. My head was just spinning. . . . I get to work . . . and I go into a conference room. I tried to call Mom at my desk, and I couldn't get through to her. . . . I just kept trying and trying. I was kind of frantic at this point. I just needed to know what the heck this meant.

Could this be real?

Finally, I get through to her and I said, "Mom . . . we need to talk." She said, "Oh, it's your father, isn't it?" She thought maybe something had happened to my dad. They were divorced, had been for many years. So that was kind of a funny thing for her to say. I said, "No, it's not Dad."

I said, "Mom, are you sitting down?" And she said, "Yes." And I said, "Mom, did you have a baby before me?" And there was just this moment.

She said, "It was a long time ago . . ."

And then she said, "It was a Black child."

It was like, oh, wow, like a whole new wrinkle to the story because Mom had said so many times over the years how intolerant her parents were of racial differences. Like, very. They were notorious, by the stories that Mom told.

"Whoa, what happened to the child?" And she said, "I gave him up for adoption. . . . I couldn't support him. I was working as a telephone operator at night. I couldn't see a future in this, not for him, and not for me." I was just stunned, and I just said, "Mom, I'm so sorry, let's talk later. . . . I'm so glad that you told me." We hung up, and I tried to go back to work, but I couldn't. So, I went home, and I just sort of spun out for the rest of the day.

• • •

Like any interesting yarn, this is a story with multiple threads. Edward (Skip) Mitchell, the man mentioned on that first phone call, was born in 1959 to parents of different races. It was the same year that Richard and Mildred Loving were arrested in Caroline County, Virginia, and banished from the state for breaking a state law that forbade White people and Black people from marrying one another. Several years later, the Lovings would successfully take their case all the way to the US Supreme Court, where in 1967 the justices ruled unanimously that such laws were unconstitutional.

But in the 1950s, laws and social norms disdained interracial unions throughout the US. Even the freethinking state of California had long had an anti-miscegenation law on the books, dating back to 1850. Nearly a century later, with the state supreme court's ruling in the 1948 *Perez v. Sharp* case, California became the first state to permanently strike down anti-miscegenation. Even so, interracial couples continued to face flagrant discrimination in housing, schooling, employment, and public accommodations like restaurants, hotels, amusement parks, and clinics.

Edward grew up as a minority within a minority, a brown-skinned, mixed-race kid unsure of who or where his birth parents were. I interviewed him and Diana on separate days from different locations. However, it felt like they were talking not just to me but to each other.

ED: The story's pretty simple. I wanted to find my mom and at least figure out why I was the way I was. . . . I was forty-five years old, and I had all kinds of weird issues. And I thought, I gotta go on a mission and figure out what's going on with me. And so, I went to a therapist, and she asked me, "Have you ever thought about looking for your family?" And I said, "Well, of course." I thought about my mom ever since I was a kid. A social services agent came and told me that my dad passed away. I never thought about looking for my dad. But I always wanted to look for my mom.

I figured maybe she's dead . . . but I thought, "You know what? I got to figure this out." And so, I went out looking. I found an agency on a Saturday night. It only took a couple of days for them to find her because they had a birth certificate. And they said, "We found this woman that we believe is your sister."

After Diana's mother confirmed that she had indeed given up a child for adoption, Diana began reflecting on her own childhood and connecting the dots between incidents that suddenly had a new and different context.

DIANA: I was looking at the underside of everything. I was seeing the underlying meaning of things and the underlying causes of things that had happened in my life that suddenly made sense or were explained.

My mom raised me as a single mom. My parents divorced when I was ten, and Mom and I were basically this pair. We moved frequently. When I was about age ten, we moved to a rural area in Colorado, and we just were very close. And so, I thought that I knew everything there was to know about my mom. Clearly, I did not. I just didn't.

It kind of clarified the sensation of this explains A, B, C, and D, and why these things were said. I remember as a teenager, I said something about, "Mom, you're a great mom," or, "I love you," or something. And she said, "Well, I think I've done pretty good, you know, considering." And I thought, "Considering? Considering what?"

I never really delved into that with her because Mom could be quite testy and rather unpredictable and moody. So, I just thought, "OK, next topic." I remember my stepmother once saying, "Your mom has done a terrible thing, and I can never tell you what it is, and I hope you never find out." And I relayed that to my mom and that impacted my mom so strongly that that's why we moved to Colorado.

ED: Monday morning I called [Diana]. I actually called her by accident. . . . I had an old friend. It was my brother's ex-girlfriend. We were roommates for almost two years, and I always called her my sister. And I wrote down Diana's phone number on a piece of paper and then wrote my sister's number above Diana's number. I accidentally called Diana, and I said, "Hey, sis." When I heard [Diana's voice], I thought, "Oh my God." I said, "Sorry, wrong number." And I hung up.

DIANA: Around 10:00 a.m., the phone rang and I picked it up and it was a man. And he said, "Oh, hi, I'm looking for my friend Deondra." And I was like, "No, this isn't Deondra. There's no Deondra here." And I knew right away who it was. I knew immediately. I just had a feeling.

And my first thought was, "Oh, he wants to see what I'm like. So maybe he's pretending that he's looking for Deondra." I said, "This is Diana." And he said, "I'm sorry." And then he hung up. I thought, "Huh, that was weird because I was fairly certain I knew who that was."

ED: It was the wrong number. And then I thought, "If I don't call her [back] now and clear this up, she's going to think I'm some kind of weird creep, you know?" So I called her. It was very tense, and I could tell that she was speculative. I told her I thought she was my sister.

DIANA: He said, "Hi, this is going to sound weird. But I think I'm your brother." And I said, "I know who you are. I'm so glad you called." It was immediately like long-lost relatives and also strangely like, wow, this is crazy because he started to talk to me about himself.

ED: [She] says, "Oh my God, I have a brother." 'Cause she was an only child. Or she thought she was an only child. And then I said, "Well, did she tell you about the rest of us?"

DIANA: And then he said, "Well, yeah, there are four of us."

ED: I guess Mom only told her about me. And so, I told her, "Well, why don't you go talk to your mom and ask her if she had a kid named Skip."

DIANA: [Mom] kept referring to the child as *him*. "I gave him up for adoption." She didn't mention the others. There was just him. I think maybe she was hedging her bets that the others wouldn't come up in the topic of conversation, like maybe that was just too wide to open the door for her.

Mom didn't say four. And still, there was a little part of me that was like, I know this can't be real. I was still having a sense of suspicion because once again, the facts were not lining up from what Mom had told me to what this complete stranger was telling me. But he started talking about them. "I have two brothers and a sister." And he said, "We're all really creative. My brother is a musician and a painter." And I thought, "Oh my God, these are Mom's kids." 'Cause Mom growing up was very creative. She was an actress, a beautiful singer. She had a gorgeous voice. When I was a child, she went to school for interior design. And so, her art was on the walls and art books everywhere. It was very much an environment of creativity. This is absolutely ringing true to me.

ED: I guess I kind of expected something different. I thought she would have known about us and would have been really happy to hear from her family members. But she came from the other side where she was the only child and the center of attention and didn't know she had any brothers and sisters, and so she was much more protective.

DIANA: Then I had to call Mom, of course, right? I said, "I want you to tell the truth." And she said there were four. My mom admitted that she'd had four mixed-race children in the late 1950s and early 1960s whom she'd put up for adoption because she couldn't support them alone. Their fathers weren't reliable parents, and my mom's parents weren't open to having mixed-race grandkids. I had just had, like, a thirty-five-plus-year secret crack wide open the day before. And that was like a tectonic shift in my understanding of life. I was like, "OK, maybe one." But four was like, "What?!" And again, why did she feel she had to lie? Why couldn't she have just said there were four?

ED: My take on this is just really simple. I think this was kind of the way things were done back in the day. You know, a lot of things were kept secret and were taken to the grave, especially where color lines were crossed.

DIANA: My mom grew up in a small town in Northern California called Willows, on a farm. My grandmother actually was present in my mom's life, but she wouldn't even call the babies her grandchildren. She would come down to the Bay Area, and Mom said she would camp out in the kitchen and just pick Mom apart. She wore Mom down. I mean, the story is that Grandma persuaded Mom to give the kids up. She says that my grandma really talked her into giving up all the kids to a family that lived in East Palo Alto, and her condition was that they all stay together. . . . So, they grew up together in East Palo Alto with a foster family.

Ed, known as Skip in childhood, is now a successful investor in Florida who works in real estate and has other business ventures. He was three years old when he and his three siblings were sent away to live with another family. His older brother was four and a half, his younger brother was eighteen months old, and his baby sister was just two weeks old.

ED: I grew up in a foster home. It was a pretty brutal place. My foster dad was the grandson of a slave and my foster mom was the granddaughter of a slave, and they brought violence into the household. That was kind of how they taught us. "Do your chores. You didn't do them? We're going to beat you. Break the rules, we're going to beat you." So, there was a lot of physical violence, and because we were mixed kids, we caught a lot of flak.

Most of the people that I grew up with ended up going to prison, selling drugs. I actually ended up with a really bad crack cocaine habit, which I was able to deal with in my twenties. And then in my late thirties, I was done with it. I went to AA. I did all that stuff, and I've been sober for a few decades now, but I had a really troubled start. I wanted to do things like go to college, and I did. I think I went to college for almost eight years. And I've never graduated. I've gone back to college three or four times and have had successes without a degree. I guess that's the best way to put it.

But I kept having all these problems. I had problems with women. I had anger problems. I had really low self-esteem. I still have low self-esteem. You wouldn't know that by meeting me or talking to me. Everybody says they think I'm the most confident person. And I just go, "That's just because I've been beat up so bad that nothing scares me anymore."

But I wanted to meet my mom. And I just wanted to know who I was, and I wanted to know why I was the way I was. I completely rejected the family that I was with. I grew up with these people, and they weren't my family. And I think it's the thing that saved me psychologically because I see people that have been brutalized by their maternal family, their genetic mother and father, and they get pretty damaged from that.

But for me, I always thought these aren't my [people], this isn't my mother, this isn't my father. These are people that I live with, that are getting paid to take care of me. . . . I experienced a lot of anxiety, and I don't know why. I've made millions of dollars. I live in Miami Beach in a penthouse [that] overlooks the water. I got more cars than I can park in my garage. And I still wake up in the mornings, worried it's all going to hell and something's going to go wrong. And I know where that comes from. It just comes from growing up, feeling unsafe.

I just wanted to know who I was and where I came from, who was my family?

DIANA: Mom is a genius, and I'm not exaggerating. She had her IQ [measured]. She's like 156 IQ. Mom is absolutely brilliant. I'm constantly blown away by, "You've never heard of this writer?" or, "What about this book?" Or, like, "The ancient Sumerians did this." So, Mom is—what's that type of brain that just knows so many things? Polymath?

Diana, Ed, and their nephew Leon Pierce, Jr.

She was very talented. And she grew up in this little farm town where there was really no place for that. She grew up in a farm family who didn't know what to do with this child. What do you do with the daughter who's brilliant, smarter than anyone in town? There's no money for college.

But Mom decided to leave Willows. She went to Chico State for a while, and then she dropped out and moved to San Francisco, and she lived with her sister, my aunt, Marty, who was a San Francisco lesbian in the fifties. . . . She just had this really colorful life.

Mom was twenty-six or so when the first [child] was born. She was quite young, and they were spread out over a period of about five years. The story that Mom told, it's quite personal, but what she told me was there are two different dads. The first father she met, he was quite a bit older. He was like ten years older than her. They were together long enough to have had my two oldest brothers. And then the way she tells it is that she was in the hospital having [her second child, Ed], and when she came home, [her partner] had moved another woman into the apartment and thought that was going to be OK for all of them to live together or something. Mom said, "No, absolutely not." I don't remember exactly how she left that situation, but the first father had a cousin, and his name was Jesse. And so, Jesse started helping Mom. He started taking care of her . . . and bringing food over. She had a little tiny toddler and a little tiny baby. Mom tells me that he was the love of her life. She fell in love with him, and they lived together and had the next two kids.

The circumstances in the sixties, when I think she was having relationships with these men, when it would have been at the very least socially frowned on. There were only certain people that they could hang out with. There's no structure for a single woman to support four children easily in the 1960s as a telephone operator. There's just so many heartbreaking elements of the story.

• • •

A few weeks after their initial phone call, Ed and Diana made plans to meet in person—with their mother, who by then was seventy-two years old.

DIANA: It was around Thanksgiving when [Ed] and his wife came to see me in Oakland, where I was living at the time, and Mom came down from Sacramento and was staying with me for us all to meet.

ED: I told my older brother, and he really did not want to meet my mom. He didn't want to get involved in any of it. He just thought it was [too scary]. And it's really interesting because my older brother was a big gangster-type guy that went to prison and everything. But when me and my brother pulled up outside, he tells me, "You go in and come out and tell me if it's OK."

He was so afraid. . . . All my time growing up, he was always a big kid. I was always a runt kid. I got put up a grade, and I ended up in the same grade and classes as my older brother. And he hated it. He looked like Antonio Banderas [back then] and he's six foot two and he's this beautiful, light-skinned Black guy with long hair. The girls just loved him. And I was just this little bucktoothed runt. So, I always looked up to my brother. He could fight, and he hung out with all the tough kids, and he did all the tough things, and it was so amazing to see him turn into this squeamish, scared person just to go meet his mom.

DIANA: They drove up, and I remember [Ed] coming up the stairway and seeing him for the first time.

ED: I just remember it was at night and my mom was sitting on a sofa and then I came in the door and there she was. And Diana was kind of standing off [to] the side like an observer.

DIANA: [Ed] came in. [Mom] was sitting on the futon in my living room, and they just hugged, and it was very quiet. I remember her crying.

ED: I don't know how much you know about AA. I'm an AA guy. I did a lot of step work to sober up. And one of the first things I had to do was work on my relationship with my mom. I blamed her for so much in my life. And I realized that I had a part in all that. And my part was that I made her the reason. I always can use that excuse. "My mom abandoned me," blah, blah, blah.

And when I finally worked that out, I realized that I had amends to make to my mom, and I needed to go apologize to her for making her the cause of all my problems. And so, when I met her, the first thing I did was I had to get that off the table. I said, "You know what? I'm so sorry. I made you the cause of all my problems."

I'm sorry, I'm having a little moment right here.

• • •

There is a long silence before Ed can continue. It sounds like he needs a tissue. I can hear light sniffling on my end of the phone, and I tell him that he can take all the time he needs, or we can continue later. He wants to continue; he says he just needs to find his breath. When we pick up the conversation, he is right back in that room, describing the moment he met his mother for the first time.

ED: She started crying, and so did I. I gave my mom a big hug. She was so happy to see me. She cried like a baby.

DIANA: I just remember watching them embrace. She was sitting on the couch, and he was just hugging her. I remember just thinking what a blessing to be able to witness that and what a gift that she's still alive and that he got to meet her again, and they could have a reunion.

We sat down after that, on the floor. [Ed] and I were sitting on the floor and joking, and he sat right next to me and we were just all talking and it just felt comfortable right away.

ED: We look alike. We have the same arms and hands. We have long arms and big hands. My mom is tall. I think she's, like, five ten. We have kind of the same face. By the time I met my mom, she was already crippled from neuropathy. So, I've never seen my mom walk. All my family, we have this very interesting walk, even Diana . . . all my brothers, my sister, my daughter, we all have the same walk. We kind of lurch from side to side. . . . But [mainly] it was just the way she talked, the way she said things. It just sounded like me. And really literally sounded like me if I was in an older woman. After that we had such a great relationship. But my brother and my younger brother—my younger brother passed away about two years ago—they never really hit it off, and I think it's because they still held and hold resentments.

Even my older brother has rarely talked to my mom. I mean, they talk—every once in a while. When I go to the Bay Area, I'll grab him and say, "Come on, let's go visit Mom," and he'll go with me, but he won't go alone. You know, he just doesn't have any kind of relationship with her.

So, I was really lucky that [reunion] happened.

DIANA: I think it was harder for [Mom] than she let on. And if I remember correctly, not too long after that, she had a little stroke. I remember the doctor telling me that she had potentially had a stroke. They weren't able to figure it out exactly. But I think it was a lot for her.

This would have been about 2007, but after that, [Ed] and I were in contact regularly, and he would call Mom and they would talk on the phone, and he really got the opportunity to have his mom in his life. And they really got along quite well.

Well, I'm really sorry to say that it's not like that now.

Things changed.

One thing that happened was that her dementia progressed and has been progressing. She has a neuromuscular condition (called Charcot-Marie-Tooth disease.)

Diana and Ed with their mother to celebrate her seventy-eighth birthday.

And so do I. It's genetic, which has meant that she basically is, like, a quadriplegic. She cannot walk; she can't use her hands at all. . . . And so, she was in a wheelchair and then she started getting these little strokes and she wound up unable to care for herself. We sort of talked about her moving into skilled nursing and moving closer to me. And that's what happened around 2016.

A few years before that, my brother [Ed] had moved. He got a divorce, and he just moved away and more or less disappeared. I didn't really have much contact with him after he moved.

ED: I haven't been able to get into the nursing home [due to Covid]. We used to go and stand outside her window. And it was really hard because she can't really hear us or see us. So, it's kinda like, well, we're there, but we're not really there. My sister [Diana] has been bugging the crap out of me, "You need to go see Mom, you need to go see Mom." And I'm kinda like, well, but my mom is so senile now. It's kind of like, she doesn't know when I'm there or not.

I think Diana is mad at me because I'm kind of a free spirit. I kind of show up whenever I want.

Shirley Stasko

DIANA: It's really been heartbreaking. I think everyone might have a different idea of what family is. And I had some ideas about it that, I mean, I will say what happened last summer [2020], I feel impacted our family, with the police killings of Black people. And I don't know if I'm imagining it, but I know that there are family gatherings that I'm not invited to and I'm not a part of. And I understand. . . . Part of being raised an only child means that large family gatherings freak me out a little bit. And I do really good with a few people, small gatherings, but big gatherings where I don't know people and I don't have history with them, it's a little challenging for me.

So, yeah, sometimes I think they don't want me there. I'm a White lady, like, why would they want me there? It's hard. She [Mom] wants to know where they are. Why are they not visiting her? And I had to tell her, you know, that Skip moved away.

ED: I know that my mom did the best she could for me. So, I don't hold anything against her. She's explained to me a couple of times probably because she feels guilty, but it didn't really matter to me. All I needed to know was that my mother loved me.

DIANA: I always have thought that our story is such an American story. I don't know of any other place where a story like ours might happen in the way that it happened.

ED: I think this is a very American story. I don't think this is some unique story. I think there's lots of us out there that are being found. . . . This story would be very different if my dad was White. My grandparents would not have rejected my mom. None of that stuff would have happened. You know, my mom ended up living in one of the bad neighborhoods in San Francisco. She actually lived about a block from the corner of Haight and Ashbury for a while, and it was not the best neighborhood at the time. But she had to live there because she couldn't live in White neighborhoods. They wouldn't accept the kids or her boyfriend. So, yeah, it is all about race. I worked in a mortgage bank from 1990 to 1995. And I was with all the senior executives, went up to some boardroom in some hotel or something. And there was a mirror on the side of the wall, and I looked up and I realized I was the only Brown person in the room. And that's been my story. . . . I go back to my neighborhood. I talk to my friends. They say, "Man, how you deal with them people?" And I said, "I just infiltrate." I go in. I've learned the language. I speak the language. I speak it better than they do. I've learned their game. I play their game sometimes better than they do. And then I just come back home. And so it is. It's always been about race, always, always.

DIANA: Everyone in our family has their version of the story, but it really is a story of the heartbreaking effects of racism in our country, but also there's a redemptive quality to our story where we were actually able to all meet again and be sort of a family.

I wanted people to know that there was a time when things like this happened and someone thought it had to be kept a secret and it doesn't have to be a secret anymore. I want [Mom] to know that she created this legacy of kids who are amazing. And, I think this is part of the story, too.

• • •

I never had a chance to speak to Diana's mother, Shirley, but I did get to hear part of the story in her own words. Diana filmed her mother ten years ago talking about the children she gave up. In the video, Shirley Stasko is wearing a lavender sweater and leaning back on a pillow. She describes the day that a woman came to take her four children away.

SHIRLEY [MOM]: I remember that day very clearly that the worker came for them . . . to take them away, and I packed their clothes and everything and put them in the car. I . . . I guess it was just such a shock to me to see them actually go. Up until that point, I . . . I was only thinking about how overwhelmed I felt and how I could not take care of all these children. And I had no money and no prospects of a job or anything like that that would pay enough to support us all. So, I decided as a last resort this is what I had to do.

• • •

Shirley Stasko (who at that time went by Shirley Coe) didn't see her children again for forty years, until Ed picked up the phone to call a woman who turned out to be his sister. In the video, Shirley says she thought her past would never be revealed.

SHIRLEY [MOM]: To keep them a secret from Diana, I . . . I think that it was just inappropriate to bring her into that other life. And I didn't see any way to make her understand. So, I just kept it to myself and, uh, never conceived the notion that it someday would come out in the open. I just kind of carried it around like a lump for all those years.

• • •

Not long after I did the final series of interviews with Diana and Ed, they reconnected—at first on the phone, and then later over a long lunch. It took a while for Ed to get to a place where he could go back to see his mother. He battled fears that he would lose her all over again, this time for good as her dementia progressed. But in 2022, he began visiting occasionally, talking with her at the bedside even if she could not answer. He and Diana worked out a schedule so she would not have to carry so much of the load when it came to monitoring their mother's care.

Notice that I said "their mother's care." When I first began talking with the two of them, they each referred to Shirley Stasko as "my mom," as if they each entered her life through their own separate portal, and in a sense they did. But over time they began calling Shirley "our mom." A small but significant shift of the heart.

• • •

On January 22, 2023, their mother, Shirley (aka Winifred) Stasko, passed away. She was eighty-seven years old.

The birth certificate read Gerald Marx

Sara Nielsen • Austin, TX

My grandfather passed away, and his birth certificate read "Gerald Marx." We only ever knew him as Gerald Nielsen. Did my grandmother know? Who was Gerald Marx, and where was his family from? Are we Jewish? Was the story of his abandonment/ adoption true, or was he the Gerald Mars of record, listed as an orphan in Brooklyn the month he was born? Where is his half sister, Beatrice/Beatrix/Beverly? Where is my family? Who was my beloved grandfather? What is my home?

Grandma sent $100 when we broke up

Anonymous • USA

"Halfbreed." Grandpa died. Not his beliefs

Catherine Adams • USA

Race doesn't scare me. Clothes do.

Robin Smith • Newburgh, IN

I'm only Jewish when it's safe

Dan Tappan • Portland, OR

I'm Asian. I pretend I'm White

Anonymous • USA

I look Black: never felt it

Janetta Stringfellow • Brookline, MA

I grew up in Cape Elizabeth, Maine, in the 1970s with a White mother who denied I was adopted. Found my birth mother when I was thirty-one, who is also White but at least had a story about a Kenyan grad student she hooked up with on her eighteenth birthday in 1964. Denying I'm Black has been the catalyst for most bad decisions in my life. When I was a kid, *nobody* talked about "identity." And Obama certainly wasn't president. I used to be the only person with this story—now there are so many. I wish I could have spoken about it sooner.

I can pass, my mom can't

Katy S. • Seattle, WA

You are dirt. So, I scrubbed.

Melody Rabassa • NY

Mom's racism took my love away

Anonymous • USA

They ask me What are you

Ashley Yee • Boston, MA

Too sad for words. White mom.

Ann • Chevy Chase, MD

Bigotry stole 30 years from us

Jennifer Berry • USA

I am a White woman who has loved a Black man almost my entire life, since I was eleven years old. We are now forty-eight. Due to the prejudice and bigotry of the members of both our families, but predominately those in my family, our relationship was forbidden when we were in our youth. We attempted to sustain a relationship, but the incredible pressure that my family placed on me to end this relationship took its toll, and at age fourteen, I felt that I was forced to make a decision that changed the course of my life forever. I broke off the relationship but never stopped loving my man. Now, over thirty years later, we have reconnected and are still as much in love as we ever were. Neither of us ever married or had biological children, although I did travel halfway around the world to adopt my two beautiful Asian daughters. I am now struggling with the emotional devastation of realizing that I should have tracked down my one true love years ago—he was there waiting for me all along. My head knows, understands, and accepts that our lives have probably turned out as they were supposed to, but my heart hurts deeply knowing that I lost the opportunity to spend my entire life with the only man I have ever truly loved, and that I was forced to make such a devastating decision at such a young age in order to feel that my family would not disown me, all over the color of someone's skin. I am thankful, and feel quite blessed and fortunate, that at least we are able to be together now, and we hope to spend the next thirty years growing old together.

Will my children look White enough

Monique • LA

Would my Grandma still love me?

Samantha • Cincinnati, OH

I don't know any Black people

Brendan Uhl • Sioux City, IA

The melting pot is a lie

Joe Slattermill • WY

FOCUS ON ME.
NOT YOUR BOX.

Stefanie Maynard-Collier • Manassas, VA

STEFANIE MAYNARD-COLLIER GREW UP as the Brown daughter of a White mom and a dad she knew nothing about. She didn't know his name. Didn't know where he lived. She didn't even know for sure what race he was. Growing up in California's San Fernando Valley in the 1970s, she says, "People [were] quite often trying to figure out what box to put me in." With tightly coiled brown hair and cappuccino skin, she didn't look like her mom or most of her classmates, so people could not figure out what category to slot her in. She had a hard time even figuring that out herself. Doing paperwork at the beginning of each school year, Stef never knew which box to check for her race. And, as her mother instructed, she left blank the line where her father's name was supposed to go. "You don't have a father," her mom told her. And that, for many years, was that.

As Stef got older, there were more and more of the dreaded boxes—on job applications, census forms, even on the document for getting her Covid vaccination. For years, she checked "Black," not only because that was how she felt people saw her, but because that was what her mom suggested she choose. Even though her mom, Ann Maynard, was White, checking that box didn't seem like an option. It wasn't hers to claim, and deep down, it wasn't how she felt. For a while, she switched to "other," or just left the boxes blank. She hated those boxes, not only because they were confining, but because they constantly resurfaced the nagging mystery of her father.

"My mother had me out of wedlock," Stef says. "I was a surprise, in that I was Brown, to my family. My mom didn't tell anybody my father was Black, so that came as a shock" to the rest of the family. Stef's mom, who was "a bit of a loner," hadn't told anyone who the father was. She raised Stef as a single mother far from her own family, with no college education and no spouse to help carry the load. No one in her family supported her dream of being an artist. Instead, she worked in blue-collar factory jobs to pay the bills.

Mom and daughter were a tight-knit duo. "I was her prized possession, and the person she centered her world around," Stef recalls—which sounds lovely, until you realize this was just another kind of box. "She didn't share me with anyone, and she wasn't trying to share herself with anyone other than me, either." Perhaps for that reason, her mom never divulged any details about Stef's dad, but simply told her that he hadn't wanted anything to do with them. "I think that possession, the desire to have someone to love that would love her, meant that I was deprived of knowing myself, understanding where I came from," Stef says.

Over the years, out of respect for her mother, Stef never asked questions about her father—and her mom never brought him up. On the very few occasions she said anything, she used the term *we*, as in, "We don't have a daddy," or, "He didn't want us." In her mom's mind, she and Stef were a package deal, and nobody else was welcome into their private world.

Once, when she was in her early teens and had started to learn about where babies came from, Stef gathered up the gumption to ask an awkward question. "So, like, what was the situation, even?" she recalls asking. Her mom told her that she and the man (she never used his name) had worked together in Los Angeles as janitors, cleaning a medical building on the overnight shift. The two didn't date, and in fact, the night they spent together was a onetime thing.

"*Ew.*" That was enough for Stef.

No teen wants to talk about her mom's sex life, so the two of them laughed nervously and that was that. No more questions.

And so, the years rolled by. Stef was a strong student who earned a scholarship to a private high school. She was popular and had a tight circle of friends. But she felt a growing resentment toward this man who had so cavalierly abandoned her pregnant mother. The mother-daughter duo stayed close, and Stef admired Ann for having raised a child as a single parent. When Father's Day came up on the calendar, Stef celebrated her mother to help fill the void. "I would always give her Father's Day cards," she says, "and tell her she was more of a parent than two parents could be."

Then, Stef decided to go to college in Saint Paul, Minnesota. Ann felt hurt and angry. "Mom was unhappy that I left California," Stef says, then corrects herself: "That I left *her*." Making matters worse was the fact that she hadn't even told her mom she was applying to schools out of state. And, she'd done it for the worst possible reason: to follow a boy. "That actually began the real rift between us," remembers Stef. "The thing that she hoped to avoid, which was to have a Black man separate us, is the thing that actually happened."

At the predominantly White Macalester College, Stef started hanging out with students from the Black Student Union, hoping to find her people. She had a Black boyfriend and felt "this need, this desire to feel

more a part of this thing that I clearly was in the world, but which was elusive to me." She sometimes felt judged by students who came from more urban areas in Chicago and Detroit and wore their Blackness with a pride and ease she envied. Her friends at Macalester started asking her questions about her heritage, and Stef had few answers. They didn't understand why she didn't press her mother for information, and over time Stef started to wonder herself.

After college, the confusion around so basic a question became a throbbing irritant. Whenever the topic of family came up, friends and colleagues in her postcollege world were surprised that she didn't know anything about the man who had fathered her. Some practically implored her to at least try to find out, if only for health reasons.

More years rolled by. Stef, now in her thirties and living in Chicago, fell deeply in love with a man who adored her. A Black man. Walter Collier III had two children from a previous marriage, and part of what captured Stef's heart was his total devotion to his son and daughter—something she'd longed for but never had. They married, and about five years later, Stef got pregnant. Her mom came to a baby shower given by her coworkers, and during the party, one of them asked Ann why Stef didn't know anything about her father. That coworker later told Stef that her mom had replied, "Well, she doesn't really care to know." When Stef heard that, something inside her snapped.

She remembers becoming undone while watching the animated film *Frozen*.

"She never once asked me, 'Hey, this is probably hard, that you don't have a father,'" she says. "Like, 'Are you OK? Do you want to talk?' That was never, ever our experience. We didn't talk about it." When Stef became pregnant, she decided it was finally time to ask her mother about her dad and keep asking until she got the information she needed. At an OB-GYN appointment, a doctor asked questions about her racial background and family health history she herself could not fully answer. "I was very nervous, but felt the pregnancy legitimized my need to ask questions," Stef said. One evening, while Stef was with her husband at an IHOP restaurant, her mother called and began spilling details. Stef was sitting in a booth waiting for her pancakes and wondering, "Why now?" But she knew better than to shut down the conversation.

"He had family from Louisiana, and a sister, I think," her mom told her. She said that he was twenty at the time. She was thirty-three, and she lost track of him (still no name) when their shifts changed at work. She said that she had tried unsuccessfully to track him down. And that she didn't know of any health issues Stef should be concerned about.

Stef was knocked out by all these revelations. "I was surprised to get so much information that I didn't think existed," she recalls. "Why had my mother, whom I was so close to, not shared all the information that she had?" Stef wondered. "Why had she not inquired about how I was feeling or dealing with it through these different moments of my life?" Stef wondered, had her mom not understood how challenging it was to grow up as a Brown child in a sea of White people, with no connection to Black people or her full heritage? The questions gnawed at her, particularly as Stef started having her own children. Becoming a mom herself made her appreciate even more what Ann Maynard had done for her. But Stef said her feelings about having been kept in the dark "would pop up in the most random ways, like a lightning strike."

In particular, she remembers becoming undone while watching the animated film *Frozen* with her two youngest children. "It might have been the first Disney movie where true love was not going to be the prince and the princess. . . . The thing that saved the day was this love between sisters." She ached to know what other family she might have. "And then my husband would say, 'You've got to look. We've got to try. It's eating away at you.'"

But Stef was convinced that trying to track down her dad would be too hurtful to her mom. "I don't think your mom will feel the way you think she will," her husband insisted. A former Chicago police officer, Walter was ready to rev up his detective skills and track down some answers. "Maybe you won't find him, but maybe you'll find siblings," he'd tell her. Stef realized that she could be passing people on the street who were relatives and not know it.

Finally, all the speculation, the family rumors, and the gnawing feeling wore her down. Now in her forties, Stef decided to confront her mother, who by that time was slowing down and had moved in with her family. Stef wanted to know if Ann could at least tell her what her father's name was.

"Of course," her mom said. She walked into the next room, then quickly returned holding a folder. Inside was a court document from the 1970s, a filing her mom had prepared asking for child support. Her father's name, according to the document, was Louis Gardner.

"It didn't even take digging," Stef says, still sounding incredulous. "Like, it was just the most matter-of-fact, as if it was just sitting right there waiting for someone to ask." Just talking about that day brings back a storm of emotions. "I was just really angry, actually. I was floored at how nonchalantly she gave it to me." Stef was on the edge of rage, but after a lifetime of tamping down her feelings, she played it cool. She simply thanked Ann before giving the information to Walter so he could immediately track the man down.

Walter dug around for months, but he came up empty. There was a snag none of them knew about at the time. The lead was cold. The name was wrong. Stef's mom had apparently misremembered it, an explanation that, all these years later, barely makes sense to Stef.

Two more years went by, and "this feeling I had was not going away," Stef says. "If anything, it was more than it was before." She needed to know who her father was, so she went back to her mom and asked for his name again, in case she'd written it down wrong the first time. Her mom picked up a Post-it note, jotted down a name, and handed it to Stef. The same name, Louis Gardner. The name that had produced no lines leading to Stef or Ann or her story about connecting with a man who, like her, once pushed a broom at night.

Stef took the Post-it note and stuck it to her desk.

• • •

In 2019, Stef turned forty-nine—and that Christmas, Walter gifted her an AncestryDNA kit. After nearly half a century of searching, wondering, and waiting, she questioned whether she should even bother. But in February 2020, she finally spat into the little vial and sent it off in the mail. One night about two months later, as she sat with her husband and kids at a restaurant, she started scrolling through the app to see what had come up.

"The matches started coming in," she says. "You can see your connections to thousands of people all over the country. Fifth cousins, sixth cousins. So, I started weeding through those trying to get closer." And then, two women's names popped up with the words *close match*. Hands shaking, Stef scrambled to find out what exactly that term meant. She discovered that *close match* meant these women—Crystal and Kaishia—were either her aunts or her siblings.

Crystal had uploaded a photo, and it appeared in a thumbnail-sized box next to her name. "I kept trying to see if she looked like me," Stef says. "I was holding it over to my husband: 'Does this person look like me?' And he was like, 'Yeah, it could be a resemblance.'" She kept scrolling, then saw the words *parent-child match*.

Her eyes were not playing tricks on her. It actually said, "Parent-child match."

"I could not actually process it," she says. "I said, 'Look, what is that?' to my husband. And he said, 'Ah, that's your father.'" Their DNA relationship showed 3,170 centimorgans across 72 segments. In Ancestry language, that meant that he was an identical twin or a parent. Bingo! Stef had found her father. But his name was not Louis Gardner. It was Louis Gordon. Stef burst into tears right there in the restaurant, just as the server came to take their order. "We sat there for a long time," she says, "and I definitely was shaking, and I . . . I just couldn't even believe it."

How do you reach out to the family you don't even know? Where do you start? Ann had created a tight little cocoon for herself and her daughter, and suddenly Stef's family tree was sprouting in several directions. Stef always prided herself on her writing, but how was she going to craft a message to Louis Gordon's family that wouldn't scare them away or make it sound like she wanted something from them—even though she did want something from them? She wanted desperately to be embraced. It took about a week before Stef worked up the nerve to write to one of the two close-match women. "Hi, I see that we are connected in some way," she messaged through the Ancestry app. "I'm interested in talking to you to find out more." She included the URL for her LinkedIn profile, thinking that would validate her existence somehow. And then she waited.

When a couple of days went by without an answer, she started poking around on

Facebook. And that was when she discovered something strange. Kaishia, the older of the two close-match women, was Facebook friends with one of Stef's daughters. She called her daughter and asked how she knew Kaishia Gordon. "I have no idea," came the response. "I just assumed when she friended me that it was someone I went to school with." That was an interesting discovery. Clearly, Kaishia had been doing some sleuthing of her own, trying to find out more about Stef. So, Stef decided to message Kaishia through Ancestry—and that was when the breakthrough finally occurred.

Kaishia wrote back within a day, confirming that she and Crystal were Stef's sisters and revealing that they had another, older sister with a different mother. Suddenly, Stef, who'd been an only child for all her years on this Earth, had three younger sisters. Stef was the oldest, and all of them were excited to invite her into their lives. She felt overwhelmed and excited. And there was more to come: Kaishia told her that their father couldn't wait to talk with her.

How do you reach out to the family you don't even know? Where do you start?

Her father was finally within reach. But Stef had mixed feelings. She called Kaishia and said, "I'm not angry. I'm not trying to point any fingers. I just want to understand." Stef explained that her mother had said that her father didn't want anything to do with her. Kaishia listened and then said, "I hear you. . . . But I need to tell you that Daddy didn't know."

Stef was dumbfounded. "Of all the things I had felt over the years," she says, "I didn't anticipate that at all." He . . . didn't . . . know. Which had to mean that her mother hadn't told him. And that apparently meant that her mother had lied to her all these years.

After hanging up, Stef told Walter, who urged her to focus on the positive pieces of news. "You found your father!" he said. "You have sisters!" And, Kaishia had given Stef their dad's phone number, so now she could finally connect with him. She could hear his voice, hear his side of the story. But she still couldn't bring herself to pick up the phone and make that call.

There was so much to process. Stef spent the next couple of days just trying to get her head around it all. Kaishia would text her and say, "Daddy's still waiting for you to call," but Stef wasn't ready yet. She doesn't even know why. She just wasn't ready.

And then, on a Friday, her phone rang. She thought it might be one of her coworkers, but when she answered it, a man said, "Hi. It's your dad. I couldn't wait any longer." Stef could barely believe what she was hearing. She had spent a lifetime thinking this ghost of a man had flicked his family away like lint on his shoulder, and here he was saying that he wanted to hear from her. This man, who she'd always believed wanted nothing to do with her or her mom, was so eager to connect that he called her. "In an instant," she says, "my heart felt whole."

Now imagine this scene. Stef, with cell phone in her hand, ran upstairs, sped through her bedroom, dashed past her husband into the bathroom, then shut the door and collapsed onto the floor. "The two of us just cried on the phone for what seemed like a really long time before either of us could get any words out," she says. Stef's father asked why she hadn't called him, and she explained that she was too afraid. "I didn't want you to think I was angry, or that I was holding any resentment toward you, or that I was critical of the decisions you made," she told him. Louis Gordon just kept saying to her, over and over, "I didn't know. I didn't know."

Stef decided that she did not want to share any of this with Ann. "I didn't want her to have any part of it," she recalls. "It was like finding something shiny that . . . was mine, and I didn't want to share it. It was my treasure to hold. The treasure she kept from me." She still felt hurt and confused by her mother's omissions. Her dad told her that, before she was born, he had tracked down Ann's number and called her after hearing rumors that she was pregnant. In his telling, she had responded strangely, saying, "I'm not sure what you mean. What are you talking about?" He'd gotten angry, feeling like she was pulling his chain, and had hung up. That was the last contact they'd ever had. It just didn't add up.

Stef wanted to meet her dad and her sisters, but by this time, Covid was raging across the United States. They finally made plans to meet up in August 2020, and that was when Stef decided to tell her mom.

Standing in her home office—the same place she'd stood six years earlier, when she first got up the nerve to ask for her father's name—she said, "Mom, I've found him."

"Oh, well, that's wonderful," her mother replied.

"Yeah, it is," said Stef. "And I have three sisters, too."

"Oh, that's exciting," came the deadpan reply.

Stef took a deep breath and kept pressing on. She told her some of the details her dad had shared—that he'd called her mom to ask if she was pregnant, that he never knew his child had been born—and her mom just answered in a flatly emotionless voice, like she was talking about someone else's story. Stef began to get frustrated. "I don't think you understand the scar that left on me, perpetrating a lie . . . about the person that I believed my father to be," she said. But Ann just repeated calmly a story she was sticking with—that she had believed he didn't want anything to do with them, and that she had tried to do the right thing. "And that was it," Stef says. "I felt almost let down by the lacklusterness of it all."

Stef and her mom still have a good but at times strained relationship. She has tried hard to protect it and maintain it. She didn't want to gain one parent and lose another. But something shifted that day. Something deep.

•   •   •

On August 23, 2020, Stef flew with her husband and kids from Virginia to Los Angeles, where her father lived. Despite the raging pandemic, she and her dad were desperate to finally meet. "God forbid either of us would get sick, now that we'd found each other, and not get the chance," Stef says. So, everyone in both families agreed to get Covid tests and then meet at Louis's house before spending a week at an Airbnb in San Diego.

Crystal and Kaishia surprised Stef and her family at the hotel after missing them at the airport. The next day they drove to "Daddy's house," as they called it. The oldest daughter, Adrieene, was already there, and when they arrived, she opened the door. The sisters had all done Zoom video chats together, but Stef and her dad had chosen not to. They wanted to see each other for the first time in person. As she walked in, he was standing behind Adrieene, and as soon as Stef saw him, she fell into his arms and the weeping began. Both of them sobbed.

"We're both huge criers," says Stef. "Everybody thinks it's very funny, actually—like, we cry about everything, when we're happy, sad, angry. He just held me. And we cried." After a time, everybody moved into the family room, where Louis had turned the room into a gallery. Dozens of family photos were displayed—daughters, nieces, nephews, grandchildren. "I had sent him pictures from growing up," Stef says, and to her surprise and joy, "my pictures of me in my cheerleading uniform were put up in the house."

Louis's wife had cooked a down-home feast, and everybody talked and laughed around the table for hours. "You're so much like your auntie Tomellar," one of Stef's sisters said, and her brain reeled in wonder. "No one ever said that to me," she says, weeping at the memory. A lifetime of photos with Ann Maynard's family show Stef as the lone Brown face surrounded by loving White relatives with buzz cuts and Breck Girl hairdos. But now, someone had seen their people in *her* face. Stef recalls thinking, "I look like my aunties!"

Stef had found her lost tribe. There is a clear resemblance with the sisters, and when you look closely, you see that Stef's looks favor her father. It's in the smile and the bridge of their nose. It's in the way their eyes turn down toward those high cheekbones when they grin. With his coffee-colored skin and meticulously trimmed hairline, Louis Gordon is a man who can still turn heads. And he was crazy about the daughter he never knew.

Stef and her family stayed in San Diego for a week, and she had adventures with her new family that she'd never dared dream of. When the ceiling fan at their Airbnb broke, her dad stepped in to help Walter fix it, taking her along to the hardware store to get the necessary parts. "It seems like a small thing," she says, "but in my imagination, every little girl goes to the hardware store with her dad." He taught her how to make Louisiana tea cakes like his mother—her grandmother!—used to make, taking care to show the secret to getting the sugar-cookie-like confections to plump up in the oven. Because he loved to fish, they rented a boat and went out on the water together. And there was one other pastime he wanted to share with her.

"Girl, you probably can't play Spades," he teased. "Oh, yes, I can!" she said. They spent hours playing, laughing, and cutting up around the big dining room table while passing plates of fried fish and chicken wings. "I got to see where my competitive spirit comes from," Stef says. It was all delicious.

Even small moments held huge wonders. "I would hold his hand," she says, "and I would look at his hand, and it is like my hand." He showed her old family photographs, of aunties and grandparents and of himself as a boy. This felt like coming home. This was a homecoming. "It was the thing I longed for," Stef says. "It would probably break my family's heart to hear me say this, but it felt different. It felt very different. I felt like I belonged there. My sisters, they grew up in California; they're exactly like me. They're so different, but exactly like me." Everything felt comfortable in a way she'd never known before.

When the time came for Stef and her family to fly home, she felt not just sad, but nervous that the magical closeness they all felt together that week might fade. Her dad got in his car to drive home—the same exact car that Stef drives. She got into the passenger seat to say goodbye and sat with him in the front seat, hugging and crying and holding his hand. "I knew we would keep in touch," she says. But would the connection stay strong?

Back home in Virginia, Stef would sometimes refrain from picking up the phone when her dad called, just so he could record a message on her voice mail. "Hello, my daughter!" he'd say. "It's your dad!" She'd play those messages over and over, as if still needing to convince herself all of this had really happened. "He was literally everything that I wished for," she says. "He was like the perfect dad for me."

A year later, the family took their Covid tests and gathered again. This time, Louis, Crystal and Kaishia, and Kristopher, Stef's seven-year-old nephew, flew out to Massachusetts, to spend a week at the beach house where Stef and her family go every summer. At age seventy-three, her dad kayaked for the first time. They all fished together and argued about the best place to reel in the big ones. They sipped cocktails while watching the sun go down. And one afternoon, they all played baseball in the front yard—a big, happy family, scrapping and teasing one another while Louis watched it all and videotaped from the porch. Another perfect family vacation.

Stef pictured with her three sisters: Adrieene standing, Kaishia in yellow, and Crystal in white tank top.

Two months later, Louis went into the hospital to get a stent put in. He'd had heart troubles previously—they run in the family—but this was supposed to be a simple procedure. Unfortunately, there were complications.

"My [fiftieth] birthday was October thirtieth," Stef says. "And I talked to him the day before, which was when he had gone in for this procedure. He had been calling me to find out if I had gotten my birthday card yet. He was in the hospital when I talked to him, and he sounded fine. And on my birthday, he sang me 'Happy Birthday,' like he did the year before. And I kept asking, 'Why are you still in the hospital? I thought this was in and out.'" He told her, "Oh, they are just making sure before I go home that everything's fine." A couple of days later, he was still in the hospital—and now he was on oxygen. "Should I come out?" she asked his wife. No, she told her. She'd let her know if the situation changed. "And then on the morning of November fourth, I got a phone call from Adrieene he had had a cardiac arrest," says Stef. ""And that his heart had stopped three times, and they had revived him, and his wife was essentially saying, 'You need to come.' So, I did."

Fifty Years Crammed into Five Hundred Eighty-Two Days

She flew to Los Angeles, and by the time she got to the hospital, her dad was intubated and unconscious. He'd had a pulmonary embolism, blood clots resulting from the earlier procedure. Stef stayed in his hospital room all night, praying that his situation would improve. At one point, he did become more lucid. "I do believe that he saw that I was there," she says. "He tried to raise his hands a few times. I know he wanted to say something, but he couldn't because of the breathing tube." Sitting at his bedside, she talked to him. And then she began to sing.

"He always liked to say I got my beautiful voice from him, and so I sang to him," she says as tears start to flow. "I promised him that I would look after my sisters. And I told him what a gift he was to me. And that my heart was completely healed and how much I loved him. And I held his hand"—the hand that looks like hers.

He made it through the night, but the next morning, he had another cardiac arrest. That afternoon, he died. "Fortunately, I was able to get to him before. . . ." Stef says, trailing off. "But just a gut punch. So unexpected." Five hundred eighty-two days. That's how long Stef had with her dad.

"Fifty years crammed into five hundred eighty-two days," she says, "and with the exception of only one or two things, I feel like I did everything that I would have wanted to do. I had more than so many people have with their parents."

At her father's funeral, Stef got to meet even more members of her family: aunties, cousins, nieces, nephews, and his lifetime friends. When it was over, she couldn't bear to go back home. She didn't want to leave California because "I felt like if I left, I was leaving him all behind." So, she stayed on for a couple of weeks.

While she was there, Stef received this text from her mother: "I wish I knew what to say."

In all those 582 days, her mother never once spoke with Louis Gordon. And Ann Maynard rarely spoke with Stef about her new connection to that side of the family. So, when Stef got the text, she stared at it for a long time. And eventually, she replied, "'I know. And I love you.' Because I think that's perhaps always been the case, that she just didn't know what to say. And so, she didn't say anything."

There it is again. The child protecting the mother.

Her mother sent one more text before Stef returned home. "Tell your sisters sorry to hear about your and their father," she wrote. "He helped give me you. Love to all."

Louis Gordon and Stefanie Maynard-Collier

Together in California, the sisters talked about how things could have turned out, if only Stef's mom had behaved differently. But Crystal, her youngest sister, said, "Promise me that you're going to go home and not be angry with her. I know you're hurting, but she's what you have left, and [promise] that you will just be kind." Sister love is a splendid thing.

"I said, 'I will do my best,'" Stef says. "And I actually have. I do feel differently, definitely feel softened in that regard, maybe because of what Crystal has asked me." Her relationship with her mother hasn't fully healed, but as she says, "It's never too late. I know that sounds clichéd, but it's never too late to say the thing or right a wrong.

"My heart is broken," she says. "But it's five sizes bigger than it was. . . . My sisters have created true belonging, and no matter what happens, even losing our father, nothing can ever take that away."

It's okay to
see my color

Yvonne Durant • NY

I know that they are well-meaning, but when
White people say, "I don't see color," it makes no sense.
I think they mean they're not prejudiced because color
does not count to them. It does to me.

Photo of gravesite KKK on headstone

Wendy • Kansas City, MO

I was flipping through some old family photos, inherited from a long-gone grandparent. One photo was of two men I didn't recognize standing on either side of a grave in a distant, small-town cemetery. On the back of the photo was a handwritten note: "The stone had 3 K's on it, but we had them sanded off."

When I realized that *3 K's* meant KKK, I experienced the oddest mix of emotions. I was horrified to know that a member of my family was so proud of his association with the KKK that it was engraved on his headstone, and relieved to know that subsequent generations were ashamed enough to have it removed.

I hesitated because she was Black

James • Chicago, IL

I am "White," and I helped a "Black" person today, but I almost didn't. I went to a doctor's visit at the hospital where I used to work. As I was walking to my car, I passed a woman who was walking with a cane but with great difficulty and a look of pain and fear. I just knew she needed help, but for a second, I hesitated. And then the spirit of this project kicked in.

I knew that it was a chance to do the unexpected, to bridge a gap with compassion. I asked if she needed help, and we instantly connected. She said her neurologist had told her to go to the ER, and she was trying to get there without falling. She took my arm, and we crossed the street to the entrance, got a wheelchair, and made it to the security desk. An aide offered to push her to the ER a block away.

I shook her hand and wished her well. She reached up and kissed my cheek and thanked me. I almost missed a chance for a beautiful experience. We do not go through this life alone. I will look for ways to walk the talk and not perpetuate the fears that our society seems to thrive on.

Dad fired the housekeeper, my fault

Sandy Balazic • Tempe, AZ

The year was 1960, and I was four years old. My parents had a housekeeper/babysitter to help while they both worked. One day, my father noticed that she would sneak off behind the basement door on the landing where she kept her personal belongings. When he asked me about this, I told him quite casually that I had told her to bring me pink and red jelly beans every morning, as those were the only ones I liked, and that she would separate them for me.

He asked me if there was anything else she would do for me. I said, "Yep, everything." So, he started watching us. When I wanted a doll from my room upstairs, I would just tell her to go get it. She would stop what she was doing and go get my doll. I could sit on the couch and bark orders, and she would obey. One day, he called us both into the living room.

He was visibly upset. He asked her about how she felt about the differences of being Black and White. She was from one of the Southern states and had just moved to Washington State. She spoke of walking down a street and if White people were walking toward her, she would have to walk out into the street, even into oncoming traffic, so the White people would not have to share the sidewalk with a Black person.

I remember feeling sick and not being able to move. She had been taught that White people, no matter the age, could tell a Black person what to do, and it was expected they

You should be ashamed of yourself

Lauren Russell • Springfield, MO

Words my babysitter told me when I was seven years old. I remember—she sat me down one day, studied me for a moment, and then spoke cold and low, "I found out about your real father, and I know he isn't White. You should be ashamed of yourself and ashamed of your mother."

And then she wrinkled up her face in disgust and told me to go outside. I remember how it made my stomach hurt. She barely spoke to me after that, and any words she did utter were said with contempt. I didn't tell my mother until years later.

do it or lose their job, or worse. He asked her if she wanted to lose her job now. She replied that she did not. In front of me, he told her that she was the adult and I was the child.

She was to be respected, and I was to obey the rules. Skin color was not important. He asked her if she could comply with those rules. She said she could not do that. My father pleaded with her to understand that she was not in the South anymore, and that he really liked her and wanted her to stay on. I will never forget when he looked at me and said that I would remember this moment for the rest of my life, and to learn the lesson well.

He told her that we are all human, no matter the skin color. We all get up every morning having to use the bathroom, take a shower, and brush our hair and teeth and that we put our pants on one leg at a time. Color was not a factor in any of that whatsoever. Then my father did something that shocked both her and me. . . . He fired her. He told her that because I was so young, he could not allow me to grow up thinking that the way she treated me was right.

He owed it to me to show me that racism is wrong. If she could not help him teach me that, then he would have to let her go so I could not continue to misuse her. She cried. I cried. She got her things. She walked out the door.

I love my father for the lesson because he refused to let me grow up thinking that I was more important than anyone else.

Hello. This man has your daughter.
Karen Button • Middletown, CT

Phone call from the neighborhood grocer—followed by my husband on the line asking me to come down to the corner store to verify that he was, in fact, the father of our biracial infant daughter. They were used to seeing me with her and were refusing to let him leave the store with her. (Location: Suburb of Boston, 1983)

3 percent Irish? How'd that happen?

Lateesha Renee Green • Lithonia, GA

I would love to find the answer to that, and many other questions...

I'm not just a dot-head

Swapna Mony •
Winter Haven, FL

I've tried so very, very hard never to play the race card. Not in the face of my friends jokingly calling me a dot head, not when a coworker talked about "filthy foreigners who don't know how to use bathrooms properly" (two days ago). And not even when I hear whispers from strangers shooting glances in my direction and hear words like, "dropping kids like rabbits . . . too many people in her country so she comes here." I'm Indian, and I love everything that means, but this project makes me feel like I can finally put down a burden I've been carrying for my last thirteen years—the years I've called America home.

Protecting son from cops and criminals.

Renee Hubbard King • Staten Island, NY

I am a Black American, and I prayed to have a boy child. Now that he is a grown man, I realize I should have prayed for a girl. Since he was about ten years old, I have had to make sure he walks with his ID and is mindful of the police as well as the hood criminals. How do we as Black people survive in a culture where we are not respected by cops and shot down by the criminally minded in our own communities? Today I wept.

Uncle Ed, wanted THEM all dead!

Tim Dalrymple • Gainesville, FL

I have generally resisted conformity in my lifetime. Born in Alabama in 1959 and raised in North Carolina, Massachusetts, and Connecticut, I developed a broad interest in the question of race. The South was complex: as children we were told to respect elders, yet the racist adults among us were sometimes acting and speaking in ways that I found reprehensible.

In the North, many were prejudiced against me—thinking me a racist because I came from the South. This was not a surprise, considering the issues of the day. Given my nature, I worked hard to dispel prejudice toward me in the North, and I openly stated my disagreement with Southern racists (I still do this).

Frankly, I was angry at the harm Southerner racists have brought on us all through their attitudes. After all, they were partially responsible for the negative view that some Northerners held toward me. When I later joined the Peace Corps and announced I was moving to Botswana, the response was fascinating. Some instantly got it; others felt I had abandoned them.

For me, the issue of race became even more complex living in southern Africa at the end of apartheid. I mean, I got to see Nelson and Winnie Mandela speak in Gaborone, Botswana, after he was freed from Robben Island and before he became president of South Africa.

The issues of race in Africa were not the same as the ones I knew in the US. My experience has led me to believe that most everyone experiences the question in different ways. What we should all acknowledge is that it is almost impossible to be objective on this issue.

Noticed the wipe, heard the flop

Keith • Seattle, WA

"Your hands were probably sweaty," stated a White college friend when I spoke to him about how rudely his girlfriend begrudgingly shook my hand. "Oh, I am a germophobe—I think everyone's hands are dirty," went another (white) lie. "It's nothing you've done. I'm just OCD," rings another reflexive lie.

I am a gay Black professional from the Deep South. Because of this, I have attended majority White institutions and work among White people.

I have dined with them, attended conferences with them, drank expensive liquor with them. I seek neither accolades nor quips about selling out. I am attempting to provide context—the Whites who have done the flop-and-wipe to me are almost entirely those comprising middle, upper-middle, and upper socioeconomic strata. Don't blame the White working class this time.

What is the flop-and-wipe? It is a reflexive and/or intentional act White people do after shaking the hand of a Black person. Usually the facial grin appears forced, the hand grip is supremely timed (as it should be), and the loss of grip is immediately followed by an audible—usually overt—flop to the White person's side.

The flop can be mischaracterized as the hand wiper simply returning to a balanced standing posture with a snap—the recipient of the microaggression knows the flop indicates fake hand cleaning. It reeks of a reflexive need to ensure

Only White countries must embrace diversity

Ken • Cincinnati, OH

"Anti-racists" are not pushing diversity onto Black countries.
"Anti-racists" are not pushing diversity onto Asian countries.
"Anti-racists" are not pushing diversity onto Arab countries.
Only White children are told to look beyond skin color.
Diversity is a *genocidal* scam.
Anti-racist is a code word for anti-White.

the Blackness doesn't rub off; the pathogen of non-Whiteness does not survive the brief touching. Hyperbolic? Not as much as the flop-and-wipe sound waves against the bones of my inner ear.

My spouse is a White man. I cannot tell you the number of times White people have subtly and overtly done the flop-and-wipe to me and not done it after shaking my spouse's White hand. I know for sure my hands are not sweaty during every handshake I have with White folks. I will not accept that every White person I encounter—either in Atlanta, northern Virginia, or Seattle—is a germophobe or otherwise has OCD. Stop lying to me—and to yourself.

It is reflexive, the Whites' flop-and-wipe. I am an MBA and MPH by training. I have admirable handwashing hygiene. "They" surely do not. While hopping from coast to coast while employed by an East Coast organization, it would terrify the powers that be at the Centers for Disease Control and Prevention to learn how many (White) men emerge from stalls and urinals and planes, even, without washing their hands. As a public health person, I notice these things. For the few who stopped by the sink, they engage in hand wetting—forgoing any use of hand soap.

It didn't matter if I were at SAN, MSP, ATL, DCA, PDX, JFK, MCI, SFO, MDW, SEA, DEN, or SLC—the nastiness reared its head. Yet, the gay Black guy is the one with the dirty hands. The mindset driving the flop-and-wipe is prejudiced and foolish. The predictable and incessant defensiveness following attempts to acknowledge this discriminatory behavior intensifies the string of the original microaggression.

Wash your hands. Brown is dirty

Michele C. H. • Boston, MA

When I was a little kid, in the 1970s, my family were the only Black folks most of the people around us had ever seen. Every day in my elementary school, I got some ignorant comment. "Are you Brown 'cause you eat brown bread?" and the like. The worst was from the old lady who served us snacks. When it was my turn to help her, she made me wash my hands to get the brown off. Over, over, and over.

Two Black lesbian daughters. Say what?

Shelly Ferrand • USA

After the initial shock of their coming out, I realized that *they* are the long search for fruits of my 1960s labor and radicalism. So, when I see the economic travesties in our community, after I pledged on campus forty years ago to give it my all to help end my people's suffering and we suffer still, I think of my daughters and realize their courage is that long-awaited fruit, no matter how small the piece out of the whole pie.

Gay, but at least I'm White

David Trahan • NY

Someone once told me in conversation that even though I was gay, at least I'm White. As if I wasn't allowed to feel oppression and struggle because White trumped gay. There's another side to it, I know. In some ways it can be harder to be gay and Black, but I'd rather not bring the race card into the gay community.

I (don't) fit. Don't look closely

Emery Boyle-Scott • Milwaukee, WI

My Whiteness is always sidelined when people learn about my lesbian moms. Don't look closely and I have all the privilege. But then it disappears. . . . There's no box for my diversity.

Would Martin Luther King Support Gay Rights?

Anonymous • USA

Mixed baby coming soon in-laws afraid

Thomas Campbell • Allentown, PA

A child knows when injustice exists

Rob Jones • Ocean Ridge, FL

I remember as a six-year-old in downtown Tampa in 1953, having seen colored drinking fountains and bathrooms for the first time, that it was not right.

Met your daughter now it matters

Charles McCoy Owens • Chicago, IL

Throughout my life, both professional and private, White people who are friends have said to me that race doesn't matter and that they see me as Charlie, a person just like everybody else.

Interestingly though, when I am the same age as their daughters or sisters and a friendship begins to develop, my Blackness comes very clearly into the focus. On one occasion when I took my first teaching job, I was at dinner with the headmaster and his family, and the race conversation came up. They assured me that I was seen as Charlie, who is a great teacher and has a funny personality. At that point I'd had enough and said, "Cool, do you mind if I date your daughter?" The headmaster's quick reply was "Watch it. . . . You're treading on dangerous ground."

I'm glad he was finally able to see that I am Black, as should anybody else who encounters me because it isn't a hindrance to my identity.

It's a wonderful thing to be a Black man.

Mom placed newborn in front row
John Butterworth • Boston, MA

My mother had just graduated from nursing school in Boston and moved to Maryland in the mid-1950s with my dad, who was in the army at the time. Mom found a job at a nearby city hospital in the maternity ward. Mom placed a beautiful newborn in the front row of the viewing window. The newborn-viewing area was designated as Whites only, and the baby front and center was an African American among the White newborns.

Mom was completely caught off guard and never fully accepted either the reaction or the explanation provided as part of the subsequent request to move the baby and told us the story more than once as a cautionary life lesson about right, wrong, equality, and the reality of the day. Imagine that this was the way lives began. . . .

White. Asked to leave shoe store
Steven Smith • Lake Grove, NY

While on a business trip to Atlanta in the early 1990s, I wandered into a shoe store. After a few minutes a salesperson told me, "I think you're in the wrong store." Puzzled, I asked, "What do you mean?" He responded, "Your store is across the street." I looked around and noticed that I was the only White person in the store. It never even occurred to me I was the only Caucasian. You know what? I wasn't angry or hurt; I was surprised and saddened. It made me sad that racism was still so prevalent that people of color were forced by racist Whites to stake a claim to a shoe store. This is Atlanta. . . . Isn't this type of bullshit supposed to be in the past? Respectfully, I left the store.

They Should All Be Like You
Shelagh Mullins • Coral Springs, FL

A White supervisor said this to me in 1965 when I was the lone "Negro" working in a white-collar job for a large international corporation in San Francisco. I am a naturalized American with light skin (yellow) who was born in Jamaica, I was well-spoken, quiet (shy), and most of all, made no waves. I did not take this as a compliment and only wish I had the courage at that time to tell her she had just insulted me and a whole race of individuals!

Turban, Assumptions, Fear, Perpetually Foreign, Resistance

Simran Jeet Singh • New York, NY

My visible Sikh and South Asian identities have shaped my experiences with racial and cultural identities. Upon seeing me, people mark me as different and make various assumptions about me. Associations assume (but are not limited to): foreign, violent, conservative, uneducated, terrorist, victim, uncivilized, and dogmatic.

2

How It Grew

I AM STILL ASTONISHED that it all began with postcards: little pieces of paper floating through the postal system with six words that could make you gasp or smile or wonder about the full story behind that brevity.

I remember when they first started arriving in the mailbox I rented at the UPS Store. The guys who worked there would immediately head to my mailbox to grab a stack of postcards as soon as I walked in the door. They knew what I was there for. After a while I asked if they ever read the stories. Of course they did. How could they ignore a stream of humanity flowing through their door with no protective envelope preventing them from seeing words you don't hear people say out loud in public?

I grew up scared of myself
Mom was a Democrat until 2008
I think I am becoming racist
AIDS killed mom. More moms coming
DNA testing changed who I am
Good Asian girls don't get raped
Hate handed down like family heirlooms

Sometimes people would hand me the cards at book events or lectures when I traveled, but mainly they arrived via the mail with a colorful stamp in the upper-right-hand corner.

Today, most of the 6-word stories arrive through the online portal, but I will always have a soft spot for those little postcards. They represent effort. Someone had to find a pen, then find their courage, then find a stamp, and then find the time to drop the card in a mailbox. The size and shape of the penmanship tells its own story. The trepidation you can see in teeny-tiny letters. The confidence of big, bold strokes. The way some people turned their cards into works of art with drawings and stickers and watercolor paint. And, because there is no backspace or delete function on a postcard, you could sometimes see someone's thought process.

The man in Pittsburgh who at first strung together a list of words that must have been important to his outlook or life story: "Jesus. Ignorance. Blending. Different. Education. Culture." That's written in what looks like a ballpoint pen, but it's crossed out with two thick black lines from a heavy marker. That same dark marker is used to spell his replacement 6-word story: "I am the cool White guy."

Remember, I started this exercise because I thought no one wanted to talk about race.

In the beginning, a lot of the cards were earnest and aspirational. A lot of people asserted "there's only one race, human race" or quoted some version of Rodney King's plea, "Can we all just get along?" But over time, the stories got deep, especially when we began receiving large numbers of cards online and posting them on the public-facing website. It was as if that set the rules for engagement. Depth begat depth. Candor invited introspection and honesty. It was as if people read someone else's truth and decided that they, too, could unburden themselves.

I have never been involved in a project that sparks such eager engagement. Online. Via snail mail. In person. On social media. In seminars on college campuses. In workshops at global companies such as Apple, Accenture, or Capital One. In football locker rooms and on factory floors. In hundreds of high schools and colleges, where teachers began assigning The Race Card Project as a writing prompt or a tool for navigating discussions about tough topics. In a Florida courtroom, where a judge in the 13th Judicial Circuit Court conducted a Race Card Project exercise over several years so that her colleagues and others, including attorneys, court interpreters, magistrates, case managers, and outside counsel could talk honestly about race. In a place as surprising as the Justice Department, where Assistant Attorney General Karol V. Mason asked to use The Race Card Project to facilitate a difficult discussion with members of her team. At the time, she said workers at the Justice Department were experiencing a range of complicated sentiments, including defensiveness, anger, exhaustion, or even trauma after investigating a series of high-profile police shootings. In all these places, people make connections and are moved toward introspection through their Race Card Project experience.

When I first started handing out those little postcards, I had no idea how the project would grow. Remember, I started this exercise because I thought no one wanted to talk about race. It turns out that it became a trusted vehicle for a lot of people to do exactly that.

•   •   •

Early on we were invited to visit Marietta, Georgia, by an Episcopalian pastor who wanted to reach out to a neighboring church but didn't quite know how to do it. He was White, and he led a church that was founded by slave owners in 1842. Right next door, separated only by a funeral home, stood a Baptist church also founded in the 1800s by families that had been enslaved. Though Zion Baptist began in a small, modest building, it had grown into a large and ornate sanctuary that almost dwarfed St. James Episcopal Church. Zion has a massive congregation that packs the building for community events and Bible study almost every day.

The two churches had been lightly tethered on occasion in the years after Georgia accepted integration. The choirs sometimes sang together, and when St. James was going through a renovation, Zion let St. James use one of their spaces for worship. But the link between the two houses of worship was thin. In truth, the parking lot next to the funeral home that separated their two buildings was much like a moat.

When Reverend Dean Taylor reached out to me in 2011, he said that after he read my book *The Grace of Silence*, he could not stop thinking about the sign he passed every day in front of Zion Baptist. It read, "1866. Founded by Former Slaves." They are proud of their origin story, Taylor said. "I am not sure we even know how to talk about ours."

Taylor asked if I would come and speak to his congregation with the idea of using the visit to invite his neighbors across the way. How could I say no to that? Over coffee and caramel cake, the two congregations came together in the basement of St. James to listen to my story and then share their own. At first, it felt like kids from different schools sharing a cafeteria. People tended to sit with their own until Taylor and the late Rev. Dr. Harris T. Travis from Zion moved about the room suggesting people "mix it up." This was in the infancy of The Race Card Project. We were still collecting stories only by postcards, still stepping gingerly into this space of candid dialogue.

I was not so much worried about a conflict between the congregations. These were, after all, church people. I was more concerned that people would censor themselves and hold their tongues or ride comfortably on the wave of saccharine Southern hospitality that typically obscures deeper, truer feelings. The way Southerners can say, "Bless your little heart," and make it sound like an air kiss when they're really telling you to go jump in the river. It did take a minute for people to warm up, and when we passed out those little black Race Cards asking for 6-word stories, the room got quiet. Really quiet. But then women started reaching into their handbags for pens; people began to peer over to see what someone else had written. Eventually some stood to read some of their stories aloud. "Hate overwhelms us; love is submerged." "Race is our burden and opportunity." "Tomorrow's promise, yesterday's shame, today's discussion."

The two pastors stood together and beamed, but both were pragmatic enough to know that it was just a baby step toward building a strong enough bridge to create true and lasting connections. However, the churches did begin communicating more. There were some shared children's programs and cross registration for vacation Bible school, and the choirs joined together again. Progress.

When I spoke to Taylor again recently, he said small steps were nonetheless monumental. "In the conversations that followed at those tables around the room, new friends were made, community ties strengthened, and I believe minds were changed," he said. "Some personal relationships thrived into friendships." But Taylor, who has since moved on to other congregations, was also honest.

As the nation became more divided, as so many Georgians enthusiastically supported Donald Trump and his rhetoric, re-creating that kind of multiracial community event would be riskier and more challenging even as it was perhaps more necessary.

•   •   •

That same year, I was also invited to return to my hometown to help settle a dispute over, of all things, a dog park. A passel of newer, younger White residents had moved into a Southside Minneapolis neighborhood filled with Black families who had integrated a previously largely White area. This was familiar turf. I grew up about a mile away from the Kingfield area, and my parents were also part of that wave of Black families who were seen as integration's invaders. Now, decades later, a new invasion of sorts was taking place with gentrification that brought hipster coffee shops and bakeries that sold raisin bread as pain aux raisins. This new crowd wanted to introduce a dog run in a local park named for Dr. Martin Luther King Jr. The Black families were incensed. The idea that dogs would run and romp and defecate in one of the few Minneapolis public parks named for a Black person, and an icon at that, was unacceptable. For some, the image of dogs and Dr. King was also problematic because of the way police canine units were used against civil rights demonstrators. These were Black families who built lives in Minneapolis, but for many, their migratory roots were in the Deep South.

One resident would later remark in his 6-word story, "Bull's bullshit came back to bite," referring to Birmingham police chief Bull Connor, who ordered his officers to use vicious police dogs to corral teenage civil rights protestors in the sixties.

The meetings to discuss the proposal were getting heated. That whole Minnesota-nice thing was tossed out the window. My aunt Doris Christopher—always one of my biggest cheerleaders—told the group that I had just written a book about race and suggested that I come to mediate the discussion. She implored everyone in the divided dialogue to read the book so they would better understand how tough it was for Black families who integrated Southside Minneapolis neighborhoods.

I wasn't there when this suggestion was made, but I can just see Aunt Doris elegantly taking over the conversation. She has always been in several book clubs and was active in city politics. When she speaks, people listen. It also helped that I was a host of a popular show on NPR at the time. A hometown gal who has gone to the big leagues. Aunt Doris would later joke with me, "You know White folks love them some public radio."

These little postcards were bricks that could build bridges across cavernous divides.

Even in this early stage of The Race Card Project, we had begun to see that these little postcards were bricks that could build bridges across cavernous divides. I will forever be grateful to Mayor R. T. Rybak, Elizabeth Glidden, my aunt Doris, and her get-it-done posse that included folks like Andrea Jenkins and Sandra Richardson. *The Grace of Silence* was selected for the city-wide One Minneapolis, One Read program (another thank-you, Aunt Doris), and we created a roster of ways people could use the book and the project to create community engagement. High school students interviewed elderly people in nursing homes about what life was like when they were young. Neighborhoods were asked to put together time capsules to capture the current culture of their areas. Residents across the city were encouraged to share their 6-word stories.

The sharing of those stories is what helped break the logjam over the dog run at Rev. Dr. Martin Luther King, Jr. Park. At an evening meeting at an artisanal bakery called Turtle Bread just blocks from my childhood home, residents on all sides of the issue packed the room for an evening of building bridges. The discussion started with the park but quickly skidded into broader territory—how shopkeepers treated Black kids, how Ethiopian and Somali newcomers to Minneapolis were treated on the street, why some people barbecue in their front yards, what residents knew about the restrictive covenants that determined who could or could not buy homes in parts of Minneapolis.

It was a hard-edged conversation, and yet it was ultimately productive. Elizabeth Glidden—at the time the city council member for the district—said the night set the course for the creation of an MLK Park legacy council and an eventual agreement for the city to transform the park into a place that honors Dr. King's life and ideas beyond just placing his name atop a green space. The dog run was created elsewhere, and today the Rev. Dr. Martin Luther King, Jr. Park is a beautiful oasis: a space where kids learn about Dr. King and civil rights history while they whimsy around the playground.

The kiddie climbing wall is meant to look like you're reaching toward a mountaintop. The jungle gym contraption that usually looks like a turtle's hump is modeled after the arches over the Edmund Pettus Bridge in Selma. There is a little yellow playhouse shaped like a fruit stand with an inscription honoring the Black Minnesotan named Frederick McKinley Jones who invented the machinery for mobile refrigeration on food-delivery trucks. And the little stationary choo choo train at MLK Park includes a placard about other Black inventors, including Elijah McCoy, whose enslaved parents had escaped captivity. He invented the oil-drip lubrication cup that revolutionized travel by steam locomotives in the 1800s, an invention that was so preferred over old models that train manufacturers began boasting that they'd installed "the real McCoy."

I was floored when I saw that the stair steps to the slide at the park are made from a stack of oversize books authored by notable Black writers. My own book, *The Grace of Silence*, is wedged in there with W. E. B. DuBois and Maya Angelou. I cried fat, ugly tears the first time I saw that.

The Race Card Project team played only a small part in bringing the neighbors together. The real credit goes to the Building Bridges group, the MLK legacy commission, and the Kingfield residents who pushed past their discomfort and disagreement to confront their defensive tendencies. Some of the squabbling continued. Some hard feelings never really healed. But they kept coming together for years, even when they walked out of those meetings in tears or with tightened jaws.

The country—indeed, the world—could learn a lot from them.

• • •

Those early years of The Race Card Project (TRCP) were a weird stretch of time for me. A lot of people close to me could not understand why I was so obsessed with the mountains of little black postcards piling up inside my house. In truth, a lot of people just could not figure out how 6-word stories could kick-start something of journalistic significance.

We proved that point after I left the host chair at NPR's *All Things Considered* in 2012. My husband, Broderick Johnson, was appointed cabinet secretary in the Obama White House, and I wanted to avoid even the appearance of a conflict of interest and protect journalistic integrity on all sides. In my new role as a special correspondent, I began producing a series of stories for NPR's *Morning Edition* based on powerful 6-word stories from the TRCP inbox with producer Walter Ray Watson. It made for riveting radio, and the small-but-mighty TRCP team (including Walter Watson, Melissa Bear, Adrian Kinloch, Steve Inskeep, Madhulika Sikka, Tracy Wahl, Chuck Holmes, and Dave Patrick) won a Peabody Award for opening up "complicated, vulnerable, and insightful discussions about race that we rarely hear in public spaces."

This was heady but also challenging. The recognition and honor were beyond fantastic. It was a thrill to watch people engage with one another around the stories online. It was surreal to watch famous people post their 6-word Race Card Project stories online. People like Don Cheadle, José Andrés, Terry McMillan, Ricardo Antonio Chavira, Soledad O'Brien, Alexander Chee, Tayari Jones, and Sue Monk Kidd. Thrills aside, we still had to find a way to keep the project alive as stories kept pouring in by the hundreds and we tried to create a website to display them and collect more. And then there was the task of moderating the comment section, which always felt like a rain of fists.

At the same time, we continued to see how The Race Card Project had utility beyond journalism as a tool for dialogue and the excavation of simmering conflicts. My TRCP partner Melissa Bear and I felt like Lucy and Ethel in the chocolate-factory episode from *I Love Lucy*, where the two women can't keep up with confections that keep coming faster and faster on the assembly line. While raising young children, we were working overtime to build the website, manage the inbox, and archive everything carefully as well as constantly seeking funding to support all of it. At the same time, people kept tapping on our shoulder asking if we could bring TRCP into their orbits to help create some kind of cultural bridge. The project was taking over our lives. It turned out to be, as they say, a good problem to have.

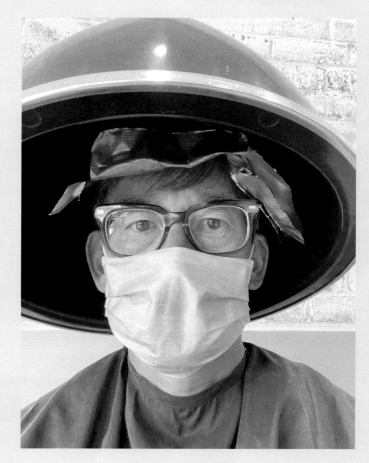

I'm not your
damn China Virus

Todd Inoue • San Jose, CA

Just what do you people eat?

Judith A. Harper • Pikesville, MD

Years ago, our family integrated a predominantly Jewish neighborhood in New Haven, Connecticut. I am African American. While walking our German shepherd, I was approached by an elderly woman who asked if she could ask a "personal" question. It was the question submitted. For a moment, I was speechless, but then replied, "Food, just like you." It has always intrigued me that people can live such insulated lives as to not realize that we are more alike than different.

White people don't season their chicken

Carter Stoecker • Warrenton, VA

It may horrify some, but sometimes I eat unseasoned chicken. I wear khaki shorts often, as well as Hawaiian shirts. I wear big, white Reebok shoes. I do all these "White people" things, and I know people make fun of it. I don't care if I fit the stereotype of a boring, corny White guy. I'm comfortable. I don't care that it's normal and funny for people to mock my race for being bland, unseasoned, and stale. If I'm not cool, I'm not cool, and that's fine.

People fear what they don't understand

Tucker Lowe • Jasper, GA

I wish I were something else

Ashley • VA

It's very hard to be proud of the skin you are in when your ancestors were terrible people.

I'm Black before I'm anything else.

Jan Miles • New Orleans, LA

I'm not a woman—I'm a BLACK woman. I'm not a writer—I'm a BLACK writer. In law school, I was a BLACK law student. If I kill my brother, it's BLACK-on-black crime. Just as White privilege is societally applied (rather than being internally rooted), Blackness is also applied by society. I don't get to just be me, the way White people exist—as the norm, as the default—I'm BLACK me.

Why do people steal from us?

Peter Chin • Washington, DC

That was the question that my daughter asked me when our house was broken into for a second time in three years. As a Korean American living and working in a predominantly African American neighborhood, I was tempted to answer her question by telling her about the long-standing hostilities between the two groups. But I didn't.

I understand the need to be honest with our children about the realities of the world, I really do. But I also understand that children do not interpret what we teach them in the subtle way in which we would like them to. I might think that I am giving a nuanced lesson in history, when all her young mind hears is "People of that race don't like me because I'm a different race." And even after all that my family has been through, I really don't think that dynamic is true, and neither do I want it to become true for her, and for others. And so, I hugged her and told her that we don't have anything that we can't live without, and she accepted that answer . . . for now.

I ate pasta, family ate rice.

Melanie Ramil • Livermore, CA

Growing up, I wanted to be as "non-Filipino" as possible and felt great achievement whenever a friend said to me, "You seem so White!" During my middle school years, I claimed to not like rice (the staple for every night's family dinner). My mom, after rushing home from work to cook dinner for us every day, relented and lovingly prepared pasta for me while the rest of the family ate rice and the evening's accompanying meat dish. Today, I long to speak Tagalog, call my mom every week for advice on how to cook Filipino dishes, and look forward to the day when I have children and can share my rich heritage with them.

I know I'm well spoken. Surprised?

**Carrington Anderson •
Indianapolis, IN**

Never sure why I get "you're so well-spoken" so often. Not sure why people look at me and expect me not to be. Being well-spoken isn't "talking White." English is my native language. Don't act so shocked when I speak it well.

"Mythical norm," is what I be.

**Donald Malchow •
Milwaukee, WI**

A friend explained to me while we were in college that I was the "mythical norm" in our society. That really gave me time to pause and reflect on what that meant. For so long, I have attempted to reject that notion, but it's something that I am coming to terms with and understand more as I grow older.

Had trouble with another White teacher

Diana Imhoff • Brookings, OR

I was raised in a White community, so I had never really seen racism. I taught school in a minority elementary school. Then a parent of one of my students who constantly disrupted class unleashed this on me. I didn't care what color her daughter was, but it was clear that her mother hated me because of the lack of color in my skin. That was about thirty years ago, and it still stings. I cannot imagine how people feel who are subjected to racism daily.

Any Black kids in your class?

Pamela Tish • Dupo, IL

When I began my first teaching job in Cahokia, Illinois, "Any Black kids in your class?" was always one of the first questions asked by friends and family. I return to that question in my own mind so often as I look across my classrooms, twenty years and three jobs later, and it still prompts the same feelings for me. My reaction is always an emotional headshaking. "No. No Black kids, no White kids. Kids of a hundred shades of cappuccino, choco-latte, summer peach, melting Hershey bar, toasty wheat crust, caramel malt." I remember the confusing moment when completing standardized-test forms together for the first time, my students and I shared puzzled looks when asked to complete ethnicity questions that had no rainbow answers.

These people want too many rights

Robert Kruk • Bloomingdale, NJ

When I was a boy (thirteen or so), my father and I were watching the news, and an African American demonstration was shown. After listening to a speaker, my father exclaimed the above sentence. Even at the time, I thought that it was one of the stupidest things I'd ever heard anyone say. Years later, now in my seventies, I realize that my father was one of the worst kind of racists: one who doesn't know he is a racist and, if he were alive, would vehemently deny that he was.

Is it because I am Black?

Renee Yates • Evanston, IL

Being Black in America means that every time you feel slighted or unfairly treated in the larger society you have to wonder, "Is it because I am Black?" It's demoralizing and exhausting.

Colorblindness will not fix societal issues

Gabrielle Elling • Philadelphia, PA

You may not see color, but the police and government do.

Dream to see, *hear, and love*

Clarence "Chet" Chavez • Taylors, SC

I am colorblind. But ignorance isn't

Natalie • Kansas City, MO

Moved south. I miss being colorblind

Natalie Voss • Lexington, KY

Not allowed to be colorblind yet
Niel Leon • Baltimore, MD

Colorblind justice is impossible in America
Michael Barone • Perkasie, PA

Colorblindness renders me invisible to you
NiCole T. Buchanan • East Lansing, MI

I don't want people to be blind to my color. Instead, I want them to see me in my entirety, including the fact that I am a biracial Black woman, and I want them to actively embrace these parts that make me whole. I believe most people have good intentions in advocating for color blindness, but color-blind ideology often results in marginalizing those pieces of me that I happen to value highly.

My family is color neutral not colorblind
Connie Tague • Holyoke, MA

Colorblind society does not help anyone
Aubrey Mathwig • Redmond, WA

No one is colorblind. Don't pretend
Joey • Glenside, PA

I don't get to be colorblind

Jenn M. Jackson • Chicago, IL

Every single day I am accused of "making things about race." I'm told that I'm "looking for racism" in everything. I'm told I must lead a sad, angsty life since I can't stop pulling the "race card." I often get this feedback from Whites who feel uncomfortable when I note their privilege or that institutional racism creates a self-perpetuating system of haves and have-nots. But those folks overlook the fact that asking me to ignore race isn't the same as asking a White person who likely doesn't face systemic bias each day. My ignoring race is my shutting out, avoiding, and silencing a central part of my lived experience in the United States. It's unnatural. It's uncomfortable. It's not me. I just don't get to be color-blind. I'm not sure I would if I could. But, most importantly, it's my responsibility not to ignore race, especially in this day and time. I'm OK with that.

3

"I wish he was a girl"

If you spread out all the Race Card stories over twelve years, one clear marker you would see is the shooting death of seventeen-year-old Trayvon Martin on February 26, 2012.

The teenager was followed, watched, and killed by a volunteer neighborhood watchman named George Zimmerman while walking back from a convenience store with Skittles and iced tea. It was the night of the NBA All-Star Game. During halftime, Martin headed to the store, wearing a hooded sweatshirt. Zimmerman was out running an errand when he spotted Martin and called the police to report a suspicious individual. Martin, who had called his girlfriend and mentioned that someone was following him, started to run. The two scuffled. Zimmerman claimed he shot Martin in self-defense.

Martin was pronounced dead at the scene.

Trayvon Martin's story did not burst into national headlines. It moved there slowly, at first getting only fleeting coverage on the local news and in a few Florida newspapers. As big a story as this eventually became, it was almost a month before it appeared on the front page of the *Washington Post* or the *New York Times*. It might have never reached that national pitch if it weren't for the fact that the Martin family's legal counsel developed a savvy media strategy to keep Trayvon's name and his case in public view. Digital activists, celebrity umbrage on social media, and a so-called Million Hoodie March on New York City streets fanned public awareness and outrage.

The story was a defining moment for the nation, the beginning of the Black Lives Matter movement, the spark that ignited a debate over stand your ground laws, the opening notes of a decade-long dirge of wailing and protest and trauma throbbing against the over-policing of Black bodies in America. It was also a marker for The Race Card Project. By 2012, the symphony of stories about police conduct that began with Trayvon Martin continued to swell, and we realized that we are not just collecting stories, we are documenting a small bit of history, creating a record of people's thoughts and perspectives on events in real time.

During the fourteen years we have been collecting Race Card stories, Americans became accustomed to watching Black death on small screens. It's become a period of hashtag activism and grieving mothers who were pushed into the national spotlight to advocate justice for sons and daughters they would never see alive again. It was a period where a daisy chain of names was burned into the nation's consciousness. Names that would forever conjure more vivid images of how the fallen died than of how they lived. As hard as the families tried to spotlight smiling pictures of victims wearing work uniforms or formal clothing, the names would immediately invoke the gasps for air, the pleading for mercy, the pop of the gun, the thud of the fall, the vacuum of silence after a life is extinguished.

The names created a requiem of dread. Trayvon Martin. Tamir Rice. Eric Garner. Walter Scott. Jordan Davis. Laquan McDonald. Michael Brown. Sandra Bland. Alton Sterling. Elijah McClain. Ahmaud Arbery. Breonna Taylor. George Floyd. Adam Toledo. Daunte Wright. Amir Locke. Tyre Nichols. And so many—too many—more.

These names were all emblazoned on the front pages of newspapers and blared across cable-news screens. But here is the odd thing. These stories create an uptick in the inbox, but the actual names of the fallen are not repeatedly mentioned in the stories people submit. People saddened or angered or traumatized by the deaths they see on televisions or on their cell phones are moved to submit personal thoughts and feelings about this litany of police killings—or, in many cases, their own experiences in life. They write about their own police encounters or fears of law enforcement officers. They write about what it's like to wear a badge and uniform in the face of so much ire. They write about concerns for their children, their angst behind the wheel, the clothes they can or cannot wear if they want to blend in and avoid drawing attention. The inbox becomes an outlet for anguish.

For Kristen Moorhead, sending six words to The Race Card Project felt like a silent scream. Her heart was so heavy that she actually wanted to wail out loud to the heavens but dared not display that kind of raw emotion in front of Che, her preteen son. The death of someone else's son had roiled her emotions on the evening she shared her story. The killing of a Black boy who, like Che, was twelve years old back in 2014. A child who had been shot dead by police at the edge of a gazebo in a Cleveland park.

Kristen and Che Moorhead

Kristen sent her 6-word story on November 26, 2014, the same day Cleveland police released a grainy surveillance video showing how Tamir Rice was killed by police responding to a 911 call within seconds of their arrival. It turned out that the child was holding a toy gun.

Kristen typed, "I wish he was a girl," and hit the Submit button.

"It was just cathartic to be able to say it," she recalls. It should be said that Kristen Moorhead didn't really wish for a different kind of child. She and her son are very close. Her words spoke to a deep-seated fear for the parents of Black children in an era where the world has seen a steady injection of Black death delivered directly on social media's small screens, as so many unarmed victims have been killed by police.

The benefit of running an archive over such an extended period is that we can witness how stories evolve. The Moorhead family still lived in Silver Spring, Maryland, and on a cold Saturday during the winter of 2021, I watched as Kristen read the 6-word story she submitted eight years ago to her son, who was then almost nineteen years old. I watched his head snap back and his eyebrows pop up upon hearing his mom read that she wished he was a girl. And then I watched his forehead settle into a deep furrow as she methodically read the backstory she submitted in 2014, pausing occasionally to find her emotional footing.

"I've always told my son, 'You can be anything you want to be,'" she wrote. "He's twelve now, almost my height, and swears he doesn't see color. His possibilities are infinite. Yes, but there is a cruel catch. You can be anything you want to be, but first you must survive, and your survival is dependent on knowing this: you are young, Black, male, perceived guilty until proven innocent. Aggressive. A demon. America's prime suspect. We all bear the burden of knowing the procedures and pathology that come with that."

Che now towers over his mother at six feet tall. When we spoke, he was a senior preparing to head off to college. He is very musical. Slightly nerdy (his words). The product of several gifted and talented school programs, he speaks like someone who has kept his nose inside books. And he no longer professes that he doesn't see color. Quite the opposite.

"My stances on things have definitely changed," says Che when it's his turn to speak. "I am very much the product of White spaces. I decided that in order to exist in those spaces, it meant that I either had to acclimate and totally assimilate to their culture and to be like them, or to refuse to believe that there was any separation between myself and them. I kind of feel like, in a lot of ways, I chose the latter. But that was obviously not a sustainable way of going throughout the world, 'cause one: it's not the truth."

Che was knocking at the door of manhood when we spoke, but he still had a boyish demeanor that winter. His voice sometimes squeaks, and his giggles spark animated facial expressions. He's a kid who knows the world is more likely to respond to him—and his size—as if he were an adult.

"I'm very much still in the habit of whenever I'm walking into a grocery store, even walking past someone on the street, I'll always say *hi* or *hello* or try to have a miniature exchange with them, just because the way that I speak tends to change people's perceptions of me," Che says. "Meaningless exchanges. Like, 'The weather we are having is so nice.' And having to always have this happy face on . . . and put up this wall that makes me a one-dimensional figure that can exist as a person, or not even as a person, but as an assemblance of a person rather than a threat."

Read that last line again: "an assemblance of a person rather than a threat." Che Moorhead was putting on a proverbial mask to survive in America long before the pandemic hit.

Like so many kids his age, he keeps to himself more in his teen years and is much more withholding about his life outside the home. And yet, during the conversation, he is suddenly on a roll, talking without hesitation about how he stopped shopping at the

7-Eleven convenience store near his high school because the clerks always followed him. He explains how he "always feels the need to represent and be every Black person ever" to leave a positive impression.

It's like the dam has broken, and all that's been pent up is spilling forth.

He talks about how he feels the burden to carry the conversation in class when the subject turns to race or diversity issues. "We might be talking about race, but the conversation is so much, so often held for the benefit of appeasing White guilt," he says. "And to know that I have to exist as this, as close to the model minority as I can. I have to be this perfect person in order for me to even be in those spaces. It's exhausting. I have emotions. I get angry sometimes. I sometimes hear things people say out of ignorance that really do offend me, and I want to respond in a way that is not palatable to me, but I've slowly recognized that this is the only way that I am listened to at all and . . . that is the most of me that they will ever be able to see."

You've probably heard of the phenomenon where Black and Brown parents give the so-called Talk to their children, advising them on how to comport themselves in the world so they can get home safe, especially if they encounter police. Well, this was The Talk in reverse—a child explaining to his mother for the first time how he has absorbed and activated all those lessons. What's a parent to feel at that moment? Pride? Anger? Frustration? Vertigo?

I know that Black skin is too often viewed as an immediate threat.

The word Kristen keeps reaching for is *insanity*.

"It's like, be free, and at the same time, don't be your authentic self," she said. "Don't be what you're feeling. Don't be your emotions. And to hear him as an eighteen-year-old now, being able to hear him process it and move closer to the mastery of operating in this world as a Black man—it's heartbreaking."

Kristen Moorhead shared her six words in 2014, and seven years later, it uncorked a revealing conversation with her only son as he is preparing to leave her nest. She knows she has done her job in getting him ready. And yet, she says there's no real pride in that task. "It's heartbreaking that the things that I was so amazed that he did not process or understand, that years later, they are so entrenched," she says. "And really, there's a level of resentment, honestly, that my kid has to learn this, and that I had to teach it to him. There's no satisfaction in your child mastering these lessons."

Don't fear me, I'm like you.

Constance Morton • Henderson, NC

I am multiracial, but what you see when you look at me is my connection to Africa. But my ancestors came from the British Isles, as well as walked tall and proud on their Native American soil. Why can't I celebrate my rich heritage with pride in your presence? If we compared our roots, we might find that we are related, and then would you welcome me without hesitation? I am ready to be received without reservation, challenged without limits, and promoted without quotas. Neither my speech nor my words betray me; so, can you readjust your focus and see me once and for all as the beautiful, vibrant woman created to change your world?

My Jacket Came With A Hood

Jayla • Wichita, KS

What we don't understand scares us

Shelley Fleming • Newark, DE

This is actually a paraphrase of a line from *Beauty and the Beast*. When I was directing it two years ago, this line weighed in my heart as a truth that I wanted my students to understand. The full line is "We don't like what we don't understand; in fact, it scares us."

I'm afraid to wear a hoodie

Derek • Pittsburgh, PA

I'm allowed to wear a hoodie

Bethany Banner • Kalamazoo, MI

I realized this today when I walked out of the grocery store, into the rain, and pulled up my hood so that I wouldn't get too wet while walking to my car. I'm a petite White woman; even with my hood pulled over my head, I'm not perceived as a potential threat.

My son can wear a hoodie

Donna Kreskey • Chico, CA

My son is about the same age as Trayvon Martin, and he often wore clothes like what Trayvon was described as wearing—that infamous hoodie. He also has an aunt in Sanford. I remain convinced that had it been my son who encountered Zimmerman, no one would have died. Why do I believe this? My son is White.

Rocky wore a hoodie. Kill him?

Michael Hubbard • Dallas, TX

I thought I was being funny

Kathy • Philadelphia, PA

I saw a student I work with wearing a baseball cap and a hoodie tied tightly around her face and I said, "You're rockin' your perpetrator look today." I didn't realize I'd upset her until another staff member told me. I was mortified.

Their age, not race, scares me

Jack Prewett • San Bernardino, CA

Many teens act like they are ten feet tall, can live forever. I don't know what happened in Trayvon's case, but I'm six five and three hundred pounds and feel uncomfortable when confronted by young adults, no matter what color they are. Standing with their hands in their pockets and they have a hoodie on is scary because I don't know what to expect.

I don't always wear a suit!

Rob West • Lakeland, FL

I am a leader in the industry and in the community, and I am well respected. Most days, I wear a suit to work, but I wear a hoodie when I run and gym shorts when I go shopping. I should not have to worry about being followed, having the police called on me, or being shot.

I want to wear a hoodie.

Nathaniel Adam Tobias Coleman • England

I am blessed
to have survived.

Trevor • Brooklyn, NY

THE PHOTO AT THE FRONT DOOR

IN SEPTEMBER 2020 I wrote a column in the *Washington Post* about one of the small things I do inside my own home to protect my loved ones from toxic attitudes toward Black lives. I was explaining to my editor Michael Duffy why I always keep a family picture on the console table near my front door. My reasoning both saddened and surprised him, and he suggested that I share the story with my readers. I resisted at first but eventually agreed, thinking that it might be useful for other families.

I keep a framed family photo next to my front door, positioned on a table, so you see it as soon as you enter. It captures a joyous moment on vacation. We're leaning on each other, smiling wide. Family Strong.

I keep that picture by the entry in case police ever enter my home, so they know that the people in that photo belong in the house where they live. That paragraph you just read is a litmus test. Some of you will read these words and wonder, "Why would she ever do that?" But some of you will read this and nod your heads in recognition. Or perhaps conclude, "Maybe I should do that, too."

Those of us in that second category are not worried about police entering our homes because the officers think we're engaged in criminal behavior. We worry—actually, we know—that we could be seen as criminals or intruders in our own homes even if we consistently and even obsessively live by the rules. A steady stream of raids gone wrong buttress those fears, and yet it goes far beyond all that.

●   ●   ●

Everyone has heard about The Talk—advice Black and Brown parents give loved ones on how to behave when dealing with officers of the law, no matter the circumstance.

No sudden moves. Hands out of pockets. Cooperate even if it feels unfair, even if you know you did nothing wrong. No hint of anger. Just make it home. Please God . . . just make it home.

But being home provides only so much protection. My social media feeds are full of stories of Black and Brown people who've had police called on them by neighbors or passersby because they allegedly look "suspicious"—a way of saying they don't look like someone who belongs in the home where they pay a mortgage and mow the lawn . . . the place where they learned to ride a bike in the driveway . . . the apartment where they just hung the drapes.

Stay calm. . . . Keep your voice lowered. Tamp down on all those justifiable emotions.

My family thought it was a bit strange when I decided to start keeping the picture by the door in case a neighbor thought one of us looked suspicious. The kids rolled their eyes. My husband, Broderick, said, "Your call." (Always a good answer.)

The picture at my door is a kind of insurance, and like most safeguards, you hope you never need it. But if you do, boy, are you glad it's there. That happened halfway through the year back in 2020. My then twenty-year-old son, a college student, up in the middle of the night. He's a tennis fanatic and watches tournaments broadcast overseas in real time, which means he is often a night owl. And like most young men, he loves a late-night kitchen raid. All of that was in play when our son, who would normally be off to college in California, was attending online classes from home because of the Covid-19 school schedule. My husband and I were out of town. He had the house to himself, and during a wee-hour fridge blitz, he accidentally triggered the home security alarm.

He was clearing dishes when he spotted police at the back-door window. They gestured for him to head toward the front. He unlocked the main entrance, and the questions began. Do you live here? *Yes.* Where are your parents? *Out of town.* How long have you lived here? *He paused to calculate our move-in date.* Are you a resident or just a visitor?

I've long fretted about a moment like this. If police were ever summoned to our home based on suspicion, would they look at my husband or my kids and calculate what I see? What I know to be true? Hard workers. Good students. Kind hearts.

I'd like to believe most officers and most people would see that. But I know that Black skin is too often viewed as an immediate threat. Studies show Black men are seen as larger, stronger, more muscular, and more threatening when compared to White men of exactly the same size.

My son has seen a steady stream of police encounters on his cellphone that end in Black death. He's standing in his foyer, wearing fuzzy purple slippers with a Baltimore Ravens logo and his collegiate T-shirt. Meanwhile names are dancing through his head. Freddie Gray, Oscar Grant, Philando Castile. He's looking at police officers

It's exhausting. I have emotions. I get angry sometimes.

and wanting to believe the protect-and-serve promise. After all, we have members of our extended family who have worked in law enforcement. But he knows that the officers standing in our foyer are responding to a 4:30 a.m. alarm, encountering a young Black man alone in a big house who claims he lives inside.

My heart breaks when my son relays this baptism into double consciousness. A bracing manifestation of one of James Baldwin's most powerful quotes: "You have to *decide* who you are, and force the world to deal with you, not with its *idea* of you."

In this case, our son remembered the picture. He pointed gently toward the hall table where a photo sits inside a silver frame. That's me, he explains to the police. That's us. This is our home.

The officers left soon after, but before they departed, they implored our son to be careful. Parents of Black children spend so much emotional energy worrying about disastrous encounters with law enforcement that a routine, uneventful exchange winds up feeling like a gift. I appreciated that the officers hovered for just a bit, repeatedly asking if he was sure he was OK.

Thankfully, he is, but what's not OK is the underlying thread in American life that automatically links dark skin with dark intention. What is not OK is pretending that it doesn't exist. What is not OK is exploiting those fears for political gain. What is not OK is that society repeatedly has one-sided conversations about policing, conversations where the people who wear the uniform don't fully participate because of union rules or liability concerns or a reflexive defensiveness. I know from all the stories we get from police officers that their input would be varied and very powerful. Yet the abiding public silence allows poisonous assumptions to fester and a system that is seriously flawed to stagger forward, weighed down by deep distrust, lost lives, multimillion-dollar lawsuits, and simmering frustrations from people on the inside who might genuinely want to reform and reimagine policing in America.

I'll keep that picture at my front door. It will change over time to accurately reflect the broadening of my son's chest.

The squaring of his jaw. The hairstyles that change by the year.

Until toxic attitudes toward Black lives and the constant perception of Black threat goes away—that picture stays.

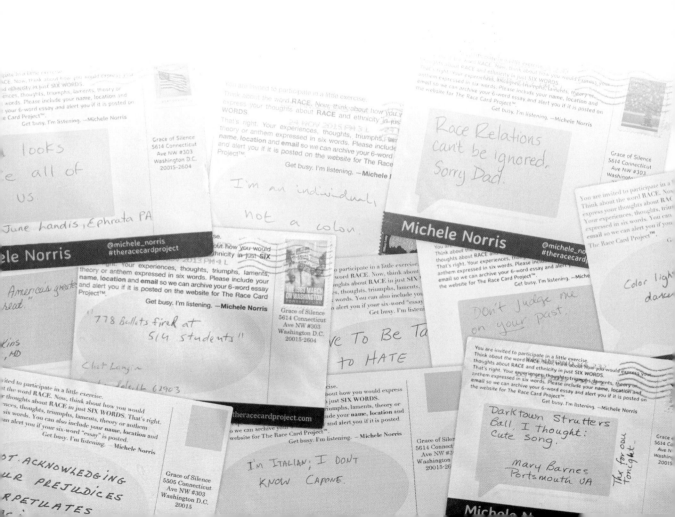

Will my son come home tonight?

Dorothy Rae • Midlothian, VA

My son just loves good food, but I worry when he says he is going out. I cannot sleep when he says, "Mom, I am going to dinner, to a movie, hang out with my friends." With his being away at school, he has been pulled over three times for no reason, held in the back of a police car, then released as the "wrong person." I should be able to rest when night falls, knowing that my son will be safe, but I do not have this assurance.

Lights flipped, pulled over, relax brother

J. C. Ousley • Houston, TX

In 1998, I bought a new red Corvette despite my mother's plea; she said the car was trouble for a Black man. On the day the car was delivered, I was driving to my parents' home to show off my new Vette when I was pulled over by three Chicago police cars.

The officers, all White, had their guns drawn as they approached me. There was a Black officer who arrived later and remained in his vehicle; I looked directly at him, and he looked away. The officers asked me where I was going and what I did for a living (I'm a medical professional). I politely told them and asked why I was pulled over. I never got an explanation. While I waited for them to check my plates and registration, I took the opportunity to have The Talk with my six-year-old son, who was in the car with me. The officers returned my driver's license and registration and told me to have a nice evening. Shaken, I continued to see my parents and I never told them of the incident.

My son, who is now twenty, never forgot it.

Hated for being a White cop

Brett Maisel • Nacogdoches, TX

As a young, naive police officer, I mistakenly thought most people would appreciate my sincere desire to help and protect the citizens of my community. I was shocked to find out that some people (who didn't even know my name, background, or what was in my heart) hated the very sight of me only because I was a White police officer.

Resisting arrest matters more than race

Jack Carson • Portland, OR

Black Lives Matter cherry-picks bad arrests and pretends that exceptions outweigh rules. It also trivializes high Black crime rates, which draws police attention. Their narrative is dishonest and harmful to the police, and especially poor (decent) people who need protection from thugs.

Running shouldn't lead to my death

Dmitri Julius • Austin, TX

I woke up in tears and a cold sweat imagining my son coming to the same fate as the slain Georgia jogger Ahmaud Arbery.

Ahmaud Arbery was pursued, questioned, judged, and ultimately executed while exercising in the suburbs, as I often do. This tragic event occurred the day after my birthday, February 23, 2020. I usually take a birthday run as a reminder to myself how lucky I am to have life and limb and of how young I feel.

I often do it at dusk and at a brisk speed. I get honks and comments (of both encouragement and anger) from passing cars. I never respond. I stick to my pace and power through with my headphones in. I can't shake the feeling that he was me. Minding his business before he was brutally executed. No human deserves to be hunted down like a rabid dog in the street. That simply isn't a punishment in this great country of ours. The only reason this young man is dead is that he was Black. The only reason those men roamed free for months is that they were White. If you disagree with that, I challenge you to imagine the situation in reverse. Do two Black men get to follow a "potentially suspected" thief in their truck? Would it be permissible to kill him on the roadside under the suspicion of petty theft? Would they be granted flexibility to remain free men for weeks with a special note from the DA stating not to arrest them? Does a video of undeniable unnecessary escalation of force need to go viral to lead to an arrest weeks later? I think not. Brass tacks is, this could have been me, my father, my best friend, or . . . my son.

I'm so tired of the senseless murders of Black men in this country. I'm tired of the terror forced upon Black mothers and families dealing with this reality daily. I'm tired of the Black form being brutalized/eliminated and the BS justification that follows. I'm tired of the endless string of examples of police ineptitude and legal miscarriages of justice that often allow killers and racists to remain free. Black and Brown lives aren't given the same value as White ones in this country, and on behalf of every Black man, woman, and child, I cry, *"Stop killing us!"* Until that changes, we implore our White brothers and sisters to be allies. That means to stop allowing

the racist comments to linger at gatherings. That means engaging in meaningful conversations on the topic of race.

That means interceding when you witness racial injustice. That means confronting internal implicit biases held by you and others in positions of power and control. That means to stop blaming the victims and using tropes and stereotypes to condemn the victims to unjustified deaths and broken families. That means developing some understanding that we hurt, grieve, and cry when another member of our community is ripped away.

You must know, we struggle daily to make you feel comfortable by not sharing our outrage at these continued transgressions! We are proud to be Black, and that shouldn't mean we might just die to coexist with you.

Men I love aren't safe here

Arlinda Vaugh • Dayton, OH

My partner is a tall, dark, muscular Black man (with a PhD). When he lived in Texas, the police arrived at a gas station that he was in and tased him eight times without warning or discussion. My brother (with a degree) has been regularly pulled over. Once, a police officer pulled him over, handcuffed him, and put him in the back of his cruiser. Then he searched everywhere for any possible warrant or person whose "description he fit." In the end, he let him go after about forty-five minutes. My brother has never had more than a speeding ticket. When he was pulled over, he was not speeding or violating any traffic rules whatsoever.

My cousin (who is a veteran) was pulled over by a city cop on the bridge in Saint Louis, Missouri. It was outside of that cop's jurisdiction, so he had to call the Illinois police so that they could search his car. He had nothing. They found nothing, but they had a gun trained on him nonetheless.

I truly feel that there is absolutely nothing that a Black man in this nation can do to be safe. If they comply, if they resist, if they are polite, if they are rude . . . all are irrelevant because if a policeman has it in his mind that they are criminals, then he will treat them like criminals. No Black man in this nation has escaped this treatment. I have serious discussions with my extended family and my partner to move to Canada. The powers that be don't want us here, anyway.

Then he died in our alley

Sue Blanshan • Okemos, MI

My family lived in segregated Georgia when I was young. A playmate's mother called the police to report a Black man smelling her clean laundry on the backyard clothesline. The police came and chased him three blocks and shot him by our house in the alley. He died there. When I got home from third grade, I saw the bloodstains on the ground and was told what had happened. I knew he should not have died for something like that.

Police harassed undercover cop wearing hoodie

V. • USA

While working undercover, I decided to duck into a burger joint to get a bite. It was cold and drizzly outside. I was wearing a hoodie. I am Latino. It was about midnight. I admit that I looked rough in a rough neighborhood, but I wasn't breaking any laws.

As I was ordering, a large White cop approached me and told me to take off my hood. I asked him why, and he said, "Because I said so." I didn't think he was serious, and I tried to ignore him until he demanded that I take off my hood. I told him no. He grabbed my arm and attempted an armlock on me to facilitate handcuffing. He said that he would arrest me. I gave in. I was hungry, after all. I told him OK, and I took off my hoodie. He won. He went back and sat down with a colleague.

After I ordered, I walked over to him and sat down with him and the other cop. I gave him a piece of my mind as I tossed my badge on the table in front of him. They said that I should have told them I was a cop, and they wouldn't have treated me like that. I said, "So you wouldn't have violated my civil rights if you knew I was a cop?" They were speechless.

"You're the reason people hate cops," I said.

Young Hispanic male, possible gang member

Jonathan Pineda • San Francisco, CA

I have been a victim of this racial profiling three times. The most recent one was the worst. I was walking home after getting out of work, and an undercover officer pulled up next to me and started asking me questions about what I was doing in the neighborhood, where I was going, and if I had any warrants. I was then searched to see if I had weapons while they ran my name to make sure I didn't have warrants. In the end, they let me go after fifteen [minutes] of my being stopped just for walking home.

Black, but I don't fear police

Rinard • Holland, MI

Yes, I feel there is an issue and a relationship gap between Black men and police. It's unfortunate what has been going on in our nation lately. I agree Black lives matter, and I can see how one may think they don't, given the recent sad events. On top of that, however, I believe if you present yourself as a confident professional, you have nothing to fear. Be tactful, calm, collected, and honest, and things will work out. I'm Black, but I have never had any fear when it comes to dealing with law enforcement.

Never been scared of the police

Kayla D. • Oregon

Please don't shoot me too, police.

Hakeem • USA

Cops beat me. Spoke up, anyway

Theo E. J. Wilson • Denver, CO

After being beaten by the police, I took an activist journey that landed me on the TED stage.

The police are following me. Why?

Otis L. Courtney • Eden Prairie, MN

If found hung, not a suicide

Mariadele Priest • USA

My adult Black sons were commenting on recent lynchings of Black men that police in several cities have labeled suicides.

Police wrong. Black violence wrong. Stop.

Carn Paggot • Cincinnati, OH

Just because my husband is White

Ferguson Police Officer's Wife • O'Fallon, MO

Just because he is a White police officer doesn't mean he's a bad person. He grew up in this community and has just as much of a right to work here as anyone else. I should not have to worry myself sick about whether he will come home every night. Protest peacefully!

Not every police officer is bad

Brooke A. Brown • Williamsport, PA

Stay on the phone with me

Becky White • USA

I was talking to my son one night as he was driving home from work. I heard him say, "What is he pulling me over for?" I realized that he was being pulled over by the police, and I felt immediate fear. I told my son not to hang up, so that I could hear what was happening. I told him to keep his hands visible and to not make any wrong movements. He said to me, "Ma, do you know how many times I have been pulled over? I know exactly what to do and not to do." A parent should not have to fear that a traffic stop could turn into something more because their child is Black.

I am scared to drive alone

Ariel Foreman • Raleigh, NC

I just moved to North Carolina from Virginia. I'm scared to travel on Highway 14 between home and Raleigh, especially at night . . . because it's heavily monitored by police. I should not be scared of a group that's supposed to protect me.

Will my son get shot too?

Nikai Mutagaana • Freedom, PA

Afraid for my Native American children

Jarret Cummings • Rockville, MD

My wife and children are members of the Cherokee Nation, but we have the good fortune to live in an area where they are unlikely to face discrimination. I worry about what may happen if my children ultimately go someplace where racial discrimination is still prevalent and how I should prepare them for that possibility. As a White male raised in Texas, I've never before had to think about racial discrimination as a personal concern as opposed to a social and political problem. Now, the thought of my wife, son, or daughter possibly having an encounter with the police has a chilling dimension to it that's hard to process.

White police officers frighten me

Erin Jones • Landover, MD

Officer, why were we pulled over?

Chandra Campbell • Mountain View, CA

He couldn't get away with this

Tracy Audette • Brooklyn Park, MN

My awareness as our son's bus driver (Black male) watched me (upper-middle-class White woman) chew out a police officer (White male) in the parking lot of our school. Long story. It was justified!

Difference between staying alive or dying

Isaiah Borders • Kannapolis, NC

My White skin; my guaranteed protection

Delaney Bicknell • Amarillo, TX

Since I am a White woman, the world doesn't see me as a threat or danger. I have the privilege of walking around knowing that the police (who are supposed to protect everyone and don't) will protect me if I ever find myself in a bad situation. That's something that our Black brothers and sisters don't have.

White, privileged,
and until Floyd, clueless

Marvin Moriarty • Belchertown, MA

George Floyd's death at the hands of police struck me hard and made me start looking into race matters more thoroughly. I found out about the wealth gap and the horrendous manner in which Whites created it and continue to systemically integrate such practices into almost every facet of life in the US. [I am] embarrassed but emboldened to help right the wrongs. Active in DEIJ [diversity, equity, inclusion, and justice] group with local land trust and using knowledge gained there to change my life practices to be more mindful of the history of my privileges, and to seek to share them across the racial divide.

Black boyfriend visited. Nana called police

Cynthia Moore • Northborough, MA

My sweet, kind, misguided, fearful grandmother called the police to report a potentially dangerous intruder in the house when my Black boyfriend first came to visit where we lived downstairs. The doorbell rang, and the police asked me to step outside. They then went inside and confronted him. I thought I was going to die of embarrassment. Up until this moment, I had no idea that my grandmother was so racially jaded. She had been picked on all her life for her Protestant upbringing and felt less than worthy due to her glass eye. I had never understood that being the victim of prejudice doesn't automatically preclude you from becoming a perpetrator yourself. It was quite an awakening for me. God bless my boyfriend, who shook it off. I'm happy to report he's still a friend in life.

Son can't speak. May be shot

Lynnisha Grigsby • Minneapolis, MN

My son has a rare form of Down syndrome, mosaic translocation Down syndrome. He wasn't diagnosed until he was two because his overall features are very "mild." He's eight years old right now. He is in a mainstream classroom and can do anything. Yet I can't see that I will let him venture out alone because he may be difficult to understand, or [people] may not understand him. If a cop can't tell he has a disability and perceives noncompliance, what then?

It's not a difference of opinion

Bryanne Smith • USA

In the Autism Community, we often talk about run-ins that we've had with law enforcement, and we all have our stories. Usually, it's because someone is triggered by bright flashing lights, or they lose their ability to speak under extreme stress. Some autistics have comorbidities such as Tourette's syndrome or a seizure disorder, both of which can cause uncontrollable movements, and cause a police officer to think that a person is on drugs or is a threat.

Some of my fellow autistics have been beaten up by police. Many have been traumatized. For my friends that are Black and autistic, the stories get more frequent, and darker. I'll share one of my stories here:

One night in 2005, I was driving through a small town on my way to my dad's house, which was about forty-five minutes away. It was right after my evening shift at a fast-food joint, and I still had on my work uniform. I was driving a big, old boat-looking car that was messy and cluttered. My hair was spilling out of my uniform hat, and my apron and shirt were covered in ice cream and grease.

Due to road construction closing the main highway, I had to drive through an unfamiliar area. I didn't slow down fast enough. Consequently, I got pulled over for going thirty-six in a twenty-five. Before I knew it, four police cars were behind me flashing their lights, and I started to panic. I quickly thumbed through my car looking for the documentation needed before the cop came up to my door and ordered me out of my vehicle. They made me stand behind my vehicle while all four of them started firing questions at me with those flashing lights behind them.

"What are you doing?" "Are you on drugs?" "Have you been drinking?" "Who are you?" "What are you doing here?"

I was so frightened. I could barely speak. I was crying. And those flashing lights were making me sick to my stomach and dizzy. My mind was racing, and I started to feel like a caged animal. One or two of the officers started walking toward me, and finally I found my words. "I'm autistic."

Those words saved me. Their voices changed from accusatory to understanding. One by one, the police officers turned off those terrible flashing lights. They asked me if I took medication. They asked me how my autism affected me. One of them said they had a nephew that was autistic. My soon-to-be several hundred dollars in tickets turned into a warning, and they sent me on my merry way, all because they believed me when I said I was autistic.

That night has been playing over and over in my head over the past several years, along with numerous questions and ways that the experience could have been a lot worse. What if they hadn't known what autism was (a very real possibility back then)? What if I couldn't speak under stress like so many of my autistic friends? What if the fast-food logo wasn't showing on my shirt and I wasn't wearing my fast-food hat?

But the [questions] that play in my head [are]: What if I was a Black woman instead of a White woman? Would they have believed me when I said I was autistic? Would they have given me the benefit of the doubt? What would they have assumed about me? And the biggest one: Would I still be alive today? I'm here to say, whether or not disabled people are being hurt and killed by police and unarmed Black people are being killed by police isn't a difference of opinion. It's a fact that it happens. I've seen it happen, and I can draw on my own experience as an autistic woman to know that it happens. Anything that involves people's lives is not a difference in opinion. When we call it a mere difference of opinion, we are erasing the stories of Black people and saying that their struggles and pain are their fault and not as bad as they make them out to be. A difference of opinion is whether Pepsi or Coke tastes better.

But, Sir, I'm the victim here

Roberta Leichnitz • Montevallo, AL

The events in Florida have brought back so many memories of the things that would happen to my son and his friends in San Antonio when he was in high school. Stopped for "driving while Mexican" in the "wrong" neighborhood, among others. The icing on the cake was when he was the victim of a hit-and-run, and when the police finally arrived, he was thrown in the back of the police car because the officer thought he recognized him. Yes, he did know my son. My son was the waiter who waited on him, *not* a criminal.

Never too old to be profiled

Ollie Daniels • Pembroke Pines, FL

I am a sixty-nine-year-old Black college professor with all-white hair. From time to time, I am stopped by police officers and questioned. It's never about speeding, but rather it's about, "Is this car yours?" I drive what I call a rather "high-end" car, and I believe that they think that it is a stolen car. I would think that after all my years as a law-abiding citizen, I would not be subjected to such treatment. Race still matters in America!

Bad time for Blue: Always Black

Tim Wagner • Fairfield, CT

This came from a conversation I was having with friends. One friend said how it was a bad time to be a cop in the United States. My other friend, who is an ex-cop, said that was true. He then said it has always been a bad time to be Black in the United States.

Bless Black skin and Blue uniforms

Tanya Adams • Durham, NC

Why is being Black a crime?

Mary Crawford • Galesburg, IL

*Thousands of Japanese Americans, like the unidentified family
in the picture above, were detained against their will in
so-called Japanese internment camps during World War II.*
(American Photo Archive / Alamy Stock Photo)

The Hiroshimas
were good Americans

Ken Prestwich • Worcester, MA

The Hiroshima family included my first friends growing up
on a small farm just outside of L.A. (they had one, too) in
the early 1950s—the parents, like so many where we lived,
had been interred during the war. They were fine people,
a second family to me (I am White).

4
Coins in the Couch

FRAGMENTS OF HISTORY ARE ALWAYS floating into my inbox at The Race Card Project—individual stories that I so treasure because these little shards provide depth and texture to the grand narratives America tells itself through collective memory.

You see, there's the history that you find in books and documentaries—History with a capital H. And there's the small-bore history that you happen upon at the supper table . . . or while rooting in some attic . . . or eavesdropping on elders in the family who whisper about things they wish they could forget.

For me, these stories are like coins in the couch. A titillating discovery, small as it may be. A reward that grows with each new excavation. A jackpot that doesn't diminish over time. After all these years a Buffalo nickel fetches far more than just five cents. And just the same, stories that are long forgotten or stuck in the shadows sparkle in a special way when they resurface.

Wading through all these deeply personal, long-hidden stories provides a kind of second sight that allows for a 360-degree view of events. An example: Whenever I hear about the World War II relocation centers that came to be generally known as internment camps where Japanese Americans were incarcerated against their will, my mind skids past what I learned in history texts—which frankly wasn't all that much—to the personal stories from TRCP's inbox.

I think of Dr. Alan Matsumoto, who described how his father, Frank, and his family were yanked away from their farm in Stockton, California, and sent to the Rohwer Relocation Center in Arkansas. Frank Matsumoto was two years out of high school when it happened. He had been popular in his largely White school. Though his Japanese American family were all Buddhists, he had started attending Christian church. He tried to blend in as much as possible, Alan explained. "There's a picture of him singing among his church friends," Alan said. "Literally everybody around him was White, and he was the only Japanese American guy there." Yet in the end, Frank's effort to assimilate didn't matter. Fear gave way to hysteria following the bombing of Pearl Harbor. Headlines in the San Francisco papers blared, "OUSTER OF ALL JAPS IN CALIFORNIA NEAR!"

When the US government began sending Japanese families away to camps in the remote countryside, none of those friends spoke up for him. He asked a White elementary school teacher who had known him from birth to write a letter to the government explaining that the Matsumoto family were good Americans and shouldn't be considered enemies. She refused. "I think that was a lifelong hurt for him," Alan says.

Decades after the war, Frank Matsumoto's high school class in Stockton held its fiftieth reunion, and the Japanese American students who had suddenly disappeared saw their White classmates again for the first time. Reunion, indeed. Emotions flowed, and so did the tears. There was hurt on all sides. Alan Matsumoto said the White classmates tried with the wisdom of time to justify or explain their silence or inaction. His father, Frank, heard confessional statements such as, "This was wartime," and, "We didn't know," and, "We were afraid that we were gonna be labeled as sympathizers to the Japanese."

I think of Zoe Kumagai Elias, who was a college student in Michigan when I met her back in 2013. At that point in her life, Zoe had decided to try to coax her then ninety-year-old grandpa to talk about what happened when his family saw the relocation order. That notice meant that they had to move from Seattle to a vast stretch of desolate high desert in Idaho 130 miles southeast of Boise. The place was officially called the Minidoka Relocation Center, but residents just called it the Minidoka camp.

Two months after the Japanese military's surprise attack on Pearl Harbor, President Franklin D. Roosevelt signed Executive Order 9066, which authorized the forced removal of people of Japanese ancestry. Regardless of whether they were American citizens, their constitutional rights were thrown to the wind with the justification that the Department of War was acting out of "military necessity." More than 120,000 people—mostly on the West Coast—were hastily shipped to ten relocation camps spread across seven states, leaving behind their homes, businesses, farms, and most of their possessions. About two-thirds of them were, like Zoe's family, American citizens by right of birth. The rest were Japanese-born immigrants. For all of them, their sole crime was their ethnicity.

ABOVE LEFT

Newspaper headline, Oakland, California, February 1942. The internment of Japanese Americans during World War II was the forced relocation and incarceration of 110,000– 120,000 people of Japanese ancestry (62 percent of the internees were US citizens) in camps, as ordered by President Roosevelt shortly after Japan's attack on Pearl Harbor. Japanese Americans were incarcerated based on local population concentrations and regional politics.

ABOVE RIGHT

Arcadia, California, April 5, 1942. Persons of Japanese ancestry arrive at the Santa Anita Assembly Center from San Pedro. Evacuees lived at this center at the former Santa Anita racetrack before being moved inland to relocation centers.

The Minidoka Relocation Center, where Zoe's grandpa Rikio landed, housed more than 9,000 people. Spread out over 33,000 acres, the camp was subject to frequent dust storms and seesaw extremes in weather: in 1942, the year the camp opened, the winter low was 21 degrees below 0 and the summer high was 104. The evacuees lived in tar paper barracks with no insulation. The camp was surrounded by a wired fence, with armed soldiers in a tall tower guarding against escape. Despite the bleak conditions, the displaced Japanese American families did their best to maintain their dignity and a sense of enterprise. They grew most of their own produce and endeavored to create a village atmosphere, with sports teams, a library, and a local newspaper called the *Minidoka Irrigator*— the name perhaps a cynical nod to that hard-scorched stretch of Idaho, where the land was so barren that it resembled Mars.

Zoe's 6-word story speaks to the gulf between her life and her grandfather's experience during the war:

My grandparents' "camp" meant something different.

"I identify as a musician, Buddhist, and writer just as much as I do a Japanese American," Zoe said. "My experience with camp is as a basketball counselor, or six weeks away from home playing orchestra music. My grandparents' camp represents unfairness that our government placed upon a race that is my own. My grandparents' camp was in the desert and meant missing out on real high school. My grandparents' camp meant packing only what you could carry and leaving the rest for the neighbors."

To prove their loyalty to America, hundreds of young Japanese men and women incarcerated at the Minidoka camp enlisted with the US military. In 1943, after the Battle of Midway had diminished the plausibility of a Japanese attack on the West Coast, the War Department changed the rules to allow Japanese Americans to serve in segregated units, using their language skills and cultural knowledge to fight against the nation of their ancestors. One of those young men was Zoe's grandfather Rikio, who by that time had Americanized his name to Rik.

All US male citizens in the camp older than seventeen had to fill out what became known as the loyalty questionnaire, which included a question asking if they were willing to serve in the US Armed Forces and a pledge of allegiance to the United States that included a renunciation of loyalty to Japan. Most incarcerated at the camps agreed on both counts, but a significant number of defiant young men came to be known as the No-No Boys because they refused to sign.

"Being a No-No Boy was really a mark of shame within the community at some level," said Susan Morita, whose family was also deported to Minidoka. The men who stood defiant were pariahs during the war, but Susan says that view has shifted over time. Susan regularly makes the yearly pilgrimage with her family from her home in the DC suburbs back to Idaho, to help heal old wounds and educate new generations about a grim chapter that has become a barely mentioned footnote to history. "You can see the younger generations coming [to the camps] and kind of reclaiming this history," she says. "They are seeing the heroes as the No-No Boys." They ask why, for instance, German Americans were not asked to sign a similar loyalty pledge during either World War I or World War II.

When the camps officially closed in 1945 and 1946, the detainees at the ten Japanese relocation sites run by the War Relocation Authority across the country were released.

They had lost wages, homes, land, and businesses that by today's calculations would be worth as much as $5 billion. And there is no way to calculate the emotional toll and the assault on their dignity.

Zoe grew up learning very little about the internment of Japanese Americans. It was mentioned briefly in a single paragraph in her Advanced Placement history text. It was rarely referenced in popular culture, and her family didn't discuss it. But that changed after she attended a Race Card Project event at the University of Michigan in the spring of 2013, a three-day gathering that included a theatrical production, an exhibition, lectures, and classroom discussions. Zoe's mom was visiting campus from California that spring and spotted a flyer advertising a Race Card Project lecture on difficult truths. As a longtime NPR listener, she recognized my name, so on a whim, she suggested that mother and daughter attend the forum.

Now thirty-one, Zoe describes that event as a line of demarcation in her life. She began thinking about her

Zoe Kumagai Elias

own identity as a fourth-generation Japanese American who grew up in largely White spaces in California. But most important, she says, is that she started asking a lot of questions. As a result, she learned for the first time about her family's own experience in the relocation camps. She learned that upon his release, her grandfather Rikio refused to go back to Seattle and instead headed for the Midwest, where he became an engineer. And that years later, Rikio received $20,000 in reparations after President Ronald Reagan signed the Civil Liberties Act of 1988, which contained an apology from Congress "on behalf of the Nation." He didn't spend that so-called restitution. Instead, he put it away for his wife. He had learned as a young man that hard times can swoop down quickly.

Zoe's grandfather was slipping deeper into dementia when she began asking him questions, and he died the following January. "There was a lot more that I wanted to ask him and didn't get a chance to," she says. "But now that I'm older, I realize it's really OK because it's a lifelong journey for me of understanding. I'm still connecting with my grandparents, with my ancestors, even if we are not talking in person."

The $20,000 given to more than 82,000 people who had been held in the ten relocation centers did not come close to making up for what they lost, says Alan Matsumoto. He believes it was significant nonetheless. The formal apology from a sitting president mattered, but the fact that it was accompanied by cash was even more important. This is a delicate point he wants to make sure people fully understand. It's not because his father valued money. It's that the US government had to give up something of value, much like an award of damages to a plaintiff from a defendant found guilty in a court of law.

I have found that when people talk about the forced internment of people in relocation centers, they focus more on how the US lost its way in trampling on those families' civil rights and less on the immense personal and psychological tolls. One reason we know so little about the vast accounting of that loss is that so many families who experienced wartime detainment stuffed those memories away. Instead, they focused full steam on building a new life. That stoicism followed the traditional Japanese ethos of shikata ga nai—a response to tragedy that translates to "it cannot be helped."

Racial milestones in our country tend to be captured through a singular image.

"Silence," Susan Morita says, "was a big part of survival."

When I consider the world that awaited those Japanese American families after the war, I think of the story that a woman named Linda W. sent to The Race Card Project more than a decade ago. Her family, originally from the Dakotas, moved farther west during World War II in search of work. Linda said her family wound up renting "a small-farm, hired-hands shack of a house that had been vacated by expelled Japanese.

"The previous tenants still had their belongings in the back of the house, behind a curtain," Linda said. She remembers that her mother struggled to keep the kids from going back to that area to explore. "She believed the [Japanese] family would come back and want their possessions, and they should be safeguarded."

Whether they ever came back is a mystery. Linda's father was drafted and sent to Fort Riley in Kansas, so her family moved again. But the details of her story: That little house. The belongings. A lifetime of possessions protected by a flimsy curtain. A family forced to leave and live much like prisoners. A mother extending grace by keeping her kids from rooting around in the possessions another family was forced to leave behind. All of it breathes life into a history I understand more fully now.

I am particularly fond of these "coins in the couch" stories because they offer the gift of almost daily education. I've learned things I never knew, and I've gained a deeper understanding of things I thought I knew a whole lot about. My years on the education beat as a newspaper reporter, and later as a TV correspondent, were like a master class in understanding the nuances and challenges of school integration. But the inbox has been something altogether different.

I have had a chance to hear from students who were on the first wave of buses that sent White kids to Black schools and vice versa. I have also been able to hear from teachers who were on the front line when children crossed the color line in the sixties and seventies— teachers who ignored the screams from segregationists outside their windows so they could focus on the newly assembled classroom of Black, White, and Brown children.

I have heard from a real estate agent who made mounds of money preying on the fears of White homeowners in a town where integration hadn't yet arrived. But integration was on the horizon: It was on the evening news. It was buoyed by the Fair Housing Act signed by President Lyndon B. Johnson in 1968. And decades later, that real estate agent admitted to me with remorse that she had gotten quite good at advising White families to get ahead of that curve by selling fast.

As she tells it, she was part of the wind that propelled White flight, telling those homeowners that the prices of their properties would plummet if a single Black family moved into their vicinity. She now thinks her actions were wrong, even though the warning was technically correct. Government policy worked in lockstep with prevailing racial attitudes for the five decades leading up to 1968. The Federal Housing Administration (FHA) refused to insure home mortgages that were within or even near African American neighborhoods. And, yes, a single Black family daring to move into an all-White neighborhood could sink the area's FHA rating—and along with that, the overall property values. Years later, as she thinks about her role in all of that, she says the regret rises like bile in the back of her throat.

As she tells me her story, I am hearing my own, as the daughter of postal-worker parents who were the first Black family to move onto our block on the far-south side of Minneapolis. In the months after our arrival, "For Sale" signs popped up in front yards like spring crocuses. Although *blockbusting* technically was the term used to describe how unscrupulous Realtors used fear to fuel White flight, my parents proudly saw themselves as "blockbusters." When I hear how they have appropriated that term, I think of them with brooms or shovels, clearing the path for a wave of integration. And indeed, they did, as middle-class Black families flowed into a previously all-White enclave in south

Minneapolis and created a diverse community near Minnehaha Parkway—a model of stable integration that still exists today.

Racial milestones in our country tend to be captured through a singular image. A monument on the side of the road. A picture of Lyndon B. Johnson signing a piece of legislation. An FBI missing persons poster with the faces of Andrew Goodman, James Chaney, and Michael Schwerner. Cesar Chavez with a bullhorn. Bull Connor and fire hoses. Jackie Robinson with his bat. A little girl with braids marching toward the school-house door, surrounded by federal marshals in fedoras.

Learning about integration by considering court orders and judicial directives and old news archives is one thing. But learning about the end of legal segregation and, really, almost anything else, is altogether different when you examine it through the prism of personal experience.

Jeff Fraser grew up in a two-family duplex in Lowell, Massachusetts, in the 1950s. He didn't realize his family was in the vanguard of America's march toward integration until a happenstance encounter at a dance he attended while he was still in high school. He saw an old friend take the stage as the lead singer of a band. The kid's name was Dennis Rivera, and Jeff was stoked to see that his childhood pal had done so well for himself. "I proudly told my friends that he had been my best friend, and that we lived in the same house," Jeff recalls. To his surprise, someone asked with incredulity, "You lived with Puerto Ricans?"

Jeff had been four years old when Dennis Rivera and his family moved into the downstairs unit of his family's duplex, and the two boys spent four years palling around side by side, like cheese and macaroni. Rivera was a name that stood out in this mostly Irish neighborhood, but Jeff was just a kid and didn't understand the stick-with-your-people tribal allegiances that ruled so many aspects of adult life in 1950s America. It wasn't until a decade later, when Jeff saw Dennis at that dance—or, to be clear, when he viewed his old pal through his high school friend's eyes—that he had a revelation. Jeff said, "I looked at Dennis, and for the first time saw a Spanish face."

By the time he got home after the dance that night, Jeff's mind was flooded with memories of Dennis and his family. "I realized that I had lived with Puerto Ricans," he says. And he decided with a shrug that it was no big deal. "My mother confirmed it and laughed," Jeff says. But then she got quiet and told him to sit down.

You see, there was more to this story.

His mom told him that "all hell broke loose" in the neighborhood when they rented the other half of their duplex to the Riveras. "Though Mom and Dad were lifelong residents of the neighborhood and active members of the local Catholic parish, they were harassed mercilessly by many of their 'friends' and neighbors for their treasonous act," he says. There were flyers and petitions. There were even threats. Jeff's father, Jack, was a decorated veteran and a former pilot. He dug in and told everyone to "go to hell." However, the Rivera family decided that it was easier to move on and purchased a single-family house a mile away.

Eventually, the Fraser family also left the neighborhood; Jeff's dad sold the house to someone who planned to open a liquor store on the ground floor, since the duplex was in a mixed-commercial zone. His thinking, according to Jeff, was, "Let's see how they like this new neighbor." His father's attempt to use real estate as a retort never came to pass. "The community eventually blocked the liquor store, robbing my father of his revenge," Jeff says.

Jeff Fraser shared this story with me after a book event in Brookline, Massachusetts. He was emotional as he asked me to sign a copy of *The Grace of Silence*, my family memoir, which includes a chapter about my own family's experience crossing a color line in their Minneapolis neighborhood. He wanted me to dedicate the note inside the front cover to his dad, a principled man who had lost so many friends but gained his son's enduring respect. Jeff said that if he hadn't seen Dennis onstage at that high school dance, he might have never learned about his neighbors' nasty response to the Riveras.

"Why the secrecy?" he wondered, and then answered his own query. "I can see why they would want to shield very young kids from the ugly events at the time," he said. "But why never speak of these matters again? The answer was in the heaviness and sadness of my mother's tone. She was not just angry at these friends and neighbors; she was ashamed of them. These people and their children populated the church and the Catholic school that largely defined our social (and previously, our moral) existence."

Jeff wonders how many other stories his parents "accidentally or intentionally" forgot to tell him. "Maybe I know enough," he says. "I'll trust their judgment on the ones that got away."

Black clients funded our white flight

Jane Meacham • Washington, DC

My dad is a lawyer in Kansas City, Missouri, who always had mostly Black, working-class clients. When the city school district started to decline in quality in the early 1970s, we moved to a nearly all-White suburban school district nearby. So, I realize now, all these years later, that his African American clientele's fees inadvertently helped us flee the changing complexion of a busing-integrated school system.

1960s Dearborn will haunt me forever

Bonnie • Empire, MI

I watched in horror at the treatment of the *one* Black family that had the *nerve* to move into town while I was a preteen. It was a surreal time and place.

Mom stayed when Whites took flight

Victoria Browne • Mundelein, IL

My mom considers it one of her finest gifts to her children that when the Austin neighborhood of Chicago began to "change," she stayed, made friends, and urged the church to take a stand against White flight.

Busing: White girl, Black schools, lonely

Clara Silverstein • Boston, MA

As one of the White children in Richmond, Virginia, in the 1970s whose families willingly participated in busing, I had few friends of any race. What we could have used at the time was leadership instead of racist rhetoric, White flight, and school administrators who cancelled all after-school activities. The possibility of an interracial dance horrified them. The longest-lasting lesson: race is a malignant social construct. Many of us wanted to reach out to one another, but generations of misinformation and mistrust stood in the way. I have written about my own experiences and also use my background to help teens of all races express themselves in writing—their struggles to fit in and find a place for themselves—when fear too often silences all of us.

I'm from Detroit; well, *near* Detroit

Susan Hayes-McQueen • Seattle, WA

Anyone who understands the White flight issue surrounding Detroit will understand this. It's code for, "Well, I'm White, so I didn't grow up in Detroit; that's where the Black people are." White people are in the surrounding suburbs.

I hate hearing, "The neighborhood changed."

Glenny Brock • Birmingham, AL

Always code. In fact, most of the people I've heard say this were people who themselves *changed* neighborhoods by leaving.

Only fools would first consider race

Brian Ellis • Glendale, CA

I grew up in a segregated suburb of Detroit (Dearborn, Michigan), where our Catholic family was a minority. My father, a physician, was contacted by the local homeowner's association, who chided him for entertaining Black guests at our house (namely other physicians). My father (who'd grown up in Detroit) told them to go to hell. That was my first realization that some were different and there were people who didn't approve. During the Detroit Riot of 1967, my father, who was medical director of the American Red Cross blood program, worked long and hard to handle the outcome of that tragic episode. While our neighbors stayed away from the inner city, he went down each day to do his job.

White flight and racism trump integration

Robert Robillard • Roanoke, VA

I teach at a White flight private school that now aims to be diverse. In Tuscaloosa as it is in Roanoke or Richmond, Black families who have the means (not just money but social capital) frequently get their best and brightest into successful county schools or private schools. This brain drain from the city school districts adds another challenge to improving test scores. Educating all our students well is the most important problem we face as a society.

White flight child knows no brother

Jeffrey Kingdon • Danville, IN

Whether my 1950s-era parents chose their life in the suburbs due to racial considerations or were simply following the trend to find affordable postwar housing, the effect was the same. The west suburban central Indiana communities were largely small farming towns rapidly on their way to becoming bedroom sprawl to their larger urban neighbor. These communities were almost homogenously White. Growing up there, I knew no one of another race. And how did this affect my life? Well, I didn't think too much about it. As a child, adolescent, and young adult, it seemed normal. My schools were White. I chose to go to a small college, Presbyterian and predominantly White.

When it came time ultimately to find a place to raise our family, we moved home . . . to west suburban Indianapolis. Still White after all these years. However, primarily through the work world, I began to "come to" and realize that my White world wasn't the only reality. I find myself today sometimes saddened by not knowing the "other." This breeds fear and distrust when there need not be any. We have not enjoyed one another's company or shared different food or taken part in varied family and cultural traditions. In very tangible ways, we have missed out by holding ourselves apart. Why? It didn't seem consciously done; we just gravitate to what we know, what feels normal and comfortable in making life's choices.

Our kids, however, are making different choices. Both live in large urban centers. They engage in this life with their spouses and enjoy it completely. They have opportunities to live side by side with every ethnicity, gay or straight, young or old. How did this happen? I do not know. Their lives will be more complete, richer. Good for them, and good for all of us.

Lifetime in slipstream of White flight

Richard Bacon • Chicago, IL

Mid-1970s, living in perfectly nice middle-class neighborhood in northeastern Dallas. The desecration, by busing, of the neighborhood school (which was mediocre, anyway) caused about half the families with school-age children to move out in one summer. My best friend moved. Those of us who stayed were dispersed to private schools or lived in families that "didn't care." It was like surviving a plague—half the people you knew were suddenly gone. By high school, I was back in Dallas public schools, at a superior high school with multiple academic magnet programs and about 40 to 50 percent White kids. But by early 1980s, it was clear that the "best" White kids had moved to the suburbs or private schools. Dallas Independent School District is now only 5 percent White.

As an adult, I moved to Chicago, to the South Side, for grad school, living in a neighborhood surrounded by a sea of neglected and abandoned neighborhoods, beautiful places with tree-lined boulevards, right by Lake Michigan, that White people fled a generation earlier.

Then I married a South Side Irish/Polish woman. Her entire extended family and friends had fled multiple times, moving en masse and replicating whole streets in a new suburb, only to flee that new refuge when a Black family moved in. And every move, some get left behind, and the familial and social connections get frayed a little more. For three generations, White flight has been [an] organizing principle of this population. I now live in one of those abandoned/neglected South Side neighborhoods, not wanting to repeat the White flight story of my life. It's a wonderful street, rehabbed and wonderful dwellings, with wonderful neighbors. But I still feel like a refugee. I don't blame Black people for all of this. I blame the White folks who disrupted and dislocated our lives. They wanted to be "safe," but they created a self-fulfilling prophecy with their fear.

Yes, I'm Black, but not angry

Ellise • Riverside, CA

My race is not what you see. It is what I feel. Do not let your stereotypes fool you. I am happy, beautiful, and peaceful about who I am. I used to be angry with who I was. I have been told I was "pretty for a Black girl" all my life. That made me ashamed of who I was. I could not hide from what God intended [me] to be, so I embraced it. I saw other Black women embracing their beauty, and it gave my joy. I want all little girls to see that beauty in themselves. Despite how I may feel, each day is my opportunity to inspire all girls of all colors to embrace how God made them. God does not make any mistakes. First embrace the beauty in your heart, then allow it to shine through your skin.

Sometimes I feel like a traitor

Paula Durant • Dearborn, MI

As a second-generation Mexican American, I sometimes wonder if I'm "Mexican enough." And does anyone else wonder the same thing about their heritage? Is being me, a proud American, enough? And no, I couldn't say all that in Spanish!

Fostering Racism for Generations to Come!

Kenneth Powell • New Kensington, PA

As a thirteen-year-old White boy, I grew up in Jacksonville, Florida. At my grammar school, I was a proud school crossing guard. One day while on duty, a Duval County deputy sheriff's car pulled up. As two deputies got out and engaged me in conversation, a Black man came walking down the road. He seemed to be a tradesman, as he had concrete dust on his clothes. One of the deputies told me to throw a rock at the "nigger." I refused, picked up my bike, and pedaled home as fast as I could. I never told my parents or teacher about that incident. Now that I'm seventy-five years old, I know what those men were doing: trying to teach me that Black people should be hurt and put "in their place," but more importantly, racism was acceptable and should be fostered. That incident instilled in me a distrust of police and an understanding, though a limited understanding, of what Black boys and men endure. Those cops failed in their mission that day.

I feel guilt for my ancestors.

Lindsey Lovel • Brooklyn, NY

I FLOURISH FARMING ANCIENT TRIBAL LANDS

Ed Kaufman • Morris, MN

EVERY DIRECTION I LOOKED in the place where I grew up, I was surrounded by the majestic cadence of words connected to Native American culture. The city, the state, the meandering creek at the end of my block, were all graced with multisyllabic Indigenous words. And yet, I was reminded of how little of that Indigenous culture made its way into my formal education when I flew home in 2012 to deliver a lecture at the University of Minnesota Morris, a campus near the middle of the state in a town that prides itself on being encircled by some of the most fertile farmland in all of America.

Looking out over an audience of more than three hundred people, I saw young faces and old, locals and college kids, many of them Native American students from the Great Lakota, Dakota, Nakota Nation, sometimes still referred to as Sioux. What I didn't know was that this gathering held the descendants of people who'd fought a bloody war with one another in 1862.

Sitting in the audience that night was Ed Kaufman, a White former pharmaceutical executive who'd come back to Minnesota to run a family farming business. Ed carried one of the little black-striped Race Card Project postcards home with him that evening. However, he didn't send the postcard back right away. He mulled it over for almost two years and then returned it with these six words:

I flourish farming ancient tribal lands

Farmers say the land speaks to them, and as Ed was in his fields one day, he had an epiphany. "It dawned on me that these [acres] must have at one time been occupied by Indigenous peoples," he recalls as he thinks back to that moment when he imagined "the Sioux or the Dakota and other more ancient tribal people." Ed was making lots of money off this land, growing and selling so-called row crops like corn and soybeans. And he knew his good fortune had come at the expense of others—of, as he puts it, "one racial group having benefited from the exploitation of another."

Ed had heard about the US-Dakota War of 1862 from his sixth-grade Minnesota history class, but he didn't know much about it. He didn't know the war led to one of the state's most infamous historic events, the simultaneous hanging of thirty-eight Dakota men from a single massive platform. To this day, that collective hanging is still the largest mass execution in US history. "I don't remember hearing about the hanging, certainly not from school," Ed told me. He grew up in a small Minnesota town, where he can't recall ever seeing Native Americans. "It was as if they didn't exist," he said. But of course, they exist—and they remember.

Oddly enough, two years after that visit to Morris, Mariah Sazue, a college student from the University of Minnesota Morris campus, also sent me her 6-word story and a few paragraphs explaining why she settled on that collection of words:

Dakota, Lakota, Native, Land, Pride, Immigrant.

I am a Dakota/Lakota Sioux who is Native to this now American Land, but I feel like I am an immigrant in this country. I grew up in the public school district, where I was not taught a thing about my Dakota/Lakota heritage. Besides the traditional Thanksgiving, Native Americans were not mentioned in my years of school. I was once ashamed of my race because I always heard classmates taunting the Native accent and the assumptions of the Native American stereotypes.

I came to learn my culture through my grandparents and oral history. Coming to find out how this country really came about, I was confused and upset. I still felt like an immigrant in our "Native America." I was mad at myself for being ashamed, I was mad at those classmates for disrespecting me and my culture, I was mad at the school system for not acknowledging the true history of these lands, and I am still mad to this day.

I still feel like an immigrant mostly because we've been treated like immigrants since the first contact between the Natives and Europeans. I now have the utmost pride in my race and culture because who we were as people before assimilation was amazing. There were once millions of Indigenous people surviving on Turtle Island (present-day North America) simply on their own in their own ways. Who we are now as "American Indians" is because of what was brought upon us; who we are now is because of "America." That's why I feel like an immigrant.

Growing up on a reservation in neighboring South Dakota, Mariah knew very little about her connection to the state where she decided to attend college. After being admitted to the school and applying for financial aid, she was informed that she would receive a tuition waiver as a student of Native descent. Not until she arrived on campus would she fully understand what led to that generosity: it was an act of atonement.

The campus sits on land that was once a boarding school for Native American children. Founded in 1887, the Morris Industrial School for Indians was part of a network of similar institutions across the country that were funded by the federal government and meant to help assimilate Native children. Originally founded by an order of Catholic nuns called the Sisters of Mercy, the school mainly enrolled Native America children from surrounding tribes who often were "recruited" despite protests from their families against an education based on full cultural assimilation. Eventually, the federal government took control of the school, and as with other assimilation schools around the country, Native American children were forbidden from participating in cultural traditions. These Native American children were not allowed to speak the first languages they had learned within their tribes. In many of the federally run or federally funded assimilation schools, the children's traditional garments and regalia were confiscated. Their hair was often cut short, and Native song and symbols were prohibited.

The goal of the Morris Industrial School was to "civilize the Indian." In other words, teach them how to be White. "The curriculum emphasized the value of the White man's way and at least implicitly the evil of the child's home," wrote the late Wilbert "Bert" Ahern, a professor emeritus at the University of Minnesota Morris who conducted extensive research on the former boarding school.

UMN Morris is now a place of pride for Native American students, who make up more than one-fourth of the student body. It is a place of uplift and opportunity. And, in recent years, it has become a place of candor, as the university has confronted its past and launched an investigation into conditions at the boarding school. The campus is also confronting the very real possibility that former students from the assimilation school might be buried on or near the grounds in unmarked graves.

As Mariah learned more about her university's difficult history, she also faced up to her own. She left South Dakota to attend college in a neighboring state, but in a fundamental way, she was also returning home. Like Ed Kaufman, she, too, was tethered to the US-Dakota War of 1862. Before that bloody conflict, Minnesota, she would learn, was the land of her people.

．　．　．

The history of struggle between Native Americans and the Europeans who took their land is violent and painful. American Indians have long asserted that their losses and their trauma are compounded by the fact that this history has been erased or reduced to little more than a fringe element of our understanding of how this country came to look the way it does.

In the decades leading up to 1862, the United States had taken land, sometimes acre by acre and sometimes tens of millions of acres at once, from the Native tribes that had thrived there for centuries. The lands were often transferred by treaty, and while that makes it sound like Native Americans willingly handed over their land in a fair exchange, the reality is that agreements that began on honorable footing slid toward something that was more complicated, less likely to be upheld, and resulting in the increased forfeiture of land and nullification of tribal rights.

In a 2018 report on funding shortfalls for Native Americans called *Broken Promises*, the US Commission on Civil Rights stated:

> In exchange for the surrender and reduction of tribal lands and removal and resettlement of approximately one-fifth of Native American tribes from their original lands, the United States signed 375 treaties, passed laws, and instituted policies that shape and define the special government-to-government relationship between federal and

tribal governments. Yet the U.S. government forced many Native Americans to give up their culture and, throughout the history of this relationship, has not provided adequate assistance to support Native American interconnected infrastructure, self-governance, housing, education, health, and economic development needs.

That spiral often began with treaties that were sometimes established under coercion with the threat of military action or gradual starvation. The late Elden Lawrence, former president of the tribal Sisseton Wahpeton Oyate, was a leading scholar of Dakota history. He asserted that other pressure tactics were used as well, including browbeating, brainwashing, and exaggerated claims. Lawrence is noted for becoming the second Native American to receive his PhD at South Dakota State University in 1999.

During his life, he implored Minnesota schools and the Minnesota Historical Society to be more transparent in describing the conditions under which the treaties were signed. In an interview with the historical society, he described how the Dakota Sioux were given an impossible choice when trying to negotiate: "If you sign this treaty, you're not going to ever have to work or hunt again; we'll take care of you. Everything will be provided. Every year you'll get so much money to buy your needs, your pots and pans and stuff, but we'll also have food coming in every month, or once a year for you. The other alternative is—look over here, this is what's going to happen. We're going to drive you all the way to the Rocky Mountains where you're going to starve to death and we'll never have to worry about you again."

Given this "choice," tribal leaders understandably opted to sign the agreements.

By the time Minnesota became a state in 1858, the Dakota had ceded most of their land in exchange for payments from the government that were well below established value, and even then, the US kept most of that money and doled out meager interest payments that were sporadic or rerouted as payment to traders and merchants who claimed outstanding debts.

Shunted from the vast land they'd occupied for centuries into smaller reservations, the Minnesota Natives could no longer roam freely in search of wild game and had to reluctantly turn from hunting to farming. Contrary to the Native Americans' increasing confinement, new settlers who occupied what were once Indigenous lands hunted with abandon and killed much of the wild game. The tribes slid into starvation and debt, and by 1861, despair turned to desperation. The crops failed in the summer of that year, and so the tribe had inadequate food stored for what would come to be known as the "starving winter."

Back east, as the Civil War was raging, the US government was distracted or disinterested. In either case, it failed to make payments that were due to the Dakota tribe.

Traders of European descent were accustomed to selling goods to the Dakota on credit, then recouping the money when treaty payments rolled in. But that winter, they showed little mercy, refusing to allow the tribes to buy food on credit in light of the government's late payments. A trader named Andrew Myrick was infamously callous, dismissing the mass starvation with the words "If they are hungry, let them eat grass." Famished, broke, cheated, and dismissed by the government and powerful local traders, the Dakota began to go on the offensive. On August 17, 1862, a group of young Dakota men attacked and killed five White settlers in the township of Acton. Taoyateduta (Little Crow), the chief of the Dakota, is said to have ordered attacks meant to drive settlers out of the Minnesota River Valley after heated debate inside his tribe.

That incursion launched the violent US-Dakota War. Hundreds of people, Natives and Whites alike, perished in furious battles across the southern Minnesota frontier. Not all Dakota supported the charge to war, but those who did seemed intent on avenging decades of mistreatment, slashing and burning their way through settlements, displacing hundreds of settlers, and killing women and children along with the men. Among the first to die was Andrew Myrick, whose body was reportedly found with grass stuffed into his mouth.

After weeks of mayhem and bloodshed, the war headed toward its end in late September 1862 in the final, decisive Battle of Wood Lake, where US forces defeated the Dakota. The following day, Little Crow fled with a band of followers to Canada, and on September 26, the Dakota surrendered, handing over the nearly three hundred prisoners they had captured. The war was over—but the trauma for the Dakota was far from done.

US forces took roughly 2,000 Dakota into custody. Of these, more than 1,600 never fought in the war—and many had even opposed it. A series of speedy military trials followed, sometimes as many as 42 in a single day. The Natives had no legal representation. "Justice" was swift: by early November, the US government had sentenced 303 Dakota men to death by hanging. When word reached President Abraham Lincoln, however, he asked to personally review the trial records. As he explained in a December 11 message to the US Senate, he was "anxious to not act with so much clemency as to encourage another outbreak on the one hand, nor with so much severity as to be real cruelty on the other." Lincoln commuted the sentences of all but 39, one of whom would later receive a reprieve. (Two more would be put to death three years later, in 1865.)

In the end, thirty-eight Native men faced execution by hanging. It was to take place simultaneously, on a massive timber gallows erected in the Minnesota town of Mankato.

As reported in one newspaper account, "The gallows is 24 feet square . . . and is so arranged as to afford room for the hanging of ten Indians on each side. It might have been larger had the President been less squeamish, and even then justice would have been defrauded of its dues." Yet not everyone shared that reporter's ire; some newspaper editorials denounced the executions, arguing that they were a miscarriage of justice since treaties had been broken and trials had been abridged.

A crowd of nearly 4,000 people gathered to watch the mass execution, some sitting high on tree limbs. At 10:00 a.m. on December 26, 1862, the condemned men were marched from their prison quarters to the scaffolding. As they ascended the steps, they chanted a Dakota song, their voices growing louder as each reached the platform. Soldiers placed white muslin coverings over their faces as the thirty-eight men reached out their arms to clasp one another's hands. A military drumbeat pierced the crisp morning air as 1,400 soldiers surrounded the gallows on all sides, creating a kind of human fencing. The executioner that morning was Captain William Duley. The hangman was also a grieving father. Captain Duly was a White settler with three children who had been killed during the conflict. They were ten, six, and four years old. His wife and two other children were taken prisoner by the Dakota. It was Duly who raised his axe to cut the rope that was holding the floor of the scaffolding in place.

Witnesses said a loud click rang out when the axe fell and the massive hinges below the gallows snapped open. The floor of the scaffolding dropped—and so did the men with nooses around their necks.

• • •

Remember Ed Kaufman, the White man whose family farmed the ancient tribal lands? When he sent us his original six words, he also submitted a second story:

"My great-grandfather stood witness at Mankato."

Yes, Ed's great-grandfather Henry Mills witnessed the hanging of those thirty-eight Dakota men in Mankato. Mills was a member of the Minnesota infantry—the same infantry that after the war drove thousands of remaining Dakota Sioux out of Minnesota in a forced relocation to reservations such as Crow Creek, in South Dakota.

And remember Mariah Sazue, the young Dakota/Lakota woman who was a student at UMN Morris? She lives on the Crow Creek Indian Reservation. She is descended from the people who were driven from the land.

"A lot of our ancestors were involved with the Dakota Thirty-Eight," Mariah says. "I was told that after the Dakota Thirty-Eight hangings, the women and children were forced to walk or move to South Dakota"—some, quite possibly, under the watchful eye of Ed Kaufman's great-grandfather's regiment. "That's how we ended up here," she says.

Mariah is peeved that she learned so little about her people's history in school. She feels robbed. From her grandparents, she learned the language of her ancestors and her lineage. But it wasn't until much more recently that she fully learned about her connection to the events of 1862 and how they led to her living in Crow Creek.

"My boyfriend is from the same reservation, and his dad's side is really knowledgeable in our history," she says. "So, that's how I learned about our ancestors being at the Dakota Thirty-Eight and being moved here."

Mariah moved back home to "the rez," as she calls it, after graduation, and she's now an elementary school teacher at another reservation near her own, in a place called Lower Brule. The Crow Creek reservation she calls home is a little more than 400 square miles, and the population is small. "I think our tribe as a whole has about forty-five hundred members, but there's, like, twelve hundred living on the reservation," she says. "And we're about an hour or so away from any type of town, any major grocery store or store. And so, it's really kind of rural and desolate. It's really impoverished. The unemployment rate is super high." (Figures from the 2019 Census show about 2,200 people are listed as official residents of the Crow Creek Reservation.)

Some tribes have found fortune through operating casinos, such as the Shakopee Mdewakanton Sioux Community in suburban Minneapolis, where every adult member has at times received as much as $1 million each year thanks to gambling proceeds. The Dakota who live on the Crow Creek reservation can barely imagine that kind of largesse. Crow Creek struggles with high levels of substance abuse, unemployment, and suicide. Prosperity and even stability are usually out of reach.

And yet, Mariah says, "It's really a beautiful place. Like, we're right on the Missouri River. So, in the summertime—any time—it's really beautiful." But yes, there also are overwhelming signs of blight. "We also have a lot of boarded-up houses. We have a lot of homeless, and things aren't very well taken care of because our tribe doesn't have the funding to keep things up. And we haven't had any new construction of any buildings or homes in a really long time."

A decade has passed since Mariah sent us her six words about feeling like an immigrant in the land of her people. That hasn't changed.

"I still feel the same," she said. "I kind of feel like racism and that kind of stuff has gotten worse," especially, she said, while the Trump administration was in office. "It's been really bad here in South Dakota. Just the blatant racism. People aren't really scared to be, or aren't ashamed to be racist here, and it's . . . it's upsetting." She pauses, collecting herself. "But I'm still here, and I'm still gonna be here. It's my home, so . . ." Her voice trails off.

The reservation is in a "food desert," lacking in grocery stores, pharmacies, or butcher shops, so Mariah and her family have to travel to a Walmart an hour away to get supplies. With their dark hair, darker complexions, and the facial features common to her tribe, they stand out when they head to town. It's both irritating and exhausting, she says.

"We always have to go and show our receipts to make sure we paid for everything," Mariah says. "I don't know if they're intrigued by us or intimidated, but we just always feel that energy, like someone is watching." The vibe, she says, is "we're not supposed to be here." She and her family, including her now eleven-year-old daughter, think carefully about appearance when they make those trips. She says they "try to dress as White as possible, to just try to fit in and not be targeted or stared at. You know, we try to look as normal as everybody else as possible, but we're also so very prideful in our culture."

Forced to abandon the windswept plains where the Minnesota and Blue Earth rivers meet.

With the onset of Covid, the family was careful to wear masks in public, some with tribal marking or decorations. This, too, leads to stares and even scorn. "We get looked at like we're dumb, or we're sheep," she says, noting that some of the highest rates of Covid infections are on the reservations in South Dakota, and Mariah's grandmother was one of the first to die from the coronavirus. Of the people outside reservations, Mariah sighs with exasperation. "They don't know," she says. "They don't care.

"I just want people to know that we're good people," Mariah says. "We're intelligent; we're very resilient. And we just want to get along with everybody. We want to just strive and be able to help these next generations move forward and be who they're going to be. That's all I really want people to know." Even though their histories are intertwined, a vast gulf lies between the experiences of Ed's and Mariah's families. Ed's great-grandfather Henry Mills received free tracts of land from the US government after serving for the Union side in the Civil War. Another great-grandfather, Jacob Kaufman, immigrated to the US from Germany during the nineteenth century, and that side of the family, too, acquired large tracts of land. Although his ancestors were immigrants, Ed sees himself simply as an American.

Mariah's ancestors have lived in North America for centuries and were forced to abandon the windswept plains where the Minnesota and Blue Earth Rivers meet. She is indigenous to this country. Her people predate its founding, and yet she is the one who feels like an immigrant.

· · ·

Why was the story of the Dakota 38 not taught in schools? Why is it only now creeping slowly into curricula and history texts? Why have Native Americans, such as Mariah Sazue, had to learn their ancestors' history piecemeal, through precious snippets gathered from the kitchen-table conversations of grandparents and friends? In the same way we talk about reconciling and recognizing the history of slavery, we as a country must figure out how to examine and lift the history of Indigenous peoples. We live on their land. Our towns and boulevards are named in their languages. Our traditions are wrapped up in theirs. And yet, across this country, there has been an erasure of unfathomable magnitude.

The Dakota have their own ways of keeping alive the memory of the Dakota 38 and the two who were executed later. Since 1972, tribe members have held the annual Mankato Wacipi powwow, a massive event that includes drumming and dancing and welcomes non-Natives. The goals of the large event are to excavate and surface memories, honor traditions, and build stronger relations between the Mdewakanton Dakota and non-Mdewakanton communities. A smaller, private powwow honors the men who were executed. And several monuments have been erected in the area, replacing one that people on both sides disliked: a giant granite monument that once stood in the center of Mankato, engraved with the words "Here were hanged 38 Sioux Indians. Dec. 26th, 1862." Removed by the city of Mankato in 1971, the monument lay in a parking garage for more than two decades before disappearing for good in the mid-1990s.

OPPOSITE

Pipestone, Minnesota. Riders on Route 34 at the South Dakota–Minnesota border on Wednesday, December 18, 2019, on the eighth day and 167th mile of a 325-mile memorial ride to Mankato, Minnesota, site of the largest mass execution in US history. The riders call themselves the Dakota 38+2 to honor the thirty-eight Dakota Indians and, later, two chiefs who were executed following their uprising against the US government.

One of the most moving memorials began with a dream. In 2005, a Dakota tribesman named Jim Miller had a vivid dream of riding his horse from his home in South Dakota to the hanging place in Mankato. When he awoke, he decided to make the dream a reality. Every year since then, a group of Dakota ride their horses the 330 miles from Lower Brule, South Dakota—where Mariah Sazue teaches middle school—to Mankato. They start in early December, then ride for days through snow, sleet, wind, and freezing temperatures. And every year, they arrive at the square in Mankato at 10:00 a.m. on the day after Christmas, the exact date and time their ancestors were executed.

It's no surprise that the Dakota take these steps to remember their own. But what about the descendants of the White settlers? What obligations do they have to keep the memory of these events alive?

Trauma cuts both ways in times of war. Amnesia, however, tends to be more one-sided.

. . .

"I've been wondering about ways in which we could acknowledge the fact that much of our good fortune stems from these unfortunate events," Ed Kaufman says. "I've been doing a great deal of thinking about how my family might acknowledge this inheritance from ancient people." Over the years, Ed and his parents endowed several scholarships at the University of South Dakota. He's retired now—in fact, he sold the farm and lives in Santa Barbara, California—but he'd still like to endow several more, specifically for Native American students. And he's thinking of doing it at the University of Minnesota Morris—the school where he heard me speak back in 2012. "I recognize that I'm standing on the shoulders of a lot of people," he says. "Some family members, and many not."

Mariah Sazue continues to teach young Native Americans at the middle school in Lower Brule. She makes sure her students learn about the war, about the Dakota 38, and about the forced relocation of their forebears. And although that history is soaked in sorrow, she teaches her students about the lessons of resiliency and pride that can be gleaned from survival.

"It's horrible that it happened," she says, "but once I did learn about it more, and how the women and children survived—I wouldn't be here if my ancestors didn't survive moving from Minnesota to here. So, it's empowering at the same time." Mariah uses that example to inspire her students. But, she tells me, it's the students who inspire her and help her through the low points when the generational trauma creates a thick emotional fog. "I love working with kids," she says. "I feel like that really helps me to keep going, to overcome all this trauma that we all carry. Because I see them, and they're just so inspiring; they're all so full of life. They just love being here, and they love who they are. So that really helps to keep me going."

•   •   •

In the fourteen years I've been working on The Race Card Project, I've noticed a trend. When people gather, they will pay homage to the Indigenous peoples on whose land they stand. In Massachusetts, the convocation begins with gratitude to the Wampanoag of Gay Head (Aquinnah). In Syracuse, it's an honor for the Onondaga Nation. Respect is given to the Navajo in Arizona and New Mexico. In Colorado, it's a roll call for the Pueblo, Arapaho, Comanche, Apache, Kiowa, and Southern Ute. Though it sometimes seems a bit performative, it's also earnest, and it's certainly righteous. Yet so often the very people who are being honored are absent from the rooms—underrepresented in educational spaces, civic gatherings, and cultural events like film festivals and the like.

Native Americans have been made invisible by the erasure of their history and culture, by the lack of opportunities through education and employment, and by the fact that so many live on sovereign lands—on reservations that through their original design were separated from the rest of the country. If there ever was an example of an out-of-sight-out-of-mind government policy, this is it. Yet as America developed, it embraced Native nomenclature even as it attempted to subordinate Native American culture. Of America's fifty states, more than half have names rooted in American Indian history.

The word *Minnesota* comes from a Dakota phrase meaning "sky-tinted water" or "land where the water is so clear it reflects the sky." So yes, the state—my beloved home state—takes its name from the language of Indigenous people whom it forcibly removed from the land.

Take a moment to take that in.

While researching this story, I realized I have my own odd and tangential connection to this history. Growing up in Minneapolis, I attended Alexander Ramsey Junior High, named for the Minnesota governor during the US-Dakota War. When the fighting broke out in 1862, he's the man who declared that "the Sioux Indians of Minnesota must be exterminated or driven forever beyond the borders of Minnesota." Ramsey also later directed his administration to offer bounties for Native scalps. He was one of the governors who, after the US-Dakota War, allowed volunteer scouts to be paid twenty-five dollars per scalp. Individual citizens could claim two hundred dollars if they could prove that they killed a

Dakota. I don't recall being taught much of this, but years later, a group of students did learn about it and led a campaign to change the school's name. In 2017, Ramsey was renamed Justice Page Middle School in honor of Alan Page, the former Minnesota Vikings football player who went on to become the first African American justice on the Minnesota Supreme Court.

The other connection is even more personal. Fort Snelling is a historic landmark just southeast of Minneapolis on the bluffs near the confluence of the Mississippi and Minnesota Rivers. An international airport serving the Twin Cities is right next door to Fort Snelling. When I was a kid, my dad used to drive us to the airport. We'd grab a cola inside the terminal, and sit by the windows to watch the jets soar toward the sky during takeoff. We'd sit there for what seemed like hours and make up stories about imagined destinations.

In the days before TSA checkpoints, you could walk all the way to a departure gate and sit on the chairs facing the tarmac along with travelers lugging their Samsonite suitcases. (No one had yet dreamed up suitcases with wheels.) These jaunts to the airport allowed my ever-frugal father to serve up a cheap thrill on a weekend afternoon. I believe that he also wanted me to see myself in those travelers and imagine the day when my own adventures would take flight.

Dad is buried in the military cemetery near the end of one of those runways. The rows of all those granite markers greet me from the sky whenever I fly home. In researching this story, I learned that Fort Snelling served as a prison camp after the 1862 US-Dakota War, a place where more than 1,600 Dakota noncombatants, mostly children, women, and elderly men, were kept in filthy, inhumane conditions. As many as 300 died there during that harsh winter.

Like the farmer, we all should learn how to listen to the land.

If you live in Minnesota, this history is all around you.

If you live in America, it surrounds you on all sides.

You just have to listen.

And then figure out how to order your steps.

Grateful granny called me Black boy

Kevin Adonis Browne • USA

I was grateful; granny was prophetic,
almost making me out of clay,
caressing my tar with old love.
Black before it was a color.
we come from an oily family,
our skins sticky to the touch.
we, who gushed from the oilfields:
she didn't want me digging holes.
she didn't want us digging holes.
she remains, now, a 45-minute recording—
my own ghost in the machine—that I listen to often,
but not often enough.
she named me.
I think it was so that every time I say my name,
I say it with her tongue:
"Black boy."

I tend to scare White people

Enrique Guzmán • Tucson, AZ

I also tend to scare those that are of a higher social class, the elderly, and the people that believe the way I speak English is not the correct form of English. Overall, these people tend to be White. It's a shame, really. It's terrible that the color of my skin is associated with something so terrifying that you have to clench your purse, grab your children, and lock your doors when I appear. I am a good person.

There are more good colored people around us than those that scare you. Every time you look scared when I approach, you send the message that I am up to no good. That's why some people find it necessary to have an employee follow me at the store. I am a good person. But the White people, higher-class populace, elderly, and educated tell me I am not through these pathetic microaggressions.

Stop this! Because those good colored people will get tired of this and get angry. Some will fight against it through positive advocacy and activism, but others may become bad people.

I am a good person.

Today I applied for a passport

Larry Smith • Saint Louis, MO

I look around and see White fear of Black people (especially Black men) on the rise as reflected in the rise of White gun possession. I also see things staying the same or getting worse for Black people in terms of economics, education, and housing. I would just like to live out my remaining years in an environment where I feel like a human being. Sixty-six years of this crap is enough for me!

Construct. Sure— easy, if you're White

Anonymous • West Grove, PA

My granny said no White girls

Clinton Browning • Fayetteville, GA

8 miles grown from cleanest toilets

Thurman • Memphis, TN

I live eight miles from where my mother used to clean a house in an affluent gated community in the deep suburbs just outside of Memphis. The town is Germantown. I now live in a bigger home, in a nicer community, in a deeper suburb called Collierville. I used to drop my mother off at the Exxon because they didn't always want us to drive in. I had to wait in the car until she finished cleaning or the garage/laundry room if she wasn't ready. Despite the long struggle, I now live within running distance of the toilets she cleaned that put me in my first car (she took a loan from them—free working days, one per week for two years) and supported me when she had it [money] through the University of Memphis, and now I can *buy* their house *if* I wanted it. But I don't. They were good to my mother and simultaneously dismissively arrogant. She was The Help. But we were better than that.

She was more than that. I proved it. I live it. I tell her. I show her. I showed them.

I'm just a kid from Memphis, but I am so much more than that. I can run that sixteen-mile loop because my knees aren't worn out. My job is easy on my bones. My back is strong, and my kids are getting my best.

She can barely walk from all the stooping. I'm carrying her now. The weight is lifted. Momma, we made it.

I can't help being born White

Christina Sinclair • Warren, RI

I try my best to stay out of the line of fire when it comes to race. As far as I'm concerned, as long as my own thoughts and opinions are private and locked away if they aren't socially acceptable and I'm not hurting anyone, then why can't I think the way I do? Why do I need to change? I didn't do anything wrong, so it's not fair to those of us who just don't care about any of it.

I can't trust White people fully

Mr. Jones • Kalamazoo, MI

I feel that it's very hard to trust White people due to their past/present global-destructive and deceptive nature. I know all White people aren't bad, but I feel that I have to be on guard around them. I still see negative qualities in them that my grandad talked about from his young years. He's eighty-nine, by the way.

Often ashamed of being White male

Anthony Whittum • Portland, OR

As I get older (fifty-six), racism seems more prevalent or at least more "advertised" by those that hold racist beliefs. Or perhaps as my childhood, young manhood, and middle age fade into the rearview mirror, my awareness of all things grows. It seems that racists are most often categorized as "White men."

After all, that's what we see on television! Those that hold political office and that hold racist beliefs are most often middle-aged White men, seeking power and speaking cleverly, covertly, and even out loud about their racism. From a young age, I have disliked anyone "assuming" that I am one thing or another, and now it feels like I am being lumped in with a stereotypical, unsavory, hateful crowd of White men/racists.

I wasn't racist until BLM rioted

Rick • USA

I am White. I went to public school K–12 where 30 percent of kids were Black. I was on athletic teams where 50 percent of my teammates were Black. My best friend was Black. In college, three of my roommates were Black. My college girlfriend was Black. I started a business, and 90 percent of the employees were Black. I managed six hundred apartments, and the residents were 100 percent Black. I lived on a street where 35 percent of the residents were Black. Now, a *woke* movement says I am a racist!

Who knew? Crazy!

Proud to be a slave's descendant

Eva Elisabeth McFadden • Stone Mountain, GA

Why do so many people the world over deny their African Heritage? What is so wrong with being Black?

Raised by racists in denial.

Amand S. • McPherson, KS

The people in my life have no idea how motivated by prejudice they truly are; I often fear I don't, either.

It's okay to be Black, promise.

Maureen Shaw • Durham, NC

This is a photo of my mother's family. I look at it and feel so proud of this photo. We let ourselves believe we are people with shattered history. I've discovered this is not always the case, and if so, it's not the end of the world.

They burned Roscoe's house last night

Paul J. Mercer • Lakewood, NJ

I recall a day as a five-year-old when my father took me to see a house that was being built by a coworker's son. It was a typical bright, sunny day as often childhood memories are, especially ones with special significance. This was one of those days. Seeing that house, which was set in a beautiful wooded area, smelling the newness, seeing the big wood-and-glass sliding doors and the joy on the faces of the young couple greeting my father and me that morning was all that I needed. I knew someday that I would build one myself.

My dad, seeing my exuberance over the experience and probably to shut me up, presented me with a Handy Andy tool case a few days later, complete with a little saw and hammer. I was on my way!

Well, fast-forward a few months. One night, my father, who was never late for anything, came home late from work. I was in bed already, not asleep, and heard him say to my mother, "They burned Roscoe's house last night." I was perceptive enough to realize that "they" indicated that it was not accidental. Our little house did not conceal sound very well, so my sobs and his words were audible.

He came to my bed to address my exposure to an ugly part of what had been a very sunny world for me until then. There was no consoling; he just put a big arm around me and simply said, "There are mean people that did not want Roscoe to build his house there." I did not understand it then, and I still do not. I did not understand it when the same thing happened to a teammate while in high school in the midsixties.

This did not happen in the Deep South but in central New Jersey in 1953 and the latter incident in 1966. Also, I found out later that Roscoe had served in World War II. That war where Americans lost their lives fighting the evilest of prejudice.

I'm White and pay the price

Jim Zeirke • Sussex, WI

I've faced more overt racism than most Blacks. While much of Black racism is discreet, I've been told to my face that I'm not getting opportunities because I'm White. In the mid-1970s, I applied for a job, and when I went to the job interview a guy came out and told all of us gathered there that "White males can leave now. We aren't even interested in talking to you."

I applied for a scholarship when I was in college and was told that, while I was one of the top two candidates, I was denied the scholarship because the committee had decided that a Black person would get one of the two awards. I applied for a job with a city and was told that I couldn't even fill out an application because I was White.

When I complained to the EEOC, the Black person that I talked to laughed and basically told me to get over it. There have been other cases where I was told flat out that they did not want a White person for the job or other opportunity. When Whites are discriminated against, it is always overt. Yet, despite the discrimination that I've faced, I have no problems with Black folks in general. As another White guy told me once, "If a guy does me wrong, it is him and not his race that I have a problem with."

Tired of dream; Where is plan!

Nathaniel U. Jackson • Partlow, VA

Please explain race to a blind girl.

Lenna • New Orleans, LA

Always under the skin of America

Andrew Lundberg • Cleveland, OH

Don't hate me
for being white

Martha McKinney • Hector, NY

My Quaker great-great-grandfather was a conductor on the
Underground Railroad in Pennsylvania; my Quaker great-grandfather
fought against slavery in the Civil War; my Quaker forebears refused
to buy pretty Southern cloth because it was made by enslaved people.
Precious stories came down the generations. I want so much to
engage in healing conversations, yet I sometimes feel a barricade.
Please don't assume I'm a closet racist because I'm White.

MY ANCESTOR'S SLAVE'S DESCENDANT CONTACTED ME

Richard Reed Watts • Burke, VA

GWENDOLYN REED'S OFFICIAL TITLE is paralegal, but what she really is, at heart, is a sleuth. She lives in Jacksonville, Florida, but grew up in nearby St. Augustine. Back in 1994, Gwen, as she is called, decided she wanted to learn about her family roots. She's seventy-two years old, and all her life, it pained her that she had no pictures of her ancestors and only bits and scraps of information. She had been raised by her great-aunt Cornelia Lue Ricker Reed, who she knew was born in Blackville, South Carolina, in 1901. So, after doing some preliminary research online and writing letters to a few people, she decided she needed to visit Blackville—a town she'd never set foot in.

"I know if you go to any small town, if you reach out to a Black undertaker or the sheriff's department, they can help you," Gwen says. "They know everybody. So, I picked out a Black undertaker. I went to his office. I told him what I was doing. He reared back in his chair and put his foot on his desk. He said, 'I know your people.' And he called them on the phone."

That's how Gwen found part of her extended family in South Carolina. That undertaker connected her with the descendants of her great-grandfather Riley Reed, and Gwen found herself welcomed into a big clan that met every year for family reunions, rotating among South Carolina, Florida, North Carolina, and Washington, DC. She relished these reunions and was thrilled to have reconnected with family who embraced her like someone who'd always been at their big table. But it wasn't enough. She wanted to dig even further back.

Captain Samuel J. Reed

"In order to find African American families on the census, you first had to find the White family," Gwen says—meaning, of course, the White family who owned them and kept them in bondage. "We didn't exist by name before 1870 on the census records." To the extent that enslaved people were recorded, it was on ledgers, wills, and legal documents.

Gwen's last name is Reed, and she didn't have to look very far from Blackville to find White families who carried that same last name. She quickly discovered that the Reed Plantation, an eighteenth-century home and property owned by Samuel and Mary Clark Reed, was just ten miles down the road in a town called Barnwell. Enslaved people often took the surnames of the families who owned them, so this was almost certainly the family who had owned her forebears. She kept digging, and through the census and probate records, she was able to deduce that her great-great-great-grandfather David Reed was owned by the Samuel Reed family. His name was listed on a probate record that dictated the distribution of "assets," Gwen said. "It was listed along with the cows and the chickens and the pots and pans."

And then, through research on Ancestry.com, she was able to find living descendants of Samuel Reed.

That was the first leg of Gwen's journey—an excursion through names and dates and old documents from the past. She wanted to explore where the branches of the Reed family tree might lead to find people still alive today.

In March 2008, Gwen located some members of the Reed family. She decided to reach out to a few of them, emailing out of the blue. One of them was Richard Reed Watts, a great-great-great-grandson of Samuel Reed.

•　•　•

Gwen wrote:

> Allow me to introduce myself. My name is Gwendolyn Reed and I am a descendant of David/Dave Reed, b. @ 1843 and was owned by the family of Hugh Reed, Samuel Reed and/or Hugh's daughter, Anne. As you are aware, researching the history of African Americans before 1870 is almost impossible. What I do know is on the 1870, 1880 and 1900 census for Barnwell County, my AA [African American] Reeds were residing near land where Samuel Reed resided.
>
> I have two questions. Do you have ANY documents where I can connect my Reeds to your family, i.e., deeds, wills, land records, birth records, etc.? #2—Can you give me the names of plantations which were owned by your Reed family in or near Blackville? It is my understanding that there is/was a "Reed Plantation" near

Dally Road and Sunshine Rd., near the church my family attended (Sunshine Baptist Church).

To Gwen's relief, Watts responded. He was the only family member who did. A civics teacher who goes by his middle name, Reed, he replied:

> It is so strange receiving your e-mail . . . it was not a week ago something had me thinking about being a kid up in my grandparents' attic, looking through old family papers, reading through court records, property lists, and remembering how odd it was reading people's names with dollar amounts beside them . . . and I swear, wondering whether I would ever happen to meet any of their descendants . . . I am literally speechless.
>
> Perhaps it would be easier if we just spoke over the phone to see what we know and what connections we can make . . . Feel free to contact me at home, anytime . . . if it would be easier for me to call you, just let me know a good time and number to reach you . . . While living in Arlington, Virginia (Washington, DC) since 1999, I was born and raised in South Carolina and my entire family still lives there . . . I regularly return home so documents, etc. . . . can be shared with little difficulty . . .

•   •   •

Slavery is something White Southern families are not always keen to talk about, especially with the descendants of those who were enslaved. But Reed was willing to dive in. The two of them soon got on the phone, and Reed gave Gwen more information about the documents he'd discovered in his grandfather's attic. He and his brother had found "an old, fragile parchment that was a list of property owned by Samuel Reed at his death during the Civil War," as he recalls. "On that list were the names of his 'Negroes,' with a dollar amount to the right."

"I remember even as a kid just thinking how strange that was, and how totally odd" to have prices assigned to humans, Reed says now. "It just struck me as sort of the history slapping you on the face a little bit."

Despite the awkward historical circumstances that led to their meeting, Gwen and Reed hit it off right away. "He made me feel at ease. It was really easy to talk with him," says Gwen. Reed went a step further: "It's funny because it's almost like the relationship that we've struck up, we treat each other almost as family," he said. The two became Facebook friends and continued to swap information about their mutual ancestors. Reed sent Gwen pictures of him with his wife and dog and even more photos when his two children were born. "I just thought it was so cool that in the twenty-first century I was being contacted about this," says Reed. "So neat. So crazy."

Not all of Reed's family felt the same way. Growing up in South Carolina in the 1980s, he was surrounded by overtly racist relatives and friends. "I grew up as a kid using the N-word," says Reed, now fifty-one years old. "There was no stigma attached to it whatsoever." Even so, young Reed had a different, more open attitude about Black people than his elders did. One year, when Reed put a poster of Dr. Martin Luther King Jr. in his room, his grandfather told him it "wasn't fitting" for a White man to have a picture of a Black man on his wall. And in the fourth grade, when Reed wanted to bring home his Black best friend for a sleepover, his mother emphatically said no. Decades had passed, and some attitudes had changed, but many of his family members still jumped to racist conclusions about Gwen's intentions.

"When I would tell this story," he says, "everybody would be like, 'Oh, was she asking for money?' And I never even thought that for a second." But others seemed unable to imagine that Gwen might just be interested in discovering her family history.

But she was—and so she kept on digging.

In 2017, twenty-three years after she first began her quest, Gwen took a DNA test through Ancestry.com. She was hoping to learn who her father was, but when the results came back, she wasn't all that surprised to discover something else. Gwen had a significant percentage of White ancestry. She and Reed were connected not only through a presumed shared family history in South Carolina—DNA matching showed that they shared blood relatives.

Now, Gwen remembers passing along this information to Reed at that time. But Reed doesn't remember it. He does recall that she started asking him to take a DNA test himself, which he couldn't quite get around to doing for all kinds of reasons. She wanted him to take it to have 100 percent confirmation that they had a genetic connection, but Reed didn't register how important that was to Gwen. He just thought she was urging him to do it for curiosity's sake, or to fill out the White branches of the Reed family tree.

After her DNA results posted to Ancestry.com, Gwen was able to find another White Reed relative, a man named Thomas Reed, who lived in the same South Carolina county that Reed Watts's family originally came from. Gwen contacted Tom, who, like Reed Watts, was related to Civil War captain Samuel J. Reed. He responded to her email within hours and said he had gone over estate papers to find the list of enslaved people owned by some of his ancestors. "I see where item #63 was a man called 'Dave' who had a value of $850," he wrote, explaining that it was unlikely that Gwen's great-great-great-grandfather David Reed had worked as a field hand. He and Gwen got on the phone that same day. "He took the first ten minutes telling me what a scoundrel Abraham Lincoln was," Gwen says, chuckling. "He was still fighting the Civil War in his head."

Gwen thought Tom Reed, who said he was seventy-six years old, was trying to provoke her. She didn't take the bait. "It was just funny to me to see where his head was at," she says, though her hackles did rise when he pointed out that Gwen's great-great-great-grandfather David, who had been valued at $850 in 1862, would "have a dollar value" of about $25,000 in 2017 when they spoke. "I said, 'Yeah, come on now. Don't go too far.'" What bothered her was hearing him so cavalierly suggest a modern-day price tag. "I didn't want him to get mixed up with history and present day," she says, "because there's no [monetary] value on my life today. Not like it would've been in 1862."

Gwendolyn Reed

At one point Tom asked Gwen how she'd gotten the last name Reed and posed it as a question whose answer eluded him. Now, the answer to this question would have been obvious enough even if her ancestors had simply been owned by his. But the fact that he asked, even knowing that they shared the same DNA, was not just surprising but also offensive.

He was getting on her last nerve, but Gwen held her tongue. She just let Tom talk because she needed information about the White branch of the Reed family, and she didn't want to alienate one of the few people who could provide it. Her patience paid off. She received a treasure trove of family history and old letters from Tom Reed, and he gave her his home and cell numbers and told her to call anytime. All the information he provided lined up with the years, locations, and work histories of the Reeds in her Black family tree.

Meanwhile, when Gwen told Reed Watts about all of this, he automatically assumed that she had been talking to his uncle Tommy Reed, but he thought it odd that his uncle Tommy never mentioned it. Reed's uncle was in his seventies and still lived in South Carolina. He thought about contacting his uncle but decided to leave that alone, thinking it was best not to poke a hornet's nest among family members who had questioned Gwen's intentions. He lost the chance to ever have that conversation when Tommy Reed passed away in 2019.

By early 2020, Reed Watts still had not taken the DNA test, but he and Gwen occasionally connected online. That spring, she invited him to join one of the family reunions on the Black side of the Reed family tree. Reed Watts was stoked to get the invitation and decided to go with his two daughters, who were then in their tweens. "I told the girls, 'We might be the only White people there, but we're going,'" he says. "And that's when Covid really flared up." Gwen ended up canceling her plans to go, so Reed and the girls didn't go, either.

And there the matter stood until January 2022, when I invited Gwen and Reed to join me for a video conference call to talk about all of this.

I had first learned about this story in 2014, when Reed submitted these six words to The Race Card Project: *"My ancestor's slave's descendants contacted me."* He went on to write about how Gwen had emailed him and how shocked he'd been to hear from her. He ended his submission with these words: "In a very real sense, I consider her part of my family, and I dare say she feels the same." His words were prescient.

> **"I think more troubling is if there was a consummation between master and slave."**

What became clear on our video call in 2022 was that Reed still didn't realize they were related, even though Gwen had been trying to tell him about her DNA findings for several years. The two greeted each other like old pals, talking and laughing. They discussed Gwen's childhood, her trip to Blackville, the various branches of the Reed family trees. Then they got on the subject of the Thomas Reed Gwen found through Ancestry.com, the name that showed up with a little green leaf—an ancestry ping—that indicated there was a DNA match. And that was when the light bulb finally went on for Reed, who leaned his face right up to the screen.

"Now, wait a minute," he said. "I think this is maybe the first time I'm hearing this. So, there's a DNA match? Which means that we truly are family?" He paused, eyebrows raised. He shook his head in astonishment, and then he started laughing. Gwen was sitting quietly, lips pursed together with a look that said, "I've been trying to tell you this!"

"Now, see, I'm not troubled by the fact that my ancestors owned slaves. But I think more troubling is if there was a consummation between master and slave," Reed said.

"Well, there was a consummation," Gwen replied. "But I don't know between who. It had to be one of the owners."

A consummation. This whole conversation had had an easy-breezy feel to it. But this was a charged moment that speaks to the gaping hole in American history. A "consummation"—such stiff and formal language to describe a sexual act between an enslaved woman and the man who owned her. The halting silences that speak to the dark aspects of sexual violence that were a common thread in American slavery.

Reed was still chipper, but he was clearly shook. "That, to me, would be more troubling because you'd have to question the circumstances in which that would arise. Which, in my mind, I can't imagine there being good circumstances that would arise—"

"No," said Gwen. "As they say about Sally Hemings and Thomas Jefferson, there was no love. It was master and servant."

This was a tough exchange to witness. Throughout the conversation I had decided to remain quiet in this three-way video call as Gwen and Reed waded through thorny turf. I wanted to see how it all would naturally evolve. "I mean, I love the fact that me and Gwen are related, truly," Reed said. "But it's just troubling to know how."

Reed swore this was the first time he'd heard this news, and he seemed totally sincere in saying this. Gwen, on the other hand, distinctly recalls telling Reed about the DNA several times, and it is hard to imagine that her memory is fuzzy because in each conversation I have had with Gwen, her powers of recall are evident. She rattles off addresses and dates and plot numbers from archival documents. Clearly, they were talking past each other. When Gwen persisted in telling Reed that she had informed him about the DNA match, he allowed that "maybe you told me and the magnitude of what you said just didn't sink in." Then he laughed—Reed laughs a lot—and said, "Well, cousin!" Reed has a gregarious personality, and this was meant to be a moment of comic relief. Gwen was not really laughing.

Eventually, Reed reached for the words of Dr. Martin Luther King Jr., as many people do when they're trying to soothe the wounds of race with a verbal balm.

"The reason why I love this whole thing is because, to me at least, our story is the story of America," he said. "I mean, truly. It is the fulfillment of Martin Luther King's dream. Where he says, 'In the red hills of Georgia, I want to see the sons of slaves and the sons of former slave owners, we come together in the table of brotherhood.' And I just think it's so cool that Gwen would contact me. . . . It's just such a great commentary on what this country should be."

When I asked Reed whether he thought the rest of his family would be as welcoming about this discovery, he chuckled.

"Truthfully, I don't know. I would think that they would be troubled by it, and I want you to understand that I'm still troubled by the act that made it so," he said. "I mean, the kinship was born potentially at least out of an act of violence. . . . Nobody wants that."

And Gwen said, "The beginning of America was from an act of violence."

"Yeah, you're right," he said. "Even with that being part of the story, I think that it perhaps even more closely resembles the story of America."

Given the attitudes about race among his family, what would they think about having blood relatives who were Black?

"I don't want to sell my family short," he said. "And I don't want to sell my mother short because my mother's a loving, caring woman." He said he absolutely planned to share the news with her. He did admit, however, that his grandfather wouldn't have taken the news well. "Don't get me wrong, I loved my grandfather with all my heart. But he was a racist, no doubt about it. . . . They say, 'Where you sit is where you stand,' and my grandfather sat in South Carolina his entire life." Reed remembered his grandfather telling him that "miscegenation, the mixing of the races, was something that should not happen. . . . He did not approve of it, let's put it that way."

And yet, miscegenation was likely right there in his own family tree. Even if he never knew or acknowledged it.

What about Gwen's family? How did they react to this new twist in the family tree? No real qualms, she said. It was what they expected to find.

"My family loves it," said Gwen. "I had to keep them off Reed because I've got a lot of family. I was protecting you like you were my brother," she said. This time they laughed together. Their fondness for each other was evident. Through distance, they had developed a bond.

"Take that DNA test," Gwen said. "Everybody else can lie, but DNA doesn't lie."

Almost a year later, Reed did take a DNA test, but the results were not as conclusive as Gwen may have wanted. There was no DNA match between Reed and Gwen, but when the two focused on the Thomas Reed with whom Gwen did match, they discovered a conundrum. The Tom Reed whom Gwen had been speaking with—the man who had lived in Sumter and was related to Samuel J. Reed, the man with whom she had a direct DNA match and who sent her a treasure trove of info about her enslaved ancestors, who also may have been genetically linked to Captain Reed—did not appear to be the same person as Reed Watts's beloved uncle named Tommy Reed. Gwen sent Reed a photo of the man she had been speaking to—the man Reed Watts assumed was his uncle—and it became clear that there were two Tom Reeds around the same age, both descended from the Civil War captain. Gwen and Reed were floored. And confused. And determined to try to find answers.

During another three-way call, I sat back and listened to the two of them hash out possible explanations. Gwen's Tom Reed and Reed's uncle Tommy Reed had both lived in the same South Carolina county and had connections to Sumter and Blackville. Weird. And as Gwen rattled off the info she had collected from her Tom Reed, Reed Watts kept noting that all the information tracked with his own family tree. Even weirder.

"He was very into his genealogy, and he was the caretaker of the family cemetery, of the Reed Cemetery," Gwen said, and Reed quickly answered, "I know exactly where you're talking about."

Gwen continued, "And this one email tells me that one of the sons was John Reed, 1792 to 1854, who was his third great-grandfather. And one of their sons was John's brother, Samuel, who married Elizabeth Boylston."

Reed Watts chimed in, "Yep. That's my great-great great-grandmother."

This went on for some time until they realized that there could have been another branch of Captain Samuel Reed's family tree that Reed Watts did not know about, knowledge he now has because, as he said in his six words, "My ancestor's slave's descendant contacted me."

As we said at the outset, Gwen is a bit of a sleuth. Upon hearing that the man with whom she had a DNA match was named Thomas Reed, they both assumed that it had to be Reed Watts's uncle. They were wrong. Gwen and Reed compared their DNA results, and she was able to untangle the various branches to figure out that Reed Watts is a direct descendant of the Civil War captain Samuel James Reed via his son David. And the Thomas Reed who shared his trove of family documents with Gwen is a direct descendant of John Reed, the brother of the Civil War captain. Both men were sons of another Samuel Reed who lived between 1751 and 1823. When she shared all this information, Gwen added the hashtag #makeitmakesense.

That hashtag could apply to a whole lot of antebellum history around race.

Gwen is urging Reed to attend the next reunion of the Black side of the Reed family tree, and if anything, Reed is now more interested than ever. He is looking forward to bringing his daughters as he had intended before the pandemic changed their plans. Gwen welcomes the chance to meet Reed in person. She is still hoping that he might go back into the attic at his family home in South Carolina to see if there is any information about her great-great-great-grandfather David Reed. More than anything, she wants to know who his mother was. "I just feel like there is something out there somewhere," Gwen said. "I just need to know her name."

Don't act your color? We're radiant!

Avis Danette Matthews • Glenarden, MD

"Don't act your color." I recall hearing that phrase a lot while growing up in the 1960s in Prince George's County, Maryland, a Washington, DC, suburb. On a fifth-grade field trip, as the school desegregation debate boiled on medium, one of my beloved Black teachers gave us that instruction as we prepared to get off the bus to tour one of DC's many monuments and museums. For the first time, the thought occurred to me, militantly: "How come? Why not act our color?!" In a flash, I envisioned our school, my classmates, our parents and siblings in our warm and loving homes within our nurturing community, our trusted teachers and perfect principal, our weekend campfire and scout activities, our backyard kickball and football games, our annual go-kart race, our parents moving their cars so we could have the whole street for sledding in the best of snowstorms, our summer dashes to the ice cream truck—and I felt adamant that *we should act our color*. I didn't say all of this to my teachers on the bus, of course. Years later, seeing those same teachers at funerals and celebrations and such, standing adult to adult with them, I realized that they had known it, too—we *were* radiant.

Black and beautiful
with breathtaking strength

Sidni Sera Goodman • Eastpointe, MI

Being Black in America is more than just challenging. There are so many highs and so many lows. I dealt with one day feeling Black and proud, seeing how other cultures love my culture, style, flair, music, etc., then other days, I see how my Black brothers and sisters literally get the cops called on them for absolutely no reason at all and it seems like nothing is being done about it. I literally see how the US government is against us, but then I see our God-given strength and it takes my breath away. It takes my breath away that you still see us smiling, dancing, and saying, "Thank you, God, for giving me breath in my body." Still being polite, still being professional in the most racist workplaces and establishments. The sad thing is, it's like really nothing has changed since my ancestors got free via the Thirteenth Amendment in 1865, but I still see that same strength our ancestors had back then, and it still . . . takes my breath away.

Black is beautiful. LOOK AT US!

Robin Massengale • Washington, DC

This country was founded on a profound falsity, the vestiges of which remain today. That falsity? That Whites are superior and Blacks inferior and therefore slaves, second class, exiles. But look at us! *Look at us! Look at what we have done from whence we've come!* Not only do we matter, *we are beautiful!* And when we carry that *inside*, we can bring back *Black* pride, and we can stop waiting for a culture that perpetually lies to itself to save us. *We save us because we are, and we are beautiful!*

Prayed God would make me White

Amber • Atlanta, GA

I was raised in Tennessee. I grew up ashamed of my Blackness. I heard the N-word for the first time in elementary school. I prayed every night for God to make me White. At the age of seventeen, I was told to go sit with the rest of the Blacks by the people I grew up with. The Blacks had only arrived in my school system after rezoning enabled more minorities to attend. I only embraced my color in college. The only time I feel really American is when I am abroad. I hoped that my children would grow up in a better world. They won't.

People, this isn't your grandfather's racism

Richard Perez • Bay Shore, NY

We tend to associate racism with nefarious intent, or White against non-White, but it's much more complex than that. The simpler days of binary race relations are no more.

I saw a group of "undesirables"

Danielle Giese • Cheverly, MD

This is what my White neighbor called a group of African American young men who were congregating outside of a local grocery store. Apparently, one of them was showing off his new baby. I wondered if that will be how my sons will be described years from now. Will they be undesirable to American society?

Why are they scared of us?

Larry Williams • Glendale, AZ

I'm not just a Black man

Jared Blocker • Gainesville, FL

Black, humbling existence to maintain dignity

Tony Williams • Detroit, MI

Change in America is slow. I find it disheartening to witness the incarceration of African American men at this current level. The battle begins after the release from jail or prison. A criminal record is just slavery by another name.

A constructed tool of the oppressors.

Phillip Johnson • Saint Louis, MO

History shows the historically oppressed are not the ones who use race to their advantage. In order to galvanize support for transatlantic slavery, one race had to be made to feel superior to another.

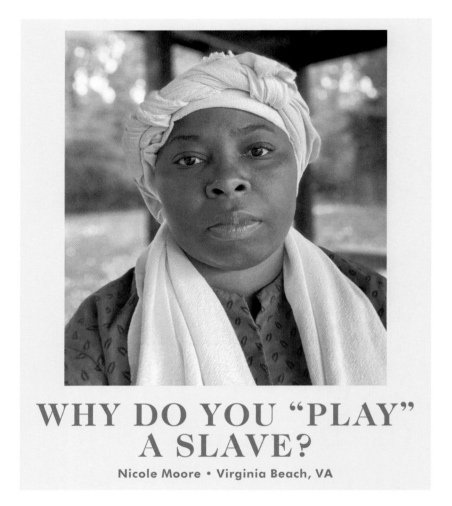

WHY DO YOU "PLAY" A SLAVE?

Nicole Moore • Virginia Beach, VA

WHEN PLANTATION TOURS and antebellum-era historic sites try to give tourists a sense of life in the Old South, Nicole Moore is someone who shows up to keep it real.

"I realized a lot of sites, they were glorifying the house and they would show you the dwelling, but they weren't talking about who made it possible," Nicole said.

Nicole is a slave interpreter, part of a small cadre of African Americans who portray the lives of their ancestors with an unwavering fidelity to detail and historic accuracy. In many cases, they have done something their enslaved ancestors could not: they've pushed their way into spaces where they were not originally part of the program, insisting that slavery be an essential part of the narrative presented at former plantation sites, just as it was a central part of life in the antebellum era.

If this has a skunk-at-the-garden-party feel to it, Nicole is just fine with that because while the history is indeed odious, in her view, it needs to be told. And more specifically, it needs to be told from the viewpoint of the people who were most oppressed. Her aim is to make sure that the tourists who want to experience a bit of *Gone with the Wind* nostalgia also see, hear, and experience what life on the plantation was really like.

Nicole is a public historian by training who works at the National Center for Civil and Human Rights in Atlanta. Ten years ago, she decided to venture out of her office and begin teaching people about chattel slavery in the US by transforming herself into a flesh-and-blood example. Several times a year, Nicole trades her smart business suits for the floor-length frocks made of coarse fabrics once known as "Negro cloth." Wearing a headscarf and an apron smudged with the remnants of her toil, she makes hoecakes and cooks down turnip greens with big slabs of fatback in a heavy kettle atop a fire. She does all this while tourists move about the buildings and the grounds, watching, listening, taking pictures, and asking questions.

There is something you should know about the way Nicole interacts with people while portraying an enslaved woman. There are first-person interpreters who speak in broken English or the patois of the enslaved in the 1800s. And there are third-person interpreters who act the part but choose to speak in more modern-day vernacular. Nicole says she is in the latter category, in part because she lacks the acting chops to comfortably carry off period dialogue. There's also another explanation. She uses the crisp diction of a woman with an advanced degree to make sure people clearly "hear and understand" all that she says. And she says a lot. She talks the whole time she moves about with a broom or a spoon or a shovel in her hand. She talks about the long days and the demands of the families who owned the land and the people who worked the soil. But her banter also wades toward things that are more personal and revealing.

She places herself firmly in the period and uses a present-tense framing to talk about family members who have been sold away to other plantations, about enslaved women who secretly teach their children how to read, about the ingenuity of enslaved men who have no formal education but nonetheless design and build sophisticated mechanical farm implements that save time and maximize profits—though none of that money will ever go into their pockets. "If [people] only hear about the negatives of what happened to Black bodies," Nicole says, "they miss the development of Black communities and they miss the development of our traditions and they miss how we survived, and for some of us, how we thrived in the institution that really tried to break us. When we think about

Nicole Moore

these narratives, we need to find strength in them. I don't think my great-great-great-great-great-grandmother would be pleased that I was ashamed of her existence. I think she would want me to find horror in the atrocities that she experienced, but then also find strength in her need to survive."

Tourists are often surprised to see Nicole, and she can sense them processing how, or if, they should interact. She encourages them to ask questions and then quietly braces herself for what comes next.

"I get White folks who are asking more about the treatment [of slaves] because I think they want to feel better," she says. Inevitably someone asks if there were "good" slave owners—a question she treats like a boomerang and flips back to quiz the audience. Regardless of how kindly the slaves may have been treated, is it ever right to own another human being? Do you imagine that working for free or having no agency over any decision in your life constitutes kindness? Can you be "inherently good" when you own a person? Nicole relishes her role as Trojan horse: a highly educated woman, portraying a slave who wouldn't have been allowed to read or write, dispensing knowledge to tourists who are visiting a plantation where they just expected to sip mint juleps and marvel at the architecture.

Nicole says the most common query she gets is "Why didn't they just run away?" That short question begets a long answer. Nicole explains how slave owners used a combination of physical and psychological abuse to control slaves, who might risk their lives, and their family's well-being, if they dared to run. Entire families might face harsh retribution, she says. The tourists "don't realize how psychologically this worked, where the enslaved made up the majority on the plantation," Nicole says. "[The enslaved] outnumbered White folks, but the White folks had a sense of power based on terror."

Because she is so often cooking during her portrayals, she also fields a lot of questions about food. This is the inquiry that makes her think of her own family tree—her grandfather was a cook in Charleston at the Military College of South Carolina known as the Citadel. And for her audience, which is so often White, it's the question that is also most likely to make them think of their forebears. "I don't know how many times I've been cooking over a fire and an old White man will say, 'That is exactly what my grandmother made,'" Nicole says. Those moments serve up ironic epiphanies. "Then they realize that they have more in common with the enslaved than they do with the White [slave masters] that owned the house."

In December 2021, Nicole was invited to do one of her portrayals at the Lexington County Museum in South Carolina. This is a living museum, where visitors can view structures and artifacts that show what life was like in the surrounding area before 1865. The property includes barns, a plantation house, and the home where the song "Old Time Religion" was composed. The museum's Hands-on History section includes a program that explores Life in the "Big House" and Life Behind the "Big House," where visitors learn about "the lives and contributions of enslaved workers to the household."

Nicole used the occasion of her Lexington visit to talk about the tradition of Christmastides for enslaved families. The days leading up to the end of the year were a time of respite for enslaved families; the workload was often lighter because of the planting cycle. "This is a time where they would be mending clothes and mending tools," she says. "You're still probably working, but it is not as arduous as planting during the harvest. This is a time where you would get passes. You might get a pass to see a family member or a spouse" at a different plantation. "This was a time for families in the community to really bond together," she says, "because [they] knew Heartbreak Day was January first."

Most people associate New Year's Day with celebrations. Champagne and fireworks. Kisses and confetti. Resolutions for a better year ahead. For the enslaved, the passage to a new year was filled with dread. "That's when people might be sold or rented out to settle debts," Nicole explains to a wide-eyed audience, most of whom are hearing about the weight of this day for the very first time. I'll bet some of you reading this passage now are also just learning about Heartbreak Day. "At the end of the year, you have planters who are settling their books and making sure that everything's good," Nicole says. "And if they come up short on money, they're going to look at what property they can sell off or rent out to balance their books with no real regard to the actual person who's impacted by it. January first, it was basically fair game. You didn't know if you were going to be separated, and when you're separated, you have no idea if you are going to see that person again. You have no idea really what your future is going to be. It's important for me to get visitors to understand how much it meant to spend time with loved ones, and how much it meant to strengthen those bonds," she says, "because some of those memories would hold people.

Some of those memories are what newly emancipated folks [after the Civil War] would use to try to find loved ones and put out ads looking for family members."

Nicole relays all this with a placid grin that's distinctly at odds with the cruel heartbreak of this tale. She tries to keep something of a smile no matter what she is discussing. Is she trying to make this history go down easy? Is she hiding her own pain? "Don't get it twisted," she tells me, explaining that she has to draw folks in so they can fully absorb both the horrors and the inhumanity of enslavement. You might find this odd when considering the content, but it's admirably strategic if you understand her mission. As I speak to Nicole, her work calls to mind a passage from the classic poem by Paul Laurence Dunbar:

> *We wear the mask that grins and lies,*
> *It hides our cheeks and shades our eyes,—*
> *This debt we pay to human guile;*
> *With torn and bleeding hearts we smile.*

Why Do You "Play" a Slave?

The six words Nicole sent to The Race Card Project reflect the question that is so often hurled at her. Nicole is proud of her work, but she knows that some people are aghast when they see her or learn about what she sees as a calling. Especially Black people. Her own people. It cuts too close to minstrelsy. A Black woman in a role that feels too close to the caricature of White folks donning blackface. That hoopskirt and headscarf make folks shudder. To call someone a "handkerchief head" is not a compliment among Black Americans. It's one step removed from the insult "Uncle Tom."

"It's the look," she tells me. "It's the true disgusted look of 'Ugh, it couldn't be me. It wouldn't be me.' And I'm like, 'Great. It's not you, and I get it.' I never in my life thought that I would be doing this work and love it." She understands why her work would rattle Black people. But she makes an impassioned defense, arguing that she can remind all who see her that the enslaved women she portrays were human beings with beating hearts and calloused hands who had dreams and loves and hurts, and sometimes even triumphs against great odds.

"The Black folks that I run into that are ashamed, they're like, 'Why are you doing this?'" Nicole says. "And they come from enslaved people. I'm just like, 'Without our ancestors surviving long enough for somebody to be born that would create us, we don't exist.' Why would we deny their story? Why would we find shame in their story? Their strength is what got us here. Awful things happened. Unforgivable and unspeakable things happened, but [that] somehow your ancestor found a way to survive or push through enough so that the seed could be planted so that you could be here is something that we need to consider."

Nicole knows this view is out of step with the people who'd rather see former plantation sites shuttered for good rather than used as a backdrop for weddings and wine tastings. Instead, she urges the sites where she works to hire more than just slave interpreters. She implores them to hire Black employees and contractors, and she asks that they take some of the money they earn from visitor fees or from renting out their white-columned buildings and funnel it into surrounding Black communities.

She calls this "reparations by another form." The irony is that for someone who spends so much time exploring the lives of the enslaved, Nicole has limited knowledge of her own ancestors. She spent most of her childhood in Virginia Beach and Hawaii, but she was born in Charleston, South Carolina. A point of pride for her family is that they are related to Ernest Everett Just, the Charleston-born pioneering biologist who did groundbreak-ing work using sand dollars and sea urchins to study the development of embryos. Just, the grandson of enslaved people, attended Howard University and became a world-renowned scientist. His and Nicole's grandfathers were first cousins, which makes Ernest Everett Just her first cousin three times removed. Nicole's grandfather and all his siblings were beaming in the audience in 1996 when the US Postal Service dedicated a thirty-two-cent Black Heritage stamp with his image.

But when I ask her if she feels any kind of magnetic pull to learn more about their shared familial roots, her answer is surprising. "The information is so limited, it's almost like I don't want to open the can of frustration knowing that I would hit so many walls," Nicole sighs. "The big thing in our family is the story of Ernest Ever-ett Just. That is our go-to story. But what about the oth-ers?" It's a question she can't answer. "I know how hard it is to dig into the genealogy of African Americans," she says. "It's almost like I don't want to open myself up to that. It's something that I wrestle with because I'm at these sites, and I'm telling somebody else's family history, and it would be dope if I could tell my own."

That remove is what might make her work possible. She is portraying a slave in someone else's family tree. Would it be harder to do if she knew that the name, the birthday, the spot where someone had worked were tied to one of her own ancestors?

Nicole has several titles that describe her work, but do not call her a slave reenactor. "I'm a public historian, and I am a living historian," she says. For many reenactors, the point is simply to dress and carry themselves in the way previous generations did. "But for me, it's not just let me dress up and play," she says. "I'm an educator. I want to make sure I can bring down every wall and answer as much as I can."

This work comes with hazards that go beyond prickly or uncomfortable questions. People have called her derogatory names. They have leered at her. They have jokingly barked out commands, slipping into something she calls "master mode." When that happens, she will first send a look that says, "Don't test me." "To do this work is to know boundaries," she says. "It is to be able to say 'no' and to really remind people, slavery has been abolished.

"Sometimes I will ignore it," she says. "Or I'll have somebody else take over and walk off because it becomes too much." But she tries to stay in place and stay in character. "It's really just kind of making sure that when people are hearing me . . . that it resonates in a way that will make them go back and remember what I said."

Once people are in her realm, she says, they cannot easily escape her presence and her stream of words the way they could change a channel or close the cover of a book. "It's a different way of teaching," she says. "People aren't going to read the books. They're not going to read the narratives. They get uncomfortable; they get squeamish. People have a harder time walking away from a human being that they're face-to-face with, who's able to answer their questions, who's able to help them process their feelings, and their thoughts, and work through the anger and the tears."

Nicole says her work has taken on greater urgency, or perhaps even peril, with recent efforts to police or significantly limit how slavery is taught in schools. Some of the museums or plantations where she works have programs specifically aimed at schoolchildren on field trips. It's hard to imagine that parents who are screaming at school board meetings about the dangers of critical race theory and lesson plans about slavery that might cause feelings of guilt or discomfort would willingly sign permission forms for a field trip where students meet a walking, talking slave interpreter.

But the adults, they keep coming—sometimes by the busloads. Like magnets, they are drawn to the plantations, with their long promenades draped with Spanish moss that bows down toward the soil as if in a curtsy. Three or four times a year, or more if her schedule allows, Nicole Moore will be there waiting for them. And at the end of those days, when she snatches off her kerchief and removes the sackcloth dress that weighs almost five pounds, she gets in her car and puts on loud music to decompress. Really loud Frank Sinatra or bass-thumping deep funk to bring her mind back to a more current century.

And sometimes she whispers to herself, "Man, I hope I did y'all proud." Not the people who employ her. Not the tourists who ask questions. The ancestors whose names she does not yet know.

5

Memory Wars

JUST AS THIS PROJECT IS BOOKENDED by the ascendance of Barack Obama and Donald Trump, it is also bookended by the embrace of the phrase *post-racial* and now, more than a decade later, by the umbrage over the way history around slavery and civil rights is taught in schools. An army of parents has mounted a highly organized campaign against so-called critical race theory in American schools, though that actual academic thread known as "CRT" is taught only in higher education, and particularly in law schools.

We are in the midst of a new round of memory wars—a skirmish over how, or if, the full story of America will be told.

In retrospect, the sudden and intense rejection of "CRT" and the sudden injection of wishful post-racial thinking a decade ago have something fundamental in common. Americans are so often looking for ways to erase the mountain rather than scale it.

Vergangenheitsaufarbeitung

Shortly after the National Museum of African American History and Culture opened in 2016 on the National Mall in Washington, DC, I was speaking to some patrons of a successful nonprofit about the importance of candid racial dialogue in politics and in the places we live, work, and worship.

One of the participants had recently toured the museum and had a pointed question. Why, she wondered, were all the exhibits that visitors first encounter dedicated to slavery? Among other things, she was referring to a reconstructed cabin built by former slaves from Maryland and a statue of Thomas Jefferson next to a wall with the names of more than six hundred people he'd owned. "Couldn't the exhibits begin with more uplift?" the woman asked, arguing that Black achievement was more worthy of the spotlight. She suggested that the museum should instead usher visitors toward more positive stories right from the start, so that if someone were tired or short on time, "slavery could be optional."

Her question was irksome, but it did not surprise me. I'd heard versions of the "Can't we skip past slavery?" question countless times before. Each time serves as another reminder that America has never had a comprehensive and widely embraced national examination of slavery and its lasting impact. Yes, there are localized efforts. But despite the centrality of slavery in our history, it is not central to the American narrative in our monuments, history books, anthems, and folklore.

There is a simple reason: the United States does not yet have the stomach to look over its shoulder and stare directly at the evil on which this great country stands. That is why slavery is not well taught in our schools. That is why the battle flag of the army that tried to divide and conquer our country is still manufactured, sold, and displayed with defiant pride. That is why any mention of slavery is rendered as the shameful act of a smattering of Southern plantation owners and not a sprawling economic and social framework with tentacles that stamped almost every aspect of American life.

We can read about, watch, and praise documentaries and Hollywood projects about the Civil War, or read countless volumes on the abolitionist or civil rights movements. But these are all at a remove from the central horror of enslavement itself. From the kidnappings in Africa to the horrors of the Middle Passage, the beatings and the instruments of bondage, the separation of families, the culture of rape, the abuse of children, the diabolical rationalizations and crimes against humanity—no, we haven't had that conversation. We have not had that unflinching assessment, and we are long overdue.

America experienced 246 years of slavery before it was officially ended with the ratification of the Thirteenth Amendment. That was followed by decades of enforced legal segregation and oppression under Jim Crow, followed by a period of willful blindness and denial. A tourist from a foreign land might well conclude that the Confederacy had actually won the Civil War based on the number of monuments, buildings, and boulevards still named for heroes of its defeated army. The real truth of our shared history was a casualty of that war, and as with any wound left untended, the results can be catastrophic.

A full accounting of slavery is one of terror and trauma, and for decades, the natural

inclination was to ask, "Why would anyone want to claim that history?" But at a moment when the United States is dangerously divided, when we are having bitter and overdue conversations about policing, inequality, and voting rights, when marauders fueled by White nationalist rhetoric can overwhelm the Capitol proudly waving the Confederate battle flag, the more important question is this: What happens if we don't?

Historians often look to collective memory—how groups of people typically recall past events—to help decipher a nation's identity and soul. These memories can change over time, and there is evidence that people remember things that never happened. But collective forgetting can be just as revealing.

The United States is not the only country with an evil antecedent that was swept aside, forgotten, or minimally examined. That list is long, but one country offers a powerful alternative path. Barely three generations ago, Germany hosted horrors that killed millions and left the nation split in two. This was not a legacy that most Germans were inclined to honor. And yet, today, less than one hundred years after the rise of Adolf Hitler, Germany has made a prodigious effort to come to terms with its past with regularized rituals of repentance and understanding.

This collective culture of atonement is captured in the eight syllables and twenty-six letters that comprise the German word *Vergangenheitsaufarbeitung*. It's a mouthful that translates loosely to "working off the past." But its full meaning goes deeper than even that awkward phrase suggests.

Vergangenheitsaufarbeitung refers to Germany's efforts to interrogate the horrors of the Holocaust and the rise of Nazism. It has been a decades-long exercise that accelerated in the 1960s to examine, analyze, and ultimately learn to live with an evil chapter through monuments, teachings, art, architecture, protocols, and public policy. The country looks at its Nazi past by consistently, almost obsessively, memorializing the victims of that murderous era, so much so that it is now a central feature of the nation's cultural landscape. The ethos of this campaign is "never forget."

"There isn't a native equivalent for this word in any other language, and while many countries have in one way or another tried to confront past evils, few if any have done what Germany has done," said Susan Neiman, a moral philosopher and the director of Berlin's Einstein Forum who has long studied the social aftermath of World War II in Germany. An American Jew raised in Atlanta, Neiman has spent most of her adult life in Germany and is the author of a book about the inquiry: *Learning from the Germans: Race and the Memory of Evil.*

"They got right the idea that a nation has to face its criminal past in order to become whole and strong and not riven by unsaid guilt, unsaid resentment," she explained. "They got right the idea that here is a process that one can go through, that it takes time, but that you come out better in the end. And they got right the idea that it has to happen on several fronts."

What ushered in the era of Vergangenheitsaufarbeitung? There is no singular hero or postwar epiphany you can find in the history books. Germany came to it slowly and, it must be said, reluctantly. And it took a different generation born after Germany's surrender to stoke the idea. It is important to remember that Germany did not immediately reach for atonement after World War II. Former servants of the Third Reich drifted back into government. And even with the Allies' strict protocol of war crimes trials and denazification—a process that at the time was often called "victor's justice"—Germans often cast themselves as victims in the decades immediately following World War II. The televised 1961 trial in Israel of Adolf Eichmann, a chief architect of the Holocaust, and the Frankfurt Auschwitz trials of former Nazis from 1963 to 1965, began to alter that view.

These and other postwar trials helped awaken public interest in the previous generation's horrifying immorality. The Auschwitz tribunal was sometimes billed as the "trial of the century" in Europe, and it stirred an appetite for a deeper explanation of what happened between 1930 and 1945. It also sparked questions about why so many everyday Germans willingly marched along that dark path.

The trials culminated in a period when the world was entering an era of protest and social unrest as postwar baby boomers agitated for a new guiding sensibility. Unsettling questions about the country's past also reverberated in private homes as children raised by people who had survived the war demanded a greater accounting of their relatives' roles. Were the people at their kitchen table, at the desk in front of their classroom, at the cash register at the corner bakery, connected to the atrocities described in those televised trials? And the questions raised by those real-life courtroom dramas created an urgency among historians, artists, and government officials to research what happened while simultaneously looking for a path toward acceptance and respectability. By the mid-1960s, West Germany's economy was beginning to hum, but the country still carried the stench of history.

Would anyone in the world buy those affordable little rear-engine Volkswagen Beetles if they came from a place that was indelibly branded with hatred and genocide? "As Germany got to be a little bit wealthier and people began to be able to travel within Europe," Neiman said, "young people did start hearing the other side of the story, not just, 'Poor us, we lost the war.' They realized how uncomfortable it was to be a German visitor in France or in Holland or elsewhere in Europe. Vergangenheitsaufarbeitung came into use in the sixties, an abstract, polysyllabic way of saying, 'We have to do something about the Nazis.'"

A good deal of the energy that fueled the rise of Vergangenheitsaufarbeitung happened at the grass roots with individuals changing the landscape by literally putting their hands in the soil, digging up the weeds that had grown over abandoned concentration camps and unearthing underground Gestapo torture chambers in the middle of Berlin.

In today's Germany, children learn through their teachers and textbooks that the Nazi reign was a horrible and shameful chapter in the nation's past. Cadets training to become police officers in Berlin take two and a half years of training that includes Holocaust history and a field trip to the Sachsenhausen concentration camp. With a few exceptions for the sake of education, it is against the law to produce, distribute, or display any symbol of the Nazi era, including the swastika, the Nazi flag, and the Hitler salute. It is also illegal to deny that the Holocaust was real.

Instead, memorials of remembrance are ubiquitous and honor the vast array of victims of the Nazi regime: Jews, gays, Roma, the disabled, and those who were viewed as disrespectable, antisocial, or traitors. Some of the monuments are impossible to miss; others catch you by surprise. Many do both: The Memorial to the Murdered Jews of Europe covers more than four and a half acres in the heart of downtown Berlin, prime real estate set aside by parliament when the Berlin Wall came down, despite a long line of real estate interests that were eager to develop the property. The former Neuengamme concentration camp in Hamburg features a sculpture of a twisted, bald, and naked human form that conveys the soul-crushing history and the backbreaking work of camp prisoners in a brick factory. If one looks down into a large glass oculus-like opening cut into the pavement at Berlin's Bebelplatz, you will see a sunken library—featuring rows of empty white shelves that symbolize the thousands of books burned by Nazis. A bronze marker bears the inscription: "That was but a prelude; where they burn books, they will ultimately burn people as well."

Many, if not most, of the memorials are far more subtle. Plaques and markers in many German cities note the locations of synagogues, schools, and Jewish neighborhoods that were raided and razed by Hitler and his legions. Roughly 90,000 small brass "stumbling stones," known as Stolpersteine, are embedded in the streets and plazas of hundreds of towns and cities throughout Germany and elsewhere. Each begins with the phrase *Here lived* and is followed by the facts of someone's life—their name and birth date. And then that etching is followed by the grim facts of their fate: exile, internment, execution.

The Dying Prisoner *sculpture on the grounds of the Neuengamme Concentration Camp Memorial.*

Two Stolpersteine (stumbling blocks), commemorating Holocaust victims, are pictured in front of Fehrbellinerstrasse 86 in Berlin on January 5, 2017. The small plaques the size of a child's hand state the fate of a mother and daughter who lived in a small apartment in the garden wing: fifty-year-old Taube Ibermann and Lotte, nineteen.

Imagine traveling through an American state and coming upon small embedded memorials that listed key facts about the lives of the enslaved. Their names. Their fates. Their birth dates. The number of times they were sold. The ways they were separated from their families. The conditions of their toil. Imagine how that might shape the way we comprehend the peculiar institution of slavery, its legacy and its normalized trauma. Imagine if there were similar embedded memorials for Indigenous peoples, who were forced from their lands, relegated to reservations far from their normal ranges and regions. Imagine stopping to fill up the tank at a roadside gas station and noticing the reflection off a gleaming brass marker that bore the names of the tribal elders who once lived where you are standing.

I am not suggesting that slavery and the Holocaust or the forced removal of Native American peoples are all in the same vein. They are each distinctly diabolical. But comparing these two countries' paths forward from a dark past is instructive because it sheds light not on comparative evil but instead contrasting redemption. The United States helped dictate the terms of Germany's future after the war. In the decades after that,

Germany outpaced the United States in coming to terms with a shameful past that collided with the country's preferred narrative.

By the time West German president Richard von Weizsäcker delivered a speech marking the fortieth anniversary of the end of World War II in May 1985, the landscape had already shifted. Weizsäcker, then sixty-five, was a leader in the center-right Christian Democratic Union, a former Wehrmacht captain whose father was the chief career diplomat for the Third Reich. And yet, there he was, gray-haired and solemn before the Bundestag, altering the conventional narrative by asking his country to reconsider and remember the true nature of the nation's past: "We need to have the strength to look truth straight in the eye.

"The young and old generations," he said, "must and can help each other to understand why it is vital to keep alive the memories. It is not a case of coming to terms with the past. That is not possible. It cannot be subsequently modified or made undone. However, anyone who closes his eyes to the past is blind to the present. Whoever refuses to remember the inhumanity is prone to new risks of infection."

Those words should reverberate and haunt us today in America, where a resurgent wave of White nationalism is widely visible. At a time when politicians and activists have waged a war against the teaching of so-called critical race theory in schools, it is hard to see how our governing leadership could possibly reach consensus about acknowledging and examining the horrors of slavery. Could someone in the conservative camp challenge the party's prevailing ideology and demonstrate the introspective courage shown by Weizsäcker? I wish the answer were yes.

Yet it is important to remember that Germany's path to truth was not swift or easy. It was halting and imperfect, and some efforts to make reparation were awkward and meager. While there are now thousands of memorials across Germany, not all of them strike the right note, and debate continues as to how to provide something in the way of balm to families who still contend with public shame and private grief for loved ones lost in the war. And Germany is better at acknowledging its crimes in its big cities than in smaller towns far from the capital.

Nor has Vergangenheitsaufarbeitung been able to fully extinguish the forces of racial and ethnic hatred inside Germany. The country's police and security agencies have been plagued by far-right extremism in the ranks, and as in many parts of the world, a strong anti-immigrant bias has taken root in activist groups. "The most thoughtful Germans,

East and West, are reluctant to praise German Vergangenheitsaufarbeitung," notes Neiman. "They are too aware of its flaws."

But if Germany's reckoning with its Nazi past is a sprawling, complicated, messy, ongoing process, it is an active process. And because of that, its national compass remains pointed toward a more just and humane future. Our compass for charting a new course from a difficult history is shaky, and we should just admit that as we begin our own journey toward truth.

When Barack Obama was first elected president in 2008, there was an expectation that he would lead some kind of national conversation about race. We don't place the same expectations on White leaders for some reason, but we should. President Biden was in Tulsa to mark the hundred-year anniversary of one of the most vicious acts of racial violence in US history. In 1921, an angry White mob attacked a thriving Black community known as Black Wall Street. A thirty-five-block stretch of homes, churches, and prosperous businesses was ransacked and burned; as many as three hundred people died. Until recently, the Tulsa Race Massacre was missing from history books and rarely discussed. Biden met with survivors who were children when that terror was unleashed, and he spoke directly about White supremacy in a way few presidents have. "Great nations . . . come to terms with their dark sides," he said.

That is a start. Biden should keep his foot on that pedal and launch an official inquiry about uncomfortable historical truths and do it in a way that ensures that it will extend over years, if not decades. Because it is time for the United States to convene its own version of a truth-and-reconciliation commission and fully examine the horrors of slavery and their continued aftermath. And it is time to do this with the full expectation that a whole lot of people will cry foul, howl at the fringes, and try to undermine every aspect of the exercise.

That should not stop the effort. That is the very reason the collective American narrative needs a strong dose of truth. We need clear eyes and firm spines, and then we need to chart a new path forward. That kind of step would also launch reexaminations of the treatment of America's Indigenous peoples, the eugenics movement, and the forced internment of US citizens and noncitizens of Japanese descent during World War II.

And yet, we are in a moment when hard truths are not just inconvenient, they are challenged and dismissed with great fanfare. A growing cottage industry is taking root among those who use their animus to stoke the fires of White grievance and feed the false claim that the hidden motive of all truth seeking is to elevate people of color by making White people feel bad about themselves.

It is not surprising that some White people would be reluctant to dive into this history. We still have textbooks where the enslaved are called "workers of Africa." And while racial fatigue is a real thing leading to real tensions and discomfort, it sometimes seems that people claim to be exhausted by a conversation that has never really taken place. I wonder whether people are just repelled by the idea of this conversation or they are really rattled by what they might hear.

I also find it deeply ironic that there is such a fierce battle to evade and erase historical teachings about slavery because, in the time of enslavement, there was such an assiduous effort to document and catalog every aspect of that institution, much in the way people now itemize, assess, and insure their valuables. The height, weight, skin color, teeth, hair texture, work habits, and scars that might help identify anyone who dared flee were documented. The menstrual cycles of enslaved women and their windows of fertility—because producing more enslaved people produced more wealth—were entered like debits and credits in enslavers' ledgers.

A startling example comes from Daina Ramey Berry, Michael Douglas Dean of Humanities and Fine Arts at the University of California, Santa Barbara, and the author of *The Price for Their Pound of Flesh*. Berry compares the sale of two "first rate . . . prime males" named Guy and Andrew sold in 1859 at what was believed to be the largest auction in US history. They were the same age and size and had similar skills. Andrew sold for $1,040 while Guy elicited a larger sum of $1,280. The difference was that Andrew had lost his right eye. A writer covering that two-day auction in 1859 noted that the value of a Black man's right eye in the South was $240.

Amnesia gets in the way of atonement in America. But *amnesia* is actually too benign a word because it sounds as though people just forgot about the horrors of slavery, forgot about people who were forced to work in the fields literally until their deaths, forgot that as many as 2 million Africans died during their forced migration to North and South America in the way one forgets where they placed their car keys or their passport.

We've been through more than a willful forgetting; we've had instead an assiduous effort to rewrite history. We've built monuments to traitors and raised large sums of money to place the names of generals who fought against their own country all over highways and civic buildings. We've allowed turncoats to become heroes of the Lost Cause instead of rebels desperate to keep people in bondage.

On a personal level, this false narrative about America is another act of cruelty, even a kind of larceny. I view the real story, the genuine history—ugly as it is—as part of my people's wealth. This country was built on the backs of African Americans' ancestors. Our contributions—in blood, sweat, and bondage—must be told. Our children—indeed, all of America—deserve to know what we have endured and survived to understand the depth of our fortitude, but also to understand that, despite centuries of enslavement and years of black codes and brutal Jim Crow segregation, our contributions are central to America's might. The erasure is massive in scope.

Our inability to face this history is a stick in the wheel of forward progress, a malignancy that feeds the returning ghost of White supremacy, a deficit that paves the way for bias to return. We find ourselves pulled backward in time, reliving some of the same challenges that inspired the civil rights movement seven decades ago—restrictions on voting rights, police assaults on Black bodies, racial disparities in health outcomes, in particular for almost everything pandemic-related, from deaths and infection rates to access to vaccines.

Poster announcing a slave sale, 1856.

We know the countries that combine truth and resolve have the best chance to reconcile with a difficult past. Truth is the most important ingredient, and it carries a special currency after America endured an administration that peddled falsehoods without apology and has leaders who continue to use a series of big lies to justify a war on our democracy. It is long past time to face where truth can take us.

Pride is part of our brand in America. So, too, is strength. Shame doesn't fit easily into that story. The Germans decided that discomfort could make them stronger by creating guardrails against a returning evil. We instead have reached for blinders.

There is no equivalent concept for Vergangenheitsaufarbeitung in our culture. It doesn't even translate easily into English. One might be tempted to think of it as working to shed the past—as in dropping pounds or paying a debt. But it really means something more prospective, like trying to build an ever bigger, ever-more-complicated structure off a foundation with serious cracks. Those flaws must be addressed, assessed, fixed, and made sturdy before the foundation can take more weight.

To address something this monumental, we often look to our biggest institutions to lead the way. But if we are to actually learn from the Germans, we have to widen our aperture. Yes, we will need leaders who have the courage to face this history to use their platforms and their muscle in government, business, religion, philanthropy, and academia. But the reason Vergangenheitsaufarbeitung took root in Germany was because its most ardent and committed proponents were closer to the ground. It wasn't limited to the ivory tower, the C-suite, or the pulpit. History was challenged from below.

Take the stumbling stones: The stories are researched by neighbors, schoolchildren, and church or civic groups. They raise the money and track down the victims' relatives and, as protocol dictates, invite them to a modest installation ceremony. These small acts of atonement and grace led to a national willingness to confront an odious history.

Could we ever open our eyes here in the United States to confront the lies in our founding myths? Could we comprehend the strength that comes from learning the real story? Do we have the fortitude for a reckoning that goes so much deeper than placing a Black Lives Matter sign in the front yard or insisting that fidelity to the Confederate flag is really about honoring Southern heritage instead of an institution based in hatred? Can we hope to produce a generation of leaders who can speak and be heard and perhaps even be embraced by people who occupy those opposing terrains? Our future as a united country of people ever more divided depends on it.

When I first learned about Vergangenheitsaufarbeitung, I kept thinking about the encounter I had with the woman who had asked me if "slavery could be optional" within a museum dedicated to Black life in America. She wanted it swept from the story like an unsavory item on a menu: I'll take a serving of patriotic history, but please hold the whippings and the bondage.

But no, slavery cannot be an optional part of the national story. It should not be excised from the narrative we teach our children about who we are and what we have become.

We must admit to, examine, reflect, lean in to, and grow through that history. All that history.

What is the word for Vergangenheitsaufarbeitung in English?

We must find it.

Postlude

Inspired by this article, the Arlington Historical Society in Virginia and the Black Heritage Museum of Arlington created a program to recover the large unknown history of enslaved people in the suburban county of Arlington just outside Washington, DC. According to the historical society, of the 1,000 people who lived in Arlington County when it was a European settlement in 1801, approximately 300 were enslaved. Inspired by the Stolpersteine project in Germany, a team of researchers plans to use so-called stumbling stones to bear witness to places where the enslaved lived and worked. The plan is to include their names and, whenever possible, the dates of their birth and death and a brief description of the conditions of their toil. The Arlington Historical Society will also develop teaching materials with local schools and plans to create an interactive online map with the locations and names of those who were held in bondage.

BELOW
*The Memorial to the Murdered Jews of Europe, Holocaust Memorial.
It consists of 2,711 cuboid concrete steles.*

He shot at us, but missed

Evelyn Ingram • Leesburg, VA

It was October of 2008 and I was taking the girls to school in Chantilly, VA. My son was in the car as well (he had just survived open heart surgery and only a few months old). Before our exit, I heard multiple shots (did not know they were shots at the time), the girls screamed, and I yelled "seat belts off and get on the floor." I pulled over, called my husband, then the police. We ultimately ended up at the police station where one of my daughters gave the details of an older white man pointing his gun at our car. She did not know how at the time to pronounce "Toyota" but she spelled it for the officer.

Yesterday, I cried typing these words, and I couldn't click Submit. I think I'm stronger today. I can't wait to pass this along.

Studying slavery makes me feel ashamed

Sam Henry • Asheville, NC

As a White male social studies teacher, I always have a difficult time teaching slavery. From what I know about my family tree, I don't have any family members that owned slaves, but that is hardly the point. It is a shameful period in our history but one worth studying. I want my eighth-grade students to know the truth.

My ancestors massacred Indians near here

Bruce Hawkins • Northampton, MA

Ambivalent, because my family owned slaves

Charles H. Sides • Westminster, MA

I always felt superior because my great-great-grandfather Sides was conscripted against his will or support into the Confederate Army, deserted, was captured by the Army of the Potomac, and was imprisoned at Elmira, where he died. Then, as I learned more about my personal genealogy, I discovered that every other branch of my family owned slaves in North Carolina, a national conversation that still is largely ignored.

A White minority during my youth

Jean Millard • Milford, MI

I wanted to be part of the Black culture around me because I could see the tight family ties they had. I was bullied by the kids I wanted to connect with. I remember when the first Black family moved into the neighborhood. I was shocked by the comments I heard from the neighbors. I could not understand why the new family was judged by their skin color. They had done nothing wrong. But has anyone asked me how I feel before they assume I am a Black hater? No. I am me, and you are you. No color, no sex, no culture, no size, no religion, no class. Using our brains and not what media or what history tells us to learn more about the person in front of us. We might even make a new friend.

Anti-Asian racism is America's tradition

Ken Yamamoto • Santa Barbara, CA

Left crying on the bathroom floor

Charlie • USA

I brought my car in for an oil change (in the predominantly Black area I live in), and they told me that it'd be an hour before they could get to it. "No big deal," I thought. "There's a shopping center across the street." As I made my way down the sidewalk, a man catcalled as he drove past. I didn't think much of it as I crossed the street and headed toward Big Lots. However, he had turned around and was now pulling into the parking lot.

"Hey," he said, getting out of his vehicle. "I don't wanna come on too strong, but you're really beautiful." At this point, I was flattered. I had recently had my daughter and was feeling uncomfortable in my own skin due to the weight gain.

"Thanks for saying so, but I'm married," I replied.

"He's a lucky man. Are you happy?" he asked, following me up the parking lot. His remarks began to get invasive and personal, making me extremely uncomfortable. I gave him a sterner no, and he had seemingly gotten the message. He hung back and didn't follow me as I walked into the store.

Less than five minutes after I entered the store, he came in. I told myself that I was being paranoid, that he was probably planning to come in regardless. Not really wanting to face him again, I made my way to the back aisles and tried to focus on shopping. He soon found his way to the opposite end of my aisle, basket empty. I tried to pretend that I hadn't seen him and went to the furniture section. Yet again, he had somehow ended up within ten feet of me. Even though it could have still been an uncomfortable coincidence, I decided to just purchase the phone charger in my basket and head to a different store.

As I was handing the cashier my card, he came up to the register next to mine, only a pack of gum in his hand.

There was a grocery store attached to the Big Lots, so I made a beeline for it. He entered the store soon after I did, and I was beginning to have a hard time believing he wasn't following me. Despite my obvious attempts to lose him, he managed to be in or near every aisle I was in. I was beginning to get frightened, so I went to the women's bathroom at the front of the store. A female employee saw the look on my face and asked worriedly, "What's wrong?" I explained the situation to her, and she asked for his description so they could call the police.

The moment I mentioned his skin color, her eyes dulled. Suddenly, her responses to me were short and a bit annoyed, as if I was wasting her time. She told me to wait and she would see about getting her manager, so I did. I sat in that bathroom for thirty minutes before I realized that no one was coming. From a different perspective, I understand that I might have looked like a racist White woman (who is in reality half Mexican) wanting to cry wolf about a POC harassing me. At that moment though, I didn't care how I looked. I sat on the floor and cried, terrified of the possibility that the man was still in the store. Sad that the employee (who was also Black) saw me as a racist, not a frightened woman who genuinely needed her help. Angry with her for leaving me alone while he might have still been out there.

Thankfully, the store manager (who was also Black) happened to walk in on my sobbing. After explaining to her what happened, she informed me that no one had mentioned the incident to her at all. She called the police herself and sat with me at the café area until they had arrived. Luckily, he left, but the manager didn't leave my side until the police officer confirmed it. As mortified as I was at the situation and the employee's inaction, I'm forever grateful to the manager who saw the problem and not my race and helped resolve the situation.

Propitiating the shame: my maiden name

Mary Bunce Benson • Lufkin, TX

My maiden name is Bunce, because of which on my wall beside my bed hangs a tapestry with the words of "Amazing Grace." Pride in the family stories of several great-grandfathers back, New England sea captain Harvey Bunce, turned to horror when I learned that slaves were his homeward-bound cargo, and even more horror as I read in Caryl Phillips's *Color Me English* of our family's Sierra Leone Bunce Island legacy. Amnesia, Michele, has *also* been *my* family's coping skill, as our family secret has been kept tucked back under generations of family rugs. None of us can rid ourselves of our genetic heritage, including our birth names, so maybe forgiveness of one another in the here and now is the only propitiation. I beg for yours.

[Bunce Island, just off the coast of Sierra Leone, was a major post in the transatlantic slave trade. Tens of thousands of Africans were kidnapped and brought to Bunce Island, where they were loaded as "cargo" on slave ships heading for the West Indies and North America. According to the World Monuments Fund, "The rice-growing skills of Africans from the west coast commanded high prices from rice plantation owners in North America." John Newton, who wrote the hymn "Amazing Grace," was a slave trader who worked mostly in Sierra Leone. Newton wrote the song after becoming a devout Christian later in life after leaving behind his work as an enslaver.]

Men tortured by great-great-grandfather torture me

Robert Carroll Rogers • Boston, MA

Wounds this deep take honesty, imagination, and all our resources to heal.

Grandma feared Blacks. Grandson IS Black.

V-Anne Chernock • Rio Vista, CA

My grandfather would hate my children.

Chad Oiastad • Madison, WI

I'm glad social norms have changed. Anyone who views my mixed-race kids as anything other than just kids is now the outsider, at least where I live. It's better this way.

My father endearingly calls us "Cottonpicker"

Thais • TX

My father, age eighty-three, born in a small town in northern Louisiana, has always called my siblings, cousins, and me cotton picker. My father is the grandson of Old Man Bass, as they referred to him, a slave owner, and Grandma Meli, short for Amelia, an enslaved African American woman who lived to see freedom. Grandma Meli had several children by Old Man Bass, one of which was my grandfather Elisha. Elisha was born years after slavery ended. Many of the African American men, or shall I say "colored" men, in his era had no other choice but to be sharecroppers. But my grandfather and his wife, Rosa, owned eighty acres in Louisiana where they primarily harvested cotton—one of slavery's trademarks.

My father was the eleventh of fourteen children born to Elisha and Rosa. The family fled from Louisiana to Oklahoma for safety, after an altercation between my father's older brothers and a White man who mistreated their mother, Rosa. My father, Dorris, was just months old when they left. A few years later, the family moved to Central California, better known as Chowchilla, California, in hope of making a better living.

One might think they escaped cotton picking. But as my father tells it, there was more cotton in California than in Mississippi or Louisiana. My father woke early to tend to the farm animals. After school, he'd pick cotton. And lots of it. He picked cotton from a young boy to the age of about twenty-five. Even at that age, any money he earned was handed over to his mother.

One day, he got tired of picking cotton. He up and moved to Pasadena, California, along with his wife and two children, who lived with him on his parents' farm. He eventually landed a job working as a construction worker for the City of Los Angeles for over thirty years. He tells about how when a White man was hired, it was his duty to train him—and then a week or two later, that White man would become his boss.

He is retired now. His voice still rings in my ears, while playing with cousins out at the family reunions: "Come here, you little cotton pickers!" And we all ran to his lap. I had no idea until I was in my twenties that he was calling me what some might consider "a little slave."

Fearful of offending, I say nothing

Sherry Buss • Bethlehem, PA

Mom's people owned slaves. Dad's were.

Andrew Dunn • Meridian, ID

My four-times great-grandfather was born a slave in Virginia. My three-times great-grandfather owned slaves in Missouri.

Grandfather's funeral. Only one Caucasian attended!!!

Mike Middlebrooks • White Bear Lake, MN

My grandparents and parents are from Ocilla, Georgia.

Grandfather would not teach mom Cherokee

Jonathan Dearman • Wagoner, OK

Why wasn't I taught this sooner?

Ryan Mearig • Fountain Valley, CA

School does a great job of giving you the surface-level depiction of slavery. It took twenty-two years to learn that every foreign race was oppressed and that we thought it was OK.

My history is beyond the classroom

Ryann Mellion • Washington, DC

Why do school textbooks only talk about slavery? Black history doesn't start or end with slavery.

Being Jewish in the 60's hurt.

David Wandel • Madison, WI

Found my ancestors and grief too.

R. Henry Goins • San Francisco, CA

I am a genealogist. I have been researching my North Carolina family for about ten years now. I found my great-grandfather's family in some notes held at the State Archives of North Carolina. The family lived in Belews Creek and Sauratown. Sauratown sounds like sorrow. I found a ledger with the name of the overseer of the plantation written in it. When I first read it, it looked like grief. I actually think the overseer's name was Greif, but I could not help but see it as grief. Grief is here. Grief will not let me go any further until I acknowledge it. Finding grief stopped me in my tracks.

Must we forget our Confederate ancestors?

Jesse Dukes • Charlottesville, VA

This question was on my mind recently, when I wrote an article for *Virginia Quarterly Review* about Confederate reenactors at Gettysburg. I don't actually have any Confederate ancestors I'm aware of, but most of the reenactors do. All the reenactors I talked to considered slavery to be an abomination, considered Jim Crow to be evil, and espoused no prejudice against people of color.

But they feel a powerful connection to the Confederacy because of their heritage, because their great-great-great-grandfathers marched up a hill in Gettysburg or some other battlefield and watched their friends get shot or got shot themselves. They're proud of their forebears. They imagine their ancestors as brave and noble people and say things like, "Those boys weren't fighting for slavery; they were fighting for state's rights and freedom." And in certain individual cases, they might be correct, even if the Confederacy collectively fought to preserve slavery.

Historical arguments aside, if White Southerners wish to oppose racism today, what responsibilities do they have toward the past? Must they forget or renounce their Confederate ancestors? Is there a way they can honor their memories and the vastness of their sacrifices while still acknowledging the racism of the nineteenth-century South and the horrors of slavery?

Slavery's legacy broke my family pride.

Kate Byroade • West Hartford, CT

When I was a child, my Southern grandmother took great delight in the fact that she was a Jamestown descendant and DAR (Daughters of the American Revolution) member and saw her membership as part of her legacy to her granddaughters, ensuring our social success. She was matter-of-fact that the family had owned slaves in the past but emphasized that we did not come from plantation-type families, that our slaves had been trusted house servants. At first this seemed OK to me because it was OK to her, but eventually I understood that the domination of another person's free will was unacceptable. I became more and more uncomfortable with the legacy of my White privilege, knowing that it was tied to something I see as reprehensible.

Earlier this year, a wonderful, elderly distant family member shared some interesting history with me. Our mutual ancestor, Harriet Hamilton Austin, immigrated to the US around 1845 from Ireland. Here is the story that broke my heart:

"I had the only record, which was the original bill of sale to Edward Clegg, who purchased that little eight-year-old girl at a slave auction in 1844. Edward Clegg was bidding for his mother-in-law, Harriet Hamilton Austin.

"The Van Buren Courthouse burned completely down in the 1870s, and all records were destroyed. Harriet later gave the little girl to Maria Jane Austin Clegg, her daughter. Harriet, the slave girl, later became little Maud Clegg's nanny. Her name was Harriet after her original owner, a custom in those days.

"After Maria Jane's death, little Maud was sent back to Arkansas, and it appears that Austin H. Clegg, age sixteen, and the slave girl Harriet took little Maud back to Arkansas. Sydney Clegg Austin became the guardian of Maud, and Sydney gave Harriet her free papers so she could make the trip without problems. Todd told me Harriet was allowed to disembark at Van Buren, but her husband was not allowed to because he did not have free papers. This happened in 1860. Harriet and her husband returned to Van Buren after the war."

My five-times great-grandmother, then middle-aged and upper-class, comes to the US, and almost immediately, an eight-year-old child was purchased for her use. What was the heartbreak she left behind? Why was my great-grandmother's need of a servant greater than that heartbreak? We are very shy in this culture about calling out the great wickedness of slavery, and we should not be; we must not be.

Great-granddad was called the slave

Ronald Ball • Peoria, IL

In her last years of life, my mother and I often reminisced about her family roots. One of the stories that really interested me was when she talked about her grandfather. She said everyone around the Easton, Maryland, (Tuckahoe) community referred to him as "the slave." His son became a sheriff's deputy, which had to be significant in those days. Mom said that Great-granddad lived to be 110 years old. I'm not sure whether or not he lived to watch my mother and my uncle graduate college. He would have been very proud.

The "haves" have not a clue.

Daniel A. Palmer •
Kettering, OH

I am not an exotic creature

Hana Peoples • Seattle, WA

Being of Japanese and African American ethnicity has brought many interesting comments from people. Because I have an "ambiguous look," I get many guesses from people about what I am. I have gotten Mexican, Filipino, Nepali, Chinese, but rarely can people guess that I am both African American and Japanese. When I do finally come out and say what I am, people that have played my guess-my-race game wrong are shocked and amazed. They act like I am some exotic creature, inhumanely mixed to even be a person. They say things like, "Wow! That's a cool mix," or, "You are gonna have really cute babies." Comments like these make it feel like to the outside world I am just an exotic creature, not a person who is biracial. I identify with both and proudly call myself Blackanese. I don't choose sides, and I don't have to.

He's my dad, not the gardener.

Kelly Stuart • Brooklyn, NY

I was five when my mother married my stepfather, Alfred Brown Jr., in 1980. My stepfather, or as I think of him, my father, was twenty-one years older than my mom and had already raised a daughter by the time he met me, but that didn't stop him from getting a second job at the Ford plant in Mahwah, New Jersey, so he could give me what I'd asked him for when he married my mom: my own room and a backyard with a swing. He got me the room and the backyard and the swing, but what came with moving from the city where we were to a small rural town were a different set of understandings, like when I went from a place where I knew other mixed-race families to a place where kids used to throw Oreos at me on the bus to school to symbolize my Black-and-White family. Even after the Oreos stopped flying in middle school, I dealt with people's fear of and prejudice against my father every day.

Now that I am grown and my father has passed away, and people see the blonde, blue-eyed, upper-middle-class, NPR-listening, Brooks Brothers–employed me, people think they know who I am and who I must have come from. This was brought home to me recently when someone looking over my shoulder as I tried to find a picture on my computer pointed at my computer and asked me whose house was in the picture that was currently on my screen. I said that it was a picture of the house in which I grew up. My dad was also in the picture, pulling weeds, and the person looking over my shoulder said, "And was that your gardener?" I said no, that he was my father, and in that moment, I was so angry at the implication of the assumption, and yet, I was so, so very grateful that I got to claim him again, publicly, as the man who made me who I am.

6

How Do You
Define Racism?

I USED TO KEEP A NOTES FILE in my phone filled with various definitions of racism. It wasn't because I didn't understand the meaning or origins of racism. It was because so many people kept asking me to serve as their dictionary on the topic.

As The Race Card Project grew in scope and size, I was often meeting with potential stakeholders or people interested in supporting our archive or diversity efforts in general, and I began to notice how many would ask some version of the same question: "How do you define racism?" I didn't think much of it until it happened a third and then a fourth and then a fifteenth time. These questions almost always came from White people. Black and Brown people generally don't need a definition of racism, but apparently a lot of White people do.

This happened so much that I used to add to that cache of racism definitions in my phone the way bakers rack up recipes for different methods of making a piecrust. Some of the definitions were academic or anthropological. Some quoted icons I rely upon for wisdom, sages like James Baldwin, Toni Morrison, Wendell Berry, or Clint Smith. I engaged with these questions. I would listen, take a deep breath, and then explain with both patience and eloquence how race or racism could be defined.

"An institutionalized system of economic, social, political or cultural frameworks that ensure one racial group, regardless of intent, maintains power and privilege over almost all aspects of life."

"Any attitude or behavior used to explain or justify bias or prejudice against racial or ethnic groups on the basis of perceived inferiority."

"When a person is excluded, disadvantaged, harassed, humiliated, threatened, targeted, profiled, harmed, bullied, terrorized or ignored because of their ethnicity, race, religious beliefs, sexual orientation, age or gender."

"When good people stand silent watching any or all of the above happen before their eyes."

"It is the arrogant assertion that one race is at the center of value and object of devotion, before which other races kneel in submission."

Racism is a shape-shifter. It is not the same thing today as it was yesterday.

I look back on that period as an unfortunate one. Serving as some kind of walking, talking cultural dictionary was a waste of my mental energy and certainly my time. It's not a question that even deserves an earnest answer. As I look back, I clearly see that the query was often an act of avoidance. A chin-stroking inquisition that allowed for engagement from a safe distance. A way of kicking the possibility of any kind of real involvement down the road. A way of perhaps making sure that whatever the definition was, that it didn't apply to the person asking the question. These were people who perhaps had good intentions, but my strong hunch is that they were hoping that they would not see themselves in the answer. But the question itself was, to say the least . . . revealing. And for me it became exhausting.

How do you live in America and not understand how to define racism?

I have stopped referring to that folder. I no longer want to scroll through its contents. But if someone asks going forward—and I realize that writing this is an invitation for people to indeed ask going forward—they are likely to get a crankier version of me providing an answer. I don't find it productive to repeatedly have Socratic discussions about how to define racism unless there is the same degree of energy or enthusiasm directed toward trying to combat it. Racism continues to tear our country apart. It is the flame that threatens our mutual well-being, and even if you think you are protected from the heat because of education or social status or the goodness of your heart, just know that the impacts of racism touch everyone. Stifling opportunities for some stifles our collective economy. Poisonous rhetoric in some quarters creates toxic eruptions that can undermine everyone's safety. Creating a false sense of superiority based on skin color might provide a jolt of instant satisfaction, but that temporary high carries a high price. As Booker T.

Washington famously said, "It is not possible for one man to hold another man down in the ditch without staying down there with him."

So, if I have to settle on a simple, bite-size definition, perhaps it's this: Racism is a shape-shifter. It is not the same thing today as it was yesterday, and it will not be the same tomorrow or ten years from now. That's shorthand for the academic definition that describes racism as a "multi-dimensional, highly adaptive system that ensures unequal distribution of resources among racial groups." The group that controls the levers of power and distribution of resources weaves their interests into the gears of that system.

The key element in that description is the phrase *highly adaptive*. Changes in society bring about new forms of discrimination: algorithmic bias . . . a pandemic that reveals the inequities deeply embedded in our social fabric. It shows up in new systems and presents in new ways, but it's actually the old thing. The same thing.

And what is that . . . thing?

I could define it for you. I could ask you to head to the dictionary or some volume to look it up for yourself. But here's another idea. Try talking about racism without ever actually using the word *racism*.

I was part of a roundtable discussion years ago where we were asked to talk about the condition of impoverishment without using the words *poverty*, *poor*, *economically disadvantaged*, or *low income*. Then, sometime later, I was at a conference in Palisades Tahoe where innovators and disruptors from the tech sector were trying to help people understand how failure can be the rocket fuel for innovation. To help the attendees shed their fear of failure, they asked people to discuss what it means to fail without using the word or many of its related synonyms. I was reminded of this linguistic tool when talking to Ta-Nehisi Coates about his novel, *The Water Dancer*. Ta-Nehisi wrote an entire novel about enslavement but only mentioned the word *slavery* twice, and even then, it slipped past him during the editing process. Ta-Nehisi said he thought Americans needed language to confront what enslavement entailed: "I was trying to get as far away as I could from other renditions of what slavery had been." I fully understand what he was trying to do. Readers could focus more on the people and the conditions of bondage rather than engaging in that reflexive instinct to reach for that stock imagery stored away in one's mental database under a cognitive file marked *slavery*.

Talking about something without using the word for that thing is a brilliant concept, and it is particularly useful when discussing a taboo subject like race or racism because so many get the heebie-jeebies when the subjects come up or reflexively slide into a here-we-go-again mentality. It's the whole reason that the phrase *playing the race card* gained currency, because it became an easy/lazy catchall to note that the conversation had drifted into a space of discomfiture or disdain. It becomes easier to say something is about race or class and gender broadly without getting a bit more granular to describe the greater dynamics that are at work. It's like saying that a person has been harmed by some gauzy, ill-defined force, as opposed to saying outright the origin, impact, and individual or institution that caused the harm. This much I know. You can't tackle or even spot racism unless you can learn how to define it for yourself.

Go ahead. Try it. Describe racism without using the word or any of its closely related cousins like *bias* or *prejudice*.

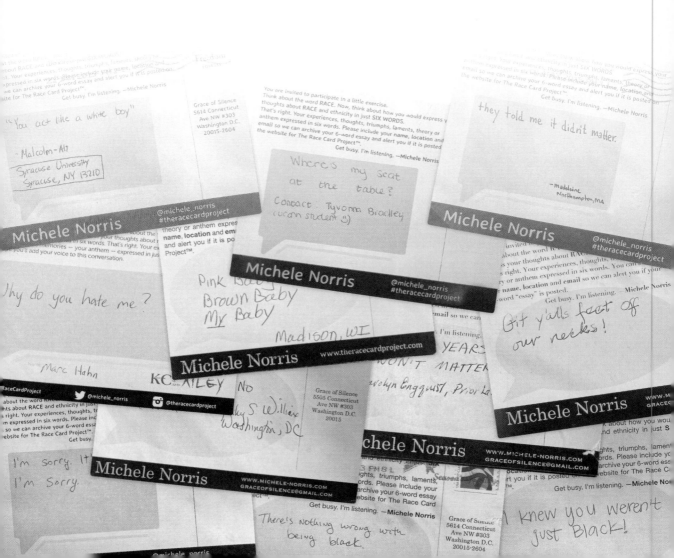

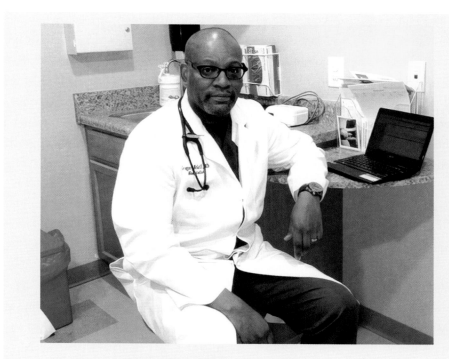

55 MPH MEANS YOU, BLACK MAN

Gregory McGriff • Rutherfordton, NC

DR. GREGORY McGRIFF HEARD ABOUT The Race Card Project while listening to NPR, and he knew exactly what his six words would be: "55 mph means you, Black man." At the time, McGriff was working at a hospital in North Carolina, and his 6-word statement was a reference to the long drives he took in his 7 Series BMW, as well as the slower pace he had to use as a Black doctor in a largely White community.

"I am an Ivy League graduate and board-certified medical doctor," McGriff wrote when he sent in his 6-word story. "The subject of race comes up all the time, but the conversation that should follow is usually very short. When I see the speed limit sign on the road announcing fifty-five miles per hour (or whatever the legal limit is), I know that posting is meant for me. My White counterparts can proceed a bit faster. I live life at fifty-five miles per hour lest I get pulled over, and then almost anything can happen."

Dr. McGriff wound up being the subject of a radio segment himself when I interviewed him for a feature on *Morning Edition*. Originally from West Hartford, Connecticut, McGriff excelled in school and studied economics and premed at the University of Pennsylvania, and he graduated from Wake Forest University School of Medicine. He did his internship at Yale and his residency at the University of Connecticut. It's the kind of residency that would put some strut in your step, and yet that fifty-five-mile-per-hour statement is a metaphor for how McGriff had to move carefully. He said any kind of display of confidence or success made his colleagues and his neighbors uncomfortable. He countered that by moving slowly and trying in some ways to make himself small.

"If you have to do fifty-five miles per hour in life all the time, you are not going to get very far," McGriff said. "And if you look around, everyone else is moving a little bit faster." With a quiet voice and a strong working-class New England accent, McGriff described his experience as a Black man in a white coat. He described the day he was called into a hospital administrator's office because a patient had issued a complaint. Dr. McGriff said he was told that the patient claimed he had used language that was foreign to them.

"A family was upset with me because I was uppity," McGriff explained. "This is something that I'm sure none of my partners—because I asked them—they've never gotten that particular complaint. And so, it's never my desire to be uppity. It's my hope, rather than be condescending and speak down to anyone, to just speak a natural language. And if there's a word or two that's a little above your vocabulary, it is not because I'm better than you; it is not because I have more education. I'm certainly not trying to lord my intellect over you. I'm simply trying to communicate. I'm sure that this is something that doesn't always happen with my White counterparts."

But because McGriff had to travel a different path than his peers, he wound up practicing a different kind of medicine. At a time when rules around managed care and hospital efficiency were encouraging doctors to move through their rounds with greater speed, that wasn't an option for McGriff. Over the years, he'd had patients who had gotten up to leave when he walked into the examination room. Or they had pointedly asked him to vacate the space. Yes, they asked him to leave his own place of employment because of their bias. So, McGriff developed his own style and pace of doctoring when he worked as an admitting physician in an emergency room.

"I make a point to do something that many of my partners don't do—most physicians don't do anymore—I sit," McGriff said, explaining that he slowly enters a room, scoots up a chair, and before he gets to work, asks his patients to tell him their story. He sits in part because he has a bum knee from his days playing sports, but mainly he takes a load off so he can be closer to the patient's eye level. "Sitting tells them I'm not leaving. I'm not already exiting the room before I've even started. Sitting, I hope, communicates that I'm interested in what they have to say, and I want to get to the bottom of their problem."

His technique usually worked. Even White patients who were visibly shaken by standing in front of a Black man while wearing one of those flimsy robes that don't cover their backside would relax and start telling their tale.

"I'm really interested in these stories, by the way, and every client I meet has a very interesting story," McGriff said. "But once I get their history and they're finished, I conduct a brief but thorough exam. And this may take about twenty to twenty-five minutes. And so, I have a well-deserved reputation as being one of the slower physicians. But what I can't do is walk into the room, announce that I'm your doctor and I'm going to do a superfluous exam. My partner might be able to get away with that, but I cannot. And so, with each and every encounter, I'm aware that I have to go a little bit slower, have to communicate a little bit more to make up for any perceptual problems."

He'd had patients who had gotten up to leave when he walked into the examination room.

Perceptual problems. That's a rather fancy way of describing a double standard based on bias. When we aired Dr. McGriff's story on NPR, we covered a lot of ground, but even so, there were things we didn't have enough time to share. We did not include the things he told us about playing video games with White friends who would forget themselves and yell "Get that nigger!" when trying to target a dark-skinned foe on their gaming screen. We did not include the story he told about how he keeps a duplicate copy of his driver's license in the visor of his car, so he doesn't have to reach down toward his pocket for his ID when he is pulled over by police. Notice that he said *when* and not *if*, because traffic stops by police have been common all of McGriff's life, and especially when he was driving his BMW in the South.

When I spoke to McGriff, he was planning to train his teenage son to do the same thing. I have appropriated his idea and have implored my own sons and nephews to keep a photocopy of their driver's license in the visor for the same reason, fearing that reaching down might lead a policeman to mistakenly assume that a young Black man is grabbing a weapon. That fifty-five-mile-per-hour metaphor has broad applications for men of color everywhere.

McGriff became an instant celebrity when his story first aired a decade ago. His Facebook page exploded. Television cameras showed up at his home and at the hospital.

But then things got strange. Remember what McGriff said about walking small? Instant celebrity is not consistent with that. For several reasons, McGriff eventually left his job at the hospital. "They made it clear that staying was not going to be an option," Dr. McGriff said.

I was mortified. We hoped that people would speak their truths, but we certainly never wanted anyone to lose their job because of that. McGriff was surprisingly calm through that ordeal. He said he felt like he was speaking for more than just himself. Doctors of color all over the US had called to thank him. A hospital had invited him to do grand rounds—a presentation where a doctor gives a talk about his expertise or experience. He prefers now to stay below the radar and did not want to share his more recent experiences at work or in life. It has not always been easy.

"I said what needed to be said. I'm good with that," McGriff said. "I hope people on the other side of this experience will hear me, too. Probably not. But . . . just maybe."

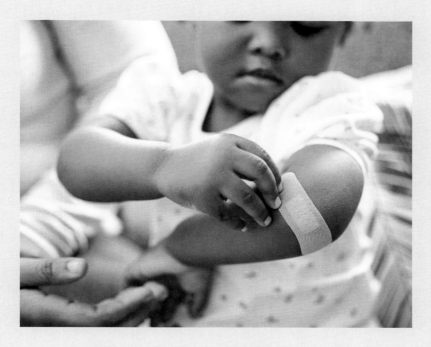

Racism is a Flesh-Colored Band-Aid

Gretchen • Portland, OR

It's different, shopping with Mom

Chas Sundling • Tillamook, OR

These words were spoken by one of my two sons. They were spoken a few years back and led to quite the conversation about race, about people's first perceptions based upon appearance, about acceptance, about prejudice, about self-identity, about belonging, about privileges, perceived or otherwise, about entitlement and self-entitlement, about rights, about struggles, and about love. My ex-wife and I are both born and raised in San Francisco. We moved up to the Pacific Northwest some years back when I accepted a position with Nike. I am White, and she is of Puerto Rican ancestry, and our sons are a blend of the two of us.

One time, when leaving the store, one of my sons made mention that I speak with and greet a lot of people in the store and that people do the same with me, which prompted me to reply, "Why, how is it with your mom when you go to the store?" to which one of them replied, "It's different, shopping with Mom."

The way it was spoken, the way he said those simple words, told me that there was something much deeper at play here than I was expecting to hear, which opened the door to the conversation that I have mentioned above. Probably forgotten by him, those words, "It's different, shopping with Mom," have never left me.

What opened my eyes: "flesh-colored" bandages

Irene M. Pepperberg • Swampscott, MA

I was in high school, a racially integrated one, in the 1960s, discussing racial issues with a contemporary Black woman, an honors student, headed for a fine college. I asked her why she was so angry, what kind of discrimination she felt, living in a middle-class community, going to a good school. Her answer, spat out at me, made me realize that discrimination was occurring at the very basic levels of her life, in ways I couldn't ever experience.

Great-grandparents were white illegal immigrants

Robin Shudak • Wilkes-Barre, PA

Both sides of my family are Polish and escaped from the rise of fascism. Their destination: the US. My maternal grandfather's family, who were Jewish, were denied entry. My paternal grandfather's family, fleeing because they were caught as part of the resistance and his brother was already "sent to Germany," were also denied entry. No refugee status or asylum. But they got in because to return was death. Both families, now without homes or countries, thought they could hide out here until the war was over, but the Soviet takeover of Poland made that impossible. So, as a little girl in the 1980s, I was called a communist by teachers and severely disciplined for speaking Polish (which everyone thought was Russian). Now, we have the opportunity to move back and are considering it. Because in our experience, we believe American Whiteness also has a pecking order.

In our experience, unless you're a Daughter of the American Revolution or some other vintage of "heroes" that formed this country or towns in it, you are looked down on. I can't even imagine how much worse it is when your ethnicity is on full display, and not just in your last name.

For my kind, it's a non-issue

Lani Bersch • Baltimore, MD

When I was sixteen and on a date, my friend saw my dad and hissed, "You didn't tell me your father was Black." He wasn't. . . . My dad is Hawaiian, but a very dark Hawaiian from years in the sun. My dad heard and later said to me, "What's the matter with that boy? Doesn't he know I'm Hawaiian?" It would take an afternoon to unpack this story, but the incident propelled me into a fierce stand to break racial norms in my family. It didn't happen. . . . I wasn't strong enough to sacrifice my entire seventy-five-plus-member family to marry my Black twenty-one-year-old boyfriend and follow him to wherever the army sent him. However, there is progress, at least in my family. My daughter is about to be engaged to a Haitian man. And to my adult children, it's an issue not even on their radar.

I am dead to my father

Debra Taylor • Bolton, MO

Fourteen years ago, I married a Black man. My father told me my child and grandchild did not exist because I was dead to him.

Postlude: Though Debra's mother and her second husband (Debra calls him her Bonus Dad) were less than happy when she married Harry O. Taylor, the two eventually embraced him and were at Harry's bedside when he died in January of 2017. They both had a chance to whisper their goodbyes, and Debra's mother asked Harry to find her deceased parents in heaven. Debra is beginning to form a bond with her biological father. She says they are "attempting a relationship," but he still cannot fathom her decision to marry a Black man. "He said he guessed he would never understand," Debra said.

Some of my best friends are...

Steven Shimberg • Washington, DC

I envy our kids, who seem to be color-blind and take diversity for granted. Having grown up in the 1950s and '60s, I regret that my ability to understand fully, appreciate, and relate to some of my friends' life experiences is limited. Divides based on socioeconomics are significant, but divides based on race seem to be more significant and harder to bridge. If we can't make the divide smaller, we need to build more bridges.

If I married a Black man—disowned!

Debbie Jensen • Everett, WA

Being comfortable is my unearned privilege

Miriam • Arlington, VA

It strikes me that among my peers, White kids talk about race much less. Being White is not only about avoiding judgment, it's about being comfortable. I'll never have to walk around with this weighing consciousness of my race. I'm comfortable wherever I go, and my skin color never feels like it's dragging me down. Being color-blind, and ignoring the issues that race brings up, is thus the luxury of the privileged.

That Black girl lost her magic

Saniyyah • Philadelphia, PA

I can't leave without my receipt

Nathaniel Kittrell • Beebe, AR

I can't ever go anywhere or buy anything without needing to have a copy of my receipt with me. I promise that what I buy isn't stolen.

Excuse me, do you do landscaping?

Ricardo • Oakland, CA

I was recently asked at a garden store if I did landscaping. I am a Mexican American male, who is also a sergeant for a medium-sized city police force in the Bay Area. I must say I was dressed shabbily, driving a small pickup, a lime tree in the cab, a shovel in the back with planter pots. The question was an innocent one, in my opinion, asked by another Hispanic male who wanted to know if I was happy with my truck. He wanted to start a landscaping business. The case made me smile, but I did give a lot of thought the rest of the afternoon about the interaction. Would I have been so gracious with a White person, an Asian person, etc.?

Why does my race cause fear?

Steven • Aldie, VA

I feel that because of my skin color, my race, and all the characterizations that have been made about both, there is a fear when people see me. Some of it is ignorant, like seeing a well-built Black man being some type of demon or beast. Like how the police officer portrayed Michael Brown. And with the kind of work I do, I sometimes wonder if my clients or employer sometimes fear letting a Black face represent them and their interests. Why do White men fear what Black men will do to their women and children? Why is that fear still there with all the interracial marriages and families that have blossomed over the years? Why does *Black* equal fear in society but is celebrated in fashion or finance (where staying in the black is good)? Why does my five-year-old, a ball of energy, draw concern from parents when playing on the playground or basketball court? Why is that fear still there?

I pray for my son everyday

J. Hill • Canton, OH

I am the proud mother of three children, two girls and a boy. They are all adults now. Every mother worries about her children. But I feel especially concerned for my son. He has done everything well so far in his life, entering his senior year in college, no kids, hardworking, respectful of his parents, kind. He is sweet, funny, smart, and well-spoken. But when the world looks at him, before he can open his mouth to present himself well, he is a young Black male, a potential threat. We live in a predominantly White neighborhood. When my son was home on break, he wanted to go out for a run early one morning. I discouraged him from running through our neighborhood, afraid someone would see a Black man in sweats and a hoodie and mistake him for a criminal. It could literally cost him his life, and it won't matter to anyone that he was my sweet, handsome son. I pray for him every single day!

New Brand of Racism is worse

Anna Berch-Norton • Pittsburgh, PA

Yeah, when White guys call their friends "my nigga" and people say to their Vietnamese friend, "It's funny 'cause you're Asian," that doesn't mean that we're totally over that whole racism thing. It means that people are subscribing to the hipster theory of racism that you can say really racist, disgusting shit all you want as long as you do so ironically just to show that you actually are completely tolerant. And just because you're Black doesn't mean you can make Holocaust jokes in the presence of an agnostic half Jew who isn't a big fan of genocide. My mixed-race ex-boyfriend made some of those because he thought he was entitled. What is so funny about systematic ethnic cleansing, anyway? Would it also be hilarious if you got harassed by the police every time you went to the corner store? Being a (very) White young female, I don't even get a second glance. And I don't deserve that invisibility any more than a Black guy in a hoodie. We make so many assumptions, so many judgments, based on so little. But seriously, White hipster kids: Please don't try to ironize your way into nonracism. And stop telling me about how many minority friends you have to make up for it. Because when it comes right down to it, you're not much different from your great-grandparents who dressed in white and burned crosses. You're just better at hiding it.

Cop can't see us with you

Alexander Hileman • Commerce City, CO

People are afraid in parts of the USA to be seen with White people. I was down in Texas, and a couple of Black kids asked us if we wanted to play some basketball. We said yes, and we played for about an hour and a half until they said something. "We need to go before seven because the cops come around and they will be concerned if they see us with you." At that point, I didn't know what to say. We were just having a good time.

Invisible Black woman. Microscope on me

Devin Horton • Los Angeles, CA

Invisible but also having the world simultaneously watch and critique my every move with microscopic precision. It can cause serious anxiety.

There's more than what you see

Josephine Kim • Cambridge, MA

When it comes to race, we need our eyes to hear and our ears to see.

All power I see is White

Erin • Saint Louis, MO

In my world today, I associate power with people who are White. All my teachers and school leaders: White. My parents: White. The police in my area: White. All forms of power and authority in my life are White, and this is how it's been since I was little. Fear those who are colored or different; respect and look up to those who are White. It's a cruel world, but it's reality, and it's been drilled into my life since infancy.

Twitter trends hashtag White girl problems

Kitlyn Gravatt • West Long Branch, NJ

Whenever I click on Twitter, I see #whitegirlproblems. How is Starbucks running out of my favorite drink a White girl problem? How is my eyeliner on one eye not matching my other eye a White girl problem? It is hurtful to be put into this stereotype that we care more about superficial things over bigger issues. The White-girl-problem hashtag goes more in depth with the idea that if girls are interested in something then that means they are a certain type of person. My interest in Starbucks or makeup should not make me a superficial White girl. People should not make me feel bad for my interests or make it a joke on Twitter. I should not be wondering if I get on line in Starbucks or post a picture with my drink is someone going to call me a basic White girl.

Sipping lattes, we call it racism

Michael • Livonia, MI

It strikes me over and over again that we confuse the problems of being poor with racism. Dr. Martin Luther King Jr. understood the problem isn't race: it's economic. The reason we see a deepening divide, and a growing sense of racial tension, is because more and more middle-class White folks—the factory workers—are being disenfranchised by neoliberalism. The jobs they used to have—the ones that paid for the snowmobiles, Jet Skis, and little camps up north—have been shipped overseas. Now, these poor White folks have nothing to do but get hooked on opioids and listen to their protofascist leader tell them it's the government's fault they don't have work. And all the while he bloviates, their leader works with the rest of the bourgeoisie to make sure their pockets grow fatter.

These same poor White folks are the ones lighting tiki torches and blaming the Black folks for their problems. To fuel the feedback loop, university professors write papers and books about our screwed-up criminal-justice system and conclude it is racist cops who are to blame. And in the poorest parts of our cities, children can't read or write, yet cling tenaciously to the hope of "becoming somebody" by playing basketball or football. Meanwhile, the rest of us worry about whether our skinny lattes will be warm enough and that the kids won't be late for soccer practice, and every once in a while, we'll give a few scraps from our excess to help out the poor kids in the city.

We would do well to remember why Dickens wrote *A Christmas Carol*.

I am glad I'm not Black

Prudence Runyan • Philadelphia, PA

In the late 1990s, a colleague and I needed to go about ninety miles away to a client meeting. We each took our own cars, as it was the weekend and we were heading off in separate directions after the meeting. He planned to follow me, as he hadn't been there before. He told me, "Don't speed." I replied, "Don't be silly, Brian, everybody speeds on the New Jersey Turnpike." "Not me," he replied. "I will get arrested for 'driving while Black.'" That's the first time I had heard the term. I didn't know what to say. As we made our way north to Secaucus, I saw that what he'd said was true. Nearly every person the police had pulled over was dark-skinned.

Oh, where's your accent from?

Martyna • Manassas, VA

"Basic White girl" who's not White.

Betsy F. • Minneapolis, MN

I grew up wishing I was White. I was raised to hate my culture, my eyes, my language, and my background. In middle school, I was known for being the most "basic White girl" who wasn't actually White. I did what every other girl did, wore, and ate. I bought Bath & Body Works lotion and perfumes. I wore yoga pants, UGGs, Converse, etc. I drank Starbucks and loved pumpkin spice lattes. Any basic trend, I would hop on the bandwagon. I'm aware now of the nuances of the term "basic White girl" and the intersectionality that comes along with being female, but I'm focusing on the race aspect. Being adopted into a Caucasian family, I have no ties to the culture I was born into. To put it simply, I'm not White, but I don't feel connected to my Asian ancestry. Growing up, it was incredibly difficult and confusing about what my identity is, and even now I'm still figuring it all out.

Adopting AA started needed conversations

Susan Kosior • Fredericksburg, VA

7

"Black babies cost less to adopt"

WHEN YOU'VE SPENT MORE than a decade collecting hundreds of thousands of tales and testimonies about a topic as prickly and vulnerable as race, people naturally want to know which one is your all-time favorite. I don't much like that question. There are already too many rankings and hierarchies in matters concerning cultural identity. I'd rather not add to that by serving up a single story as the sizzling example of our racial fault lines.

However, when someone asks about the story that hit me the hardest when it landed in The Race Card Project inbox, one answer immediately springs to mind:

Black babies cost less to adopt.

I remember with clarity the day that 6-word story arrived in my inbox. It was a Saturday, mid-January in 2012, and it hit me like a sharp jab to my rib cage. At that point, we were still collecting a large number of our 6-word stories via little black postcards sent in the mail, but this was a digital submission sent through an online form. It came from a woman who identified herself as Michelle P. in Covington, Louisiana, and she explained why she chose those six words when she submitted her story to The Race Card Project archive:

"We decided to adopt a child years ago. We are not infertile but felt like it was a great way to add to our family while loving someone who needed us. Our research showed us that African American children, especially boys, are the least adoptable in our country.

We decided to adopt via a nonprofit agency, a child of any race. In the US, whether you use a nonprofit agency or a for-profit agency, Black children are cheaper. I have read the reasoning behind this, but I really don't care to repeat the rationalizations here. My son was cheaper than if he'd been White. How will he feel if he ever finds out about that?"

I had to just sit inside those words for a long time, lingering at my desk in the third-floor attic, staring at the screen while my own Black babies, who were at that point entering their tweens, were running back and forth in the hallway one floor below. I was familiar with the variegated fee structure in adoption that's tied to the race and skin color of a child. Back in 2002, I had done some reporting on that practice while working as a TV correspondent for ABC News. Yet even with that foreknowledge, those six words from Michelle P. stung.

The straightforward economy of that sentence—"Black babies cost less to adopt"—packed more of a wallop than any policy paper or twelve-minute investigative broadcast report. The juxtaposition of the words *babies* and *cost*. The cruel addition of the words *Black* and *less*. And all of it yoked to adoption—a process that is supposed to be saturated with love and altruism. An act in which society, through the generosity of the heart, hopes to find its best self.

Those six words revealed an ugly aspect of a beautiful tradition, and in the following months and years, I kept hearing from parents who expressed similar sentiments—a combination of bewilderment, confusion, disappointment, and anger upon discovering that growing their families through private domestic adoption would cost less and could be fast-tracked if they were willing to accept the discount that goes along with choosing a Black child.

• • •

Dawn Friedman and her husband, Brett, who are both White, decided to try to grow their family through adoption. They also decided they were open to a transracial adoption. Upon hearing that, a social worker told Dawn that if she was willing to adopt a Black baby, the agency would share her profile only with women who were giving birth to babies of Black descent. She then told Dawn, "You may as well get the fee break."

Dawn was stunned that the social worker referenced this "price cut" without a hint of regret or discomfort. "I said to her, 'Well, maybe we should just pay full price,' like somehow that would absolve us," Dawn said. The social worker declined that offer and placed Dawn and her husband in the program—a separate program—for adopting Black children.

A family therapist in Columbus, Ohio, Dawn has written a popular blog for several years, in which she explores the challenges of parenting, including in her own family. She wound up participating in what she calls a "half-price adoption," and within a year, she and her husband welcomed a beautiful biracial baby girl. Their family also expanded in other ways. They opted for an open adoption, so their youngest child's birth mother also became a frequent presence in their family life. Dawn is grateful that both are now a part of her life, but she says she will forever be uncomfortable with the role race played in how—and how fast—it all happened.

What justified a system for adopting White children where the fee structure was almost twice as much as it was for adopting Black children? What explains the discount?

•   •   •

After years of trying to conceive, Caryn Ward Lantz and her husband decided to explore adoption, and from the start they were also willing to embrace children of another race. They live in the suburbs of Minneapolis. The Twin Cities is a place where transracial adoption has been fairly common since the 1970s, but despite seeing so many transracial families at the shopping mall or the movie theater, one aspect of the process was shielded from public view.

The Lantzes, like Dawn and Brett, were shocked when social workers started talking about the discount. One told Caryn in no uncertain terms that many of the private adoption agencies had two different tracks. On the one hand, adopting a White, Latino, or Asian baby would be a slower process because long lists of White parents were waiting for those babies, especially newborns,

Those six words revealed an ugly aspect of a beautiful tradition.

and there weren't enough available to satisfy demand. On the other hand, there were long lists of Black and biracial Black children who needed loving homes, yet there weren't enough families willing to adopt—and more specifically, willing to adopt Black children.

Lantz recalls a phone call with an agency in Florida. She was sitting in her kitchen, and she could barely believe what she heard. "The social worker was telling us about these different fee structures that they had based on the ethnic background of the child. And not only the different fee structures, but they also had sort of a different track for adoptive parents. If you were open to adopting a full African American child, there was what I refer to as a fast track, although I'm sure it's not the appropriate terminology. But they have this fast track that allows you to move through the process quickly and take placement of a child relatively soon. And that is because they have children of color wait-ing," Caryn said before describing the alternative route to adoption that was presented to her on that day. That track, described as the "traditional" one, was for children who were biracial, Latino, Asian, or Caucasian. The agency explained that the traditional route would entail a slower process because there were more parents in line for those children.

...honestly, I hope reading about this does make you squirm.

"And I remember hearing this and just sort of being dumb-founded that they would segregate—to use a loaded term—segregate these children by ethnic background before they were even in this world," Caryn said. "That's when I started realizing that, OK, being a parent to a child of a different ethnic background, this is going to be some work. There's going to be a lot of work on our end in order to be successful parents and to get our child ready for this world."

Caryn lives in a community where Black Lives Matter signs are placed in front of churches and on lawns outside some of the homes in her neighborhood. Those signs pro-claim something that has not always been obvious in a country where a history of bond-age, bias, and bloodshed has belied the grand assertion that "all men are created equal." That "truth" has not been self-evident in America. Certainly not in the world of adoption.

Now, I know that honest conversations about race can make people uncomfortable or send them into retreat—especially when America is teetering on a knife-edge about matters of race. But honestly, I hope reading about this does make you squirm. It should make all of us queasy, particularly since there are other ways to incentivize families to par-ticipate in adoption. Some agencies in states like Nevada, New York, Ohio, Florida, and Massachusetts have used a sliding scale for fees based on the adoptive family's income. But sadly, after more than twenty years of tracking this issue, there are still pockets within the adoption industry where these discounts stay in place, even though almost everyone cites broad disdain.

"You have to think about supply and demand, even if it turns some people's stomachs," said Elizabeth Raleigh, a professor of sociology at Carleton College and author of the book *Selling Transracial Adoption*. Raleigh is herself a transracial adoptee, born in Korea and raised by White parents in Massachusetts. She says the market forces of supply and demand are not the only reasons agencies have offered what she calls the "dark-skinned discount."

The agencies themselves have served up a constellation of excuses. In some cases, the tiered system was introduced to make the expensive process of adoption more afford-able to a wider range of families—especially families of color, who are more likely to participate in foster parenting or informal kinship adoptions, where families take in children of direct or distant relatives. (It should be noted that White families, despite this recruiting effort, still represent 90 percent of international adoptions, and almost 80 percent of domestic adoptions.) The fees for Black children are lower, some agencies say, because African American birth mothers tend to be poorer and therefore qualify for Medicaid and other forms of assistance. They posit that this lowers the overall adoption fee because the government is sometimes footing part of the bill.

Conversely, some agencies have argued that the fee structure for White, Asian, and Latino children is higher because adoption facilitators have to spend more money on advertising and recruitment to find pregnant White mothers interested in adoption. However, one snag seems to refute this assertion. Some of the agencies still apply the discount if pregnant White, Latino, Asian, or Native American mothers give birth to a part-Black biracial child. It's like the old one-drop rule. Black lineage of any kind means Black categorization.

Raleigh notes that some adoption providers justified the two-tiered system by saying that Black children (full Black and biracial) were harder to place because fewer families were willing to participate in transracial adoption. But she and other adoption scholars scoff at that logic. They argue that, under traditional market standards, the extra work done by agencies finding homes for allegedly "hard-to-place" children (more staff hours, bookkeeping, and operating expenses) would be passed on to the consumer in terms of higher fees. "When agencies implement tiered pricing schemas, it is never the easy-to-place White children who cost less; instead, they cost more—a lot more," Raleigh asserts in her book.

How much more? When the Lantz family was going through their adoption process more than a decade ago, they were told to expect that fees for adopting a White child would be in the $35,000 range, not including legal expenses and travel. But when the calls started to come in for Black children, the fees quoted were between $12,000 and $18,000.

One of the saddest things about the discounting of Black babies is how neatly it fits into the narrative of American history and the devaluation of Black lives in their youngest stages. The demeaning characterization of Black children as pickaninnies, criminals, and menaces to society. The idyllic portrayal over centuries of childhood innocence as the sole province of children with snowy skin. And in modern culture, the drumbeat of news stories and cultural tropes in which Black children are overcriminalized, oversexualized, and overexaggerated as threats instead of being represented as treasures.

• • •

In June 2013, I produced a radio feature about the 6-word submission "Black babies cost less to adopt" for NPR's *Morning Edition*, as part of a series of conversations about The Race Card Project. We featured Caryn Ward Lantz in that story. And though she and her husband eventually adopted two Black sons from Nevada—a state where fees for adoptions are often based on the family's income, rather than the race of the children—Caryn explained in detail how they navigated the race-based discounts.

I knew the story would have an impact on listeners. After all, I never forgot the way those six words hit me. What my NPR producer, Walter Ray Watson, and I did not fully comprehend until years later was the impact the discussion would have on the adoption industry.

Radio is a powerful medium, enveloping a listener with the aural intimacy of the human voice. But it was a feature of the accompanying online story on the NPR website that really shook the audience: a screen grab from one of the agency's listings of "available adoption situations," where it was all spelled out in black-and-white.

The segment drew an avalanche of response, and in the years since, audiences often gasp audibly if I give a lecture that includes those six words: "Black babies cost less to adopt." But only when I was doing research for this book did I fully understand the hand-wringing caused within the industry when journalists, pundits, and bloggers suddenly turned the spotlight on the fairly common practice of applying that dark-skinned discount. Disturbed by the fallout, some agencies dispensed of the two-tiered system altogether, but some just took the practice behind a paywall. Only those who have formally registered can see the fees for available adoptions.

• • •

"Since that broadcast and the outrage that followed, racial pricing seems to have gone underground," Raleigh notes in her book. But it has not gone away. Though not as common as it used to be, the discomfort and the discount continue.

Over time, the supply-and-demand market forces that contributed to that so-called dark-skinned discount have lurched in significant ways that created something closer to parity within pricing structures. Adopting a baby of any race is much more difficult and much more expensive across the board than it was two decades ago. Part of that is due to a greater emphasis on family-reunification efforts that seek to help mothers find the support they need to keep custody of their biological children. Another factor is the steep drop in international adoptions as countries such as Russia, China, Guatemala, Ethiopia, and South Korea have instituted much more restrictive policies. At the peak, in 2004, there were almost 22,987 international adoptions, according to State Department records. By 2021, that number had dropped to 1,785—a 92 percent decline.

Cultural forces have changed, as well. Magazines are filled with celebrities and their African American children. And same-sex couples have stepped into the market in large numbers and in many cases showed a greater willingness to participate enthusiastically in transracial adoption.

The discomfort or outright shame over a system that discounted dark babies may have helped tamp down on the practice, but in the end, the thing that made the biggest difference was the combination of cultural trends and a closing of the border for international adoption.

"The market forces have changed things," said Michelle Hughes, a longtime adoption lawyer based in Chicago who asserts that the pool of available adoptions has shrunk so much that it doesn't make financial sense for agencies to offer discounts as incentives. "If I'm an agency, why am I going to discount if I don't need to?" she said.

So, why do some outfits still do it?

Caucasian baby due late October: $28K + $8 in legals

Biracial (AA/NA) girl due August 18th: $22.5K + $2.5 legals + medical

African American baby due any day: $17K + legals

(Data for available adoption situations posted online when the story first ran in 2013)

. . .

Pulling this unfortunate aspect of adoption out of the shadows helped lead to uncomfortable, yet necessary, conversations. But this is not just about process. Ultimately, it is about people, and this is where I once again feel something akin to a jab to the ribs.

I remember meeting a sharply dressed young Black woman on a college campus in Oregon. She complimented my work and said she'd been following The Race Card Project for some time. Then she paused for a moment before offering up some personal information. "You know, I'm adopted," she said, before giving me a look I still remember but can't adequately describe. It wasn't anger. It wasn't anguish. It was something in the way the smile faded from her face as if to say, "I know who you are and I know what you did and I live with how that made me feel."

I still feel the ice just recalling that story. You see, stoking a national conversation about the discount means putting the spotlight on the people—the children—to whom that discount is applied.

Angela Tucker has experienced the adoption process from all sides. A transracial adoptee in a transracial family, she has worked inside the system as a caseworker and outside it as an activist, mentor, speaker, and consultant on shows such as NBC's *This Is Us*. Her search for her biological parents was detailed in the documentary *Closure*, and she hosts a popular podcast called *The Adoptee Next Door*.

The discount expressed in that initial letter to her adoptive family hovers over Angela's life.

Angela is Black. She was a ward of the state of Tennessee for nearly a year before being adopted by White parents at eleven months old. She joined a family in Washington State with seven other children that included a combination of her new parents' adopted and biological kids. As an adult, she obtained her adoption records, including a letter the agency had sent to her parents.

"Our fee for Angela would normally be $5,000, but since she has special needs, we'll lower that [and] will also take into account your current income and the number of adopted kids already in your home," the letter read. "We'll invoice you for $1,500, but we'd be glad to receive a thousand. Let me know if you'd like to negotiate this further?"

Angela was sickened but not surprised because of her experience working in the adoption business. Processing that letter and its descending series of ever-lower discounts is now part of her therapy, she says, and it fuels her work to improve the adoption process. "It's hard to bear otherwise," she says. Asked if she thinks the intent behind the letter was altruistic, her answer is blunt.

"I think it was lazy," she says, almost spitting out the words. As an infant, Angela was diagnosed as having spastic quadriplegia, a subset of cerebral palsy in which brain damage has disrupted normal muscle function. "I don't have spastic quadriplegia," she says. "I never did, but I did have a lot of tightness in my body because of my birth mother's inability to care for herself during my pregnancy and the drugs she used."

Over time, Angela's body loosened. She excelled in school, was a standout athlete, played basketball in college, and now runs a successful consulting business. The only remnants of the conditions that led to that early, incorrect diagnosis are the small hearing aids she wears. Of all the potential parents who passed on her, Angela says, "I turned out to be what many parents want."

And yet, the discount expressed in that initial letter to her adoptive family hovers over Angela's life as a reminder of how the world first greeted her. She does a lot of mentoring work with young adoptees, and she knows both from her experience as an adoptee and her history as a caseworker that many will yearn for details of their origin stories. And in seeking those details, they often want to know specific information about their adoption fees.

"Many adoptees have this question on our minds, 'But how much did I cost?' That comes up in our head a lot because we're really trying to figure out how did this happen," Angela says. "Parents usually respond by saying something like, 'You know, we had to pay an agency a lot of fees for overhead because they needed to process paperwork. They had to hire staff.' They will go around the issue by softening it.

"And so, when . . . adoptees start talking to each other and comparing stories, that's when they start to realize, 'Oh, it differs from family to family.' And so, some of my Black adoptees find out about the difference in their fee and the process itself, and their parents kind of stutter around the issue."

Deesha Philyaw is an author and adoptive parent who has written about the thorny aspects of adoption—especially when race is involved. Her mantra is that the facts of someone's adoption, regardless of how jagged the storyline may be, should not define their worth. "Even without the price conversation, it's not uncommon for adoptees to feel like, no matter how you frame the narrative, that they were given away, that they weren't viewed as valuable," Philyaw says. "The shame of it, the crime of it, lives within our society. It is not a reflection of their worth as people. It's a trauma before you even get to talking about the money part. But just for them to know the brokenness belongs to the system. What our society has allowed to be, that's the fault of the system, and it's no reflection on them."

•   •   •

Remember Dawn Friedman and her husband, Brett—the White couple from Ohio advised to take advantage of the price cut for Black children? The couple that wound up adopting a biracial newborn? That child's name is Maddi, and she's now nineteen.

"I've been told right from birth my story about being adopted," says Maddi, "and I feel very fortunate because it's a very, very complicated one."

Maddi's parents saved all their paperwork from the adoption process, including a brochure about the two-tiered race-based system, and they kept it in a box with Maddi's baby booties and other keepsakes. As soon as Maddi was old enough, Dawn told her daughter about her origin story, including the fee discrepancies. She says she wanted Maddi to learn about it in an environment where she was surrounded by people who loved her.

"When my mom first told me, she didn't sit me down or anything," Maddi says. "It just kind of came up, like, just another way that the system has failed Brown people in general." The adoption industry "is such a disgusting thing," she says, "because it's profiting off people's situations."

Maddi still feels anger at a system that places a discount on babies who look like her, though she refuses to let that define her. But that doesn't mean it doesn't hurt. It's a wound she tries hard to ignore. "I can joke about it now," she says, displaying a gallows humor. If her mom refuses a request to buy something at the grocery store, Maddi will pleadingly tease, "You should buy me these cookies because I was half off!" Mother and daughter are able to laugh about it, but I can't help but wonder what other shoppers listening in the aisle must think of that conversation and the giggles that ensue. For Maddi's family, it's a sign that they've learned to roll through life's storms. Yet as well-adjusted as her family seems to be, Maddi says "adoptees are also survivors of trauma."

Among the challenges she has faced is the constant feeling of being an outsider—not Black enough for people who look like her, but always fielding stares when traveling with her parents and their older biological son. "I would go to my Black friends' houses or be in a part of the community where I was supposed to fit in and look like these people," she says. But "I always just felt like I was pretending in a way." She felt ashamed that she didn't fit in, especially as a child. "When I go home, I'm not going home to my Black mom. So, I felt like an outsider in my own culture, which was really, really difficult."

Her parents did what they could, particularly on the sometimes tricky subject of Black hair. "Hair has been a pretty big challenge," Maddi says, laughing. "I would go out with my dad places, and he didn't really know how to do my hair. So, we always kept rubber bands in the car for him to just really quickly pull my hair up into a bun. Because the only person who did [my hair] was my mom, and when she didn't do it, it was a little looking like a bird's nest."

Maddi wishes adoption agencies would focus more on educating parents in transracial adoptions. "I think when placing a child, you have to know that that family's going to be willing to learn," she says. "And I don't think it's helpful to have the attitude of sweeping something under the rug, or color blindness . . . because, you know, that is a child's life and that is their experience, and it's really easy to feel out of place."

• • •

Transracial adoption has always had its critics. It was outlawed for years when anti-miscegenation laws were common across America in the all-out effort to prevent "race mixing," and later came under harsh criticism from people like the scholar Dorothy Roberts, whose studies find that a disproportionate number of Black children were being torn away from their families for infractions that would elicit more empathy or family reunification efforts in White communities.

The National Association of Black Social Workers also decried the rise in transracial adoption, releasing a strongly worded policy statement in 1972 claiming that Black children raised in White homes and White communities were "cut off from the healthy development of themselves as Black people." Some of the organization's leaders likened that loss to a kind of cultural genocide.

Maddi still feels anger at a system that places a discount on babies who look like her.

Yet today, transracial adoption is a fact of life. In the five decades since the social workers decried the practice, it has become common, it has become normal, and we are likely to see more of it without debate or fanfare. Over the last fifteen years, transracial adoptions have increased by more than 50 percent. Ninety percent of Asian adoptees, 62 percent of Hispanic adoptees, and 55 percent of Black adoptees are raised by a parent of a different race.

If you dig a little deeper into the numbers, the story around transracial adoption of Black children becomes more complex. While there's been a significant increase in the number of Asian, Hispanic, and multiracial adoptees, the number of Black adoptees has dropped by 61 percent. Even so, Black children are overrepresented among children living in foster care or with relatives other than their parents.

Behind all these figures is the cohort of families willing to open their homes and hearts to adoptive children. That group is overwhelmingly White (77 percent) and tends to be older, better educated, and more financially secure than parents raising their own biological children in America.

The rise in transracial adoption is generally presented as proof of progress, and I tend to agree with that view. It represents an important shift in racial attitudes and ensures that children who might otherwise languish in the system have the opportunity to find loving homes. But transracial adoptees in many cases have a more cautious outlook, imploring the agencies that handle adoptions and the families that decide to travel down that path to take a more realistic and courageous attitude toward understanding the challenges such adoptees will face.

Asked if the growth of transracial adoption was a sign of progress, Tucker answers emphatically. "No, no, it's not good at all," she says, which may be surprising to anyone who has tracked her success as an adoption advocate and consultant. Everything about Angela's presentation—big Afro, dazzling smile, fashion-forward clothes, high-profile projects with her equally accomplished filmmaker husband, tell-it-like-it-is success in the media world—suggests that she has made it. But the scars are there if you look closely, she says, because she spent so much time cut off from her own culture, surrounded by people who didn't understand her hair, her standards of beauty, her cultural interests, and her potential.

A child of color shouldn't be a family's only non-White acquaintance, nor should he or she be their first.

"It's just an incredible amount of cultural loss for a whole generation of folks who would say, 'I don't know where I belong,' and the adoptee suicide rate is really high, and I attribute that to the loss of culture, belonging, to feeling like a token, to the incredible pressure put on these kids to be like a spokesperson for their race because they're so alienated, all the while their parents get a lot of praise," Angela says.

As part of her consulting, Angela works with prospective transracial families to help them prepare for bringing children of another race into their homes. She's held workshops where parents invite up to eighty members of their community—friends, family, neighbors, teachers, coaches, fellow congregants, and even local shop owners—to prepare them, too. You have no doubt heard the proverb that "it takes a village" to raise a child. Angela takes that to heart.

"It's because the neighbors need to know, or when the kid goes out to coffee or gets a hot chocolate with their aunt, their aunt needs to be able to be prepared—to have conversations with the barista, who says, you know, 'Where'd you get them?' or, 'How much did they cost?,' which people do ask."

The research on long-term outcomes for transracial adoptees is somewhat muddled. Some studies show higher rates of dysfunction and mental health challenges for adoptees who have limited contact with their biological parents or links to their ethnic or racial culture.

But one thing is clear: the growth in transracial adoption needs to be coupled with a greater effort to ensure that families who adopt across color lines understand the challenges that will most certainly come their way.

This is a sentiment expressed not just by Black adoptees, but by Native, Latino, and Asian adoptees who get caught in a swirl of cultural crosscurrents. All the color-blind love in the world won't adequately prepare transracial adoptees for the color-specific quandaries, questions, assumptions, and outright bias they will likely face in life. Nor will it help them embrace, elevate, and revel in the glorious aspects of their root cultures that may not be evident or attainable when they are always the outliers in their communities.

In too many cases, out of discomfort or naivete, there seems to be an effort to excise any examination of the meaning and impact of race in transracial adoptions. But a child of color shouldn't be a family's only non-White acquaintance, nor should he or she be their first. The impulse to be color-blind, as altruistic as it might seem, erases a crucial part of a child's identity and lineage and fails to prepare that child for a world where people not only see color, but make both intentional and implicit decisions based on it.

Imagine the difficulty you'd have navigating your town's streets if you didn't pay attention to flashing red or green lights as you approached an intersection. I wish people would think about that when they're inclined to say, "I don't see color." Seeing color doesn't mean conceding to racism.

I say this not as an outsider wagging a finger at adoptive parents whose lives I could never fully understand. I have too much respect for parents, and especially adoptive parents, to try to dictate rules of engagement. I share it as someone who has spent more than ten years listening to transracial adoptees and biracial children talk about their challenges and the changes they desperately want to see.

Pediatricians will sometimes tell young parents to get down on their knees and navigate their homes, to understand where toddlers might roam into dangers, such as running into sharp edges on coffee tables or reaching for knobs on cabinets full of toxic cleaning products. A similar effort perhaps should be made to understand the world that awaits a child from another cultural realm. Because what seems like a great school or a fantastic neighborhood might look different if viewed from the perspective of a child who's always the only lonely presence in that world.

• • •

In our national conversation about adoption, the voices that are most muted are those of mothers who give their children up for adoption, and that is true when it comes to the use of lower fees to help find homes for children of color. In some cases, birth mothers have no idea their children are placed in a discounted category.

In that Ohio household where Dawn and Brett and their nineteen-year-old adoptive daughter, Maddi, decided to have an open conversation about the discrepancy in fees for adopting Black children, they are well aware of a cruel irony. The last person in their extended family circle to learn about the so-called dark-skinned discount was the person who birthed Maddi in the first place. The agency, which has since ceased operating, never bothered to tell Jessica Boutte.

Jessica had no idea that her child would be adopted for less money than other children when she agreed to work with an adoption agency. She was a high school student in Washington State coping with an unplanned pregnancy. She would eventually give birth to a child who would find a loving home halfway across the country.

"My daughter's conception was not a consensual one," Jessica says quietly. "The week I graduated high school, I went to a party. I got separated from the group. And the next thing I remember is hearing a garbage truck back up and smelling like I had been dumped into a garbage can."

Jessica got herself to an emergency room, where the police and hospital staff confirmed that she had been sexually assaulted. "And I was just kind of left out to the world after that," she says. When she found out she was pregnant, she had little support from her family. "That was a journey that I had to kind of go through on my own."

Her father was "very disappointed in me," she says. He implied that she was at fault for having been "in the wrong place at the wrong time." It hurt his pride that his daughter had suffered an assault, since he was serving in law enforcement at the time. Jessica and her mother never discussed it. "Everybody was just kind of OK with it being a thing they didn't have to address," she says. "The weight of all of it just kind of fell on me.

"I have struggled a lot with why I became pregnant after this traumatic event happened to me," Jessica says, "and I always tried to think positive even when things were really bad." She kept in mind a quote she'd read, something to the effect that every negative event has some kind of positive outcome, and every positive event has a negative one. So, when she realized she was pregnant, she decided to create something positive out of that.

"Instead of going to have my pregnancy aborted, I thought, 'There's a lot of people out here in this world who can't have children, who want them, who deserve them.'" She decided to give her child up for adoption.

The adoption agency "had some very predatory practices that I didn't realize," Jessica says. They gave her gift cards to buy products she'd need during pregnancy, then warned her that if she changed her mind about giving up her baby, she'd have to reimburse the agency for all she spent. "At the time, I was homeless," she says. "So that wasn't something I could do."

The agency also never explained the options that might have allowed her ultimately to keep her baby. "I wasn't told until we were in the hospital . . . that I had the option to place her into foster care until I got myself together to take her," she says. When Jessica asked why she hadn't been told this, the adoption worker said, "That's just the small print," before reminding Jessica again, right there in the hospital, that if she changed her mind, she'd have to immediately reimburse the agency for the cost of everything she'd been given during her pregnancy.

"My nineteen-year-old mind went into adoption very naively, not understanding the long-term effects that it would have on myself, my family, my child," she says. "I didn't think about any of that. It was just, like, panic mode for me. And I believe that my adoption agency preyed on that, and here we are." She laughs dryly.

"That's just the small print."

Jessica said she didn't understand that adoption was "an industry." And though she was estranged from her family during her pregnancy, there were no clear risk factors that someone might try to use to justify an automatic discount for her child. (As if it's ever justifiable.) She was healthy. She was a good student. She came from a middle-class family.

Though Jessica had hoped to place her newborn with a Black family, her options presented by the agency were limited. She ended up choosing a White couple—Dawn and Brett. And while she respects and appreciates the stable and loving home environment they gave her child, Maddi, she feels that Black families don't get the same opportunities. "I think there are Black families that want to adopt, but the opportunities to do so are not as open to them as [to] White families." The cost can be an impediment. And adoption is a sector where agents are called upon to make judgments about lifestyles, language, and fitness of duty. And since so many of the caseworkers, lawyers, home inspectors, and office staff are White, those judgments can get complicated when directed at families of other races.

In the end, Jessica's adoption process didn't go quite as she expected, but in Dawn, a Jewish White woman, she met someone who felt like a partner. Unlike in most adoptions, Jessica had frequent contact with Dawn, the adoptive mother. In fact, the two women grew close even before the birth. "I had maybe three months left to my pregnancy, and

Dawn and I talked on the phone as family members," Jessica says. "When I went into labor, the first person I called was Dawn."

Jessica has been impressed by how hard Dawn works to provide the cultural support Maddi needs. "Dawn knows how to cornrow hair," she says. "I don't know how to do that. I've been asking her to do my hair forever," Jessica says with a chuckle. "She did the work to try to find out those things and to make sure that her Black daughter didn't miss out on those parts of being a Black child."

Jessica came to realize that Dawn's efforts were unusual in the adoptive world. And beyond that, she perceived that these added layers of work and cultural acclimation were part of the reason behind the fee differential for Black babies.

Dawn Friedman candidly admits that the price cut they were offered made a difference.

"When people want to add children to their families," she says, "if they're all the same color, it's less questions . . . and I would assume that there would be some sort of premium pricing for that. Like new car versus used car. I'm not saying that it's right, but I would assume that would be the mindset around it. And I think that this country, the way that we're treated . . . I believe it reflects a value system," she says.

So, what advice would she give to those who work in the adoption industry?

"I would ask them to consider the long-term damage, which that type of mindset and practice can cause," she says, "not only for the children but for the mothers that are placing their children with these agencies." She admits to feeling "just a little bit spiteful" about it, adding that "if I passed my caseworker in the street today, she wouldn't know who I was. So, maybe consider these human beings over the bottom line or whatever bonuses you'll receive to place children. . . . Think about the human part of it."

All the same, she feels fortunate with how her own story has turned out. "My daughter's adoptive parents have always considered me as a human being and a person who brought their child into this world," she says. "Like I'm part of the unit of parents. And I'm very grateful that that was my situation." Too many adoptive parents, she says, have a "savior complex, like they saved this child from this life and these people. And I feel like that mindset needs just to stop."

Jessica also feels fortunate about one other part of her story. Her father, who reacted to her assault and teenage pregnancy by telling Jessica she was "in the wrong place at the wrong time," had an evolution of the heart. For years, he showed very little interest in his granddaughter Maddi. But when Jessica's brother got married, Dawn and Maddi flew out to attend the wedding as family. "My dad got to meet Madison for the first time," she says. "And then I feel like that changed his whole mind about the adoption."

Unbeknownst to Jessica, her father established his own relationship with Dawn and Maddi—a connection that sadly ended in February 2021, when he was killed in the line of duty. It wasn't until the following July, five months after his death, that Jessica came to realize just how close her father had become to his granddaughter.

Jessica's great-uncle passed away around July Fourth, and Madison flew to Washington State and stayed for the summer. Jessica said her "aunts called and tried to introduce themselves to her. And Madison said, 'I already know who all of you are.'" Jessica laughs at the memory of what Maddi said next. "'Grandpa Michael has been sending me pictures.' She was able to name everybody who was on the phone, and all of us just started crying. It was a really beautiful gift that he left all of us.

"He did a lot of work to build a family tree for her," Jessica says, "because somehow he understood the importance of that for her." This triad of stories—of the adoptive parents, the adoptee, and the birth mother who gave up a child—shows the triumph and the heartbreak in adoption. Yet they also underscore a painful reality. You see, here's the thing about that discount for the adoption of Black babies: it can be effective.

The option to save money in an expensive adoption process does create new options and new pathways. Dawn Friedman candidly admits that the price cut they were offered made a difference. At a time when she and her husband were in the early stages of their careers, it made adoption more affordable—less expensive, even, than the insurance costs when she delivered her biological son.

For the adoption industry, the discount for minority children was a useful but noxious instrument. Its gradual decline is justly heralded as a long-overdue correction, but as with almost anything linked to adoption across color lines, there are complexities that are compounded by race. The same laws of supply and demand that are helping to even out the variegated fee structure have also caused the overall fee structure for adoptions to soar. Fees and legal costs from agencies can push the price tag somewhere between $45,000 and $50,000. And a new crop of so-called "facilitators" have entered the process, sometimes charging as much as $25,000.

Adoption is now too expensive for a wide swath of people, and many of those families locked out of the process are communities of color. "So, when you ask me, is it better or worse that there's no longer a uniform differential—one could argue both ways," says adoption attorney Michelle Hughes. It's progress, to be sure, but there's a big asterisk, she says. "I would argue that if you look at it from a Black perspective, if you adopted twenty years ago, that discount meant I could afford to adopt a child that looked like me. The effect is that Black babies are not as likely to get Black families. There are a lot of Black families that want to adopt, and they get priced out," Hughes said.

That barrier to entry often applies to Latinos, Native Americans, and anyone who does not have deep savings, big salaries, or generational wealth. Those families that cannot afford adoption often move toward the foster-care system instead, and when all works well, children find loving and supportive homes. But foster care is a temporary commitment.

. . .

The so-called dark-skinned discount may be in decline, but it has not disappeared, and its memory and lingering reality should haunt us.

It is an offense explained as some kind of necessary adjustment, a ranking that stinks of bias even as it offers the hope of loving arms, an assumption based both on indelicate facts and enduring attitudes about Black life, Black motherhood, and what is presumed to be a dim trajectory for Black children.

It is also a mirror that reflects back to us a landscape much broader than just the adoption industry. When Black babies cost less to adopt over decades, that's an indictment of a system and of a society that fails to recognize the shimmering possibility in a newborn Black baby's eyes, regardless of the circumstances of that child's birth.

My Children jumpstarted my racial identity

Johnny • Concord, MA

As a gay Asian man married to a White man with two adopted children of color (one Black, one Latino), I came to understand my own racial identity through the experience of welcoming our two children into our family. It's taught me that to really provide a strong racial identity for my children, parents need to do the work themselves—including White parents.

My race does not define me

Kristin • Palm Bay, FL

I was put up for adoption before I was even born. A loving White family of seven took me in and treated me, a mixed-race infant, as their own. They soon adopted a Black child so that I could have a sibling my age to grow up with—they were always thinking about what was best for all of us kids. . . . I'm a very lucky person. I'd like to say I'm sorry to all my family for everything they endured because of adopting me and my brother. I'm sorry that both of my parents' families disowned them. The last thing my dad said to his family after they told him that I would never be one of them, was "Get the f*ck out of my house." I'm sorry the Catholic church shunned them and kicked us all out.

My very religious parents never stepped foot in a church again because they felt so betrayed. I'm sorry for the big black cars that sat outside our home watching us. I'm sorry for the crosses that were burned in our yard. I'm sorry for all the eyes that turned our way in disbelief and disgust. But I'd also like to say thank you. Thank you for bringing me into a fantastic family. Thank you to my dad's brother and very Irish mother, who stuck by my dad and his decisions. Thank you to my sisters, who took me to show-and-tell. Thank you to my brothers, who always joked, "You know, we can always return you if you don't stop crying"—that would always make me laugh. Thank you to the one pastor from the church that gave us the boot, who baptized me in a warehouse and wrote a caring letter to me that I still have to this day. Thank you, family, for making sure I knew how much you loved me and how special I am. Thank you for pushing me to be the best I can be. Thank you for teaching me that race is not important. Thank you for loving me for me and giving me a chance to grow up in a loving, caring family environment.

May I please touch his hair?

Ryan Harrell • Holland, MI

Our adoptive son, Tagg, clearly is not a biological member of our family. In his two years with us, we have encountered the entire range of reactions from loving acceptance to ignorant comments to outright disgust and disdain. But through it all, the fact is that we represent the new reality of the hodgepodge of racial and familial identities that is the United States. And the most common reaction we get, whether at church, in line at the grocery store, or at a playground, makes us laugh and enjoy the humor in *everything*: "May I please touch his hair?"

Closed adoption: racial mystery and more

Linda Spoon • Wellsville, PA

I enjoy being a grab bag

Melissa • Holland, MI

I was adopted at three days old and know nothing of my biological heritage. I enjoy feeling as if I'm a mixture of many different ethnicities.

At least my mother is real.

Shoshi Shaw • Denver, CO

In middle school, I saw nothing wrong with being honest about my past, so anyone who asked I would tell, "I'm adopted." One day in math, I was correcting a classmate's work on the whiteboard, and on my way back to my seat, I heard the boy say under his breath, "At least my mother is real."

He's American. Why do you ask?
Terry Savage • Kailua, HI

This was my standard response when "insignificant others" inquired about our then very young adopted son's origins.

White. Wait, no! Turns out Cherokee
Stephanie McCleery • Portland, OR

Adopted at birth, assumed White, found out one-fourth Cherokee at age forty when I found *my* birth mother.

Cousin's adopted Guatemalan, still my family
Annabell Standfor • Louisville, KY

She is more American than me
Judy Goffena Boogman • Billings, MT

When I was young, there was a girl adopted by a couple in my small hometown in Montana. She was Native American and her parents were not. Matter of fact, the whole town was not. She seemed angry and out of place. One day I was waiting on the courthouse lawn on Main Street. My mom was probably inside. Robin, the girl, was also sitting there on the grass. The next thing I know, I am facedown, and Robin is sitting on me with my arm pulled behind my back. She demands that I declare out loud that she is more American than me. I had to shout it loudly, and then she was gone. I have always wanted to tell her that I believed she was right.

Who does your little girl's hair?
Ernest Fabrizio Garcia • New Fairfield, CT

Neither of us are African American, but our children are. There seems to be a conception that doing Black hair well is partially genetic.

International Adoptee. Parents praised. Children unwelcome.
Lindsay Van Nostrand • USA

I'm still discovering who I am
Barry Kyrklund • Flowery Branch, GA

White dad, Black son, daily frontiers

Rick Kraske • Las Vegas, NV

We adopted our son Joshua as an infant. His mom, also White, and I later divorced. He is now twelve, and his understanding of race in America is now growing at a rapid pace as he is reminded of the manner in which he is treated with us and away from us.

Will I ever meet my mom?

Colin McKearnan • Missoula, MT

A question that my eight-year-old son asked me on the way to school. We are White, and my wife and I adopted him and his brother from Ethiopia seven years ago. We also have two birth children.

Adopted Black son; more confused now

Andrew • Tacoma, WA

We adopted our son when he was two weeks old. He's seven now. My naivete about race has only gotten clearer and clearer these last seven years.

Family matters; race, not at all

Phyllis Kedl • Little Canada, MN

Ours is a multiethnic family. We have fourteen grandkids, only five of whom are ethnically related to us. The rest? Two African American, three Hispanic, and four Chinese. We are anything but vanilla, and I wouldn't have it any other way.

You'll find your real parents someday.

Alessa Abruzzo • Philadelphia, PA

Biologically I'm Korean. Ethnically I'm Irish German Italian. I was adopted at four and a half months old, at which point I flew from South Korea to the USA and into the loving arms of my parents, who happen to be White. To put it plainly, I was raised by White people. My entire immediate family (and most of the extensions) are of European ancestry. I really hate having to go into the Asian enclaves of the city to do certain grocery shopping or go to certain restaurants.

Conversations always start with questions. "You [insert East Asian race here]?" (No to everything but Korean.) "Oh, you're Korean! You speak Korean?" (No, I'm adopted, and my parents are White.) "Ah, adopted!" And then comes the polite nod, the comforting pat on the shoulder, the smile that's supposed to tell me that it *will* be all right, even though it's currently not. "You'll find your *real* parents someday!"

That's the instant I'm reminded that race, what's on the outside, is what's "real." Ethnicity is learned, culture is a side effect of being around people. But race is skin-deep, which is as far as most people look at first glance. My parents can't be real because we don't look alike. Real is apparently over 6,500 miles away, in the faces of two people I've never really met. That's race for you.

You two are such good people

Erin Morris • Tempe, AZ

My husband and I have two sons adopted from South Korea. When people feel compelled to mention our race difference or the obvious fact that our children are adopted, it is often along the lines of what "good people" we are, or how "lucky" our children are to have been adopted and brought to the US. This line of reasoning disgusts me.

The world is overpopulated, and there are children sitting in foster care and orphanages around the world who have little to no chance of having a supportive family structure. Yet, many Americans spend years and tens of thousands of dollars to conceive babies that are genetic matches to themselves through a variety of unnatural medical procedures.

No news story on infertility, IVF, Clomid, or surrogacy should be complete without mention of the other option to becoming a parent: adoption. It is unfortunate that people who face infertility by adopting their children should be viewed as "such good people."

Yes, they really are my children

Corrie Bugby • Murray, UT

I am a Caucasian woman who adopted three African American sons. I love them. I cherish everything about them. And I hate it when people assume that they aren't my children. Like the woman who asked me, "Don't you think you'd love a biological child more?" I have come to embrace their ethnicity as a part of my own life. And I am a better person for it. And with open adoptions, their birth families are now a part of my family, too. People say that my kids are lucky to have me. . . . No, I'm the lucky one.

I am not what you see

James Moore • Sterling, VA

No one told me when I adopted my baby girl that I was no longer White. I had to find out the hard way. One friend at a time. Sadly.

Needing to introduce myself as "adopted"

Anonymous • Morris, MN

Black babies cost less to adopt

Heidi Gold • Germantown, WI

When my spouse and I began the adoption process in 2011 with a national agency, I was shocked to discover that the fees for domestic adoption were subsidized if we adopted an African American child. It broke my heart. When completing our questionnaire, we were open to adopting a child of any race or ethnicity. Our first match was a biracial Black and White baby boy, but [it did not work out]. We've since adopted two children of mixed races who appear Caucasian. I often reflect on how our lives would be if our first adoption was successful and often pray for the well-being of that baby boy, who is now nine years old. He will always be in my heart.

I am conflicted on whether acknowledging my children's heritage (Alaskan Native/Caucasian and Mexican/Caucasian) on census forms or other forms is exploitation since they will likely benefit from White privilege being raised by White parents and will likely be assumed to be White due to their appearances.

A transnational adoptee, consumed by "in-betweenity."

Rebecca York • Takoma Park, MD

Fighting for visibility and validity, in White and of-color spaces, is perpetually exhausting. Transnational adoptees are at the heart of America's racial, cultural, and nationalistic legislation and cultural beliefs. Stop gatekeeping and let us join the conversation.

CHINESE ADOPTEE
WITH TWO WHITE MOMS

Ting Goodfriend • Austin, TX

TING GOODFRIEND'S 6-WORD STORY is simple and descriptive. It explains who she is. Or more specifically, who she is to the outside world. That is the story she settled on when a professor at Willamette University asked the class to think about their 6-word stories. In truth, Ting had a hard time figuring out what to write. She thought about it for a day or two, and she zeroed in on a feeling she couldn't shake.

"I held a little bit of shame," she says. "And though I wasn't blaming my parents or anything like that, it just felt a little . . . off-putting for a minute." She decided to include a bit of backstory with her submission to explain:

"Growing up in a White household and being told to be proud of my identity from a White narrative has made the journey of my personal identification extremely hard. I'm too White to feel comfortable with my Chinese identity, but too Chinese to feel at home in White society."

Ting and her older sister, Dawn, both adopted from China, grew up with two White moms in Austin, Texas. "My parents did a really good job of trying to surround us with families that were similar to ours," she says—meaning White parents with Asian adoptive kids. During Chinese New Year, the girls would get dressed up and go to celebrations sponsored by an organization called Families with Children from China. "It felt like pretending," Ting says. "I would put on this costume and go to the event and then put on my 'normal'—like, White—clothes." She felt a split between her Chinese identity and what she calls "the rest of my identity."

"It's a weird dynamic because I am definitely more comfortable within White society and being around a majority of White people," she says, "because that reflects the environment that I grew up in." But at the same time, "There's always something that I can pinpoint about myself that differs from that kind of homogenous group."

She cites her name as one example. For about six months after she was adopted, her parents called her Ruth. But the name didn't seem to fit, so they reverted to her given name, Ting. "I always feel slightly insecure about it," she says. After growing up in an anglicized culture, she says the name to her own ear sounds "kind of funny, like a sound effect." It is a badge that screams "different" and "aggressively identifies me as 'other,'" she says. So, sometimes she removes that badge. When she goes to Starbucks, she never uses her real name. Instead, when the barista asks her name, she chirps out her sister's name, Dawn. "For the longest time, I just kind of disconnected from my Chinese identity," she says. Her parents, hoping to help Ting and Dawn reconnect to their Chinese roots, sent them to a program the sisters dubbed "Chinese culture camp."

The first time they went, when Ting was about six, she found the experience overwhelming. She and Dawn were put into an auditorium with hundreds of other children adopted from China, and counselors talked with them about Chinese culture. The kids were separated into age groups, and Ting remembers having lessons on how to use chopsticks. "We'd play games where we would move a bowl of M&Ms with chopsticks, from one bowl to another," she says.

Ting went to the camp for two or three years, and she hated it every time. "I remember telling my parents, 'I don't want to go to this. It is horrible. I don't like anyone there,'" she says. It wasn't that she didn't like the activities. It was that she felt so much more disconnected from her Chinese identity than the other kids. "I don't want to be talking about these things," she recalls, "especially with these people." Why them in particular? "We just had nothing in common," Ting says. Which is evidence in itself of how disconnected she felt because all the kids at the camp had at least one indelible and life-shaping experience in common: being adopted from China by an American family.

One of the problems with the camp was that, because campers were separated by age,

Ting was separated from her sister. "When talking about subject matter such as adoption and your background, especially if your sibling is of the same background as you," she says, "it's important to keep siblings together." The conversations, she notes, can bring up "a lot of hard emotions. And I think having someone that you have a personal connection with outside of this whole community . . . would be really beneficial."

As Ting got older, her feelings of disconnection remained. In early 2020, when she was in college and the Covid-19 pandemic began, "I really wasn't ready," she says. "Because at that point, I still hadn't addressed my Chinese identity and hadn't made space for it at all in my life." But as anti-Asian sentiment broke out across the country, stoked by a president who called Covid the "kung flu," Ting found herself facing a whole new challenge to her self-identity. "I'd wear my mask outside if I was walking to an academic building," she says. And suddenly, in a way that it had never been, her identity was front of mind. "People are going to see me wearing a mask," she'd think. "They're going to know that I'm Asian, and they're going to think I have Covid." These intrusive thoughts didn't always take up a ton of space, as she put it, but they were always there.

And because of that, she found herself tackling her long-standing questions of identity "all at once . . . being Asian, being adopted, and also Covid and the fear of getting attacked," she says. This made for a difficult, sometimes painful, but ultimately eye-opening year. "I had never given myself the opportunity to hold space for both my identities," she says. "Growing up, it just felt like, you pick one and that's the one you identify with. And thinking about picking my Chinese identity to be the one that I go with just felt way too difficult." But now, "just being able to hold multiple identities at once and know that that is completely acceptable and healthy . . . It is incredibly difficult, and it's still something that I have to work on actively every day."

So, looking back, what advice would she give White parents of Asian kids?

"Parents should recognize that they might not be the appropriate resource for their children to go to when talking about this," she says. "You might need to do work on the side to find people in your community that share your children's life experience because they are an expert in their field, and they might be able to provide children with the type of support system that you can't."

But Ting wants also to make one thing clear.

"That doesn't mean that you're bad parents," she says. "It just means that you're White, and that's something you can't change."

How did you get a boy?

Claire Wallick Moy • Maplewood, NJ

This is what I was asked in 1998 when I moved to New Jersey.
Our three children look much more like their father than me.
So many girls have been adopted from China in this generation,
but not boys. A White Jewish woman with an Asian-looking boy
is outside of people's reference points.

Need a fork.
Can't use chopsticks.

Deb Kruse • Tucson, AZ

Yes, I am "from" somewhere. Born in Korea—adopted as an infant (three weeks old to be exact). Yes, most of my family is White. Yes, I grew up on a farm in Iowa and have driven a tractor and a combine. Yes, I'm adopted. Yes, I like Asian food—Mexican food, too. No, I don't remember anything about Korea (really, you just asked me that?). No, I don't speak Korean. No, I don't know who my biological parents are. No, I'm not really curious about it. And no, I can't use chopsticks. So, give me a fork and don't make any assumptions about who you think I am or how you think I should act or be.

Are they yours? Are you sure?

Adam Connor • Washington, DC

My sister and I are both adopted from South Korea. Our parents are White. One of my memories from childhood is being at the grocery store and constantly having people ask my mom, "Are they yours?" [as they would] point to my sister and me. I remember one time someone then adding, "Are you sure?" As if my mom was going to look over and realize then that "Whoa, these kids are Asian! Thank you, stranger in a grocery store, for pointing that out to me!"

Adopted, how much did she cost?

Gail O'Rourke • Brooklyn, NY

White Mom + Chinese daughter: said right in my face, with my five-year-old daughter in my lap. She clutched me, buried her face in my chest, and sobbed. I put my arms around her, said, "Don't be disrespectful," and walked out of the shop.

People against racism made race essential

Katelyn Crombie • CA

I never cared about race until I was in college. Before then, I was adopted from China and grew up in a family that taught me to love everyone, regardless of appearances. I was also blessed with attending a high school that was racially diverse, despite our predominately White neighborhood, and these classmates reinforced the idea that personality matters most. So, I never thought twice about race until my freshman year in college, where I met people who were supposedly "anti-racist."

These people challenged everything that I knew. To them, I wasn't me, I was a minority voice. I was to be revered, defended, and protected against any "internalized majority prejudice." My natural Chinese heritage was something to be flaunted, and my adopted Scottish heritage was to be scorned as "privileged White culture." If I did anything they didn't agree with, they would express their disappointment by implying that I had somehow agreed with racists and thus betrayed my race. So now I find that I'm always second-guessing myself.

Am I being racist? Is the other person being racist? Am I defending the minority I represent? Am I wrong for wanting a Scottish-heritage event, simply because it's "White culture"? Maybe this is the price I pay for being more "open-minded."

Yellow outside, White inside, adopted Twinkie

**Karen Skillin Rojas •
San Francisco, CA**

Adopted from Korea at four and a half months old, I was raised in an entirely Caucasian family and community until I went to college. I often struggle with not identifying with my Asian exterior (yellow), which is how the world around me sees me. I find I identify so much more with my Caucasian interior (White), a testament to nurture versus nature, I suppose. I, and many others in my situation, call themselves bananas or Twinkies. Can it [be] classified as a race?!

Brother played cowboy, never the Indian

Bonni Hamilton • Eliot, ME

I grew up with two Native American siblings, whom my parents adopted when we were very small. When he was young, my Lakota brother always wanted to be the cowboy in cowboys and Indians. He knew from personal experience the Indians always lost. The memory still breaks my heart.

You can sit in the bar

Diane Graves • San Antonio, TX

My husband and I (both Anglo) were driving our adopted daughter (born in El Salvador, adopted as an infant, a US citizen since she was eleven months old) to a guest ranch in Colorado. It was 2004; our daughter was eleven years old. Late on Sunday morning, we stopped to have lunch in Alamosa, Colorado.

My husband entered the restaurant first, and my daughter and I busied ourselves at a postcard rack while he asked for a table. The White, male, college-aged host eyed our family, spotted our daughter, and said, "You can sit in the bar." My husband asked, "Why would that be? I see plenty of tables in the main dining room."

It was pretty clear why. Fortunately, a young female waitress pulled up and said we were welcome in her station. We were stunned—and grateful that our child didn't realize what had happened. She only learned about it this year, when I asked her if I could submit this story. We are glad we live in multiracial San Antonio, but still worry what kind of nation we are becoming—and if our daughter can ever be accepted as American in the rest of the country. Recent rhetoric would indicate that she will have to be alert for profiling and other forms of bias. My heart is breaking now as it did that day. How many other people of color experience this kind of bias on a daily basis? We all can do better. We can *be* better.

My kids: one White, one Brown

Sarah Day • Waynesboro, VA

I have an adopted child and a biological child. My son looks Hispanic, Arabic, you choose. I fear for him. I have seen him pulled out of line at airports for scrutiny I have never faced. Some say he has advantages, but I see no evidence of that anywhere. The world, while evolving, is still an unwelcome place for so many. Fear drives this.

White people shouldn't adopt tan babies

Kipp Jarecke-Cheng • Maplewood, NJ

One day, out of the blue, my seven-year-old son said to me and my partner, "White people shouldn't adopt tan babies like me." We were stunned by our son's comment, partly because it seemed so uncharacteristic of him, but mostly because my "tan" son is Asian, like me, while my partner, my son's other father, is White. Our son is adopted, and we are the only parents he has ever known, and although we live in a diverse community and are surrounded by multicultural, multiethnic friends and family, our son is already acutely aware of what race means in America.

We asked our son why he thought White people shouldn't adopt tan babies, and he deflected the question and dropped the subject. As an Asian man and as an immigrant, my experience as a minority in America is complicated, and I am very sympathetic with my son's experiences, perhaps more so than my son's White father. But it was still surprising that our son would express this idea to us. I wish I knew what was really behind my son's statement, but I don't.

He's not really yours, is he?

Stacey Golden • Portland, OR

I am European American, and my husband is African American. When we decided to adopt children, we adopted children that had bio parents that were the same race as us, thinking that then our children would feel more comfortable in a family that would have been like their bio family. That was until we found our last son. He was a beautiful, sweet, wonderful little two-and-a-half-year-old child . . . who did not look like he had a bit of "White" in him.

The first time we were in the grocery store and he called me Mommy, the woman behind me at the checkout stand said, with a sneer, "He's not really yours, is he?" It really caught me off guard, and I almost said, "Oh, well, he's adopted." But before I got it out, anger took over, and I thought, "Who is this woman, who does not even know me, think she is?" I looked back at her, as innocently as I could, and told her, "Why yes, of course he's mine." She said that what she meant was that he must surely have been adopted. I looked back, feigning a puzzled look, shook my head no, and assured her he was indeed my son. She began to raise her voice and stammered that he couldn't possibly be mine.

She kept on arguing, and I kept looking at her quizzically, as she tried to figure out how "this could have possibly happened." As I look back, I'm sure I could have been more understanding and said something that could have promoted racial harmony or something, but all I could feel was anger that out of all the things she could have commented on, that is what she said.

Never keep secrets from your children

I. Lulu • San Antonio, TX

I was fifty-two when I confirmed what I had long dodged: I was adopted—more like appropriated—at birth. Back then and in my part of the world (Texas), those things happened. My adoptive parents are on my birth certificate as the birth parents. What ya gonna do, right? I have very little knowledge of where I came from—just gossip.

My father died without telling me the truth, and my mother had Alzheimer's pickling her brain when I found out, so she couldn't help me too much. Therefore, I have no personal history. But I know that I belong to the great human race and that the people on this planet are related. That's all that I can vouch for.

Scared that we are not enough

Tanya • Manakin Sabot, VA

I'm White. My daughter is Black

Jennifer Berkemeier • Farmington Hills, MI

I'm a single mom. I adopted my daughter from Haiti in 2012 when she was four years old. I'm White and fifteen years older than most of her friends' moms. We get a lot of stares and unwelcome comments from little kids ("Is she your grandma?" "How come you're different colors?" "She can't be your mom. . . . She's White."). We love each other. We talk about race, her origin, being White and Black, and being a nontraditional family. I'm teaching her to embrace it and be proud of it. It's strange and painful to teach someone about slavery when you're White and she's Black.

My (adopted) son is biracial; his bio father is unknown. I will never be able to connect him with his biological African American family. There is a void that I will never be able to fill for him. This breaks my heart as his mama.

251

Adopted at birth;
family history unknown

Kristi Boehm • Spring, TX

Every year on my birthday I give thanks to the woman who loved me enough to give me up for adoption. I couldn't have asked for a better mother and father, and my family life was nothing but ordinary. As an aging adult, with no idea of whether I'm Swedish, German, Irish, or _____ (fill in the blank). Not having any history also means I have no medical history.

I would love to know more about my background, both to discover my roots and also to uncover any potential medical issues. I have jokingly said that all the women in my family may spontaneously combust at age fifty-four, so I try to make the most of every day!

PROUD FATHER OF
MULTI RACIAL CHILDREN

Dave Reising • Peoria, IL

DECEMBER 4, 1969. In the early morning hours, fourteen armed Chicago police officers storm into an apartment on the city's West Side. Gunfire erupts, roaring into a full-on shootout that seems to last an eternity. More than ninety shots are fired over a ten-minute span, and when the shooting finally stops, two young Black men lie mortally wounded. One is Fred Hampton, the leader of the Illinois Black Panther Party, and the other is Mark Clark, a fellow Panther. Neither lived to see age twenty-three.

These shootings were dramatized years later in the Oscar-winning film *Judas and the Black Messiah*. But that bloody event was part of a string of clashes between police and Black activists throughout the late 1960s. More than two dozen people died in 1967 during five days of violence in Newark when outrage over racial injustice spilled into the streets. Civil disorder was simmering well beyond New Jersey. More than 150 uprisings scarred cities across America. The spark that led to the unrest was almost always the same thing—a violent encounter between police officers and Black people. The embers stayed hot going into 1968. That year, South Carolina Highway Patrol officers opened fire on a group of more than 200 unarmed protestors in what became known as the Orangeburg Massacre. Most of the protestors were students from local historically black colleges. Three were killed. Twenty-eight were injured. Two months later, the assassination of Dr. Martin Luther King Jr. sparked a wave of protests, mayhem, and civil unrest across the United States. And with growing frustration over segregation and housing, employment, and health disparities, the unrest simmered into 1969.

A three-hour drive southwest of Chicago, in Peoria, Illinois, Dave Reising and his wife, Judy, were trying to make a decision during that same period. Dave and Judy had dreamed of having a big family, but after two years of trying, they'd been unable to conceive. So, they started thinking about adoption. The couple was White, but "as fate would have it," Dave says, "my cousin and his wife had adopted a couple of biracial children." After talking it over, the Reisings decided that they were open to doing the same, even as racial strife was flaring across the country, and despite the relative rarity of transracial adoptions. Peoria, a town with 190,000 residents, wasn't exactly a big city. It had a downtown and a manufacturing base, but Peoria had a small-town feel. A cocoon of a place where people watch out for neighbors.

The couple filled out the paperwork to begin the process, and before long, they heard there were babies available for adoption at a nearby family-services facility. The Reisings called their adoption counselor, who said, "Oh, yes, there are babies—but they're biracial."

"It doesn't matter to us," Dave replied. "If it's a baby that needs a home, we're offering our home."

After that, things moved quickly. When the Reisings were told there was a six-week-old boy available for adoption, they jumped. On the day they went to meet their son, an adoption worker approached them with a request. "I'm just going to ask you, while you're standing here, if you'd be interested in taking a second child," she said. "So, you don't raise just one biracial child by himself." Dave and Judy agreed, and to their surprise, the second adoption happened within days. Just like that, the young couple were now the parents of two mixed-race boys, Christopher and Michael.

Now, bear in mind that this is all happening long before the popularity of TV shows like *Diff'rent Strokes* and *This Is Us* and before public attitudes were shaped and maybe even softened by seeing so many White celebrities bringing their Brown adopted children along for Hollywood photo ops on the red carpet. Yes, transracial adoptions had been happening for a few decades in the United States when Dave and Judy made their decision—but not in significant numbers. In the sixteen-year span between 1960 and 1976, there were about 12,000 transracial adoptions in the entire country.

Again, not everybody was a fan of the practice. As mentioned earlier, the National Association of Black Social Workers took "a vehement stand against the placement of Black children in white homes for any reason," with that 1972 statement asserting "Black children in White homes are cut off from the healthy development of themselves as Black people." The statement further claimed, "only a Black family can transmit the emotional and sensitive subtleties of perception and reaction essential for a Black child's survival in a racist society."

The NABSW also took particular aim at the phenomenon of White parents adopting mixed-raced babies, as the Reisings had done:

> We fully recognize the phenomenon of trans-racial adoption as an expedient for white folk, not as an altruistic humane concern for Black children. The supply of white children for adoption has all but vanished and adoption agencies, having always catered to middle class Whites developed an answer to their desire for parenthood by motivating them to consider Black children. This has brought about a re-definition of some Black children. Those born of Black-White alliances are no longer Black as decreed by immutable law and social custom for centuries. They are now Black-White, inter racial, bi-racial, emphasizing the Whiteness as the adoptable quality; a further subtle, but vicious design to further diminish Black and accentuate white. We resent this highhanded arrogance and are insulted by this further assignment of chattel status to Black people.

The Reisings were acting from the heart. They didn't claim to be color-blind, but in retrospect, Dave says he could not fully see the invisible wall of judgment that circled his family on all sides. A whole lot of White people also seemed to take umbrage at the Reisings' choice. "Judy would take the kids shopping with her. . . . She had these two little African American kids in the cart, and people would see her coming down an aisle and they'd turn around and walk away," recalls Dave. "And she said, 'You know what? It would just tear my heart out. They don't know my children. They don't know the beautiful love of these little kids.'"

In 1971, the Reisings decided to grow their family, adopting a mixed-race girl they named Jennifer. In 1974, they added another daughter, Molly. Now they were a family of six—happy at home, but still facing discrimination out in the world. When the boys started kindergarten, their primarily White elementary school "wasn't ready for an infusion of children of color," as Dave delicately puts it. "I remember coming home and thinking, 'What do you mean they don't want my kids in your school?' I was floored," he said. It turned out to be just one of a series of continuing epiphanies. "Well, hello! Wake up! This is the beginning of the revelation of what you're going to face when you take those Black children."

Whenever his sons came to him with problems they faced at school, Dave would turn the question to them. "I said, 'Well, what do you want to do? How do you want to manage this?' . . . Because I didn't want to pretend to be an old White guy who knew what was going to happen or how it was going to work. I wanted to hear what they wanted to do. And that's basically how we would handle situations."

Rather than trying to push the school administration into supporting his sons, Dave and Judy decided to pull up roots and move the family to a more diverse neighborhood. It was a decision that improved all their lives—for a time. Christopher and Michael liked their new school, and the whole family became close to their new neighbors, an African American family two doors down. But soon enough, trouble came knocking again.

When the girls were old enough, they began attending a Catholic elementary school. And though they had friends, it soon became obvious that their White classmates were treating them differently. Jennifer and Molly invited their classmates over for birthday parties—but they never received invitations in return. So, once again, the Reisings made a change, switching their daughters to a public school.

By 1979, the Reisings had been parents for ten years. When you've been raising four kids, it takes a lot to surprise you. But one afternoon, when Dave got home from work, Judy said, "Can you sit down? I've got something to tell you." To both of their shock, she was pregnant; she gave birth that September to a son they named Joseph. Then, "five years later, we repeated the program," Dave notes dryly, and in 1985, Judy gave birth to a daughter, Catherine.

Now the family had three boys and three girls. But unfortunately, not for long. Christopher, the first child the Reisings adopted, had always been joyful, the kind of child who liked making people laugh. When puberty hit sometime after he turned thirteen, his body changed, as expected. His chin squared off. His shoulders widened. His voice deepened. The child started to look like a man. But the real change was in his behavior. It shifted dramatically. Suddenly, he began acting out in all kinds of ways—staying out all night, locking Judy out of the house, and even threatening her. The battles between Christopher and his parents grew so fierce that one day, Dave just leaned against his car and wept, saying, "God, what am I going to do?" He couldn't see a way clear of the strug-gle. The other children were starting to fear their brother. He had snatched the phone from their mother's hand and threatened her with a knife. Dave thought Christopher might need psychological help but could not pull Christopher close enough to take that approach together. Eventually, he and Judy made the painful decision to turn Christopher over as a ward of the court. Dave said it was excruciating.

Later, the Reisings would learn that Christopher's birth mother had been a heavy drinker and that his symptoms were possibly indicative of fetal alcohol syndrome. He wasn't diagnosed, so they can't be absolutely sure what caused Christopher's dramatic change in personality. But what is certain is that after fifteen years of trying to raise and nurture his son, Dave felt like a failure as a parent. And Christopher's own take on it was no less painful. "You guys aren't Black enough to be parents to me," he told Dave and Judy before he left their home. "So, I don't even consider you my parents."

That saying about how a parent is only as happy as their unhappiest child rings true here.

This was a gut-wrenching time for the Reisings. Dave had to consider the possibility that he could not give his son what he needed, in part because of their racial differences. He relied on his faith, but the pain never subsided. Decades have passed, and that is evident when I speak to Dave. That saying about how a parent is only as happy as their unhappiest child rings true here, even though that child is long gone, living across the country, estranged from his family, now carrying a new first and last name to further distance himself from his past. Though Christopher has been in touch sporadically with his brother Michael over the years, there has been no contact between him and the rest of the family.

Michael, the other Black boy adopted by the Reisings, confirmed that his older brother experienced psychological challenges throughout his life, and all of that, he says, may have been compounded by the ostracism and outright racism the family faced. "He was just a really angry person," Mike said. "You had to really tiptoe around him because he always had a person under surveillance [for] being disrespectful to him." Michael works as a medical technician in California, where he has four children, including an adoptee. He is proud of being an adoptive parent and sees it as a way to honor the Reising family who chose him.

When you talk to Mike Reising, he sounds Black in terms of his speech patterns and dialect. That is something he can easily flip on and off, after growing up with White parents in small-town Illinois. The ability to code-switch has made it easier for him to navigate various facets of his life: school, work, parenting, dealing with someone on the phone, talking to his White siblings. "I felt like a lucky person that they adopted us," Mike said. But he admits that his childhood outside the home could be tough. "We're super-stars during the basketball season, but we're never invited to birthday parties. I remember being the brunt of racist jokes and stuff like that. Then I go down to the Southend and play basketball at an outdoor park and get my butt kicked by a guy named Wonk who's Black, right? All because I was a yellow boy. Banana boy. Pretty boy." In other words, not accepted fully as a Black boy or as a White boy.

Christopher is six weeks older than Mike, and they were raised almost like twins, but they had very different personalities, especially when confronting the challenges around race. "He saw a clip in one of the local newspapers about my parents adopting me and him, and he looked at it like we were tokens," Mike said. Does he think his parents failed Christopher? The answer is complicated. Now that he is an adult and a parent raising four kids himself, he thinks that his dad "shouldn't really beat himself up" because he had to look out for the well-being of the entire family. In truth, he said, laughter returned to the household even though everyone was dealing with heartbreak in their own way.

That's confirmed by a story Dave Reising shared with me. He said one night after Christopher left, when the family was sitting at the supper table talking and laughing, the presence of joy underscored how much that had been absent for years in their house. "It just kind of reinforced to me that we did the right thing for the five other children," Dave said.

As life moved on, the remaining five kids grew up, got jobs and partners, some got married, and several had children of their own. Judy passed away in 2004 of a heart condition, and after a period of mourning, Dave fell in love and married his second wife, Cassie. The couple, now in their seventies, are ecstatic to be the grandparents of fifteen grandkids. They dote on their brood every chance they get. And one of those grandkids represents another special thread in their complicated family yarn.

When Jennifer, the Reisings' oldest daughter, was sixteen and still in high school, she got pregnant. She decided to give the baby up for adoption because she was too young and ill-prepared for motherhood. But the mother of the boy who fathered the child had other ideas. "She came storming into our house one day," says Dave, "and sat down in front of Jennifer and said, 'You know, Jennifer, Black children don't give up their babies.'" She used the word *children*, but she was referring to teenage moms. He said Jennifer listened respectfully and then replied, "Well, I was adopted. I was given up, and I love my life. And that's what I hope for my baby."

Jennifer gave birth to a healthy boy she named Michael after her older brother, and the big Reising family came to the hospital to see the infant. Everybody got a chance to hold the baby briefly, and Dave, a devout Catholic who eventually became an ordained deacon, took his moment with the infant to bestow a small blessing on the boy. The Reisings had just that one day with Jennifer's son. After that, he became part of another family.

Twenty-eight years went by. Then, in November 2015, Dave got a Facebook message from a man named Joshua Thomas. Joshua wrote that he'd been given up for adoption by a woman named Jennifer, and he wondered whether Dave's daughter was his birth mother. "Now, Jennifer had a false alarm before," says Dave. A few years earlier, a man who thought he might have been her son reached out to the Reising family, but it was determined through DNA testing that he was not related. "So, we were a little bit cautious," Dave said. "But I had an awfully good feeling about this." He sent a note back to Joshua and said yes, he had a daughter named Jennifer who'd given a child up for adoption. Then he asked what evidence Joshua had that he might indeed be that child. Minutes later, Joshua replied, saying that his birth name was Michael Anthony Reising and that he'd been born in Peoria. He named the hospital and the date Jennifer had given birth.

Dave told Jennifer about the message, and the father and daughter had a good, long cry. A note was sent to Joshua: "You have found your mother." Jennifer and Joshua spoke on the phone for three hours that day, and the following week, he traveled to Peoria from his home in Iowa to meet the rest of the Reisings. The whole family—except for Michael, who was living in California—gathered at Dave and Cassie's home for dinner. Dave put all the leaves in the table and brought out the extra chairs, so everyone could sit together at the meal. Dave said Joshua told the family at dinner: "All I wanted to know is what happened." Joshua tracked down Jennifer to find out why she had chosen not to raise him. It wasn't confrontational. But it was uncomfortable. Advances in DNA technology and new laws around once-closed recordkeeping have allowed adoptive children to find their birth parents and have made it harder for those parents to outrun their pasts. This is a very prickly subject in the adoption community. Jennifer was not defensive or alarmed. Dave watched the exchange with tension sending his stomach acid sloshing into his throat. He was both surprised by and proud of her calm. "I just wanted what was best for you. And I knew I couldn't provide it," she told Joshua. Then she added another detail: "I want you to know that everybody who's here held you in their arms before we placed you up for adoption."

Dave said he was in tears at that point. Everyone in the dining room was in tears. Frankly, I am fighting back tears as he tells me this story years later. Dave said he pulled himself together and turned to Joshua. "When I held you, I kissed you on the cheek and made the sign of the cross on your forehead. I prayed that God would guard and protect you all the days of your life." The tears are flowing again as he remembers that reunion and the words he spoke to the grandson he thought he would never see again. "God promises that when you bless someone, the blessing will come back to you. And it's back. The blessing I gave you when you were born has just come back to us because your coming home has repaired a hole in our hearts—the hole nobody else can repair."

•   •   •

I asked Dave what he learned about his country upon adopting four biracial children back in the late 1960s and early '70s. "Well, my first reaction to that question would be to say America is slow to change," he told me. "We can see things right in front of our face, but it wouldn't necessarily give us pause to change our attitudes and our opinions." But zooming in closer, he praised the neighbors, church communities, and friends who supported the family through trials and difficulties. In particular, he singled out the family two doors down, the Gaytons, who helped him and Judy through some tough times.

"We were neophytes. We really had no idea what we were getting into," he says. "Mrs. Gayton would just sit and talk to us and say, 'You're going to get through this. This is a temporary hurt, temporary burden, temporary hurdle.'" Looking back at those times, he says, "I think it's fair to say that what we learned came in phases, much like the stages of life kids go through." But in the end, only one thing mattered, according to Dave.

"Love conquers everything," he says. "It really does. I mean, you're going to have hurdles. You're going to have challenges. But you still have to be faithful. You have to be faithful to your core. And if your core has developed over the years as a stern, strong belief that the God who created you has never abandoned you and never will, then there's not much you can't put up with to get to the next phase of your life. . . .

"There's just so many reasons to be grateful," he concludes.

"I have healthy kids. My family's all put together.

"We've had some bumps in the road, obviously. But by and large, I consider myself just one of the luckiest men of all times." They are all adults now, but Dave prays for all his children every night. All of them. And especially Christopher.

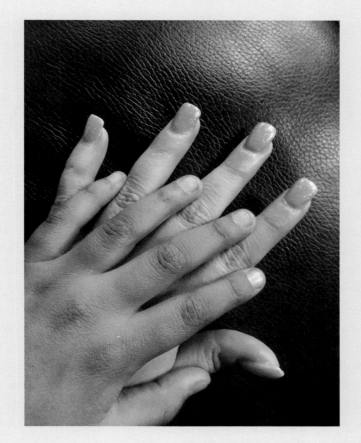

No my children
are not adopted

Beth Schumacher • Collegeville, PA

He's not your son? Oh good!

Amber Alverson • Eugene, OR

My first real encounter with my own race that I can remember was when I was in middle school. My White godparents had just adopted a Black baby. They "kept his Black name," DiMario, as his middle name and changed his first name to the "biblical" (aka: White) name Joshua.

We were in the store, and my godmother took her oldest daughter to the bathroom, so I was with the baby waiting outside. An older White woman came up to me and asked if he was my son. I exclaimed, "Oh, no no no. He's my brother." In my mind, it was a crazy thing to ask because I was obviously too young to have a baby. Her response was "Oh, good. Because he doesn't look like he has any White in him at all!" and then she just walked away like what she said didn't mean anything.

I was raised in a diverse city with many different races and cultures, but my own race was not acknowledged to me until it was compared to someone else's. His was acknowledged right away and was immediately looked down upon, all before he could talk.

Being biracial and adopted is complicated

Lauren Juanita Hines • Alexandria, VA

I am the American melting pot personified: born to a Mexican father and Caucasian (White, mostly Irish) mother, raised by a Lebanese mother and a German Irish father. I remember weddings as a child where we all danced the Middle Eastern dabke. Cousins on the other side of the family won awards for Irish dancing. Now my Mexican family blows up my phone with renditions of "Las Mañanitas" on my birthday. It's a huge family: Catholic on all sides.

Vote Obama! He looks like me!

Val Sheffield • IA

Jessica Sheffield at age eight said this. Her adoptive father wonders, "Should I be happy or dismayed by this comment?"

White. Adopted transracially. Now get it.

Ursula • Oklahoma City, OK

I did not get White privilege until we adopted. I am so sorry. This story terrifies me.

I Forget I Am Not White

Dougherty • US expat

I was adopted. My dad is Irish, raised in Texas and then California. Mom is a retired nurse. I was raised around Protestants, Catholics, Mormons, and Jews. My friends in elementary school were White. Race was never an issue. Or if it was, I have long since forgotten about it. I even speak with a slight Southern drawl if you listen carefully. You can thank Dad for that. Even in the mirror, all I saw was me. Wide, curious eyes and awkward smile and a few scars from some cystic acne. It's gone now. All I saw was a person, and that is how I saw everyone else—as people. Do you see people like I do? Or are you still wondering what race I am?

But, you are not really Chinese

Lianna Thomas • Congers, NY

I am a Chinese adoptee. I've lived in New York practically my entire life (since I was seven months old). My family is entirely White, and I was brought up in a Western culture with Western traditions. I celebrate my Eastern culture, as well, through holidays like Chinese New Year, I study the language, and I have traveled back to China many times. But to my friends, I am not Chinese. They tell me I don't know how to cook Chinese food, I'm bad at math, I can't speak the language, I do "White girl" things. So, even though I was literally born on Chinese soil (while most of my Chinese friends have never been to China, let alone been born in that country), my friends still see me as what they like to call "a banana."

My daughter isn't a "China Doll"

Debra Cope • Alexandria, VA

Adoption is beautiful, and I really don't mind helping others navigate the awkward preconceptions that accompany it. But this phrase just burns me because it equates my spunky, lively child with an object. She's not my toy—she's my daughter!

Black families don't adopt White babies

Sue Rushfirth • Sudbury, MA

It strikes me that one way of assessing just how evolved we are as a culture would be to consider the reaction of most people to a transracial adoption with Black parents and a White baby.

What country is he from? Maryland

Mike Spillman • Buffalo, NY

Strangers see Black boys walking around with their White father and often assume that all transracial adoptions are also transnational—that since our family looks strange to them, our boys must have been saved from some faraway, wretched place. "No, ma'am, we are not saviors. We are just parents of a family with beautiful kids." Then I go back to checking out my groceries.

Abandoned by my adoptive White family

Kayleen • WA

I was born in 1969 and adopted by an all-White family. In the beginning, I assumed it was OK because there were other people in the house besides me and my adoptive mother. The other kids were older than me and were all moved out by the time I was nine. It was just me and my adoptive mother. What ensued would be years of neglect, poverty, and abuse. It seemed just existing around my adopted mother enraged her. I remember calling my sister when I was about ten and telling her I was being abused, and she did nothing. I finally ran away from that home when I was fifteen. I never heard from my siblings after that. I'm now fifty-one and still have rough days coming to terms with being put up for adoption then going into the family I ended up with. I still hold it against them that they didn't protect me from her or try to have any relationship with me. I was just a kid.

Adopted. But am I still Mexican?

Kasey Nichols • Clemmons, NC

I've known I've been adopted since I can remember and never questioned my ethnicity until I reached middle school age because we had to fill out cards with "check yes if Latino, African American, White, or other." Biologically I'm Mexican and Italian, but I was raised White with my dad being Greek and mom "White." I kept asking myself, "What am I?" I don't speak Spanish well, and I grew up with a White Southern family, but my blood says Mexican and Italian. I worked in retail, and Hispanic people would assume I was Latina from my short stature, olive skin, dark eyes, and dark hair and start speaking Spanish, but they would stop when they saw the confused look on my face. Especially when I go out with my Mexican boyfriend. However, I don't resemble either culture. So, what am I? I'm an American born and raised. I'm a mixture, but I don't need a label. I am *me*. Just a person.

Two steps forward one step Black

Gerald Harmon • Southington, CT

As a biracial child, I was given up at birth by my White mother in 1960. I spent time in the hospital after my birth while they determined my race based on the development of my hair, lips, and skin tone. Eventually, I was labeled Negro and was placed in the appropriate adoption agency. I was fortunate to be adopted by two wonderful African American parents and raised accordingly. As a biracial child, you are never Black enough, let alone even considered as a member of the White race. It causes a determination to always work twice as hard and never be satisfied with your place in life or the place others think you should be satisfied with. You never stop trying to achieve more because you know it takes two steps forward to get one-step credit as a Black man. I love being Black and would not change it for the world, but why did society get to choose my race? I will not let them control my destiny.

White mom hoping Filipina daughter's prepared

Yael Silverberg Urian • Montclair, NJ

Why aren't Black adoptive parents colorblind?

Ilbersalle Fallon • Austin, TX

8

"Start with kids and mix well"

WITHIN MY LIFETIME, INTERRACIAL MARRIAGE has gone from being illegal in several states to becoming so common that you cannot turn on the TV without seeing an ad of some kind featuring a mixed-raced couple buying a car, talking about insurance, or planning a poolside vacation.

Among recently married couples, almost one in five have a spouse of a different ethnicity or race, according to the Pew Research Center. That is a whopping fivefold increase since 1967. That's the year the US Supreme Court ruled in *Loving v. Virginia* that state laws banning interracial marriage violated the equal protection and due process clauses of the Constitution. That's also the year that the film *Guess Who's Coming to Dinner* explored whether families of different races could set aside their misgivings to applaud a marriage that tested the limits of society's tolerance. As you have seen in earlier chapters in this book, consternation about interracial couplings was so strong that it led to fractured families and false histories.

That angst was often fueled by the question "What about the children?" Some of that pearl clutching may have actually been based on fears for a mixed-race child's future. But let's be honest, a lot of that consternation was also about adult worries over what the "moral gatekeepers" might think of them.

America has become a much more welcoming place both in attitude and actual life choices now.

Interracial marriage, "multiculti" dating, blended families, transracial adoption, grandparenting across the color line, and loving whom you want without fear of legal repercussion or collective condemnation is now a fact of life. Pass the champagne and toss the confetti. But this whoosh of forward momentum does not mean that the issue of multiracial coupling is free of anxieties or impediments. I know that because of the thousands of stories we have received from people who are in mixed marriages, or are the product of biracial coupling, or are observing or opining about multicultural couplings somewhere in their orbits. It is yet another example of how progress on matters of race—while cause for celebration—does not always erase cultural complications, but instead introduces new avenues for contemplation and complexity.

WITH KIDS, I'M DAD.
ALONE, THUG

Marc Quarles • Pacific Grove, CA

I LIVE IN PACIFIC GROVE, CALIFORNIA, and I chose these six words because I'm African American, my wife is German, and we have two children—a son and a daughter. We live in a predominantly White, affluent area on the Monterey Peninsula. Every summer, my wife and children go to Germany to visit her parents, other friends, and relatives. So consequently, I spend the summers alone. When I am alone, I'm treated very differently. People seem apprehensive to approach me, and most of the time, I've noticed my White counterparts almost avoid me. They seem afraid. They don't know what to think of me because I'm in their neighborhood. I oftentimes wonder if they think I'm a thug. The same does not happen when I have the security blanket and shield of my children. When my children are with me, I'm just a dad. I love being a dad.

• • •

The first time I met Marc Quarles, we were in a radio studio, and I asked him to read his backstory aloud because he was going to be featured in a Race Card Project segment on NPR. When he got to the end of that paragraph, he had the beginning of a smile as he read one of the last sentences: "The same does not happen when I have the security blanket and shield of my children."

By the time he got to the final words—"I love being a dad"—his face lit up like Christmas. I had expected that he would be irked or angry, yet he explained to me that what I saw was not necessarily what he felt. The anger and irritation were there, but it was not something he could give in to for all kinds of reasons. The smile was also part of his shield.

Quarles is a Black man with dreadlocks that reach down to the middle of his back. He is an ultrasound technician with an athletic build even though he's just turned sixty. His smile is an effective tool for inoculating himself against others' fears that he might pose a threat. He's an affable guy, and it's a natural part of his personality, but it's also part of his life survival kit as a Black man who lives in a predominantly White, affluent area. The smile is an outward projection but also an inward protection against letting random examples of bias chip away at his soul when he's followed around in stores or approached by people who ask where he's from or what he's doing in the area.

Quarles was drawn to Pacific Grove, California, because of its good schools and natural beauty along the rocky coast of the Monterey Peninsula. When he first moved into the area, he was often followed by police and stopped counting the number of times he was pulled over for a supposedly random registration or license checks. When his family relocated into a second, larger house in the area, an officer knocked on their door to ask about a neighbor's missing purse.

"The police officer said, 'The woman across the street is missing her purse.' And I looked at him, and I said, 'So you can come in and look for it if you'd like. But no, I didn't take the purse.'" Marc Quarles and that neighbor have since become fairly good friends.

The Quarles kids found more immediate acceptance in their community. They didn't experience the same kinds of stares or security stops, or if they did, they kept it from Marc and his wife, Claudia. He takes comfort in that and wonders if their comfort and ease moving through largely White spaces contributed to an overall more welcoming vibe. And since they tend to move in packs as kids, he wonders if their big, multiracial group of friends was a shield for them.

Marc also recognizes that people who question his place in their community are reacting to his skin color, his size, and perhaps something else.

"I just decided to grow dreadlocks," Marc said. He had wanted them for a while but waited until he had the house and the job and the career. When I first met Marc, his son, Joshua, was fifteen. It was a time when a growing number of Black entertainers and basketball players were starting to sport a wider variety of hairstyles: twists, buds, braids, and, yes, dreadlocks. Joshua asked his parents if he could get an earring, and the answer was "Absolutely not!" Marc's wife, Claudia, was open to the idea of Joshua growing dreadlocks like his dad, but Marc had already prepared a response to shut down that idea:

Marc says the world often ignores their White side.

"I would tell him, 'Son, I've completed my education. I have a very good career. We have a very nice home, and I did all these things before I decided to grow my dreadlocks,'" Marc said. "'The world will make assumptions about you based on your appearance. So right now, I just need you to be a clean-cut, well-dressed kid without your pants hanging off of your butt,' and that's the direction that we're going. He may think it's a little unfair right now, but we do have many, many conversations where I explain to him there is a method to my madness, and one day you will understand. And I'm looking forward to that day when he'll call me up and say, 'Hey, Dad, you won't believe what happened to me today, but now I understand.'"

That day came when Josh left home to head for college, driving cross-country in his truck with a friend to the East Coast. Josh, who by this time had begun growing dreadlocks despite his dad's concerns, was pulled over multiple times by sheriff's deputies during the trip.

"Little did they know that by doing that, they created an activist," Marc said. "Once he got to the University of Mary Washington, he joined the NAACP; he joined the Black Student Union." Marc and Claudia raised their kids to embrace both of their cultures, but Marc says the world often ignores their White side while reminding them, "Yes, you're really Black."

Josh didn't tell his dad about the traffic stops at first. He waited until he came home on Christmas break. That was more than three years ago, and since then, Marc has wondered what his kids will use as their shields to protect themselves from the bias they may face in the world. Will their confidence and comfort in spaces where they are outliers be enough? Will they, too, use their smiles or personalities to neutralize tension? Will the world evolve to the point where maybe they won't feel like they need that kind of protective shell?

Since Marc Quarles's story was featured on NPR, he became a minor celebrity in his town. Not everyone was comfortable with the way he portrayed Pacific Grove, but he said it led to some productive soul-searching around police profiling and diversity. As he moves around town with his dreadlocks and his medical scrubs these days, people tend to know who he is. That's a good thing, he says. With both kids headed off to college, he no longer has that reliable safety shield.

Postlude: In the summer of 2023, Marc Quarles cut off his dreadlocks. After working at the same hospital for years, he was preparing to change jobs and in his new position, he would be working with new colleagues who had not known him for years as the hardworking, highly professional ultrasound technician who happened to sport dreadlocks that hung past his shoulders. In the current cultural climate, he said a change seemed prudent. He said, "I know that I didn't have to cut my hair, at the same time we all know that I did have to cut my hair."

White moms.
Brown Kids.
Colorblind love.

Melanie Gilbert • Boston, MA

Love who you are, not what you are.

Because I married a White man

Patricia Osborn • Grand Rapids, MI

People are always surprised when they see me. My last name doesn't "match" how I look. Although my parents are awesome and didn't think twice about any of their children's spouses' races, my aunts and uncles made so many comments ranging from me not wanting to be a true Hispanic to saying that I was cleaning up the bloodline all because my husband is White. My kids also have a hard time because they are identified as White because of their appearances, but they know they aren't.

Our neighbor won't look at us

Angela Bennett • Arvada, CO

I married my husband, whom I met in the Dominican Republic while I was a Peace Corps volunteer. He and his son moved to the United States after a long immigration process. We moved into my parents' home, and a man who used to be a friendly neighbor stopped all communication and won't even make eye contact with us. My mom addressed him directly and asked, "What's your problem?" He said his sister had dated a Black man who beat her.

Feeling helpless the dream is dying

Ellen Asbury • Crofton, MD

How can I verbalize my feelings of nonbias to people who have faced bias and prejudice based on how they look? Even my own daughter (biracially White/ Asian) projects upon me as being not understanding and uncaring because I'm White. Please understand there are people out there that consider who you are, not what you are, without hesitation.

Parenting through a prism of race.

Rita Radostitz • Washington, DC

Who will your children play with?

Linda Hunt • CT

I am in a forty-year biracial marriage, and very early on when my children were small, my grandmother made the comment above. I said, "They will play with whomever they wanted as long as they were decent."

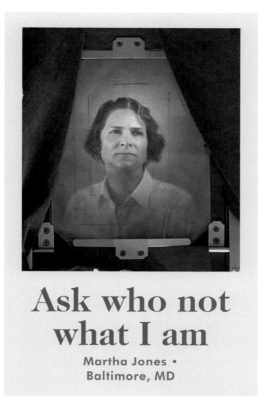

Ask who not what I am

Martha Jones • Baltimore, MD

Mom's White. Dad's Black. I'm spotted.

William Jones • Reisterstown, MD

It's vitiligo. Yes, it's what Michael Jackson had. It basically means the cells that make skin color stop doing that. Although you can't see it as well in lighter complexions, anyone from any race can develop it, and at the age of about thirty, I became one of the 1 percent of humans who do. What's funny is that, as a biracial person, I've spent a lot of time dealing with race issues, from both sides, and wondering exactly where I fit. Now that I have white spots that will slowly but eventually completely cover my whole body, the idea of the color of a person has taken on a whole new meaning . . . and a much smaller one, I think. When people ask about the spots, I explain. When people ask how I feel about it, I simply tell them that I spent the first half of my life as a really attractive Black guy, and I plan to spend the second half as a really attractive White guy.

Parents' interracial marriage seems selfish sometimes

AMW • Santa Cruz, CA

I'm tired of my biracial experience being used as proof of progress. Sometimes I think my parents were selfish to have kids and then act like everything would be fine. There are still unequal power dynamics, still racism in their relationship, and they wonder why their kids are insecure and damaged. Kids should never feel ashamed to be in public with a parent or hate themselves for being racially "other," but sadly this is common among many biracial youth I know.

The only Mexican in my family

Sarah Willis • Portland, OR

My dad is a half-Mexican, half-German man who married a European mutt and had seven children. I am the only one of the seven that he marked the box on my birth certificate as Hispanic instead of White, making me the only Mexican in my family.

Tennerican Asian passes on only Asian

Rosita Gonzalez • Madison, WI

I am not who I seem. Roads converged to make me a person of three races, of which only one sticks. My children only identify with the one that sticks. But I cannot tell them much about that race that defines them. I blog about it to examine and heal both their wounds and mine.

One White. One brown. Same parents.

Adana • Seattle, WA

I have two children. My son looks just like his papa: dark, wavy hair and alabaster skin. My daughter looks like me: golden skin and curly brown hair. When I'm out with my son, I'm asked if I'm his nanny. When I'm out with both kids, I'm asked if they have the same father. We worry, often, about the prejudices my daughter will face that our son will be spared. All because one has white skin and one has brown.

Want to publicly fearlessly hug dad

Ruth Greyraven • Redlands, CA

White mom, mixed-race Afro dad. I look White. Brothers look (knowing I'm stereotyping) Italian, Mexican, and unclassifiable. I want to live in a world where I can walk with my dad's arm around me, walk arm in arm with my brothers, dance with my cousins . . . without us getting the "White girl with Black guy" glare. In some areas, I would experience real fear of inciting an assault, just by my being loving with my family.

He said half-breed; I said Hapa

Elisa Mader • Seattle, WA

I no longer call myself hapa because I learned that it's cultural appropriation from Native Hawaiians, but the story is true as is, a moment from the early 1990s. [Elisa now lives in Germany.]

Who is your daughter's father

Itoko Richardson • Daly City, CA

I am Japanese, and my husband is Black (he extremely dislikes being called African American). Our experience alone was interesting and filled with many racist-stereotype encounters and reactions. But my experience with my daughter is interesting. When my daughter and I are out, I can feel strangers' wonder of who and what she is.

My daughter is beautiful, and I get that compliment from time to time. But such a simple compliment is to ask the real question for many people, "She is so pretty. What is she?" "Is this your daughter? She is beautiful. What is she mixed with?" Interestingly, it does not happen as often as to my husband and daughter when they are out. He said it is because he is Black. He means that people who ask our daughter's source of race want to know if she is mixed with Black. So, I answer that I am married to an American. Sure enough, I am asked what kind of American I am married to.

Our experience in Japan is totally different. In a homogeneous society, every Japanese knows my daughter is mixed when he/she sees her. So being mixed with Black or White isn't something for them to be concerned about. It seems to me that people in Japan wanted to see if I embedded Japanese (Soul of Japanese) in her because Japanese blood runs in my daughter. They showed some happiness when she ate natto (fermented soybean), spoke Japanese, sang Japanese songs, used chopsticks, believed in Buddhism, or celebrated our traditions. So, I am working hard to engage in Japanese cultural traditions more than I ever cared to do. Partly, I do not want to be looked at as failed Japanese. But mostly, I want her to have more cards in her hand, cards of being Japanese.

The Loving Index

Year in which the term *miscegenation* was coined, by two New York journalists, in an anonymously published seventy-two-page pamphlet:

1863

. . .

Number of US states that had laws on the books between 1947 and 1967 that outlawed mixed-race marriages:

30

. . .

Number of US states in 1967 that outlawed mixed-race marriages[1]:

16

. . .

Year in which the Hays Code censored the on-screen depiction of interracial couples[2]:

1930

. . .

Percentage of Americans who approved of Black/White marriages in 1958:

4

Percentage who approved of them in 1978:

36

In 2002:   In 2021:

65   94

Year in which a Louisiana justice of the peace refused to marry an interracial couple, citing concern for the children:

2009

. . .

Number of US Asian/non-Hispanic White marriages in 2010:

737,493

Number of US Black/non-Hispanic White marriages in 2010:

422,250

Number of US Asian/ Black marriages in 2000:

31,271

. . .

Percentage increase in the number of US interracial marriages between 1990 and 2000:

65

Percentage between 2000 and 2010:

32.8

. . .

Percentage of US newlyweds with a spouse of a different race or ethnicity in 2015:

17

[1] The number at the start of 1967 was seventeen, but Maryland repealed the state law banning mixed-race marriage once the *Loving v. Virginia* case was underway.

[2] The Hays Code was a self-imposed set of guidelines adopted by Hollywood studios that prohibited, among other things, nudity, profanity, rape, realistic violence . . . and "sex relationships between the white and black races."

[3] Translates to roughly 11 million people.

We don't match. Yes, we're family.
Deb Venzke • Iowa City, IA

The future belongs to the hybrids
Skip Mendler • Honesdale, PA

Never enough of a particular race
Yema Pizzuto • MD

I'm not mixed, I am biracial
Kiki I. • American Canyon, CA

Am I just what I look like?
Dane Rivas • Lubbock, TX

White interracially married sudden paradigm shift
Barbara Young • Stockton, CA

I've realized my own White privilege for some time now. But being the White female half of an interracial marriage, I suddenly experience America in a new frightening way. My husband is a six four, three-hundred-pound Black man. I have a plan worked out in my mind of how I can shield his body from police gunfire should I need to. I'm mourning the loss of my innocent and naive view of police in the USA.

Interracial marriage succeeding more than forty years
Thomas F. Costello • Binghamton, NY

Black with dreads and White husband

Tiffany Yizar • Norwalk, CT

My Blackness and Black cultural authenticity is never questioned, until people discover I have a White husband. As if his race diminishes mine and the life experience I've had in the years prior to meeting him. In fact, I'd argue being a Black woman married to a White man, a union not fully supported by either race as normal or acceptable, has made me even more secure in my Blackness.

She's so beautiful, is she mixed

Julie Newell • Lubbock, TX

Latinas don't burn, so you're White

Jessie • San Francisco, CA

I am Hispanic, half Tano (Italian Argentine) and half Danish. Very dark hair, but Whitey-Whiiiite skin. My Tano family always tries to get me to tan, saying things like, "If you were a real Tano, you wouldn't burn," or, "You look so sick."

I am the only black-haired, brown-eyed person in my blond, blue-eyed Danish family, and they only say, "She's Italian." Other Latinas in the US see me as a "typical White American," even though I am fluent in Spanish and [engage in] mostly Latin cultural practices. They frequently call me out for "co-opting" Latino culture. I also teach race and culture at my university, and students have said, "You look more Latino in your picture than in person." I constantly feel like some big disappointment. . . . I wish others could understand race and ethnicity better.

Yes I'm Black. No, not biracial.

David • Detroit, MI

To the cops, I am "White." To many others, I am "not Black." I don't try to pass, and I don't try to compensate for it by "acting" Black. I am very direct about these issues, though. I am a Black guy. How much more direct can I be? I'm not adopted.

So, let's cut to the chase. I'm one of those light-skinned Black guys that looks so Caucasian that some people think I fall in that "lucky" category. Well, I do not relate to that category, and I honestly do not like it. As much as I feel like I stand out among everyday Black people, I am Black. Not mixed, not multiracial, not this or that. Just Black. I have never felt the pull to deny this, although I grew up confused about how it's physically possible.

I've never met anyone in my family who is not Black, except some in-laws of some second and third cousins. Yet people wonder if I am truly Black, some even my own family. As funny as it is, my own son even doubted I was Black, despite the fact his grandparents he knew were both Black. It's just the genetics came out the way they did.

Little did I know that my family going back generations were fanatical about equality and ending racism. And no, they weren't just the "light-skinned ones." I learned from my family that, yes, I am Black, and no, I'm not "mixed"—at least

Bi-racial son draws Black self-portraits

Malika • Los Angeles, CA

Our son began to draw what he saw in the world very early. He wakes up from vivid dreams, grabs a sheet of paper, and illustrates the thunder and lightning, fairies and wizards, monsters and princesses from his nighttime imagination. Having grown up in America as a woman of African ancestry, so much of my life has been defined by race. I wanted my son, who is biracial (Black and White), to determine for himself who he is and what he'll become. It tickles me to see his self-portraits of a brave, dark-skinned child with brown curly hair that falls off the paper's edge.

not any more than any other Black person. In the end, I go down or up with Black people. I read a lot of comments about race, and what I notice is that people see stuff on the surface, especially regarding Black people, and compare that to their own deep, pondering thoughts on the same matter. So, I've taken it upon myself to insert myself into those conversations, passing, gaining their trust, then honestly inquiring about the whys, the hows. And you know what I get? I get either honesty or absurd, exasperated nonsense. I'm tired of hearing Whites being tired of Blacks complaining. And I'm tired of White people talking about feeling guilty. No one wants Whites to feel guilty. We want action for our society (Black and White) to improve where it's most needed.

White and Black are not polar opposites or "versions" of each other. They are just two distinct types of people. In the end, we are all people, but you cannot ignore what stands out and just pretend. Acknowledging our own ignorance, mine included, is a real effort to improve our country, world, city. I benefit from White privilege to some degree. I get the respect from cops that many Black people don't. I get Whites to talk more earnestly with me about race issues—that is, until I tell them I am Black or until I question their thinking.

In the end, I do not resent Whites or hate them. But I do hate the indifference. When there are Black issues in America, they are just that—"Black" issues. When there are White issues in America, they are "American" issues.

White father, Black kids. Eyes opened

Kenneth Klepper • Portland, OR

As a White Jewish man raised in the suburbs, everything I know about race I know because I was married to a Black woman for twenty years and have Black/mixed children. And yet, my experience doesn't stop me from having racist thoughts and attitudes. My experience simply makes me conscious of them and willing to question them. It is understandable that most White people are blissfully ignorant of today's subtle, background form of racism since they don't experience it. Yet, we take lots of things on faith without firsthand knowledge, and this should be no different. White people need to believe that racism does still exist in this country, that White privilege is real, and that, as far as America has come in repudiating its racist roots, it still has a long way to go.

I am mom, not the babysitter

Mikaela Rejbrand • San Francisco, CA

Being a person of mixed race, my biological mom is White and my biological father is Black, and having married an Irish man, my children are much lighter skinned than I am, and therefore I am often mistaken for "the babysitter." The constant theme since my children were born is that, "Oh, wow, your kids look so much like their dad!" I never understood that comment, as I see myself in my children beyond the color of their skin. With my children so young—my son is two, and my daughter is four—I have not yet broached the very complicated questions around race and the history of how people of all colors have had to endure discrimination, slavery, persecution, and hate. My children do not see color, they see people, and I hope that when the day comes that I will begin sharing stories of my ancestors, that the color of one's skin will be just that, the color of your skin.

Questioning my parents'/ society's racial preferences

Jordan • Flushing, NY

I'm Eurasian with a White father. At times I think, "Of course he was White." I wonder why, exactly. Why were Asian men not good enough? I look Asian. I have been turned down and called terrible things by Asian women because of my appearance. Am I considered better because I am Whiter? Am I considered an improvement? Am I still just inferior? Am I still just an Asian man, with the added benefit of knowing that my mother did not want one? Why did she take a White name? Why did she take pride in my looking White? I don't think I can ever get over this.

Start with kids
and mix well

Anika Fajardo • Minneapolis, MN

MY DAUGHTER'S A "TIGGIE" (REPUGNANT HALF-CASTE)

Paul Karrer • Monterey, CA

Korean Kisses

His résumé says he's a retired fifth-grade teacher, but Paul Karrer of Monterey, California, has always been a storyteller at heart. He is a podcaster, and his essays, columns, and poems have been published throughout his home state, and in a series of online posts he has chronicled a longtime pen pal relationship with a former student who went to jail.

When you talk to Paul, stories just spill forth. He's a natural raconteur. He lived in South Korea teaching English in the early 1980s and witnessed a country going through rapid change. He watched how young women in South Korea struggled to earn respect in the workplace. Feminism may have been blossoming around the world, but it hit a hard wall of resistance there. He watched the growth of the adoption industry in South Korea and saved money on some of his flights home by agreeing to serve as an official safe handler to escort infants and young children on their way to adoptive parents in the US.

And in the three years that he lived in Korea, he witnessed how hard it was to be an outsider in a country with few foreign residents. People would stop their cars and bicycles to stare at him when he walked down the street. "They had these big green buses, and it would be stopped, and every single face was pressed to the window watching me because I was like a Martian," Paul said. Sometimes Korean men would call him *monkey* or make up little songs about swinging in trees because of the fuzzy hair on his arms. They didn't know he spoke their language and could clearly understand the insult. It hurt. A White man who had grown up in America was not accustomed to being a targeted minority.

"I used to have a motorcycle there, and I got a full-coverage helmet that looks like an astronaut helmet where there's a jaw guard and a face shield that comes down," Paul said. "When I would park my motorcycle, I would almost always leave the helmet on. And then I would walk into where I was going and only then take the helmet off." He said he was tired of people commenting on his long neck, big nose, hairy arms, or white skin.

Paul met his wife of thirty years while working on the Korean Peninsula, and he had a story about that, too. His wife, also a teacher, is a native of South Korea. Theirs is a story of courtship, judgment, rejection, and ultimately the power of love that he summed up in his submission to The Race Card Project back in 2014.

But their story centers on a word that will be unfamiliar to many who read this. *Tiggie* is a derogatory term in the Korean language (튀기 twi-gi), an ugly slur whispered by people who try to police ethnic purity. In the Korean English dictionary, it translates into "the off-spring of animals of two different species" or "(disparaging) a person born of two people of different races." What the dictionary definition does not fully capture is that the derogatory term has historically been used to shun mixed-race children of American soldiers, with the presumption that a mother may have been a sex worker. It's a horribly offensive word, and though it is not widely used anymore, particularly among younger South Koreans, it is still whispered. As recently as 2019, a government official in Iksan had to issue a formal apology when a video surfaced of him using the term. Given all of that, it is extremely jarring to see Paul use that word in a 6-word statement about his own daughter. He says he was trying not to sugarcoat the harsh judgment that some children face. Paul's daughter is now grown, and she knows her father is sharing their story but asks that we withhold her name. So, she is referred to simply as Daughter throughout this story.

"My daughter's a tiggie (repugnant half-caste)"

He explained why he chose those words in an accompanying short essay called "Korean Kisses." These are his words:

> Our daughter is a tiggie (rhymes with *biggie*). She is Amerasian. Stripped to its essence, *Tiggie* is a Korean word meaning nonperson, animal, or mixed-race. That anyone could hate my child because of her gene pool is beyond me.
>
> Eighteen months after our daughter's birth, my wife, Mi-Ra, and I decided it was high time for her to mend the family fence and go back to Korea. We had, after all, eloped and brought a "tiggie" into the world. Would the two of them be accepted? I could not make it back with them because of my teaching job. I wanted to protect our daughter from what Mi-Ra and I had suffered in Korea. But even in multicultural California, things had not turned out too well for the three of us.

"He beat the snot out of her, kicking her in the stomach and pummeling her face."

> Monterey, California, harbors a world-class bay and Steinbeck's Cannery Row, but even near flowing tides of opulence, ignorance can run deeper than the submarine canyons hidden below the choppy waves. In an Asian store, Mi-Ra had our daughter bundled on her back, Korean style, allowing freedom of movement for the mother. Mi-Ra politely waited in line to check out a twenty-pound bag of brown rice. She smiled with rosy cheeks, basking in the glow of contented motherhood. Two ancient Korean grandmothers shuffled behind her, stopped, and whispered, "Tiggie, tiggie, tiggie." A shattered Mi-Ra later related this to me with a darkened soul.
>
> This is in the USA, my God, what will happen to the two of them in Korea? It made me reflect upon our own many Korean incidents in the years we lived on Cheju. But the worst of it was Mi-Ra's family. Her father had died long ago, and her five brothers ruled the roost. Once, her third brother had spotted us together. No one knew we dated, I had thought. The next day I couldn't recognize her. Her lovely head approximated the size of a pumpkin. A bruise the color of a ripe plum underlined her left eye. She walked with pain.
>
> "What happened?"
>
> "Bus accident," she lied.
>
> "Did you go to the hospital?"

"Yes. Many people did." She had lied again.

Years later, she spilled the beans, but only after that brother had had a stroke. Her brother had seen us together in the town market. He figured she'd dishonor the family by getting pregnant. Then the White devil would abandon her like so many had done during the Korean War. Then she'd have a *tiggie*. So, he beat the snot out of her, kicking her in the stomach and pummeling her face. Now she was returning home . . . with a *tiggie*. So, I was worried.

•   •   •

The phone connection wasn't that good. It crackled, and a time delay didn't help. But I didn't care. "How's the flight?" I asked as the acids in my stomach stormed.

"Long."

"How did [our girl] do?"

"OK, but she has a cold, I think."

I couldn't stand it anymore. "So, what's your family's reaction? What did your mom say?"

"They think [she] is beautiful." Mi-Ra's voice was calm, and I almost believed her.

"You're not lying this time?" I asked.

"No, I swear by the gods."

That was good. *I swear by the gods*. That was our private code. It meant the statement made was a truth to be believed at all costs.

"By the gods?"

"Yes, by the gods. My mother is holding her now."

"What about wing nut number three brother?"

"He has apologized many times. He bought [her] lots of presents. A gold bracelet and a gold ring. Korean twenty-four-karat gold, not American eighteen karat," she added. "He cried."

"I still think he's a bonehead, and I want to kick *him* in the head."

"Since his stroke, he can't walk anymore. These are not good thoughts."

"What else is going on?"

"Oh, you will like this. I walked in the market today with Daughter strapped on my back, and a street shoe vendor begged me to leave her with him."

"Why?"

"He said she is so beautiful that people would stop to praise her and buy many shoes from him."

"Hmm . . . I'll call you in a few days. Saranghae [love you]. Give Daughter a kiss for me. Say hi to your mom."

"OK, saranghae. Call in three days."

•   •   •

The connection was a little better, no crackling, but still a time delay echoed.

"So, how's Daughter?"

"She has a cold, but a funny thing happened because of that."

"She's sick, and a funny thing happened?"

"Yes, listen. . . . Yesterday, I took her to the market strapped on my back. She sniffled and sneezed. I felt a strange movement and turned around quickly. A young businessman had a tissue, and he was trying to clean Daughter's nose. He turned bright red when I caught him. I think things are changing here."

"A businessman, huh. You're not drinking maekju, are you?"

"No," she said. "Oh . . . here is another one. Today a group of high school girls kept on following Daughter and me from a distance. Finally, one of them ran up. 'Here, auntie, we bought a bag of candy for your beautiful baby.' They all smiled and ran away."

"You aren't making this all up to make me feel good?" I asked.

"It is all true. I can't make it up."

"Mi-Ra, I'll call in three days. Same time. Saranghae."

•   •   •

The connection was great. Not even a delay.

"Mi-Ra, how's things?"

"I think I'm going to cry."

The blood rushed to my face, and a quick nausea nailed me.

"To heck with Korea! Come home now!"

"No," she whispered. "No, it is good. Daughter and I were in the market for a long time. I was really busy. After three or four hours of shopping, I went home. [She] sleeps most of the time when I shop. When I took her home, I unstrapped [her], and I saw it."

"You saw what?"

"A kiss."

"A kiss? How can you see a kiss?"

"A red-lipstick kiss. Somebody in the market kissed her. I don't know who."

I was quiet for a while. "You want to stay longer, huh?"

"Can we? My mother is very old now. Your tiggie is safe."

"I suppose. I'll call you in three days. Saranghae, you two. Hi to your mom," I said.

"Saranghae," she replied.

"Mi-Ra . . . say hi to that bonehead brother, too."

• • •

As I said, Paul Karrer is a storyteller who has a way with words, and the story of his daughter's early entry into the world as a mixed-race child stirs the heart. The brothers who had a violent reaction to their sister's decision to date and then marry a White American all had a change of heart. The men have all passed away, but before they died, they were doting uncles even from afar. Paul and his wife settled in Northern California, an area with a large and thriving Korean community and where mixed marriages like theirs were fairly common. Paul's daughter was successful in school and had lots of friends. All good things.

But there was a piece of Paul's story he did not know about, something he might never have known if not for the inbox at The Race Card Project.

Five months before he submitted his story, another person with the last name Karrer had also sent in a story. A person who had the same first name as Paul's daughter. Someone who also lived in Northern California. She actually submitted two different stories within a five-minute period in June 2014.

He assumed things would be easier for people in his daughter's generation.

The first was a string of six words: "Culture, Beliefs, Family, Genetics, Language, Society." A few minutes later another submission: "I'm biracial but I don't fit in."

When I talked to Paul recently about his 2014 submission, I asked about his daughter, and his immediate reply was, "She's not going to talk to you." He said she was far too shy and withdrawn to ever share a story. I explained that I was asking because someone who shared his daughter's name had already sent a story to the inbox, and again, he was quick to respond: "That's not her!"

I explained that this person had the same last name. I repeated her first name and told him that she identified herself as someone who is now living in Sacramento. "Oh, wait, what year was this?" he interjected. His daughter was indeed living in Sacramento in June 2014.

"Are you sure it's not your daughter?" I asked. Paul said it was possible but unlikely. Then we both looked at the email she left in the contact field. "That's her. That's her," he shrieked. "Wow," he whispered under his breath, and then got really quiet. He realized something we have seen before at The Race Card Project, that two people with a shared story are communicating with us, but not talking to each other.

Paul explained that his daughter has always been closer to his wife, that maybe she had shared this sentiment with her mom. In the end, he was glad his daughter had found an outlet to give voice to something she was wrestling with. But the man who prides himself on being such an observant raconteur also realizes that he missed a story that was right at his kitchen table. His daughter might have been facing some of the challenges and feelings of alienation that he experienced as a White man living in South Korea. He wished he had a chance to talk with her about all of it. As America changed and became more tolerant of multiracial culture, he assumed things would be easier for people in his daughter's generation. He now questions why he would make that kind of assumption. Majority status, he said, sometimes comes with blinders.

There is no such thing as a do-over as a parent, but there is always an opportunity to do the right thing in the moment. Paul said there are some conversations in his future with his now adult daughter where he doesn't want to be the storyteller. Instead, he wants to just sit back . . . and listen.

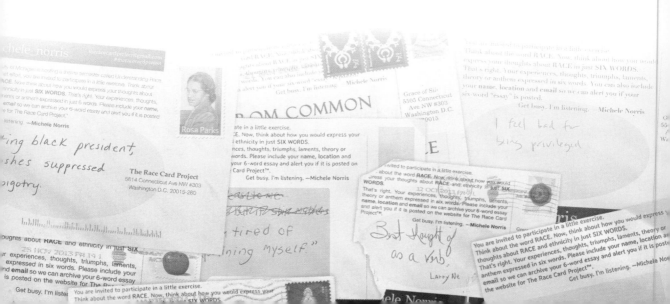

Married a White girl. Now what?

Kyle Lim • Grand Rapids, MI

As a biracial individual, I learned early on how to de-emphasize certain aspects of my racial identity depending on whom I was around. When I met my wife, Claire, we were both attending a predominantly White private college, and although she knew that I was mixed, her experiences with me have been ones where she mostly experiences my "White side." Over the course of our short year as a married couple, I have begun to realize that she sees me not as a biracial, multicultural individual, but more as a White man who tans really easily. We are deeply in love; I am not worried. But I do wish that she would/could see me the way I see myself. I am only now learning that I need to embrace my heritage and break out of the social/racialized conditioning that tells me that it is just easier and better to be White.

Don't hate 'cause I claim biracial

Fe Bencosme • Houston, TX

As the product of an Afro-Crucian and Anglo-Dominican union, I self-identify as biracial and bicultural. Some people find it "exotic," which leaves me feeling uncomfortable, although not as angry as when someone says to me: "Well, no matter what you think you are, the truth is you're Black." The retort is usually a deep, visceral reaction and always from Black Americans (African Americans, if you prefer).

I understand the many reasons why African Americans, in particular, would feel some kind of way about a Brown girl like me claiming mixed race as an identity. Yet, it doesn't take away the fact that I had a Black parent and a White parent or that I recognize them both equally. I refuse to deny either one because of a limiting and false reality some people have chosen to accept or because doing so would make others feel more comfortable about themselves. I *am* biracial. Now get over it.

I have the gift of choice

Dawna B. • Fort Thomas, KY

I am biracial and have the power in today's society to choose the race I identify as. My race and background are often misjudged or guessed at. I'm thankful that I have this option.

White culture. Black skin.
Perpetual outsider

Nicole Urbatch • Minnetonka, MN

Raised by interracial parents in the dominant White culture: internalizing racism just like every other White American. Oppressed by racism, marginalized, dismissed: just like every other Black American. Uniquely positioned to understand both perspectives. Crushed by the weight of it.

I won't disrespect my White mother!

Sabrina Price-Durling • East Windsor, NJ

I am proud to be of more than just one race (Black, White) and proud to have more than one nationality (American, German). After thirty-six years living, I still find it incredibly silly that other people feel the need to put me in a category, and more often than not it's Black folks who have more issues with my multiethnicity.

Apparently only my Black father counts—let's forget that 50 percent of me came from Germany, Czech Republic, and Slovakia. So, am I to ignore (and therefore disrespect) the heritage (*my life!*) that I received from my mother? More of the racism or narrow-minded comments I've received over the years have happened in the US than anywhere else I've been in the world (which I find ironic given we're the "huge melting pot").

I don't care what color your skin is, where you come from, or what your religion is. Don't ask me, "What are you?" if you don't expect to receive an answer of, "A human being!" If you're a decent person, we'll get along! I am proud to be a "mixie"!

I am both Black and White

Alexander Belisle • Bronx, NY

My mother is Latvian, and my father is from Belize, but all my life I passed as White. I always listened to the prejudicial biases expressed by others who were unaware of my ancestry.

My grandmother was mixed, I'm White

K.S. • Phoenix, AZ

During my childhood, I was raised to believe that I am Caucasian. I found out through a health crisis that what I suspected about my grandmother "passing" was true. In her abusive marriage to my grandfather, she lived as a White woman whom he institutionalized in mental health facilities when she tried to tell people she wasn't Caucasian. I now identify as being "mixed-race"; I don't want her to be invisible even as I am cognizant of my own "passing."

Multi does not equal NO race

Erin Yarbrough • Norman, OK

My husband is half Black and half Korean. I'm White. Our son is three races, but I hear and fear that others don't see him as any race. Multiracial is sometimes a hard way to identify.

I'm biracial but others see Black

Willie McBride • Long Beach, CA

I was born in China to a Chinese mother and African American father. I was orphaned, and an American serviceman and his wife adopted me; my adopted father just happens to be African American, and my mother is Chinese.

They also never mentioned that I was adopted, and so I grew up thinking that me and my sisters, who are also adopted but happen to be full Chinese, were blood relatives. Growing up, my parents made it very clear that we should never look at another person's color, that we should get to know the person instead. But they also made it very clear to me that people would always see my skin first and the person behind it second. I'd like to think I'm still color-blind.

Is the ticket together or separate?

Taylor Norman • Norman, OK

White man. Black woman. Two babies that look in-between. People never really think before they speak when they see my family together. For some reason they can't deduce that my mother is married to my father and my sister and I are their two girls. Instead, their eyes only see color. Brown goes with Brown, so the children go with the woman and the man is on his own.

This has always seemed to hurt my dad more than my mom. People look at him as the pervert. The thing in the puzzle that doesn't belong. When I held his hand in public, people whispered, and the situation tensed, but I never cared. Here's to hoping that interracial couples will stop being an oddity so families can enjoy outings in peace and not have to make clear that "Yes, the ticket is together."

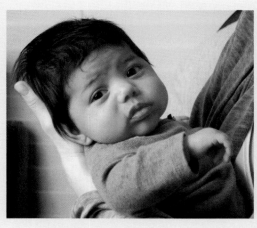

People assume my daughter is adopted

Rebecca • MO

I am White, and my husband is Indian. My daughter has my husband's complexion. When we are together as a family, people assume that she's mixed, but when I'm out with my daughter alone (which is most of the time), everyone assumes that she's adopted.

People ask me where she's from or where I got her. She's still too young to understand these questions, but I wonder how she will feel about them when she's older. I hope she won't feel less related to me just because other people make that assumption. And I hope someday people will become accustomed to mixed-race families and stop making the assumption in the first place.

Norwegian with nappy hair doesn't fit.

Wilma Stordahl • Seattle, WA

If I had a dollar for every time I was asked if my sons were adopted. It's happened a lot. A complete stranger approaches my family, usually in a grocery store or some other public location, and compliments me on my family. "Your sons are so handsome," the person will say, and by now I can almost tell what they're going to say next.

"Are they adopted?" "No," I say, "they are my biological children." The stranger looks bewildered for a moment. I can see she is trying to make sense of the puzzle before her: White parents, two Black sons, one White son. What's up with that? It doesn't fit in the tidy categories this person has in her mind. Our brains are constantly making associations and categorizing information, and when something doesn't fit, we try to make sense of it, even if it means making a fool of ourselves by asking a White mother, a complete stranger, if her Black children are adopted or not.

There are other ways this causes confusion. A job interviewer receives my son's résumé, his Norwegian surname prominently displayed at the top, and then a Black man shows up to the interview. What? No, he didn't lie on his résumé, but the effect is the same.

There's no appropriate box in the "diversity" section of a survey or census. "Mixed-race." What does that mean? Afro-Caucasian? Norwegian/Northern European and African American? At the end of the day, it means my sons are Black. That's the way the world sees them. Because of that, it means I, their White

How long have you had him?

Heather Ann Lindstrom • Buffalo, NY

My beautiful son was born to two very different parents. Me, of Swedish and Irish heritage, and his father, of Samoan and Chinese heritage. When I would take my son out as a baby, it felt like everyone I met assumed he was adopted and asked, "How long have you had him?" It always seemed like a strange question to ask first thing after hello.

mother, viewing the world from my privileged White perspective, am ill-equipped to raise my Black sons. This was never more apparent to me than after the shooting of Trayvon Martin when I suddenly realized I had not had The Talk with my sons. You know, I hadn't told them how to handle being stopped by the police.

I will never know what it's like to be a Black man in the United States. There are certain things that, because of my White experience, I will never know nor be able to teach my sons. They may not look like me, but they are my sons, my biological sons, my flesh and blood, and I have tried to prepare them for the world the best I can with love, discipline, and humor. Sometimes, when a stranger asks if they're adopted, I look at my sons with a smile and say, "No, we're still trying to figure out who their mother is."

Biracial??! Maybe. But call me Black

Tiffanie Luckett • Greenbelt, MD

I was adopted at nine months of age. My parents are Black. My biological parents were Caucasian and Black. My parents expected the world to see me as Black (or "other than White") and raised me accordingly. I was raised to see myself as Black, and I find it unsettling/ strange/uncomfortable when someone calls me biracial. I see myself as a Black woman and have never identified as biracial, mixed-race, or anything other than Black.

Successful, Black, gay. A family's shame

Karim Ali • Columbus, OH

When I read the comments of Michael Sam's father (Michael Sam Sr.) about his disappointment in his son for being gay, I was nearly in tears, as it reminded me of my own coming out with my family (namely my parents) and among my larger family, my fellow Black Americans. [Michael Sam was the first openly gay football player drafted into the National Football League.]

Mr. Sam (Sr.) was disappointed [despite the fact that] this was his only son to attend college, [a gay athlete] who will likely have a very positive impact on his family and society. Similarly, many of the men in my extended family have been incarcerated, fathered fatherless kids, and dabbled in drug addiction and crime.

I have been fortunate to have achieved the highest level of education in my family (MBA/JD). I am a partner at a large Ohio law firm and I volunteer extensively and mentor many young Black youths/young professionals, but I still sense the immense disappointment and judgment from many in the Black community in general, and from my father in particular.

My six words capture my personal struggle with being Black and gay.

BLACKCICAN
SPANISH SPEAKER
DIDN'T TEACH KIDS

Marisha Vandenberg • Menifee Valley, CA

MARISHA VANDENBERG SAYS SHE HAD never been happier in her life. She had returned to school to earn a master's degree in education after raising three children with her husband, Richard. The Vandenbergs had built a good life. They have been sweet on each other since they met in high school. She lives near her extended family in California's Menifee Valley. Her college-age children chose schools that allow them to pop back home for frequent visits. Yet, when a professor at California Baptist University in Riverside asked students to send their 6-word story to The Race Card Project back in 2017, Marisha wrote about regret.

"Blackcican Spanish Speaker Didn't Teach Kids" are the six words she chose for her class assignment.

Her first three words are like a quick bio. Marisha, who now works as an intervention specialist in the Riverside, California, school system, says she has always been taller and darker than the rest of her family and most people in her extended community. Her father was Black and Creole; her mother's side of the family is from Mexico. Marisha was raised in a tight-knit family that included her Latino grandparents, two uncles, and three aunts. They lived in a circle of houses that surrounded the Marmolejo family's upholstery business.

The next three words, *didn't teach kids*, hearken back to a decision that she now wishes she could reverse. Her husband, a mortgage lender, is White and of deep European ancestry. They did a DNA test and discovered that he has Norwegian, Scandinavian, German, and Dutch ancestors. Marisha jokingly calls Richard her Viking.

When they started their family, Marisha's mother would encourage the Vandenberg toddlers to use Spanish as they were learning to talk. When her son, Tyler, asked for water, his mother would correct him. "My mom says, 'No, agua,' and so Rich was like, 'Wait, why is she correcting him?'" Marisha said. She had always assumed her kids would grow up bilingual just like she did, but Richard was worried that they would get confused. She insisted that they would be just fine. "He had never experienced anyone being bilingual in the home," she says of her husband. "None of my reassurances helped."

Even as she protested, she had to admit that she herself sometimes still gets flummoxed when Spanish words dance through her mind as she is searching for the right phrase in English.

"Sometimes I do get confused," Marisha said. "Like, I did not know what flip-flops were. I called them chanclas my entire life. Sometimes I would forget words, like the word *pot*, like, you know a cooking pot. I would call it an olla so much at home." She sometimes slips into a version of Spanglish, and in her Southern California community, that's never been an obstacle. She assumed the same would hold for her young children.

The Vandenbergs were barely in their twenties when they faced the English-versus-Spanish decision for their children, and at the time, it felt monumental. "He [Richard] insisted they not learn both, and I caved in," said Marisha. She herself insisted that her husband's discomfort with Spanish was not a reflection of his discomfort with Latino culture. She knows people who find her story at The Race Card Project may jump to that conclusion. She says they wouldn't take that leap if they knew his heart.

In time, she agreed to an English-only approach for her children, but because they spend so much time with the extended Marmolejo family, she says she was secretly betting that her kids would learn Spanish almost by osmosis. To her regret, that didn't happen. If anything, the grandparents and great-aunts and -uncles wound up learning more English from the kids than vice versa as the Vandenberg brood grew older. "It was just, like, so weird to me that I finally realized, like, wow, these kids don't know Spanish," Marisha said.

While this was happening, the world was shifting, especially in California. The ability to switch easily between Spanish and English was increasingly seen as a skill employers were seeking—and sometimes rewarding with higher pay.

By the time their kids were teenagers, the Vandenbergs decided to change course. Part of the reasoning was to give them an eventual advantage in the workforce. But Marisha said she was also motivated by the heartbreak of seeing how much her kids missed when the family engaged in animated conversations that went right over her children's heads. "The faster we talk, we kind of get into it, and we get really emotional and start talking with our hands a lot," she said. "I could have a conversation with my grandparents, my aunts and uncles, that my kids just didn't understand." Marisha worried that they were losing a part of themselves. An essential part of themselves.

The Vandenbergs committed to making sure their three kids took Spanish in school and gave family members the green light to serve as language ambassadors. The kids are getting there, Marisha says. They can now conjugate verbs. They know the basics. They sing along with the love ballads Marisha keeps on her playlists. But she admits that Spanish or the Spanglish she so often speaks doesn't quite roll naturally off their tongues.

"Our son pronounces words with the appropriate accent," Marisha says. "Our youngest daughter pronounces words like a White girl. Our eldest daughter is adopted, so isn't Mexican at all but keeps up just fine." Ironically, after working for years in restaurants in his youth, Rich has a stronger command of the Spanish language than his kids.

"I wish my young ignorance hadn't allowed me to cave in," Marisha says. "But it's never too late to right some wrongs."

Not from here, nor from there.

Maria Sefchick • Seattle, WA

My father is American, my mother Mexican. I was born in the US, went to live in Mexico when I was eight, and returned to the US when I was thirty-nine. My kids were born in Mexico, first language is Spanish. First time I heard Hispanic as an ethnic label, I was in the US. In Mexico, I was called a gringa; here I am Hispanic. *Ni de aquí, ni de allá* is a common phrase in Spanish that means, "I do not feel I belong anywhere."

I feel more comfortable when I am with people of "color," although in Mexico, I was considered White. Being privileged in Mexico, it was a culture shock to be discriminated against here and find that I am part of the underrepresented and underserved minority. I have faced discrimination, mostly unintentional intolerance by "nice people" reacting to unconscious bias. For example, I have been told by my White male colleagues, "You know you only got your job because you are Hispanic," or, "What should I call you people? Hispanic or Latino?" Or my favorite, at a university where 80 percent of the staff is made up of White males: "We are just worried you people will take our jobs." I love many of the opportunities my children and I have enjoyed in the USA, but I am shocked at the number of poor people and the belief that we all have the same opportunities in this country. I work at a community college striving to increase access for all and awareness that there is such a thing as White privilege, that racism is alive and well, and that equity and justice must be worked for.

Ni de aquí, ni de allá.

Elizabeth Fernandez • Saint Paul, MN

The price we're forced to pay for having been born here as a minority, for having been born with the privilege of opportunity.

Don't speak Spanish but still Mexican

Elizabeth Fernandez • Saint Paul, MN

Bicultural and bilingual should be enough

Megan Medrano • Houston, TX

Growing up Latina in south Texas, I have always been surrounded with rich culture. My home was filled with both the English and Spanish languages, and I was encouraged to live both my Mexican and US Latina identities. I did not realize how important an ethnic identity was until I came to college. Discussions of, "What does being a real Mexican look like?" and, "Am I more Mexican or more American?" really pushed me to search for my identity.

The hidden criticism that people like me face begs the question of, "Am I Mexican enough to be considered Mexican, and am I American enough to be considered American?" I soon came to realize that striving to be one or the other is not who I should be, but instead I should embrace the heritage and the country that has made me who I am. I am both Mexican and American, bicultural and bilingual, and that should be enough.

Biracial boundaries separate my American life.

Joyenia Cabrera • Cleveland, OH

I am a biracial Hispanic. I have boundaries between the several races I [represent]. I am a Mexican and Puerto Rican living what I believe to be a typical American life. I don't speak Spanish. I haven't stolen an American job. I don't clean yards or create drama. I'm just Joy.

307

Ni de aquí, ni de allá

Ana Rodriguez • Antioch, IL

Selena's dad explained it best in his monologue from the 1997 film where he talks about how tough it is to be Mexican American. He goes on to explain that

Anglos jump all over you if you don't speak English perfectly. Mexicans jump all over you if you don't speak Spanish perfectly. We've gotta be twice as perfect as anybody else. . . . We've gotta know about John Wayne and Pedro Infante.

We've gotta know about Frank Sinatra and Agustín Lara. We've gotta know about Oprah and Cristina. Anglo food is too bland, and yet, when we go to Mexico, we get the runs. . . . Japanese Americans, Italian Americans, German Americans, their homeland is on the other side of the ocean. Ours is right next door. Right over there. And we've gotta prove to the Mexicans how Mexican we are. And we've gotta prove to the Americans how American we are. We've gotta be more Mexican than the Mexicans and more American than the Americans, both at the same time! It's exhausting!

United we stand, divided we fall.

Chad Beauvais • Bend, OR

I was told that there was no financial aid for me because I was predominantly White (even though I had the grades and financial need to qualify), so I joined the army for thirteen years in order to pay for college. I am grateful to have served my country, but I am 70 percent disabled because of my service. If I was any other ethnicity, I would not have had to risk life, limb, and mind just to receive an education. Where is my so-called White privilege? I traced my lineage back several generations to find that not only did none of my ancestors own slaves, my grandmother was an indentured Irish orphan servant (slave) to English foster parents.

Disabled doesn't mean helpless or nothing

Chris Gajewski • Barre, VT

I was hurt eleven years ago due to my making the worst choice a person could make. I got behind the wheel of a car one too many times while being intoxicated. After learning to walk and live again, I slowly began to repair my broken life. I clawed my way out of debt, got back to work on a part-time basis, started my collegiate career, and now I am a mere six months from having my own little chunk of the American dream with a home of my own.

Being disabled has made me more aware of my environment. When people see or find out I am disabled, they automatically assume I can't do for myself. Worse than that, it is hard to develop relationships with those people whom I would like very much to. For instance, women are very put off by my situation. I could count all the women who have been interested in me until they find out I was disabled on one hand.

I have done for myself fairly well up to this point, so people shouldn't all be fired up to help a "cripple" because they might just surprise you as to the level of help they don't actually need. Also, don't take us at face value; there is much more than meets the eye.

Universal race— being a disabled person.

Susan M. Giusto • USA

I hear this a lot from the nondisabled race(s). You are described by your disability: "The chick with glasses." "The dude in the wheelchair." "The kid with the artificial leg." In a crowd, people scan for that and then further qualify with color race labels. Some days it is hard; other days it is just normal, but it is there . . . just like the shade of one's skin.

I have been alone among many

Gordon Lee Pattison •
Napa, CA

In 1959, when I was fourteen years old, I moved from Los Angeles to Honolulu. I had just started taking French as a foreign language at my junior high school in Los Angeles and wanted to continue. However, there was only one junior high school in Honolulu at that time offering French in the ninth grade, so I got permission from the Honolulu school district to enroll there even though it was not located where we lived.

I don't think we realized it at the time, but I came to find later that it was located in one of the rougher parts of the city. When I enrolled, I met with the principal, who warned me that because I would be one of only two haole students at the school, I might encounter trouble from the other students because of my race. What he was telling me was to watch my back, at the same time making it clear to me that I was on my own.

I was about to have an experience that every White person in America should have. I know what it is like to be subjected to the mostly curious, sometimes mocking, and occasionally hostile stares and harassment that minorities often endure. I know the feeling of isolation, vulnerability, and anxiety that comes with that. I also know as a minority member what it is like to walk into a room of people and find myself instinctively looking around the room to see if there is anyone who looks like me.

I do realize, however, that my experience had one major difference from that of many other minorities in our society. I was a member of an economically dominant, privileged—albeit minority—ethnic group in Hawaii. Nonetheless, it was a very instructive experience. It shaped my life and social outlook ever afterward and gave me empathy for the minority experience in America, and for that I have always been grateful.

I help; I'm not THE help.

Eric N. Peguero • New York, NY

We, Latinos, may raise your children, do your laundry, and clean your floors, but we are not The Help. We are people like you, perhaps a little less proud of how we earn a living and very willing to earn that living honorably. We deserve respect.

Carlos, you really don't speak Spanish?

Carlos Hernandez • Seagoville, TX

I am a Hispanic of Mexican descent with an extremely stereotypical name. My first and last names are both common Latino names. So, when people figure out I can't speak Spanish well, they don't believe me, and my fellow Latinos mock me for it. I can't help that I wasn't taught the language at a young age, and I wish I knew it before.

Mexican White girl, doesn't speak Spanish.

Elysha O'Brien • Las Vegas, NV

Whites see me as Mexican. Mexicans view me as White because I don't speak Spanish. I find it interesting that we don't qualify other ethnic identities on the basis of language.

Borderlands born. Always illegal. Always home.

Chuy Benitez • Houston, TX

When you grow up at the collision of two countries, of two cultures, of two identities, you learn very quickly the different nuances between the two cultures, and you adapt to appease whichever culture you have to encounter. It makes you more observant, but of course it doesn't occur without making mistakes and having to

learn how to deal with the situation of appeasing more than one point of view at a time. If you think the social constructs and expectations of a singular culture, from even a singular city or town, are rough enough to deal with, try growing up with two very distinct cultural expectations that clash against each other on a daily basis. The languages clash, the religions clash, the politics clash, and the economies clash, but yet somehow on the borderlands you have friends, families, and lovers that exist in both worlds and that cross those borders and work with them every day.

The border is always there, the signs are threatening to the new visitor, but the borderland native looks at the border crossing like they would a McDonald's sign or a neighborhood park. It's just part of the landscape that they might use from time to time. The border is ingrained in their heads. They have a natural cultural GPS on how to act depending on which side they are on. Which language to use, which jokes to say, how much bravado or humility they should have as they walk down the street. As one book put it best, the borderlands are the laboratory of the future. If you can make it here, you can make it anywhere.

Can you speak Indian for me?

Kushal Methukupally • Pleasanton, CA

A common stereotype that is involved with Indians is the thought or belief that we all speak "Indian." This is surely not the case. There is no such language called "Indian." To be "Indian" is considered your race, not your language. Hinduism is the religion we practice, and Hindi is the most common language spoken among Indians, but even then, there are several languages spoken in India, and "Indian" is not one of them.

Suburban White kids nicknamed with Chinaman

Aaron Yeh • Las Vegas, NV

White mother, Chinese father. I was raised by my mom and don't speak Chinese. Sometimes I look in the mirror, and my Asian features surprise me. It's startling how I identify more with being "White" than anything else. The "other" box on forms asking my ethnicity has always comforted me, like there's a half-breed bureaucrat out there who understands.

Not All Asians Speak Chinese, Okay!?

Austin McGlothlin • Berea, KY

I'm an Asian studies major with a concentration in Japanese language. I have spent the only year I've been in college identifying the cultural differences in Asia that have created stereotypes about all Asians being smart or gifted at musical instruments. But I've mostly noticed the fact that no one, even in Asian studies classes with me, can tell the difference between Asian cultures. Everyone thinks that each country and ethnicity is the same as one another, and they even tend to assume that Asian Americans speak an Asian language . . . well, just Chinese. When I tell people I am learning Chinese [as well], I tend to get mocked with the typical "ching chong wong" crap that is supposed to resemble Chinese and doesn't even accurately mock any other language but Chinese. I'll even have friends that have known me for years ask me which language I'm learning again because it's supposedly so similar to Chinese that they can't get it straight. Everyone assumes that they are exactly the same and that both Chinese and Japanese specifically are all there is to Asia and anyone with tan skin and slanted eyes is assumed to be a smart, gifted Chinese person. It bothers me.

You're just like a normal couple

Kathleen J. Gagnon • New Haven, VT

We were at another couple's house for dinner. The meal was excruciatingly boring, but the man of the couple was my army officer husband's commanding officer, so I pasted a smile on my face and got through the evening.

When it finally ended, we thanked our hosts and got in the car for the short drive home. "Let's not do that again soon," I said to my husband. It was a short drive home. Many of the officers lived in the same small area of Colorado Springs. As we walked in the door of our apartment, the phone was ringing. I answered to hear our recent hostess gushing, "What a wonderful night! Why didn't we do this sooner? You and Duffy are just like a normal couple!" I am White. My ex-husband is African American.

I, White man, afraid of Whites

Mike Wyncoop • Orlando, FL

I thought we'd have gotten further

Barbara Ogur • Cambridge, MA

Celebrating racial heritage can be divisive

Rob Davidson • Lone Tree, CO

When I was studying for my PhD, I was in a class with a doctoral student who was studying education in our inner cities. This person told a story about how upset s/he was when interviewing four-year-old students because they had no concept of their racial differences. This person went on to say s/he was comforted to find that by age six students fully understood their racial differences.

Seems to me that if we truly want a color-blind society, then the four-year-olds had it right. How can we ever achieve racial harmony and equality when we celebrate our differences and not our similarities? How can we ever achieve racial harmony and equality when each successive generation learns the concept of "us and them" (in-group/out-group conflict) at such an early age? Imagine a world where celebrating racial heritage wasn't divisive. . . . The power to realize this dream lies within us.

I'm a living apology. I'm sorry

Annaleis Thibault • Bolton, MA

As a White, middle-class American, I feel
as though I owe reparations for the crimes
committed by my ancestors.

Does a fish know it's wet?

Mike Hendry • Las Vegas, NV

Almost every White person I know has no idea or won't admit they are
racially biased against Blacks. They think that since they have a Black
friend, a Black neighbor, they joked around with the Black woman in
line at the grocery store, or they voted for Obama (etc.) that they are
not racially biased.

But I hear what they say, and as tame as their views might sound
to them and others, my ears now hear something different. To me,
their views on Blacks sound patronizing and ignorant at best and even
downright racist on occasion. With as much humility as I can muster,
I'm here to say that I truly realized I was biased against Blacks, and
without going into details, that realization put me on a path to ending
those racial biases as I knew them. It started with an awakening,
followed by a new and deep understanding of myself and how *my*
environment had shaped my views.

So, through my own experience, I believe the answer to the question
is this . . . Fish don't know they're wet, as being wet is not a concept
that's easy to comprehend when your environment *is* water.

Pale freckled redhead burned by words

Marie Farrell • Brooklyn, NY

I grew up in San Diego, California, where the sun shines all the time. I was the kid that never tanned, just freckled and burned. I recall a day when I bravely went to school in shorts and was destroyed by the words of a Black girl who said, "You need to get a tan!" I was often looked at weird because of the pale skin, being told to tan as if it were that easy. I was told by a girl in my gymnastics class, "You have freckles on your knees," as if that was such an odd thing. I was called Annie, Pippi, and Strawberry Shortcake, and later I was called more inappropriate names like Fire Muff and Ginger.

Since having cancer and losing my hair, it has grown back less red, but I feel I am always and will always be a redhead on the inside and out—always feeling like a fish out of water in a hot, sunny climate, being called names that most people might not think are racist, but no matter what they thought, it stung. It burned me more than the awful sunburns I grew up with. As an adult I take pride in my "spots" and my pale skin, in my sort-of-red hair and my Irish heritage. But sometimes those words still burn.

I don't have any Black friends

Sam • Wheeling, WV

Black teen boys
scare White people

Tim McGovern • Chicago, IL

I live in a racially integrated neighborhood on the South Side of Chicago. You go to the playgrounds, and there are kids of all races playing together, parents talking over coffee and bonding over the crazy things that four-year-olds do. The public school kindergartens, first grades, second grades, third and fourth, all full of different-color faces. Sixth, seventh, eighth . . . high school: Where'd all the White people go?

"Oh, we're worried the school has discipline issues in the upper grades." "I wouldn't feel like my daughter is safe there." . . . What's going on? These are the same families you've known since your kids were running around naked in the fountain as toddlers, but all of a sudden, they've turned into Young Black Men. And that scares off White people. And we all lose out.

I will burn the house down

Eric • Chesapeake Beach, VA

1974: I was fourteen years old; my dad was in the army, and we were moving to Ohio from Weaver, Alabama. We rented the house we lived in. The owner was selling the house, and the Realtor was in the driveway talking to my dad one day. The neighbor came over to see what was happening. He was a state trooper, and when he heard the house was up for sale, he told the Realtor, "If you sell the house to a n*****, I will burn it down." Then he walked away. Stuck with me for all these years—a police officer. Wasn't he supposed to protect everyone?

I was bused. I was scarred.

Andrea Stewart • Brooklyn, NY

When I was in third grade, I was bused from the predominantly White side of town to the predominantly Black side of town for elementary school. I had had Black friends in my former school, but the new school was mostly Black, and I had a Black teacher. For once, I was in the minority. Unfortunately, my teacher made a point of letting me know that *often*. I was no one special to her. In fact, on Valentine's Day, she gave candy to everyone in the class but me. That and other incidents with her made that the worst year of my education, when it could have been an enlightening year. She scarred me.

One flight; we were not Black

Hazar Khidir • Boston, MA

"If we were in slave times, I'd whip you." He aimed his face directly at me as his small mouth fired the phrase out onto the table. Even at the budding age of six, each of us around the lunch table knew enough to stop and give the words their due weight. But I only stopped biting into the hamburger I held in my hand for just a few seconds.

The sandwich was made lovingly. From an oversize bread roll instead of a hamburger bun, with ground beef that was kneaded with copious amounts of earthy cumin and coriander seasoning, and soggy with its generous helping of condiments. I knew it was off. Not quite classically American, but rather, an earnest attempt by my mother to create something American with an immigrant's innocent naivete, an instinctual Sudanese spice ritual, and an enthusiastically, just-discovered appreciation for mayonnaise and ketchup.

Yes, I knew it was off. Just like the five-sizes-too-large socks that covered my small feet; in the shock and suddenness of the below-freezing temperatures that greeted us the year before when we'd first arrived in the United States of America, they had rushed to purchase them, not realizing to look in the children's section of the enormous mid-Missourian Walmart Supercenter. "I don't care. I'm still not getting it for you," I responded after the brief silence. The little boy had demanded that I go fetch him an item from the lunch line and had launched the sentence after I'd refused. I knew the words were meant to wound me. However, I hardly felt the sting of them at the time, and so it had to be my Caucasian American friend who had been sitting next to me and who, in a beautiful and prodigious defense of my Thirteenth Amendment right, told our teacher the dangerous sentence he had spoken.

318

I was embarrassed by my parents' reaction. Having to see them in the middle of the school day when they demanded to meet with teachers and the boy's parents, having my teachers usher me formally in front of the boy who'd spoken the words so he could utter a mandatory and airy apology, and having to be reminded once again that there was yet another thing that contrasted me from my primarily Caucasian, Christian peers; I was eager to forget about the entire incident.

Meanwhile, my parents were worried. My family won the Diversity Immigrant Visa lottery in 1996 after years of frustration with the coup-established authoritarian government of Sudan. In the 1920s, my mother's grandfather had worked hard to establish a camel caravan that journeyed regularly forty days by foot across the Sahara Desert to sell camels to wealthy Egyptian traders. The business was passed down to my grandfather and caught the attention of Western journalists, who documented the passage of the caravan across the desert in the documentary *Voice of the Whip*. After the military coup led by Omar al-Bashir in 1989, my mother watched as the business deteriorated under the harsh, inconsistent regulations and bans imposed by the new dictatorship. She also watched this same dictatorship detain my father for a short time, believing that he belonged to a political party that it had banned.

The incident in the cafeteria worried them because they realized that though we'd managed to make it to the fervently sought-after land of liberty and prosperity, we had been relegated to a minority group that was vulnerable to neglect and abuse. We were now Black. Though this seemed an obvious and observable fact to most Americans who looked at us, my parents were used to a Sudanese sociological system that did not consider them Black, but rather reserved that term for other ethnic groups in Sudan.

I talk the walk too much!

Eric Wall • Kent, WA

I was fortunate to be part of an integrated busing program all through elementary school. I went to college and got a master's degree in multicultural education. I still spend too much time talking the talk and not walking the walk. Fully understanding the impact of race is truly a lifelong journey.

Jason's Cabbage Patch doll was Black

Sarah Currier • Northfield, MN

My daughter's boyfriend Jason shared a great photo of himself at about age six or seven. He was holding a Black Cabbage Patch doll he had received for Christmas and had a puzzled look on his face. Not a typical gift for a boy in Hudson, Wisconsin, in 1990. His parents were working-class folks, not involved in any political or social groups that he knew of.

This year, Jason asked his parents if they had been trying to increase his awareness or open his mind or something. His mother paused a moment, then said, "Well . . . yes. We were." It was so understated and beautiful. They gave their White boy a *doll*, and it was a *Black* doll. Jason is one of the gentlest, most compassionate and accepting young men I know. It's possible to grow up in a less diverse culture and still be aware of the greater world beyond you.

My childhood prejudice still taints me

Christopher Allen • Worcester, MA

I am White, I'm sixty years old, and I can't shake the prejudice that I absorbed during my upbringing. It wasn't overt; it was hidden, not talked about, but very real and therefore more insidious. It was matter-of-fact, from the only "eeny, meeny, miny, moe" ditty I knew as a boy, to this day when I meet a White guy, I think "guy," and when I meet a Black guy, I think "Black guy." This prejudice is still part of me. I hate it. I wish it would go away.

Separation based on race is horrifying

Joycelyn Cole • Terrytown, LA

As a high school sophomore in 1955, I attended our school system's oratorical contest. The finalists were a White girl from my high school and a Black boy from St. Augustine High School. We attended the contest in a high school auditorium. The Black boy won. He walked out with a huge trophy. We boarded the bus together, but the boy had to sit behind a "Colored Only" sign. Made me feel sick and angry to see that. I have never forgotten it.

Not brown? Pass Go. Collect $200

Sue Ann Higgins • Portland, OR

For me, White privilege operates as unearned advantage, kind of like in the Monopoly game, where you get paid simply for showing up. I was pulled over by a police officer for the first time ever for speeding (which I do daily) the day after I turned fifty. And I was not ticketed, even for going seventy-two miles per hour in a fifty-mile-per-hour traffic safety zone where tickets double. This sort of unearned advantage influences me all the time, often without my noticing.

Get out of jail free card

R.J. • Philadelphia, PA

Being White is one reason no one ever accused me of shoplifting, or selling drugs, or cheating on tests. Even when I was.

I know rap, not Black people

Toby Johnston • USA

I grew up in Los Angeles in the 1980s, a rabid fan of all things rap. I am White, and for many of my friends (Mexican, Black, White, lower-/middle-/upper-class, whatever), rap was the music of rebellion. I got called wigger by my White(r) friends and heard a lot of hate spewed. And yet at the same time, through the love of the music, I came to understand the African American and immigrant experience through a very narrow lens.

I see this myopic perspective from a generation of kids who grew up with rap. Rap created icons of disenfranchisement easily accessible by our teenage angst and yet simplified the narrative of what race, and in many ways gender, could be.

I think this myopia is easiest to identify in the bias of those who hated rap, called it "jungle music" in the pejorative, but the misinformation worked both ways. Rap elevated a struggle but also defined an individual's potential in a very dangerous way. Don't get me wrong, I still love rap, but I don't confuse my love of the music with an understanding of those peoples and the neighborhoods that it came from. I understand rap, and its later corporate-sanitized little brother "hip-hop," as only a single voice in the discussion and not the whole choir.

Latinos overlooked in conversations about race?

Brenda Ramirez • Chicago, IL

You would think that only White and Black people exist in this country. What about the rest of us? There is no outcry for Latinos who are shot, harassed, discriminated against, whose families are torn apart, and whose children are locked up in detention centers. When will we matter in America?

Dig n***** out of my head

James Christopher Perry • Silver Spring, MD

I was raised by parents who didn't think they were racist, and by grandparents who were and didn't care. The first word I heard to describe Black people was n*****, followed by, "They'll cut your throat out." I have spent my adult life digging those words, that hatred, that fear out of my head. I work at it every day. Maybe one day I will succeed.

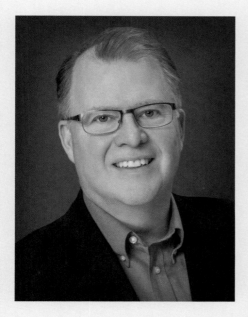

Dad was racist, I fought him

William G. Doyle, Jr. •
Castle Rock, CO

From the time I could remember, my father expressed his racism against African Americans. I fought him because of it throughout my life. Usually, it exposed itself most after we would go to church and listen to beautiful sermons about God's love for all people and then come home and he'd yell at the football game on the TV saying, "Those damn n******, they should all be shipped back to Africa."

When I was young, I didn't know what to say and felt ashamed. As I got older, I would challenge him on his hypocrisy and get into shouting matches. When our high schools in Minneapolis had race riots because of busing, I wanted to go down and protest on behalf of desegregation. He wouldn't let me and said I would disgrace his family.

Mostly, I felt a sense of embarrassment that this was my dad. These arguments continued into my adult life, and I got tired of trying to win this fight with him. My mom and siblings just wanted to keep the peace and would admonish me to keep quiet, for their sakes. So, I kept quiet and did the best I could to live a life filled with respect and love for all people regardless of race, religion, gender, and sexual orientation. My parents are gone now, but I still think about the racism that was in my home growing up. I still feel ashamed.

9

The Patterns Themselves Tell a Story

IN NATURE, YOU CAN DETERMINE the condition of an environment over time through the study of tree rings. When a tree is cut, a series of concentric rings surrounded by tree bark is nature's way of telling a story.

It's known as dendrochronology or dendroclimatology. Patterns in variation, size, contour, and invasive elements shown in those repetitive circles help scientists find clues about atmospheric conditions. In each growth season, a new tree ring helps reveal environmental patterns and the impacts of humans on the tree's surroundings.

The Race Card Project archive is much like a social tree ring, capturing people's thoughts, observations, and experiences through shifts in time and social change. It is a living portal to the human experience around race, identity, culture, otherness, and belonging. Some of those markers are monumental footnotes to history. Protests and police shootings. Political milestones and a global pandemic. Court cases. College debates. Trailblazers who change the face of an industry. And some of the markers are impossible to miss, not so much because they are the stuff of blaring headlines, but rather because they show up in the inbox so often. Scores of people all writing in about red hair and teachers who underestimate their potential. Stories that come from all kinds of places yet have a common theme—about having to decide which box to check, what clothes to wear to avoid suspicion, whether they should apologize about something that happened years ago.

In some cases, the patterns themselves tell a story.

The repetition sometimes speaks to an issue or event that resonates through many lives like an earthquake with fault lines that reach in all directions. In other cases, the stories that land in the inbox on repeat are a window into shared epiphanies or networks of hidden anxieties that people nurse largely behind closed doors. And some of these stories that land repeatedly in the inbox help us understand the ways that language can define or confine people. How a simple question or statement that may seem breezy in its tone or intent is nonetheless noxious to the person on the receiving end.

One clear example of the poison dart masquerading as a compliment: the moment when someone remarks on a woman's attractive appearance but turns the plaudit into a gut punch by adding an ugly qualifier. We have heard from hundreds of women who themselves have heard some version of this backhanded bouquet: "You're pretty for a _____ [fill in the blank]." Pretty for an Asian girl or Indian woman or a plus-size female. It seems to always be aimed at women and most especially at Black women of all ages. Over fourteen years, variants of this card have arrived almost every month. My heart breaks a little every time it happens because I know what is really at work inside those words.

Because I know that America has tried to define beauty in ways that don't include women of color, especially Black women, over centuries.

Because I know that little girls absorb those messages, even if they are never directly articulated.

Because I understand that this so-called "compliment" is meant to make the subject feel extra special because they are an anomaly. An outlier. Someone who is different from the general cohort of brown-skinned women who are not supposed to lay claim to a felicitous adjective that describes what is most attractive and desired.

And mainly because I know it is all a lie.

Beauty is not the same as beauty standards. Beauty is given upon birth to all who walk this Earth like a gift that can be nurtured, embraced, or cherished just as easily as it can be twisted, extinguished, or denied by forces that believe they wield the power to police someone's worth. Beauty standards are something altogether different—the product of a capitalist, colonialist system that through laws, customs, messaging, and media portrayals created a metric meant to elevate some by ensuring a large group of outsiders were held at a lower rung. Beauty is only partly about appearance. Too often it is an expression of power. A tool for enforcing an exclusionary social order.

Just look at their pictures on the following pages. These women are radiant. I hope they walk through life feeling as good as they look. Most of them know that the backhanded, beautiful-for-a-this-or-that "compliment" is rubbish. But just because you can see and name a poison cloud doesn't mean you can always escape its fallout.

You're Pretty for a...

Pretty
Adjective

Pleasing by delicacy or grace
Having conventionally accepted elements of beauty
MERRIAM-WEBSTER DICTIONARY

• • •

Pretty
Adjective

Pleasant to look at, or (especially of girls or women or things
relating to them) attractive or pleasant in a delicate way
CAMBRIDGE DICTIONARY

• • •

Pretty
Adjective

If you describe someone as pretty, you mean that they are attractive
Synonyms: attractive, appealing, beautiful, sweet
COLLINS DICTIONARY

• • •

Pretty
Adjective

Pleasant to look at or listen to
Synonyms: see beautiful
THE BRITANNICA DICTIONARY

You're Pretty For A Black Girl

Amari Adams • DeKalb, IL

You are cute to be dark

Secunda Joseph • Houston, TX

I've always seen the beauty in myself, even as a kid. My brother and I were the darkest of all my aunts and cousins. Around family, I was "everything good." One of my several nicknames was Chocolate Drop. Then when kindergarten started, what I heard was "with your *Black* self," "you look like an African booty scratcher," and the compliment, "you're cute to be dark"—hence went my confidence. Darkness and Africa became a shame and a flaw. I have to thank God for opening my eyes and allowing me to see the beauty in my dark complexion and my African roots. #africanamericanconsciousness

Chil', she Black BUT she pretty

Lezlie Harrison • Brooklyn, NY

You're Pretty, for a Black Girl.

Kem • Huntsville, AL

I was so shocked when a White coworker said this to me. He actually thought he was giving me a compliment!

She's pretty for a Black woman.

Mary • Detroit, MI

My dad was born in 1906 and would say this about perhaps the first Black female anchor on a Detroit TV station; I can't remember her name. I hope I replied, "Why can't you just say she's pretty?"

You are pretty for dark-skinned girl

Amber • Chapel Hill, NC

You're pretty for a dark-skin girl

Imani B. • Baltimore, MD

So, are all dark-skinned girls ugly, and I'm the exception? Would I be ugly if I was lighter? You're insulting me. Please don't.

You're pretty for a Black girl

Maya Segirah • Los Angeles, CA

You're Pretty, For a BLACK girl

Courtney • Moore, OK

I am told this quite often, and it makes my heart ache, not because I let it bother me personally because I don't. But for the other Black women and young ladies that are told the same thing and don't have the courage to say that I am a beautiful Black woman, not pretty for a Black woman.

You're pretty for a Black girl

Gloria Collins • Shreveport, LA

Every ethnic group has beauty. No race has more beauty over another race.

No offense, but you're so pretty!

K. E. Broadnax • Cleveland, OH

This was said to me while attending college. I am Black and went to a predominantly White, upper-class university (as many are, to be fair). His statement was prefaced by the question, "What nationality are you?" If I was me now, back then, I would've replied, "American."

You're pretty for a dark-skin girl

Shanyla • Beachwood, OH

What am I supposed to think when I hear this?

331

You're pretty for a Black girl
Alexis • Minooka, IL

I hate when not just other races say this about Black girls, but African Americans alone say this to individuals. I think it's an insult honestly because what are Black girls supposed to look like? Not pretty? Others may see it as a compliment, but in reality, it's not. Beauty comes in various colors, shapes, and sizes. There is no real term for the word *beauty*.

Not just for being a Black girl
Anisha (Blair) Taylor • Riverside, CA

"You're beautiful. For a Black girl." Those words spilled out the mouth of a young Black male, in my twelfth-grade math class. Only then was I reminded that being a dark-skinned Black woman, we are not considered to be as beautiful as other women. I was in second grade, attending a mostly White school and being one of the few darker-skinned children, I often felt out of place and not very pretty. I remember praying to God that I would wake up with blonde hair and blue eyes. Flashing forward to being a high school senior, and hearing someone saying exactly how I felt most of life, it was horrifying. I cried. This was not a first. I have heard this countless times throughout my life but *never* from someone of my own race. The sting of hearing those words seemed to hurt a little worse than ever before.

I eventually became more confident within myself and my skin color. I embraced my being dark-skinned and began to love myself. We are taught at an early age (when I say *we*, I mean dark-skinned Black women, mostly) that if you are not White or light-skinned you are not as pretty. It's an issue I have dealt with my whole life, and I pray that one day, if and when I have a little girl, that she never has to deal with this issue, but because I know if things haven't changed in hundreds of years, it's not gonna change tomorrow, I will be fully prepared to tell her she is beautiful and not just for a Black girl.

You're pretty... for a dark-skinned girl!

Vernae Williams • Sacramento, CA

I grew up in a family full of light-skinned people. I always felt like an outsider because, within the Black community, light skin is seen as the "right skin," and dark skin is viewed as being ugly. Growing up, I never truly felt comfortable in my own skin due to the stigma associated with dark skin. I can't begin to count how many times I have been told, "You are pretty for a dark-skinned girl." People would feel as though they were giving me a compliment, but they were doing the exact opposite. I want people to know that all shades of Black are beautiful! My Black is beautiful!

You're pretty for a Black girl

Autumn Rainey • Indianapolis, IN

I remember growing up in a mostly Caucasian area, and I was told this often. What was likely meant as a compliment to me became quite an insult as I got older. I wish more people could give a compliment without qualifying it.

But you do not look black.

Melanie Payne • Tampa, FL

I'm the Jimmy Durante of six word racial insults delivered as compliments. Among them: — You're too pretty to be black. — Well, you can't be all black. — You must have white blood. — I bet your mom was white. — But you have such beautiful hair. Each of these are real responses to the question, "What are you?" or "What race are you?" This is often the very first question a stranger will ask me! Not, "What's your name?" or "How are you doing?" Maybe it's just curiosity, I'm a reporter, I get that. But I think it's because for many Americans, what I am is more important than who I am.

Mom said brown girls are ugly

Anna • Santa Maria, CA

I am a forty-seven-year-old Filipina. I remember being constantly compared to my lighter-skinned cousins and feeling awkward to be among my own family. If I could, I would travel back in time and give my three-year-old self a tight hug and tell her how important it is to love herself and to never believe any of the BS her mother tells her ever again.

Enough to make you look pretty

Adrienne Zimiga • Minneapolis, MN

I was born and raised on the Pine Ridge Reservation my first twelve years. Upon moving from Batesland, South Dakota, to Castlewood, South Dakota, my Caucasian grandmother was concerned that my brothers, sister, and I could face social problems being part Native American (iyeska: mixed-blood/race) in an all-White community. She told us, "Now, you don't have to go around telling everyone here that you're Indians. Besides, you're just enough to make you look pretty." It was a very confusing statement for me as an adolescent. I came from a place where I was very proud to be who I was as a person, and now I have my own grandmother telling me it may be best to keep it under wraps, that "Indian" part of me. Anyone who knows me knows *that* will never happen. I'm very proud of my ancestry, my culture, my heritage, and my connection to it. It is the driving force that has made me the person I am today.

I'm not prettier because I'm White

Rhiannon Watkins • Centennial, CO

You are pretty for an Asian

Laurel Nelson • Corona, CA

Brown Girl scale, White girl scale

Kameel Mir • Athens, GA

When I was a freshman in college, an Indian American boy told me I was a certain level of attractive on the "Brown-girl scale," but on the "White-girl scale," my "rank" was lower. It fed into my ingrained notions that the Brownness of my body put me into a second class of beauty/worth that anyone with lighter skin would automatically trump, no matter the particulars. I noticed the way that boy talked to White women, with palpable awe and attentiveness, versus how he spoke to me. I did not expect him or anyone to find me beautiful, but I also did not expect to be categorically dismissed. Because he was Brown, too, it felt like a mirror reflection was parroting my worst fears—it felt like what haunted me privately also had the power to publicly humiliate me. I was new to this school that was overwhelmingly White, having come from a fairly diverse high school, and I was all dressed up for one of my first nights out. As much as I wish it didn't, that comment shaped the way I viewed my social currency, my self-worth, for a long time following.

Darker skin can be pretty too

CaMera Gibson • Birmingham and Jacksonville, AL

Being pretty for a black girl

Rachel Rowe • Chicago, IL

I've grown to love how I look but growing up in a predominantly White community at one point in my life, I heard "you're pretty for a black girl" way too often. It gave me unrealistic beauty standards to look up to.

BLACK AND FAT WHICH WAS ENOUGH!

Shari L. Burgess • Detroit, MI

How dare I be Black and then choose to be fat. Elephant, big nose, whispers and out-loud comments. At fifty-eight, tears still falling, still looking for the B in *Black* to be beautiful and F in *Fat* to be fabulous.

You're too pretty to be Black

Akira Lee •
Virginia Beach, VA

I once had a woman approach me in a restaurant and tell me that I was really pretty. It was my thirteenth or fourteenth birthday, and I had dressed really nicely and was proud that someone noticed how beautiful I looked that day. I responded politely to her and thanked her, upon which she asked me, "What are you?" I replied that I was Black, but she gave me this confused look and said, "But you're too pretty to be Black. What else are you?" At the time, I didn't understand that what she had said to me was disrespectful, and I ended up taking her hurtful words as a compliment. If I knew then what I know now, I would've known that what she had said to me was ignorance and would have simply walked away.

Grandma called me "pretty colored girl"

R. Denise Everson •
Washington, DC

My grandmother reared me. Her positive expressions of beauty being Black shaped my perception and made me proud to be Black.

You're cute for a Black girl

Leah Thomas • Florrisant, MO

I grew up in Saint Louis, Missouri, and I moved to a mainly White private school in the fifth grade. I was a "gifted student" according to my public school district, and my parents struggled to give me a better education. As I got older, of dating age, I started to get more attention from boys. That attention shaped my life in ways I never could have imagined.

I remember the first guy who liked me in fifth or sixth grade. He was Black, and we carpooled to school together. One day, he told his White friend that he liked me when I was maybe five feet away. His friend then looked me up and down and said, "Man, you can do better than that." My eyes shot down at my feet, and I walked away quicker than I knew I could. When boys liked me, it seemed like it was always supposed to be a big secret. They would ask me to see a movie outside of school but just give me a simple wave in the hallways.

It seemed like they were taught that Black women were not supposed to be attractive. I was some unusual exception because I didn't roll my neck and snap my fingers—like that was all Black women were supposed to do. I wanted to cry and run away each time I heard those six words. It hurt me even more when it came from the Black private school boys. They got sucked into the thought process that Black women were beneath them and not meant to be attractive. How could they say those words against their own race?

They came from a Black mother, have Black cousins, and maybe have a Black sister. I felt like I had nowhere to turn and nowhere to run to. I was always the "first Black girlfriend." Just some educational experience for someone who originally never intended on dating a Black woman. I want to be beautiful for a woman. I am beautiful for a woman. Not beautiful for a Black girl like I am so far beneath the expectations for beauty. I am beautiful because I am me and I am a person.

Still Black.
Still Beautiful.
Still here.

Olivia • Washington, DC

"I'M NOT THE NANNY. I'M MOM."

A WHITE MAN IN A COAT AND TIE is doing a live interview with BBC World News from his home as an expert who can help explain an impeachment scandal in South Korea. Robert E. Kelly, a professor at Pusan National University in South Korea, was speaking via Skype from a desk in his home with a map of the world on the wall behind him. Just to the right of that map, TV viewers could see a door. As Professor Kelly solemnly explains geopolitical ramifications, the door swings open with a whoosh, and a toddler comes bouncing happily into the room. She's holding some kind of snack and marching elbows out as if dancing along to a nursery rhyme. Kelly is clearly a pro at parenting and television punditry.

He barely breaks his composure to reach backward and gently swat away the child, who has invaded his makeshift home studio. But then a second—even younger—tot comes barreling into the room riding in one of those little rolling toys that help toddlers learn to walk.

"Pardon me," the man says, looking down in an effort to compose himself, while a live television audience looks on, no doubt with amusement.

At that moment, a petite, dark-haired woman comes flying into the room, crouching down as if trying not to be seen on camera. She grabs the arms of the two children and snatches them toward the door. The scene is both chaotic and hilarious, and the man can't help but laugh as the woman, who appears to be Asian, hustles the kids out and then appears once more on-screen as she lunges from her knees to pull the door shut.

Picturing this scene, where does your mind go? It seems safe to assume the kids belong to the White man since he was taping a segment in what appears to be his house . . . but who is the woman?

Clips of the incident from 2017 racked up millions of views, and commenters on social media began making jokes about "the nanny." A Time.com story described the "frenzied nanny burst[ing] in, in a cartoon-like blur." Joyce Carol Oates tweeted, "Poor nanny/au pair will be fired." There was no indication in the clip of who she was, and no interaction between her and the man. As it turned out, her name is Jung-a Kim; she is the man's wife and the mother of the children.

So . . . why did so many viewers assume she was the nanny? Why did it seem so easy to believe a woman of color was an employee of a White man, rather than his spouse? We are surrounded everywhere by interracial couples, in our lives, on television, in advertisements of all kinds, but the stories we have collected over so many years suggest that these families, though more readily embraced, still walk through a minefield of particularly painful assumptions when the parents and the children look different to the outside world.

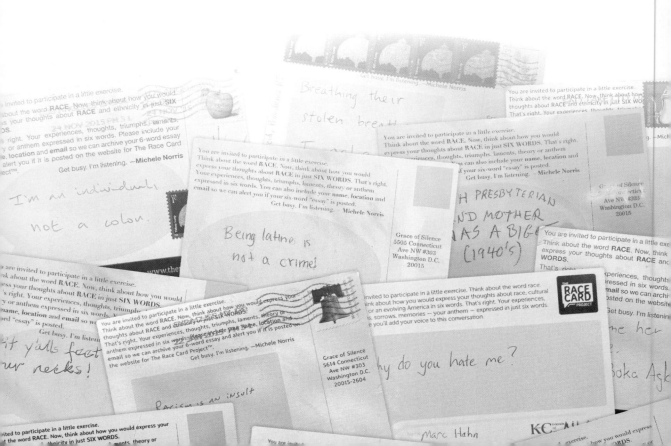

I'm his mother, not the nanny

Toya Dragseth • Saint Paul, MN

My youngest son is biracial. He has his father's genes, very light-skinned, brownish-blond hair, and when he is with just me, people look as if he is not my child but a child I may be babysitting. When he's with his dad, they look very natural together.

How much do they pay you?

Rosa-Maria Lazarovits • Santa Barbara, CA

This happened when my girls were toddlers and we played at a park. A Latino woman approached me and asked in Spanish: "How much do they pay you?" Assuming I was employed as a nanny. She gasped when I quickly replied: "nothing!" She could not conceive that these beautiful, fair skin girls were my daughters. A long-standing idea of a "malinchista," a traitor. A malinche marries an outsider. La Malinche was Hernan Cortez' translator, Mexico's conquistador. La Malinche had a horrible tradition as someone who gave up on her roots, supposedly betraying her people, but history showed us that is not quite true. She was a professional woman, with an incredible talent for learning languages, and learned Spanish very quickly. She was the mother of the first mestizo (mixed race people of Mexico). She was the mother of our future world, an amalgam between new and old, a native mother and a Spaniard father. Unfortunately, the clueless woman at the park saw other Latina women as maids, nannies, and caregivers. Like Malinche, I am a professional, I hold a master's degree.

I'm their mom, not the nanny

Allison A. • Yakima, WA

Sometimes it's nanny, sometimes it's babysitter or neighbor, but being asked if I was their grandmother was a first for me. At times, the question is about adoption: "Where did you get her?" The questions come from complete strangers, usually White people. The need to figure out this "puzzle," and what a White woman is doing at the store (insert anywhere public here) with these children, is tangible. Maybe they can't imagine themselves with three biracial daughters and want to know more. For the most part, these interactions are not malicious; it's more out of "polite" curiosity.

I'm not their nanny, I'm Mom

Michele • Ypsilanti, MI

My darling boys are Chinese and Black but look more racially nonspecific; even while I lived in Northern California, what people think of as some sort of center of tolerance, people constantly assumed that since I was Black, I was their nanny. Even though they are older now, I still get surprised looks when I pull them close and kiss their thick, black, curly, to-die-for hair.

I'm Her Mother, Not Her Nanny

Dacia Mitchell • Oakland, CA

That's my wife, not my nanny

Jonathan • Washington, DC

She's my mom, not my nanny.

Maile Siefert • Belmont, CA

No, I am not the nanny

Liliane Dizon • Tampa, FL

Each time I have been pregnant, people (mostly White women) have said the rudest things to me. Most recently, as my daughters were standing next to me, a woman said, "You must be excited to finally have one of your own!" I asked her to clarify what she meant. She pointed to my girls and said, "Now you don't have to adopt anymore."

No, I am not the nanny

Evan Shelton • USA

I am mixed. My dad is White, and my mom is Hispanic, but I look more Hispanic than White due to my coloring. I have always been proud of my heritage and loved the skin I am in. My dad remarried when I was ten years old, and they began having children. Like my father and stepmother, they are all fair-skinned with blond hair and beautiful bright-blue eyes. I love them so much! But as they continued to have children, and as I got older, my color difference began to stand out more than ever. At the end of the day, I just don't look like them. Family members, including my immediate family, began joking about how I looked like the nanny. People would give me weird glances if I ever took my siblings out without my parents—or even if I was with them—I just looked out of place. As a young girl, I didn't have the voice or understanding to process how these things made me feel, but as an adult, I now see that this "joke" was never OK. My stepmom made the nanny joke about a month ago, and I am happy to say that I stood up for myself—"No, I am not the nanny. Never say that to me again."

I've been called my sister's nanny.

Mary Carroll • Columbia, SC

I am biracial and adopted into a White family. Growing up in a very Southern, affluent area, people were always asking me if I was paid well to look after the child and if I would work for them. When I would tell them that the child was my sister, generally they would respond with a laugh and "If that's what you call it," then turn to someone else and say, "That nanny calls the child her 'sista,'" assuming I was using a colloquial term rather than defining a familial relationship.

My Daughter, I'm not her nanny

C. Fleming • New York, NY

I am Jamaican American Black, and my fiancé is White. Somehow even in a place as mixed as New York, people generally assume that I am the nanny since my daughter turned out to be very fair-skinned. I think the thing that saddened me the most is seeing the way that many Black women respond when they see me and my baby girl out together. They generally look away or whisper among themselves. I've had some comment, "Her daddy is White, huh?" and then have nothing more to say after that. White people think I'm The Help. Black people think I'm a traitor.

Graduate degree brown, not nanny brown.

Elisa Espitia • Palmdale, CA

Assumptions.

No, not the nanny…
They're MINE

Valerie Grajeda Rountree • San Jose, CA

I grew up not speaking Spanish in a very Mexican neighborhood. My mother sent me to schools out of my area to prevent me getting involved with the local gang population. I grew up with other nationalities and met my future husband in high school. He is White. Our children were very fair when they were toddlers, and at one of the parks we used to frequent, I was always getting asked if they were mine. Hispanic nannies were predominant in this area. When I assured the questioner they were mine and I had not adopted them, they always had the same response: "They don't look like you at all . . ."

YES, I'M TOBACCO-PICKIN WHITE TRASH

Tracy Hart • Washington, DC

Yes, I'm from a tobacco-pickin, Southern, White trash family, and I mean that in the most endearing way. Some stereotypes my family breaks: we were Southern but poor sharecroppers rather than slave owners. Other stereotypes my family embraces: using discriminatory language in equal measure across all those who are not White Southerners. Yes, I'm mortified, but it leaves me wondering: Is it more honorable to be a closeted racist or one who is out in the open? As for me, I believe we are all Africans in origin (ultimately—from the rift valleys), my sharing of which almost caused my family to choke on their turkey one Thanksgiving. I can only hope that my daughter finds her own authentic voice in all the cacophony.

ASK TRACY HART WHAT SHE DOES for a living, and she will take a deep breath because she needs a full gust of air in her lungs to get through all her official titles and descriptors. She's a global lead at the World Bank, where she focuses on environmental risk management and fragile and conflict states. She is also part of the Environment, Natural Resources and Blue Economy Global Practice, where she has done extensive work as a water economist in Africa and throughout the Middle East.

But when she encountered the simple question that we pose through The Race Card Project—"Race. Your thoughts. 6 words. Please send," she says she also had to take a deep breath. In that case to wade through a thicket of complicated and conflicting emotions before landing at, "Yes, I'm tobacco-pickin White trash."

Tracy is one of several people who write about that prickly intersection of class and race in America. We've received many stories from people who use words like *redneck*, *hillbilly*, *bumpkin*, *Bama*, *yokel*, *bohunk*, *hick*, or *hayseed*. Often, those stories also include the phrase *White trash*. And in almost all these cases, people are not hurling these words at someone else. They are talking about themselves—writing about the pain of hearing those words, about the expectation and stigma attached to those labels, about the ways they try to claim a pejorative term to neutralize the sting or distance themselves to avoid absorbing the stench.

Tracy was working through all of that when she sent in her six words. She attended the University of California, Berkeley, and is a trained opera singer. Her work with the World Bank has allowed her to travel all over the globe. She's now a resident of Washington, DC, but Hart was raised outside of Houston and spent summers visiting family in out-of-the-way rural hamlets throughout the South. Most had little money. Some didn't have indoor plumbing. Those Southern journeys helped shape who she is today.

However, the person she became created a distance that is not just about geography. She says her liberal views, her diverse circle of friends, her marriages outside of her family's Christian religion (one ex-husband is Jewish, the other ex is a Syrian immigrant) make her an outsider inside of her family. And even without all of that, her education, her diction and ability to speak ten different languages, her interests in books and empirical science, her history of living in or visiting big, noisy cities creates a cultural moat that separates her from people she has known all her life.

Tracy Hart was one of the people we featured in The Race Card Project series on NPR's *Morning Edition*. Because she puts so much energy into studying other cultures around the world, she brings that anthropological eye to trying to understand the cross-currents in her own family. She spoke about being bicultural as a White woman whose life story has careened between elite institutions and hardscrabble poverty.

Years ago, I asked Tracy what it feels like to go home and sit at the family table as both an insider and an outsider. Her answer zeroed in on tough responsibilities rather than tough emotions. Because of her education and ease in dealing with authority figures, she is the family fixer. She immediately rattled off three examples.

"I have an uncle who is on his deathbed right now who did not have a will, and so I was called to write the will because they couldn't afford a lawyer," she said. "So, I spent a half day looking up Georgia state law. I have another aunt who is going to scatter her husband's ashes. He died from lung cancer, and she asked me to give her directions about how to create an ash-scattering ceremony. . . . The third thing I'm doing is I have a cousin who has a child with a woman, and I think that common-law marriage is not the rule in Georgia, and he wants to establish paternity and make sure that he can get some visitation rights if they split. They cannot afford an attorney. So, I am now looking into determination of paternity and determination of parental rights between unmarried couples. . . . So, I'm like the staff lawyer. I have no legal background, but people call me up."

That was all in just one week. That was a heavier load than usual, but when I spoke with her recently, she said she is still the family's go-to problem solver. It is a lot to take on, but it's also a way for her to reach back and give back. A way of saying, even with the distance and the difference in their lives, she still sees her people with loving eyes.

Many people who heard that NPR feature saw themselves in her words, even if they did not share her race, résumé, or specific cultural background. People all over the country in all kinds of stations ride a sliding cultural escalator around class when ties to loved ones and special places are out of sync with other aspects of their lives. Black people call it code-switching. Tracy calls it being bicultural. She says it's a skill, and she is proud to have mastered it.

I have spoken with Tracy over a ten-year period, and listening to her talk about the bridges she works hard to maintain with her family provides a window into conversations we don't much hear in public spaces, like the time she tried to explain the term *White trash* to her preteen.

"I said, well, if you drive by someone's house and they've got an old car that's not working parked on the side, and they've got their washer and dryer that's not working kind of put outside in the front, and it's basically their inside has kind of expanded to the outside with an old stuffed couch on the front porch. And I said they just keep their trash around them because it still has value, and they also don't know how to dispose of it properly. That's the very literal meaning of White trash.

"But I have a great-uncle who was living near Independence, Virginia. He never had indoor plumbing. He died never having had indoor plumbing, never having had electrical wiring in his house, never having had a telephone line to his house. The water for the kitchen came from the stream through a PVC pipe, then dumped into a sink, and then there was an egress PVC pipe that took it back to the stream downhill. And that was the only running water in the house. And people have had a hard time believing that there are people who live like that in the year 2000. And yet he lived like that. That's where my grandmother was raised. That's where we've spent many summers hanging out.

"There's a lot of stories that I find related to White trash that I could tell. We did something called the rounding up of the cats. He had a bunch of feral cats, and they had kittens all the time. And once a year we would run and catch the ones we could . . . it was kind of like survival of the fittest. They were put in a bag with some rocks, and they were drowned down at the river. And I mean, that's just one of many stories where it's the kind of thing I think people read in books, except it happens in my family, and I'm pretty sure it doesn't happen in most of the people's families that I associate with in DC on a daily basis. But there's a sort of a lawlessness to it . . . the lack of embarrassment about what one has to do in order to preserve one's living the situation."

"It's all coded by class. 'We can't get the jobs that we used to get anymore.'"

While Tracy was comfortable talking openly about such a taboo term like *White trash*, it wound up creating another hurdle for her back home.

"I think my family might think that I'm being a bit uppity in saying that because I'm able to admit it because I've stepped out of it. It's where I'm from . . . but it's not where I'm at," she said. "And by the way, on my father's side, they did grow tobacco and pick tobacco. My father spent his summers laying tobacco up in the attic of the barn making sure it dried properly, etc. So, tobacco picking is literal in this sense. That's how money was made. I have never picked tobacco, but if they had not picked tobacco, I might not be where I am now."

Some of her family members will say something like, "That's just because we're White trash," and laugh. But if someone else said that, they would not be amused, Tracy said.

"They feel misunderstood because of the heavy legacy of slavery and segregation and poverty. And I think part of their feeling misunderstood is to embrace that term, which is self-denigrating. But it also says, 'We've been hurt, too. We have missed out, too, on the American dream, that we may have perpetuated segregation, we may have perpetuated slavery, but we also were hurt by those conditions, and we also are still suffering because of those conditions.' And that may or may not be true, but I believe there's a sentiment that exists that believes that's true."

Ten years after Tracy sent in her 6-word story, she said she feels like an edge walker—an outsider in all her worlds. "The price I pay for being able to fit in lots of different cultural situations is that I don't feel fully that I sit in one, but that's the price I pay for being able to feel like I can go here or there," she said.

And the edges and the rules of engagement with the people she loves are getting blurrier as older family members die. She notices that when she goes home for holidays. Years ago, she was concerned about what her child would hear at the dinner table. The conversation is still, shall we say . . . animated, but things have changed.

"I do feel, I feel like as our generations pass on, as my grandparents passed on and some of my older aunts and uncles, that, um, a good part of the overt racism in my family has passed on with them, and there's a whole new kind of covert code. But the . . . the most egregious part has passed on with those whom I shared Thanksgiving with forty or fifty years ago.

"I was just worried about the language that was used at the Thanksgiving table of my youth in terms of just racist words and racist stories and racist jokes that were freely exchanged. That kind of died off with my mom's dad and some of my uncles. And it slowly then fully died off when the few of them that were left realized they were out-numbered. But that doesn't mean that it doesn't still exist. It just means that it's gone [underground]. You know, that there's kind of people talking and I think people talking kind of class language and that it's left kind of [to] figure out whether that class language is coded for race, as well."

Tracy said she used to get into arguments about racist jokes or language at the dinner table back home, but more often than not, these days, she said she lets it slide and saves that energy for being more of an upstander in the workplace and in her social circles in the Washington, DC, area. Part of that is chalked up to exhaustion, she said. And part of it is because it is harder to pin down overt bias when she thinks her family is speaking in coded language and they think they are just telling it like it is.

"It's all coded by class. 'We can't get the jobs that we used to get anymore,' or, 'People don't get into universities the way they used to.' It's all about the shifting quote, unquote reverse discrimination that is happening in society. Our traditional American culture is under threat. This is my personal view of this. There are those who, because they're losing their status quo, would rather try to undermine a changing American society because they're losing their place in it."

Tracy knows her family is judging her, but she also knows this: Many people also judge them. *Hillbilly* and *redneck* may be pejorative terms, but they are also acceptable in common language—by people who embrace them as an anthem of sorts, and, if we are honest, by people who have a dismissive view of those who are poor or uneducated or embrace dogmatic religious or political beliefs. Tracy sometimes asks herself if she is as much of an upstander for those people . . . for her people . . . as she is for the victims of discrimination and over-policing. What would she put in her front yard next to the Black Lives Matter sign that would allow her to upstand for her Southern family with tobacco-picking roots without making it look like she was gliding toward expressions of White supremacy? Given their overt bias, do they deserve to be defended?

Years ago, Tracy told me that she sent her 6-word story never expecting that anyone would actually read it. "I wrote it to put it on the paper to say, here I stand, this is who I am. And if I'm gonna understand anyone else, I'm gonna understand myself first."

Hillbilly—
the wrong kind
of white.

T. R. Kelley • Swisshome, OR

"White trash" is a hip cultural joke.
"N*****" is hate speech. Why?

I'm Appalachian—
it's an invisible ethnicity
Catherine Vance Agrella • Asheville, NC

I'm White and by definition am associated with some of the worst perpetrators of racism. But I also come from deep Appalachian Scots-Irish roots and have a clear ethnic identity. I do know what it feels like to be mocked for my speech, or thought of as a dumb hillbilly, even though I have two master's degrees. . . .

White is not a single race
Slaton Anthony • Mount Vernon, IA

My last ancestors came to America before 1800, all from England, France, and Germany. My ancestors fought and died in almost every American war, I was raised in the Cookson Hills of rural Oklahoma, and I believed that I was part of the American White culture. While attending college in Oklahoma, I realized I was not White, but White trash. I worked hard, and after graduating law school, I was no longer White trash after I had changed my most discriminatory feature, my accent. Eventually leaving Oklahoma for Kansas City and Iowa, I realized I was again no longer White but was "Southern hillbilly." This process, along with coming out as a gay man, taught me that "White" is not a single race or culture, and discrimination occurs constantly within people, and the decision is to become a victim of such discrimination and resent it or to fight against it and find power in that fight. This feeling of discrimination or always being the "outsider" has fueled my lift.

She's nothing, but poor white trash
Patricia • Sacramento, CA

Came from a *very* poor family: mother with eight kids on welfare. I heard those words so many times growing up. I believed them; I identified with them. We were all called that, by relatives who thought they were better than us, by neighbors, at school by other kids, and I even heard it from adults out in public. I heard from every race out there, but mostly from White people. People would move away from me, like I had a disease that they would catch if they got too close. Then you grow up with that in your head and people tell you to move on, some of the very same people who treated you like trash. . . .

I'm a Redneck. Not a Racist.

Anonymous • Spokane, WA

Worldly Redneck Fighting Stupid, Class Stereotypes

Alex Loose • Conneautville, PA

I'm a Yooper, not all hicks.

Brody Sundquist • Kingsford, MI

Yoop·er /yo͞opr/: a native or inhabitant of the Upper Peninsula of Michigan.

I'm not Bohunk, I am Czech.

Kim E. Hudecek • Rochester, MN

Since I was a child, I have been referred to as a bohunk, a word that is a reference to a rough or uncivilized person. Granted, the people who referred to me and everyone in my family referenced it in a positive way, as if I belonged in a special club. I am Czech and proud of my heritage. I correct anyone who ever tries to call me a bohunk.

Can someone help me find my privilege

Steven W. Grudzinski • Clarksville, TN

Conversant in White mountain hick English

Margaret Anne East • Arlington, VA

Appalachian oppression is a minority issue

Rebekah Epling • Ripley, WV

Appalachian people are treated in this country as second-class citizens. It is perfectly acceptable for mainstream media to characterize Appalachian people in ways that would incite outrage and not be published were it about another minority group. Just because the majority of Appalachian people are White does not mean it is OK to belittle them or mock their culture and experience by employing gross generalizations.

354

Do hillbillies have White privilege too?

Anonymous • Knoxville, TN

I'm from the Mountain South, where White privilege and racism take on a range of meanings outside the mainstream. I've heard our regional identity described as a kind of "otherized Whiteness," and I think that's about right. Whatever else we were, we always knew our Whiteness was the wrong kind. That's what the images and dialogues on TV said to us, either directly or indirectly. It was plain that we were just a bunch of hopelessly dumb hillbillies who didn't speak proper English. My sister told me she worked hard to shed her accent, like me, because she said she didn't want to be perceived as ignorant. Anybody from the poor White South knows just what I'm talking about. Then there are others who embrace it, who drape it around them like a flag. My parents loved watching *The Beverly Hillbillies* and *The Andy Griffith Show*, like they reveled in the delight of seeing people who talked like them on TV, even if they were represented as rubes and degenerates. I've never really understood that. But then they always loved *All in the Family*, *Good Times*, and *The Jeffersons*, too.

On the other hand, it is one of the few subregional identities in the US that allows for the possibility of something like a "White culture." Maybe. But it has its own set of prejudices, too. My grandpa worked in the coal mines of southwest Virginia. He always talked about working shoulder to shoulder with Black miners underground, but how when they emerged on the surface, they went their separate ways with nary a backward glance. My paternal great-grandfather was a renowned banjo player in Tennessee's Cumberland Mountains, but I doubt he had any idea that the banjo was an instrument of African origin. It's never simple.

Hillbilly White Trash? I'm Oxford educated.

C.B. • WV

I grew up poor in rural West Virginia. My race, the way I talk, and where I'm from immediately make people assume I'm illiterate, uneducated, and deeply racist without ever actually talking to me. The irony . . . I get so angry at how common and acceptable it is to use hee-haw accents as shorthand for stupidity and to call people with ignorant and racist attitudes hillbillies and other names meant to illustrate that they're backward and uneducated. I'm proud of my heritage and the sacrifices my "poor, White trash" family and I made to get me to where I've been and where I am now.

Scotch tape no longer clings here

Malcolm Ian MacKenzie •
Naples, NY

My mom and dad immigrated from Canada in the early 1950s with two children Canadian-born, and eleven were born in the States. Growing up, we had a strong family identity as Canadians but knew we also had Scottish roots through our dad's family. My mom's family were Anglo-French Canadians with an Irish twist. Upon my father's death five years ago, I was reviewing legal papers and read through his birth certificate from 1921. It struck me when it said of his mother's and father's ancestry, "Race: Scotch." To think that in 1921 a birth certificate would refer to the Scotch as a race astounded me. It illustrated how quickly our impressions of culture and ethnicity and national heritage can change. I have always been a bit puzzled by the social acceptance of calling Scotch tape Scotch, when its origin is derogatory slang depicting a tight-fisted, perhaps thrifty people. Most people do not realize that today. I only recognize it because of my interest in words and their meaning, direct, implied, or acquired. This especially hit home to me a few years ago when President Obama was quoted in a newspaper article as stating that someone wanted to get off "scot-free." No editorial response was uttered by the press or the readership. This would not be the case had he referred to another ethnic/national/racial group with such an offhand and socially accepted comment. This is the background of my six-word submission. The subliminal message of Scotch tape goes by us all cloaked in a handsome tartan. The slang use of Scotch doesn't cling to this Malcolm.

Natives can only be poor or past.

Maranda Compton • Denver, CO

For most of society, the American Indian is conceived of as strictly a historical figure. People maintain images of Tonto or the Crying Indian walking alongside the highway in buckskin and feathers. And if they do allow the Indian to exist in modernity, he or she is relegated to an impoverished, alcohol-soaked cultural outpost—a Diane Sawyer interview subject.

This antiquated stereotype seems benign, but in reality, it severely limits the ability of Native Americans to be successful—and be perceived as both Native and successful—in modern American life. What follows is an exhausting struggle for legitimacy.

For most modern Indians, one's heritage is always in question. The revelation that you are Native is always met with pejorative questioning: "Are you *really* Native American?" people will ask. "How much?" Without the slightest understanding of one's enrolled status, particular tribal history, or connectedness with (or participation in) tribal government and culture, the general public will expect to hear a story from your time on the reservation or to see you wearing turquoise and feathers with your business suit to prove your "Indian-ness."

I understand that the identity of Native Americans is complex. And there is often a lot that the general public does not understand about the varied tribal and federal laws defining what it means to be Indian. But I hate that I often feel less Indian because I am middle-class, because I come from Oklahoma, where reservations are not the norm, and because I wear gold studs that I bought off Amazon (not turquoise or beads that I purchased at a powwow). It does not matter that I have a CDIB card (a derogatory card that proves that the US government accepts the validity of my Indian bloodline) and that I am an enrolled member of both of my tribes. No one ever asks if I vote in tribal elections, am informed of tribal issues, or connect deeply with my tribal culture. It does not matter that I am an Indian law attorney that works daily to protect and properly assert tribal sovereignty in the modern legal context. No, I just look like your normal, modern woman, so I can't possibly be Native. Natives can only exist in poverty or in the past.

WHITE HUSBAND BECAME IRANIAN SEPTEMBER 11TH

Maren Robinson • Chicago, IL

MAREN ROBINSON AND ROM BARKHORDAR were on a cross-country road trip on the morning of 9/11, driving from her family's house in Houston back to Chicago, where the married couple live. It was midmorning when they pulled into an Arkansas truck stop to fill up and grab a bite to eat. When they walked inside the diner to pay the cashier, everyone was staring at a TV mounted high on the wall. Smoke was rising from side-by-side skyscrapers in New York City.

"What's going on up there?" Rom asked. A large man sitting at the counter explained that the World Trade Center was under attack. Then a second man sitting nearby spat out an expletive usually directed toward people of Middle Eastern descent to condemn those thought to be responsible.

Rom looked at his wife and said, "Let's get out of here."

Rom is Iranian. His wife, Maren, is White, and that encounter alongside the Arkansas interstate was a preamble to a new, strange, and less welcoming world for the couple.

That sudden pivot in their lives is captured in the six words Maren sent to The Race Card Project: "White husband became Iranian September 11th."

She submitted her 6-word story on May 24, 2013, and provided a backstory to explain her choice of words. "I watched how my American-born, half-Iranian husband went from being perceived as White to being perceived as vaguely Middle Eastern (eliciting double takes on trains and extra searches at airports) after September eleventh," she wrote. "He is an actor, so I have also watched him play characters who are Caucasian, Spanish, Jewish, Armenian, French, and of course various Middle Eastern characters, and it is still something he struggles with feeling the advantage of, being raised White but playing other races, with other dialects and languages. I have also watched his increasing discomfort as he tries to reconcile the complex issues of race and the current American discomfort with anyone who seems to be Middle Eastern."

At the time, it seemed odd that later that same day a Chicago-based actor submitted a 6-word story: "'You don't look Iranian!' 'I am.'"

I had a hunch the two stories were connected, and years later, I discovered that two Race Card submissions came from a married couple who are both active in Chicago's theater community. Maren is a dramaturg with TimeLine Theatre Company and associate director of the Master of Arts Program in the Humanities at the University of Chicago. Rom is an actor with a long list of credits in theater, TV, and video voice-overs. After hearing a segment about The Race Card Project on NPR's *Morning Edition*, both were inspired to share their stories, but neither of them knew what the other had said. "I guess we were both looking for an outlet to express our feelings after things had changed so suddenly for us," Maren said.

September 11 wound up being a line of demarcation in their lives. "I would say that was definitely the first moment that I had just physically feared for [my husband's] safety, and that has not gone away," said Maren.

Rom said the animus toward Middle Easterners following 9/11 gave him flashbacks to his high school years during the Iran hostage crisis in 1979. He was living with his mother in Wyoming at the time, in a town where few people knew that his father was from Iran. He didn't use his father's last name during that period. "I remember being very scared during that period of having not only other students come down on me hard, but even my own friends, who didn't know I was Iranian," he says. "I was afraid that they would come after me or not understand or try to do what people do when they're mistrustful."

He began using his family name, Barkhordar, when he went to college in Montana. That's where he met and fell in love with Maren while they both toured in a traveling

Shakespeare troupe. But even with the name change, people still assumed he was a White man who was swarthy enough to play a range of ethnic roles. That changed after 9/11, when the work that came his way was most often for Arab store clerks, gas station attendants, or bad guys. The kind of roles denoted in a script as Terrorist #2.

"I'm not making this up," he says. "They were auditioning at some point Chicago Middle Eastern actors because they had run out of Middle Eastern actors on the West Coast because they had used them all in these awful roles. And that's a point where it's like, no, I'm not doing that."

The couple got used to the stares and the extra scrutiny at airports, adopting a kind of gallows humor. They would come up with names for bad TV movies to describe what might happen if Rom was whisked away to an internment camp because of his background and last name. Soapy titles like *Not Without My Husband*.

They were even paranoid in their own home. "Right after September 11th, we started getting telemarketer calls in Farsi, in Arabic, in ways we had never been marketed to," Maren said. Suddenly, mail started to arrive at their home written in Farsi. Catalogs and newspapers. Rom says neither he nor his wife speak Farsi, and the sudden influx of Middle Eastern missives was a complete mystery. As they look back now on that time, the couple suspects they were being surveilled by some government initiative aimed at making assessments about Middle Eastern men in the US.

"I mean, I have a totally clear and spotless background and record," said Rom. "They were just going by the fact that I had a certain last name that was Iranian, that I was male, of a certain age, and so I fit the profile. It felt like a wide net to gather information on those with Middle Eastern heritage and names. It felt very uncomfortable."

Rom didn't respond to any of it, and eventually the mail and the calls stopped. But two decades after the 9/11 tragedy, they still feel the sting. If anything, it made their allegiance to his background stronger, especially through their work in theater. As a dramaturg, Maren advocates for stories onstage and in film that examine a broader range of cultures and characters. And Rom has grown a beard in part to more closely identify with his culture on and off the stage.

"I was basically White prior to 9/11 and was raised White and instilled with those things that we consider White," he said. "And when 9/11 happened, the shift started changing to this other part of me that I would either just kind of, I don't want to say ignore, but just didn't identify with. As time progressed, I had to identify with it whether I liked it or not. And at some point, I just decided, let's do this on my terms so that who I project is not how others want to see me, but is how I want them to see me."

By protecting her, I'm oppressing her

Adrienne Kern • Keller, TX

My daughter was two weeks [shy of] turning one on September 11, 2001. She is one of them. An Arab (pronounced with a Texas drawl: A-Rab). A camel jockey. A raghead. She is Turkish and Saudi and Egyptian. She is not White like me, her mother, who is also mixed-race. Far from Aryan. When those people killed our people, I automatically went into that maternal protection mode where assumptions are born. I assumed people would be cruel, and so said cruelty was magnified. I heard an elderly man say, "Nuke 'em all." But I did not hear his wife say, "But most are innocent." I heard a coworker call my daughter "Osama's niece." But I did not hear my boss call her beautiful.

My daughter is not Muslim, but still it was my duty to defend her even to strangers.

But as my daughter grew, and began embracing her ethnicity, I had an epiphany: she does not need me to shield her from something that should make her proud. By doing so, I am only amplifying the prejudice that I fear. I realized that, by constantly defending my daughter's Arab bloodline, I was the only one oppressing her.

Frustrated with the concept of race

Riad Nassar • Austin, TX

Up until 9/11, race wasn't something I ever thought [about]. I didn't look at my Hispanic friends as Hispanics or my Black friends as Blacks. Being Egyptian was just a thing, and they accepted me for me and not my race, just as I accepted them for the beautiful people they were.

Then 9/11 happened, and my race was a problem. Not for my friends, mind you, but rather for other people. And for a fifth grader who had just read a book about internment camps in the US during World War II, it was scary. Going into middle school and all the way through high school, I started meeting fewer minorities and more White people, and my race was now my identity.

It wasn't because they were inherently racist and wanted me dead but because I was exotic and different. But it was isolating. I felt like everyone was studying me. I had to work hard to show them that I was intelligent, athletic, funny, and not just an Egyptian. That I was multidimensional, that you couldn't give me one label. And that seemed to make things worse because they couldn't label me as anything else. I did too many nerdy things to be a jock and too many jock things to be a nerd.

So, I started joking about the stereotypes of my race. And then every year I would try to stop but would ultimately fall back to that comedic farce. And when I went to college, I swore to be different. [But] those who had been with me through high school and middle school and went on to the same college with me ended up just bringing it back out.

I tried hanging out with other Muslims in college, but there, too, I found my race standing in the way. There were mostly Pakistanis who wanted to talk about Pakistani things. Of course, they also talked about Indian things with Indians, since the countries do have a lot more similarities than they are willing to admit. So even when my religion says race shouldn't matter, it still seems to impede my life. And that's not even the scary stuff. Walking down streets, my family members and I will sometimes get looks. Most of the time, it's not in Austin, but it still happens here. And I think, "Is it going to happen today? Will my family be targeted today? Are we going to be attacked?" Twelve years after 9/11, and I still have this fear. I hate this. Why does my race matter? Why do people care?

The invisible Arab until 9/12

Jennie Clement • Riverview, FL

I noticed how my university applications changed in the wake of 9/11, how there was all of a sudden a magical radio button for being Arab. I had previously been invisible, moderately enjoying White privilege until 9/11. I was no longer "White," which was a slight sigh of relief because I was so proud of my heritage. Now I feel it is important to relish in no longer being invisible, so that I can counteract the waves of hatred aimed at Arabs in the wake of 9/11. No longer invisible and trying, sometimes stumbling, to stand proud. No longer being invisible does come with additional scrutiny, occasional bias, and interpersonal/professional challenges.

Before 9/11...Unique, After 9/11...ARAB!

Miriam Piper • Colorado Springs, CO

Before 9/11, I was just this unique mix of who knows what. I am really Palestinian and White, but no one ever knew what I was (Indian, Puerto Rican, Greek). But as soon as 9/11 happened, and living in a large military community that was then trained on facial features, I am now clearly recognized as an *Arab*. They even try to narrow down the region I'm from, like it's a guessing game. I went from being unrecognizable to racially profiled everywhere . . . airports, military bases, government buildings, etc. A lot of racial questionnaires (bubble questions) ask, "If you are mixed, which race do you identify with more?" I always had trouble answering that question until I realized if you are being treated differently in public, you tend to identify with the race you are being singled out for.

Don't speak to me in Arabic

Christine Abraham • Santa Monica, CA

My mom is ashamed to speak Arabic
in public in this post-9/11 world.

Entered world of race after 9/11

Lesley Thomas George • Frisco, TX

My perfect little world was broken up into different races post-9/11. As an Indian American, I had escaped much of the profiling that many African Americans face. After 9/11, much of that changed.

My Tenth Birthday Was Super Awkward

Wilson Sunny • Sunnyvale, TX

I was born September 11, 1991. Ten years later, a great national tragedy happened within the United States that shook the nation to the core. It was the first time, I believe, the term *terrorist* became a mainstream word. Not when Timothy McVeigh decided to blow up a building in Oklahoma City. Nor would Americans be called such when they were first involved with fighting in the Middle East during the Gulf War. It's only reserved for when nations decide to attack America. But I digress.

When we learned about the attack, everyone was in shock. Once the shock subsided, anger arose. Anger for people who look a specific way. For those who wear a specific type of clothing, or for those who have a specific skin color. A color that I have. While the anger never led to physical violence in my life, it did lead to snide comments, especially with a birthday tied to the event. Others would ask, "Was that a gift from Uncle Osama?"

The problem with the joke is I am not Middle Eastern. My parents were born in the south of India. But we were all just blindly melded together. I should be grateful that no physical harm came toward me. But I know that there are those who did have to suffer persecution for events they had no hand in. Just as Japanese Americans had to face in the 1940s. And just as those that have suffered after the 2016 election . . .

The Day After the World Changes

Duryan Bhagat-Clark • Aberdeen, NJ

My father is an immigrant from Bombay, India. He moved here to go to college and graduate school. He is Muslim. While working at Rutgers University, he met my mother; she is Jewish. They were married within a year. As I often joke, I know there will never be peace in the Middle East as there was never peace in our home. They split when I was thirteen. Growing up, my father used to "Americanize" his name so people would not have a hard time. Instead of Abbas, he became Abe, and instead of Bhagat (pronounced Bah-gaht), we became the "Bag-its." You have no idea of the "bag-it Bhagat" jokes. Once at a summer picnic with my father's next-door neighbors, they asked what my stepmother's name was. Apparently, she, too, had been Americanized from Zulie to Julie.

When I got to college and then entered the professional world, I began to insist on being called Bah-gaht. My first name became Dur-ee-yan, instead of Dorian and the nickname Dur. I began to insist people get it right. Hanging up on cold callers if they didn't pronounce it right. Really getting mad when I was called Mr. Bagit.

I took pride in the fact I was a first-generation American. When asked my ethnicity, I often answered American and didn't volunteer any more information. If asked, I would answer my father was Indian and that my mother was Jewish American. I tend to leave the ethnic box unchecked, as American is not an option. And then September 11, 2001, happened. At the time, I was living in a small section of Brooklyn in the smoke cloud of the Twin Towers.

The day after, as I walked through my lovely neighborhood, I heard a comment following me. "Damn Arabs, I'm so [expletive] sick of them." A friend kept me moving, not allowing me to turn around. A few blocks later, I got various dirty looks from people. Was I imagining it? I asked her if she saw it, and she didn't respond.

How do you respond? I've lived here my entire life. Not only am I a first-generation American, I'm Jewish and participate in a Jewish life. I have been in Israel during a bomb attack in the 1980s. I was in the center of downtown Los Angeles during the riots in the 1990s. I have seen the pain of people attacking people. I also feel the rage of what happened at the World Trade Center. I, too, was shocked and pained by watching the second tower collapse. I, too, checked for missing loved ones.

And yet, in the aftermath, I was judged by my neighbors for the color of my skin.

I stayed overnight in colored town

Michael I. Posey • Asheville, NC

In the summer of 1973, I worked all of that June, July, and August, as I did for four straight summers, with an all–African American janitorial crew cleaning every square inch of a private school campus in Boca Raton, Florida. I was the only White person on the crew. That summer, there was one boy on the crew, the nephew of one of the gals who had worked there for years. The family invited me down to Deerfield Beach, the next town south, for a weekend stay at their house. I gladly accepted. They lived in the middle of the Black neighborhood in Deerfield. I was perhaps the only White child within miles, and I received some of the most inquisitive stares from their neighbors during my stay. I never thought twice about it. . . . I had so much fun just hanging with my summer coworkers.

When I tell this story, which occurred forty years ago at a time of some pretty significant racial strife, I say that I stayed in "colored town" because, back then, that is what we always called the part of any city where the Black families lived. Every time I think of that phrase, I feel so disgusted with myself. In one sense, I may have been the least prejudiced child in all of south Florida, while at that same time referring to where they lived as "colored town." I think of my innocence all those years ago and realize that one rarely recognizes one's own prejudices without the considerable benefit of hindsight.

Will you have an arranged marriage

Krishna Ghodiwala • Washington, DC

I am an Indian American woman who was born in Canada, immigrated to the US at the age of three, and went on to receive an excellent education that has helped me pursue a successful career in US politics and issue advocacy. My Indian heritage is a big part of my identity, but for all the cultural wealth my ethnic and geographic backgrounds have to offer to someone eager to ask questions, this one is the most common. As a Brown woman, no matter what progress I bring to the table, age-old notions of exoticism and helplessness follow me around like a sad puppy. I can't just be another young professional woman who lives a normal and independent—emphasis on independent—life. People pry for tidbits of a drama that they couldn't even dream of partaking in: "Do your parents know you date? Would they be mad? Do you have to marry an Indian? Will you have to get an arranged marriage?" Yes. No. No. No. Just no.

Mugged...Most assume Black mugger...wrong

Lynne Moffitt • Virginia Beach, VA

When I was living in Louisville, I came home from work and was mugged when I got out of my car. I had looked around before I got out, and this nice young man was walking down the sidewalk. He looked like a typical student from the University of Louisville, which was only blocks from my apartment. He didn't speed up or slow down, but we just naturally intersected when I got to the sidewalk. He told me not to say anything, and I knew then I was being attacked. I screamed, and he hit me in the face, knocked me down, and stole my purse. Many of my neighbors came out to assist me, and some even gave chase to my attacker but didn't catch him.

Whenever I told the story, I didn't mention his race, as it was not relevant, but many people wanted to know it. As if that made any kind of difference. Mostly they asked, "Was he Black?" I don't think anyone has ever asked if he was White or Hispanic or Asian. And they were visibly disappointed when I would answer no, since they wanted to talk about how afraid we should all be of young Black men. So, I discovered that those who asked usually turned out to be racist. So now, I use my story as a quick way of weeding out those I don't wish to become closer with.

My Dad is in car sales

Anonymous • Washington, DC

I was talking to an African American student about which classes he might take during his senior year. I asked him if he had a certain college major in mind. Was he interested in being a scientist? Was there a certain career that ran in his family? He told me, "My dad is in car sales," and moved the conversation forward. I thought I heard him say, "My dad is incarcerated." After our meeting, I talked to another teacher to check in about supporting this young man. This teacher explained that the student's father was in *car sales*.

This experience really gave me pause. I realized that the images I have seen on the news and statistics I have read in the paper affect the way I see and interpret my everyday experiences. I realized I had made a quick and biased assumption. I realized that it was critical for me to own up to my own biases and to actively work on unraveling them by being more self-aware of my own interactions and thoughts and by exposing myself to images and experiences that counter the stereotypes of African American men.

You're invited! You're not a minority

Rafael Rosato • Berwyn, PA

This is my college graduation picture from 1988. I received a Bachelor of Arts degree from an Ivy League university and a short while later was traveling to New York to join a management training program at a prestigious Wall Street bank. There were thirty-four of us in that class. On the first day of work, I received an invitation to a reception with executives. How exciting!

But I quickly became aware that many others had not received the same invitation. A few of my colleagues were invited, but I did not immediately put together that they were minorities. As the day wore on, that became the common attribute of those invited (about five of us). I was really uncomfortable about being classified as a minority, so I called HR to inquire about the real reason I was invited. Why? As my photograph illustrates, I am White and of a predominantly Irish heritage with an Italian grandfather. While at some point in American history my ethnic background could have been considered a minority, this was decidedly not the case in 1988. The woman from HR that I telephoned was very nice. She

Hey, are you the maintenance guy?

Mr. Jones • Charleston, SC

New neighbors moved in about six months ago. First introduction while I was sweeping the driveway: "Are you the maintenance guy?" I have a vacation home in an "upscale neighborhood," just thirty houses, and [I was the] only African American for five years. Neighborhood HOA even hired local police to do daily drive-throughs, as well. I've really had a hard time there, especially since it is the South. I have a home in Baltimore, as well, next to Johns Hopkins University. While Baltimore is much more accepting of diversity—that is a very different world. I would hate to see the neighborhood reaction if I had a family reunion.

quickly informed me that new minority employees can have problems adjusting to the predominantly White male environment of the bank. Therefore, they wanted to assign each of us a mentor to help us adjust and settle in. Also, if we were to have any problems, there would be someone looking after us. I guess they assumed my White colleagues could handle things themselves, so no mentors for them. I mentioned to the woman from HR that I thought this might seem like a good idea, but I did not understand why I was invited.

There was silence for an uncomfortable five seconds. "Well, what do you mean?" she asked.

"Because I am White, and I don't understand why the company thinks I am a minority," I said.

"But your name is Hispanic. . . . We just assumed," she said.

"No, my name is Italian" is all I could say.

I told her I would not attend the reception. I went on to successfully finish the program and enjoy a successful career in finance. In this instance during my past, I was judged based on assumptions and misplaced stereotypes. I was sized up before I arrived and thought of as "less," even though I had a degree from one of the best universities in the world and was hired to work at one of the most prestigious banks in the world. I still struggle to imagine what it would be like to deal with that type of judgment from people every day. It was a lesson. I always try to remember it when I meet new people.

PS: I still get some Spanish-language mail; it's tough to get off those lists.

Wear a suit? He's a pimp

Chris Thompson • Rochester, NY

I have been an engineer for thirteen years, and I notice that when I don the regular business casual attire, colleagues outside my department think I'm either in food or custodial services. Now I wear a tie daily, and the "compliment" I get is that I look like a pimp. Why can't I look like an engineer? Or a businessman? I'll even take lawyer. Why does a tie on me make me look like a sex trafficker, and how is that a compliment?

Being called sassy is not a compliment

Starr • Albuquerque, NM

Black women are often characterized as sassy, which I take as an insult. The root of *sassy* is "sass" or "to talk back," in other words, to disobey or not know your place with the not-so-subtle inference that your place is inferior. I've been called sassy because I am smart and do not see myself as inferior in any way to any person. That I was called this today at my job by a group of disgruntled employees because I carried out my job as requested was racist, as I informed the person who made the comment. There are thousands of ways to disrespect someone. Black folks all over the world are particularly attuned to the many monikers and mischaracterizations we are assigned when we make people uncomfortable with our inherent abilities, and in many cases, our power. Calling me sassy in the workplace disregards my skills and abilities as a professional. Moreover, it says that I am in the wrong place. Perhaps I am in the wrong workplace, but never am I in the wrong place.

Ignored Black man, looking for boss

John May • Franklin, MA

I was a salesman of warehouse equipment. On an ordinary sales call, I would drive to a warehouse and try to meet with the boss to deliver my sales pitch. Most times, I would go in a back door, loading dock, or other path that would avoid the receptionists and get me in faster. On one occasion, as I entered the loading dock, I saw two men loading freight onto pallets. One man was Black, the other White.

I walked right past the Black guy and straight to the White guy to ask him if the boss was in. He pointed to an office across the way, and I went on with my day. As I left the warehouse and passed the two guys loading pallets, I said goodbye and got into my car. And then it hit me. Why did I walk past one man and over to the other, when each one could have given me the answer? I just assumed that the White guy was the boss or knew the boss, never giving thought to the possibility that the Black guy could be the boss.

I never did that again. It was twenty-five years ago, and when I heard of your project, this immediately came to mind.

They all asked, "Was he Black?"

Amy D. • Royal Oaks, CA

One night in San Francisco, when I was walking home from my car after a late work night, a man came toward me and tried to steal my purse. My immediate instinct was to resist and call out, hoping for some intervention from those living in the houses nearby. Ultimately, he took off without my purse, but he punched my face in the process, leaving me with a big shiner and a cut that required stitches.

As I shared my story with friends and coworkers, I did not expect to hear the question that came up over and over from them: "Was he Black?" Honestly, it surprised me when it first happened but then really shocked me when it happened again and again. Although I felt I had an understanding of the pervasive endemic racism in our society, I really didn't expect this reaction from so many. It was a real eye-opener for me.

Whatever my challenges, race wasn't one

Justin Flagel • Niles, MI

Yes, I've faced plenty of challenges throughout my life. Yes, I've worked hard to earn things I've gained in life. Yes, my life hasn't always been easy. Acknowledging my White privilege does not mean those things are untrue or that I've never had problems. It just means that whatever my challenges were, my race was never one of them. "White" doesn't equal an easy life, but it does remove obstacles.

Blacks who speak Spanish confuse people

Manuelal Bernardez Kuchta • Pittsburgh, PA

It can be very frustrating at times explaining myself—or a good teaching experience, depending on who's questioning me.

Last Jim Crow Generation In Charge!

Cleo Brown • SC

I and others in our late fifties and up are members of the last generation of children to grow up under the Jim Crow legal system that required *every* White person to discriminate against *every* Black person, whether or not they were racist. This extreme inequality left a residue that caused us not to immediately "see" another person, but to first see what we thought the other person's race represented. We could see people from different races doing the same thing and think two very different thoughts about them.

We are the children whose relatives were lynched or shot, and we are also the children whose parents did the lynchings and shootings. We are the children harassed while integrating White schools, and we are also the children who did the harassing or whose parents funded lawyers to maintain an inferior education for some. We are the children whose parents' livelihoods and reputations were destroyed via the media, and we are also the children whose parents wrote and spoke to move the masses to hate in order to achieve personal agendas. We are the children of almost a whole state of Black parents who lost their right to vote in a single year, and we are the children who as adults have applied their parents' tactics to gutting the Voting Rights Act. We are the children who feared the fiery cross, and we are also the children who stood hand in hand with our fathers encircling the cross. We are the children who may have never gone to school with anyone of the opposite race. Now we work side by side, and we (and those we mentor) teach and supervise and make employment decisions; we are jurors and judges, and we set policy and political agendas. After all, we are of the age to be in charge, to set direction for others, but for many, our childhood Jim Crow foundation still frames our worldviews because we failed to challenge (or even acknowledge) what Jim Crow taught all of us and what has become a part of our automatic response system.

We can't solve what we are unwilling to acknowledge or confront.

Leave now! Hanging about to happen

Bobbie Clark • Baton Rouge, LA

My father taught school in rural parishes all his teaching career, from the 1940s through the '70s. I recall one afternoon he arrived home, and he and my mother went into the bedroom. I sat by their door to hear what was going on and heard my father crying. All "colored" people who did not live in the parish were told to get out of town, and as he and another teacher he rode with were leaving, they saw a Black man hanging from a tree, and he felt totally helpless and frightened.

A family lynching changed my life

Karen Branan • Washington, DC

Now 82, lynching at age 3

Florence L. Tate • USA

When I was three years old, I sat with my grandparents around the fireplace and listened to my father reading the *Chicago Defender* about the details of my cousin's lynching.

White people, it's not about you

Jaqui Wilridge • Bremerton, WA

So often, when having a conversation about race with a White person, they are unable to step outside themselves. They are either (A) focused on how they personally never owned slaves, lynched someone, etc., or (B) more worried about their own hurt feelings because somehow pointing out that the system of oppression that we live in gives White people a leg up is offensive and "racist" to White people (they don't know what racism even means).

Slave-owning ancestors mortgaged my future

Buford Woolley • Pittsburgh, PA

My mostly White family tree flows through South Carolina, Georgia, Virginia, Alabama, Mississippi, Tennessee, Arkansas, Texas, Oklahoma, and lastly California, where I was born. Many were slave owners. One outlier was lynched because he supported the Union and opposed slavery. The question, to me: Did my ancestors mortgage my future?

When will we just see people

Robert Williamson • Margate, FL

I was a White boy born in southwest Florida but left there at five and came back at eleven in 1970. Had a Black friend up North, had no real awareness of race until I came back South. My mother grew up in southeast Florida. She witnessed lynchings and all the racial bigotry of the day. I had a lot of problems in school with Black kids picking on me. The hatred between Blacks and Whites was an incredible shock to me, and I learned to fear.

Forty-three years later, I've raised four color-blind children. I pray for the day the only "race" we see is the human race, and the different colors and shapes are seen as variety, God's gift to us, to keep things interesting. I find that some of the most beautiful people I've seen come from "mixed" marriages. My hope is that my children's children will get there.

My stepbrother threatened to hang him

Teagan Peacock • Cuba, NY

There is only one African American family in my rural neighborhood. My stepbrother got into a fight with one of the boys in the family and threatened to hang him. I was never more embarrassed in my life.

Italians were also lynched down south

Michael Bertolone • Rochester, NY

Please be aware that many Italians and Sicilians (myself included) are considerably darker than the typical "White" person. This is why many southern and eastern Europeans oppose affirmative action programs that equate their ethnic group with the oppressors who carried out lynchings in the US. Italian Americans (and specifically Sicilians) were commonly lynched in the Deep South. In fact, one of the largest single lynchings in the US occurred in New Orleans, Louisiana, in 1891 when eleven Italians were lynched at once.

That said, it concerns me that this group is lumped into the "White" racial category, and "diversity consultants" insist that they have enjoyed "White privilege." With privileges like this one, I wonder what "punishment" looks like for this group.

Did my Southern Grandpa attend lynchings?

Barbara Bennett • Saint Louis, MO

"It's time for the DAY OF THE ROPE.
WHITE REVOLUTION IS THE ONLY SOLUTION!"

Post that appeared on a far-right online forum was included in House select committee hearing on the January 6 attack on the US Capitol.

"Arizona lawmaker speaks to white nationalists,
calls for violence — and sets fundraising records."

The *Washington Post,* Beth Reinhard and Rosalind S. Helderman, March 8, 2022

"We need to build more gallows," the speaker said, adding that such a deadly fate would "make an example of these traitors who've betrayed our country."

"Bring out Pence!"
"Bring him out!"
"Hang Mike Pence!"

Dramatic footage showing a mob chanting these words was shown at the House select committee hearing investigating Donald Trump's role in the January 6 attack on the US Capitol.

"Trump likens House impeachment hearing to 'a lynching'"

Darlene Superville and Jay Reeves, October 22, 2019

Washington (AP)—Stirring up painful memories of America's racist past, President Donald Trump on Tuesday compared the Democratic-led impeachment inquiry to a lynching, a practice once widespread across the South in which angry mobs killed thousands of black people.

"Graham backs Trump: 'This is a lynching in every sense'"

The *Hill,* Alexander Bolton, October 22, 2019

Senate Judiciary Committee Chairman Lindsey Graham (R-S.C.) on Tuesday said President Trump is absolutely right to call the House impeachment process a "lynching."

"This wasn't the right word to use and I'm sorry about that."

Tweet from @JoeBiden on October 22, 2019. After condemning Donald Trump for invoking a lynching, Joe Biden issued an apology after it became clear that he had used similar language to describe the Clinton impeachment hearings in 1998.

**"NASCAR releases image of noose found in
Bubba Wallace's garage, says concern was 'real'"**

ESPN News Services, June 25, 2020

NASCAR on Thursday completed its investigation into the garage pull rope formed as
a noose that was found in Bubba Wallace's garage at Talladega Superspeedway.

**"USF Officials Investigate Noose Found
Hanging Off Student Dorm Room Balcony"**

CBS News Bay Area, April 7, 2021

"Noose found at school in Loudoun, sheriff says"

The Washington Post, Martin Weil, March 7, 2022

"Noose found in middle school classroom in Maryland"

The Washington Post, Donna St. George, February 28, 2020

**"Dozens of nooses have shown up on U.S. construction sites.
The culprits rarely face consequences."**

The Washington Post, Taylor Telford, July 22, 2021

"Second noose found hanging at Durham pharmaceutical plant"

WRAL News, June 10, 2021

"Noose found near CIA facility in Virginia: report"

The Hill, Sarah Polus, July 18, 2022

**"This is a circus. This is a national disgrace. And from my standpoint, as a black
American, as far as I'm concerned, it is a high-tech lynching for uppity blacks
who in any way deign to think for themselves, to do for themselves, to have
different ideas, and it is a message that unless you kowtow to an old order,
this is what will happen to you. You will be lynched, destroyed, caricatured
by a committee of the US Senate rather than hung from a tree."**

Clarence Thomas testifying before the US Senate Judiciary Committee, October 11, 1991

10

So, You Want to Talk About Lynching?

LYNCHING IS NO LONGER a common aspect of American life, yet the language of lynching still hovers over us with an ease and frequency that should be alarming.

But it's not.

Justice Clarence Thomas's claim that questions about his behavior with coworker Anita Hill was tantamount to "a high-tech lynching" during his Supreme Court confirmation hearings almost overshadows the memory of the ghoulish nature of lynchings that were at one time a feature of American life.

At one point in 2019, President Biden chastised President Donald Trump for comparing the Democratic-led House impeachment inquiry to a lynching and then had to backtrack and apologize for using almost the exact same language to describe the Clinton impeachment hearings.

Americans are very loose about using the language of lynching, with talk of someone being "strung up" or "hung out to dry." It may just cruise by your ear unnoticed, but if you start paying attention, those references really add up, especially as the radical wing of the Republican Party uses violent references about domestic terror and extrajudicial punishment without apology.

We should never forget that the men convicted of hatching a plot to kidnap and hold their own version of a mock trial to prosecute Michigan governor Gretchen Whitmer, a Democrat, had written social media posts that included a photo of a noose. Those posts included the question: "Which governor is going to end up dragged off and hung for treason first?"

The repeated chants of "hang Mike Pence" will forever be a stain on this nation's history, but what gets less attention are the comments from politicians who use the rhetoric of the rope to rile up their supporters. Arizona state senator Wendy Rogers, wearing a bright-red MAGA hat, told a crowd at a White nationalist conference in Orlando that "we need to build more gallows." Rogers said the instruments of death were necessary to "make an example of these traitors who betrayed our country." The Arizona senate voted 24–3 to censure Rogers, a former US Air Force pilot, for those remarks. But she has become one of the most prolific fundraisers in the Arizona legislature, showing that there is an audience for that kind of red meat on the campaign stump.

The history of lynching is foul, and yet the language of hanging still haunts us.

In a disturbing footnote to history, a popular T-shirt at some Trump rallies read: "Rope. Tree. Journalist. Some assembly required." In July 2022, a Santa Rosa County, Florida, school board candidate said doctors who treat trans kids should be punished by hanging. At an event sponsored by a group called the Gulf Coast Patriots, Alisabeth Janai Lancaster told the audience, "These doctors that are going along with mutilating these children and prescribing hormone blockers to these kids, in my opinion, they should be hanging from the nearest tree." Those remarks were met with enthusiastic applause. The applause, the acceptance of this kind of rhetoric, the fact that these comments are all too common is an example where history seems to fold in on itself.

A report called *Lynching in America* by the Equal Justice Initiative notes that lynching "first emerged as a form of vigilante retribution used to enforce 'popular justice' on the Western frontier." The report explains that it then became a "vicious tool of racial control in America during the late nineteenth and early twentieth centuries." Mob violence that operated outside of official legal frameworks was used to maintain White supremacy and control the behavior of Black populations with terror. Most of those lynchings occurred in public spaces, watched by throngs of spectators at the time but now unmarked or unrecognized. There were thousands of lynchings throughout the United States, which means multitudes of Americans have passed by a tree or a town square that was the site of one of the most gruesome forms of death.

The history of lynching is foul, and yet the language of hanging still haunts us.

The casual use of this language has a pernicious effect, said Sherrilyn Ifill, the former head of the NAACP Legal Defense Fund who authored the book *On the Courthouse Lawn: Confronting the Legacy of Lynching in the Twenty-First Century*. "It demonstrates a failure to understand what lynching really means and what it's about, and how close it is to us in our historic timeline." What she is saying is that it minimizes something that is monstrous.

Over the years, stories about lynching have drifted into the inbox at The Race Card Project. Very personal stories about a cousin's lynching, about witnessing a hanging, about why America has all but forgotten the mass lynching of eleven Italian Americans in New Orleans in 1891. The language of lynching is often meant to explain or complain about an individual being singled out unfairly for prosecution, but I agree with Ifill when she says, "There is no such thing as a high-tech lynching or no such thing as a character lynching." Cancel culture or social opprobrium or mistreatment may feel like persecution, but it's not the same. Not even close.

"I think people don't understand what makes lynching different than murder, and what makes lynching different is what makes lynching dangerous," Ifill says. "Someone who commits murder in general tries to hide the crime. They hide the body. They bury the body. They run away from the scene of the crime. All the things that we would associate with someone committing a murder. Lynching is not like that because the perpetrators are convinced that they have the support of the community around them, either tacitly or explicitly, to commit this act. They feel like they are expressing the will of their community, and therefore, they are not afraid that they'll be caught," Ifill said.

And language played a role, sometimes a key role, in the callousness that developed in a population that was not only willing to look the other way but to stand at full attention in the face of such evil. I am not advocating for speech police or curtailing free expression, but a velvet rope around this rhetoric does serve a purpose. Casual talk about lynching is a descent toward a sorrowful slope.

If people understood the true horror of lynching—the ghastly way life leaves the body, the strange enthusiasm from the crowd, the sheer brutality, would they be less likely to invoke that awful imagery? I'd like to think that might hold true for at least part of the population, which is why I wrote the following column for the *Washington Post* during a cross-country flight in the fall of 2019.

· · ·

So, you want to talk about lynching?

OK. Let's talk.

A lynching involved a man, but sometimes a woman or a child, who was dragged from home, heels in the dirt, body contorting, convulsing with fear.

A lynching involved another man—this time, almost always a man—finding a rope and making a noose, or perhaps finding a rope that had already been made into a noose, for this was not exactly rare in an earlier time. It took a special kind of rope to hold the knot, to hold the weight. A heavy rope. Corded and coarse.

The knot took skill; the act was impulsive, but the details relied on practiced technique. The genus, health, and shape of the tree were important. Were the branches high enough? Thick enough? Healthy enough to accommodate the sudden plummet of death?

A lynching was bulging eyes and slobber and spittle.

It took a mob, a rabble, a group of several people to carry out the deed. To hold the victim. To toss the rope. To necklace the rope. To hoist the rope. To keep it taut while the body fought and then stiffened and then went limp and sodden. Heavy like coal. Dangling like earrings.

A lynching was loud, for a mob is never silent. The act itself was audible: The rope chafed against the bark. It tore open the skin. It suffocated and gagged, crushed the esophagus and snapped the neck. It made water, involuntary and foul, tricking past the knee, past the calf and the foot. A lynching was a fight against gravity. Desperate. Futile. Listless. And gravity always won.

A lynching was an act of community will. A community that showed up dressed for the outing, smiling, cheering, hoisting their children for a better view, preening for the cameras, for there were so often cameras to commemorate the occasion with postcards later sold as keepsakes. Postcards with swaying, charred bodies. Shoulders limp. Legs loose. Heads lolled backward in an odd contortion that made it seem that their souls were communing with God.

Lynching was the work of "good people." People who held positions of stature and authority. Who went to church. Who taught their children the Golden Rule about Jesus

The rope that is believed to have bound the wrists of Raymond Byrd,
lynched in 1926. His body was hung in a tree not far from St. Paul Lutheran
Church in Wythe County, Virginia. The rope was given to John M. Johnson
by a relative of a man who was present at the lynching.

loving all the little children. A rule with exceptions and bylaws and fine print. A rule that applied only to people with white skin.

A lynching was meant to send a message. Stay in line. This could be you or your son or your wife or your father. Your heart. Your pride. Your breadwinner. Your changemaker. Your dignity. Yes, there was a message. We are powerful. You are not.

A lynching was often accompanied by long-term amnesia. The people behind those acts would eventually forget this history, forget that this was what transpired in the town square or tobacco field, forget that they were engaged in what would now pass as evil because, jeez, who would want to claim that?

According to the NAACP, 4,743 people were lynched in the United States from 1882 to 1968. (Yes, 1968.) Of that number, 3,446 were Black. Lynching was a fact of life for much of this country's existence. It was the green light for decapitating the victim and the impulse to place a head on a stick and then place that stick into the ground on a well-traveled road and leave it there until the sun or the birds or the vermin had their way.

Lynching was sometimes not enough. Bodies were burned and blowtorched and branded. They were gutted and skinned like animals. They were castrated, scalped, dismembered. It was the justification for human bonfires and dismembering bodies and turning toes into key fobs and skin into lampshades.

In one particularly gruesome case, Mary Turner was lynched in 1918 after threatening to swear out warrants for the men who lynched her husband, Hayes Turner, who was wrongly accused of a crime. She was eight months pregnant, but that didn't matter. She was tracked down, captured, dragged to a bridge between two counties in Valdosta, Georgia, and hung upside down from a tree, ankles tied together. She was doused in gasoline, and her clothes were burned off.

Had enough? The mob wasn't done. One man used a hunting knife to cut open her pregnant belly. Her unborn child tumbled to the ground, where it was reportedly crushed under the heel of a boot.

Even that was not enough. They pummeled her body with gunfire before cutting her down. She was one of eleven people killed in that rampage, and her name—we must say her name: Mary Turner—now graces a project dedicated to remembering that there was no justice served for these atrocities. And that we must understand how the long arm of this history and the attitudes that fueled it still touch us today.

• • •

This is hard reading, I know. Many will not have gotten this far or perhaps have decided to put the book down or skip ahead to other pages. I am not sharing these facts for mere sensation. This is our history. **Our** history. We will never fully understand how far we've come as a nation until we accept and acknowledge the spectacular abominations that passed as normal.

Do not trifle with this history. Not unless you are willing to understand the meaning, the weight, the horror, the ardor, the hatred, the stain, the special brand of evil associated with it and the deed it represents. Anything less is an attempt at distraction.

So, if you want to talk about lynching, let's do it. Let's acknowledge it. Let's face it, even if it turns our stomachs. Let's face it as the terror and the terrorism it was. Because to face it—and face it down—is a first payment on an insurance policy that perhaps ensures we will never see this again on our soil.

If you are unwilling to do this work—and it is work—then leave that word alone.

Grandfather's poker gift a hanging invitation

Carol Zachary • Washington, DC, and Montana

Somehow, I kept blocking on three things: (A) the six words . . . grandfather, poker, three hangings, an invitation lost for almost sixty years, and my changed perceptions; (B) the fact that I've felt I should know exactly what evidence was presented against the men who were hanged; and (C) the lingering question, "Did my grandfather's actions help direct me toward family history, or did he see something in me that told him I would cherish his 'gift' and do something with it, or was it just the only unique thing he could give a grandchild for winning at nine-card stud?" When I finally realized I needn't answer B and C, at least not for your project, then I got to A.

Confederate re-enactor chose intimidation as spoils

Lillian J. Hal • Dallas, TX

I was a freshman in college. I was sitting in the dining hall with a friend, near a window. It was "Texas Day." The theme was obvious by the bales of hay, Western-wear-clad employees, and of course, barbecue on the menu.

My friend and I were chatting, when all of a sudden, two middle-aged men dressed in Confederate-era uniforms were passing by outside. The one that lagged slightly behind looked at me, looked at my friend, then stopped. He was a big guy. Burly. He backed up, turned his body to face me, propped his foot on the window ledge, and prominently displayed his rifle on his knee. Then came the staring contest.

I stared at him. He stared at me. I refused to look away, ignoring my friend's pleas. The other "soldier" finally grabbed the burly one by the elbow and dragged him away. The smirk he had seemed like a badge of honor. He was quite amused.

That was when I realized I was Black. Granted, I went to all-Black schools from elementary to high school. I chose a predominantly White school in west Texas that had a 1 percent population of Black students. My friend, by the way, was biracial, but could "pass" as White. I went to my dorm and cried and vowed to never be intimidated by a White man again.

The hatred that one encounter produced should have ruined me, but it didn't. My great-grandfather was White. He had five children with my great-grandmother in rural east Texas at the turn of the twentieth century. He allowed them all to call him Daddy in public. He was not ashamed. The society he lived in was, and they burned down my great-grandmother's house to prove it. Enough in my life has happened to cause me to hate one group or another. I made a choice to accept people as I receive them. Have you made that choice?

It is not a heritage thing

Sara Lachance • Springdale, AR

Seeing Confederate flags on the backs of trucks and outside people's houses makes my stomach hurt. I once encountered a person with the Confederate flag on their sunglasses right between the lenses, like it was staring me down. I am forced to be associated with those people because (A) I am also White, and (B) I am also from the South. The truth is, they represent hate and stall progress within America. It's not a heritage thing; it's a race thing, and it's discriminatory.

I'm not guilty, family from Norway

Michael J. • Rochester, MN

I just feel I am a little tired of feeling guilty about being a White male. My family came from Norway and Sweden. We never owned slaves and, moving to southern Minnesota, didn't even have a plantation. Nevertheless, it seems that this issue is somehow my fault, as well.

Mortified by dad's Confederate flag tattoo

Courtney Potter • Ann Arbor, MI

Southern heritage doesn't mean I'm racist

Gunner • Goshen, UT

Just because I have Confederate flags and my family comes from the South does not mean I am a racist.

Yes, I transitioned. Still White though.

Jonah Frank • Brooklyn, NY

As a transgender man, I can relate to being marginalized. But still, my Whiteness (and now maleness) affords me privilege in 99 percent of my everyday life, and I know that's still 100 percent better than what BIPOC people are experiencing.

Lie. Pretend to be less Black.

Anonymous • USA

Someone, maybe many people, in my family took on the persona of mixed-race Black/Native Americans so they could be, what? Less Black? I don't know if it was my father's generation, or his father's, or even further back. I grew up thinking I was Indian and consequently less connected to my Black friends and family. All because someone in generations past thought it would be best to create a lie for their family than make them live in what they knew as the pain of truth. Now I am deconstructing my own story as I try to create a true and strong narrative for my children.

Pessimistic poster child for post-racial promise

Carey Tan • New York, NY

Biracial (White and Asian). Partnered with a White man from rural West Virginia. We don't experience much (if any) hostility. I'm told that this is increasingly normal in society, and this demographic development is supposed to fill us all with hope and pride. But I look around at all the entrenched inequalities in our country, and the entrenched apathy toward it all, and I feel increasing despair and hopelessness.

I passed Citizenship test, can you?

Avanti Iyer • Chevy Chase, MD

I'm tired of not being seen as having the same rights as White people (especially after 9/11). I had to pay hundreds of dollars in fees and take a test to become a citizen of the US. I am curious how many native-born White people have the equivalent civics, history, and geographic knowledge of this country that they seem to take for granted.

White minority does exist in America

Gregory • Philadelphia, PA

As a Polish immigrant in America, I have been faced with many challenges, but one that has always seemed most challenging and bizarre was the issue of being White and being treated by others as a minority. As long as people didn't hear my accent, I would fit in, but once my identity was established, I would be treated differently. It seemed pretty obvious to me from day one that the attitudes to White people with accents are closely related to the feelings many minorities experience.

Spit towards my feet on train

Azeem Raheem • Chicago, IL

Happened about a week after 9/11 as I was headed home from school on a Chicago train.

Teacher this is my home flag

Randi Sin • Eureka, CA

When my dad was in the third grade, he was tasked to draw his home flag. He proceeded to draw the American flag, which the teacher told him was incorrect: his was the Mexican flag. This was met with very offending words from my grandmother, who, just like my dad, was born here. The teacher assumed that just because he was Mexican, he was born in Mexico.

Three Cultures. Two Races. No Home.

Kristen Ellerbe • Richmond, VA

As a mixed child, I have never felt at home with any culture. My mother was born in the Philippines, and my father was an airman stationed there. They are wonderful parents who are absolutely in love with each other. I am one of three children, the middle child and only girl. I am mixed. I grew up in White, middle-class America. So where do I fit in?

To America's confusion, I identify more with my Filipina roots than anything else, despite not speaking Tagalog. That is another story for another time, though. My mother and her surrogate Filipino family made up of her best friends were the people I grew up around. My nearest cousins on my father's side lived too far away and were all boys. I just could never really fit in anywhere. At the same time, I was always aware that I did not look like my Filipino friends, either. My hair isn't kinky enough, or my skin is not light enough. My speech was not Black enough, or I had never actually been to the Philippines. There was no place for me.

Furthermore, I attended a White school, and I was acutely aware of it. I remember one year, I had an angel costume. Right before Halloween, I told my father I couldn't wear it. When he asked me why, I told him that I didn't look like an angel. Angels were White and blond and pretty. And I wasn't. Instead, I had my mother make me a Pocahontas outfit because I looked like her. I am not Indian, but that was the closest thing I could find to me. I was in elementary school. And I didn't think I was pretty.

I felt like a dog in a shelter where people walk up and cock their head. Then they say, "What is it?" I had three cultures, two races, and no identity.

"BUT WHERE ARE YOU REALLY FROM?"

"WHERE ARE YOU FROM?"

Such a simple question. An icebreaker. A greeting. A gesture of genuine curiosity.

The answer can be just as simple as . . .

"From New Jersey" . . ."From New England" . . . "From the Southside" . . . "From Boyle Heights."

But . . . when that simple question is amended with a few words . . . things change.

"Where are you really from?"

"Where do you actually come from?"

"No, where are you originally from?"

"Where did your family first come from?"

"Are you genuinely from here?"

I can't speak to the intent of the person asking those questions, but I have gotten an earful from people who are on the receiving end. Over time, it's the most common submission in The Race Card Project inbox, usually sent in by people who feel that the question of their actual origin triggers a sense of alienation or otherness.

The question is seemingly harmless but carries a lot of toxicity. It is usually a clumsy attempt at hospitality, but it pokes at something raw and personal. Being a fringe dweller, an outsider, someone who does not fully belong in a space where the norms of White culture are dominant.

For many people, the question "Where do you actually come from?" winds up sounding like, "Why are you here?" Even when someone tries to answer the question, the true response is far too complex to explain in a breezy conversation. When someone says they are from India or Alabama, Boston or Brazil, that is usually one piece of a much larger tangle of class, education, intermarriage, migration, assimilation, adoption, or individual anthems.

And I know from doing scores of workshops and lectures where the frequency of this question comes up, the person asking the question (and I must admit I myself have often asked this question) has no idea that their curiosity might feel like a microaggression. This is a case where intent matters and grace can go a long way, but perhaps we can learn something from the hundreds of people who have shared 6-word stories in this particular vein. For me, the lesson is that this should not be the first question in an encounter. It's a good idea to get to know who a person is before trying to figure out "what" they are. Intentions matter and are often signaled in small ways through actual language and body language.

And when you ask someone where they are from, be prepared to accept any answer you receive, even if it does not satisfy your entrenched assumptions about lineage, geography, pedigree, or ancestry. If someone says they are from Mars, it's probably acceptable to ask a follow-up query about where they really come from. But if the man wearing a turban, the teen wearing a hijab, the dude decked out in dreadlocks, the kid with curly red hair, or the woman wearing a sari or overalls or a fashionable blue pantsuit tells you they're from Naperville, Illinois, accept that as the reward for your curiosity, until they are willing to share something more on their own time . . . and their own terms.

Swallow the instinct to press on by repeating the where-are-you-from question with some qualifier because when you inject words like *truly* and *actually* and *really* into that sentence, the subject of the inquiry might make an educated guess about where *you* are coming from with that question in the first place.

No, Where Are You Actually From?

Shagun Doshi • Naperville, IL

Coming from a predominately rich, White suburb and not being rich and White has been an interesting experience. While there is a lot more diversity within my community compared to many others, there is still a lot of hostility. The divide between White and every other race is very prevalent, as it is in many places throughout America. I never really got to know the people that surrounded me until I started working at the local Jewel-Osco. This job not only consisted of cleaning dirty bathrooms and pushing carts that were ten times my size, but I also encountered some of the most ignorant people that I lived among. I eventually lost count of the amount of times that people asked where I was from or started the conversation with some Hindi word that I didn't know. The surprising part was that it wasn't only old White people that made such assumptions; it was also many Indian people. I was offended that even though I was born in America, had lived in Naperville most of my life, went to school in America, and saw myself as an American, people were still only looking at what I represented on the outside. While my Indian culture influences a lot of my values and beliefs, the American culture that I have been brought up into also accounts for my personality and views. So yes, even though my skin color and my ethnicity are 100 percent Brown, I am actually from America.

So where do you come from?

Michael Chan • Maplewood, MN

I am half Chinese and half Caucasian, but my German- and Hebrew-language skills are much stronger than my Cantonese (my family's language). So when I get the question, "Where do you come from?" I laugh internally and typically spend a few seconds trying to figure out what exactly I'm being asked.

Different is not bad, just different

Shaida Johnson • Falls Church, VA

What is my nationality? I am American. I am as American as you are. Where am I from? Los Angeles, California. What is my ethnicity? I know you are trying to get at something with your questions. It is your way of telling me that you noticed I am different—or perhaps, more sinisterly, that I do not belong here, wherever here is at the moment. Yes, I am different from you. But there is no need to be afraid or uncomfortable. I take nothing away from you and your culture. I have no expectations of you. I simply wish for a seat at the table. I will bring my own food, my own flavor, and my own color.

I am American, no questions needed

Demetrios Pathammavong • Sanger, CA

I am an American, although my grandparents are from Laos. It is often a repeated question of where I am from. When I answer that I am from America, people then ask the same question. Sometimes I say, "Oh, I am from Laos." In reality, I was born in California. This is an ongoing matter that needs to be stopped. If we were born in America, we are American.

No, where are you really from?

Fatima Abdel-Gwad • Sacramento, CA

Yes, I'm Muslim.
Yes, I'm American.
I'm really from America.

My son's not half he's double.

Jon Letman • Lihue, HI

I'm as American as you are

J. Lim • Boise, ID

First generation American. No root anywhere.

Crissie Acosta • Miami, FL

Born of Cuban immigrants, there is a sense of loss of my heritage, culture, and traditions. My parents came to this country when they were children themselves, carrying little to nothing but the clothes on their backs and even less of their culture and traditions. They were raised in an era of assimilation instead of acknowledging cultural diversity. My brother and I were raised "American"— *Brady Bunch* and *Cosby Show* American. However, when speaking to an American, I am Cuban, according to them at least, and when I speak to someone directly from the island, soy Americana o gringa. I see myself as a first-generation American, but what that actually means I still don't know.

I am American. Stop insisting otherwise

Erin Capina • Arlington, VA

My brown skin and Asian features do not make me a perpetual foreigner. I am a born and raised New Englander. I am as American as you. Deal with it.

Native Americans America's Invisible Invisible Invisible.

Gene Tagaban • Ruston, WA

395

But where are you really from?

Christopher Lee-Rodriguez • Boston, MA

We don't live in a post-racial society. We live in a post-race society. We live in a country where in a short amount of time, there will no longer be a majority race. And race is continuing to be reshaped and redefined.

I am half Chinese and half Puerto Rican. I live in Boston, and I see dozens and dozens of couples of White men and Asian women. The half-Asian community is doubling by the decade. There are so many Black and Latino families in this country, as well.

Race is not real. It is malleable. Racism is real. It's pervasive and inside all of us. When people ask me where I'm really from, they are saying that I am not really American. Even though I'm second-generation on both sides and can really only speak English, I do not look like an authentic American. I am part of the other American. The new American. And no matter how many racist cops kill people of color or disenfranchise communities, we're still going to be around. It's time to not only reform the system but redefine what it is to be Black, Latino, Asian, and, in the end, American.

Ask WHO I am not WHAT

Jessica Hong • Philadelphia, PA

As an Asian American, people often ask "what" I am within the first twenty minutes (or sometimes twenty seconds!) of meeting me. Others feel self-conscious about asking but are visibly relieved when/if I happen to mention my ethnicity myself.

I think the question of my ethnicity wouldn't bother me so much if it was a true inquiry about the substance of who I am and what makes me *me* (including but not limited to my ethnicity). But more often than not, I find that the desire to know "what" I am seems to be motivated by an anxiety about the unknown, an anxiousness to know which category of people to put me in. This anxiety is revealed as soon as the question of my ethnicity is answered.

What that looks like is this: as soon as I reveal that I am Korean, I hear about all the other Korean things in that person's internal Korean Box—friends who taught English in Korea, favorite Korean dishes, the two words of atrociously pronounced Korean picked up along the way, family members who fought in the Korean War, or childhood best friends who were (and presumably are still) Korean. These contents of the Korean Box come spilling out, and I realize that the next Korean person this person meets may soon be hearing about me.

Love me because
I am you

David Clark • Sacramento, CA

11

Color Me Surprised

I HAD NO IDEA when I began this journey that I would be engaging in a fourteen-year odyssey of examining what it means to be White. When 6-word stories started arriving in large numbers—first as postcards and then as digital submissions—I assumed the bulk would come from people of color.

Color me surprised.

In many of the fourteen years that we have done this work, the majority of the submitted stories have come from White people. I don't really know why this is the case. I used to think that it might have something to do with the makeup of the audience from all those years I hosted a show called *All Things Considered* on National Public Radio, but the trend held true long after I left NPR in 2015. The fact that The Race Card Project is used on so many college campuses around the country where White students are in the majority was another possible explanation until we really started to examine the stories and realized that many of the White people who sent submissions had long ago left their campuses behind or never went to college at all.

I now believe this project and its tilt toward stories that come from White Americans reflect a shift that has become evident over the past decade. It's the era when America's Caucasian population has increasingly become part of a racialized cohort known as . . . White.

For decades, examining race in America meant focusing on the predicament of people of color. Under that framework, being White was simply the normative identity, and Americans in that category didn't see themselves as "raced." Indeed, the whole concept of race as we understand it today was created as a social construct to delineate a group that held power from a non-White and poor population that was supposed to be relegated to lower rungs. White people in power created the concept of race as the concrete necklace that would weigh down other people. The concept of Whiteness has been elastic over time, evolving as a line of demarcation separating a group in power from those deemed to be of lesser stock. In America that meant Native Americans, emancipated slaves, and people with dusky-hued skin. There was a time when Italians, Greeks, and Europeans from Slavic nations were not considered to be automatic guests in the subcategory of White until the carefully policed definitions broadened to allow for greater membership in the class, and consequently a greater hold on the levers of power in an electoral democracy.

Why should White people get to stay on the sidelines holding VIP tickets to a space designated as "normal"?

Whiteness over time was cemented as the foundational standard for what it means to be American, and every other group was otherized so that matters of race were the problem and province of people of color designated as "minorities." Race as a construct is made up, but racism and its consequences are very real.

Around matters of race in America, many White Americans have occupied a vague bystander space where it has been easier to sidestep ownership or participation in the fractious debates on racism and equality. Those problems were often viewed as things that were tethered to other people and other realms.

That is changing. On several fronts, there is growing evidence that for White Americans, race is no longer a thorny travail viewed from the remove of a spectator's perch. In the period that covers the elections of Barack Obama and Donald Trump and the insurrection at the Capitol ahead of the inauguration of President Joe Biden, the question of what it means to be White in America has increasingly taken center stage. This is evident on several fronts. Battles over immigration and the way the history of slavery and civil rights is taught in schools, the racially polarized electorate, the growing appeal of White nationalism, the introduction of Whiteness courses on college campuses, and the rising poverty and death rates for middle-aged White Americans with no more than a high school diploma from drugs, alcohol, and suicide in what economists are calling "deaths of despair." There are a lot of White Americans who will read that list of examples and see nothing of their experience or perspective. The heat from those flash points may not touch their lives. But even in America's more mundane spaces—in the classroom or on the sports field or the factory floor—the discourse around race increasingly surfaces with a new beckoning expectation that White Americans should more actively participate in untangling the knots left behind by a culture that was created around White supremacy.

All these years of listening to White Americans talk honestly about a topic many try hard to avoid has helped me understand the twisted conundrum that leads to anxiety and race fatigue. Because so many people spend so much energy sidestepping the topic, they only wind up dipping into matters of race when they absolutely have to. And that's usually because something has gone awry. Whether or not people want to engage in prickly matters of race, and it is easy to understand why many would rather not, the tensions and intersecting issues in an increasingly diverse culture can be hard to sidestep. We live in a world where our neighbors, our coworkers, our in-laws, and fellow travelers are increasingly likely to come from another cohort. It's one reason why a growing body of scholars argue that it's time to remove the cloak of racial invisibility around Whiteness so more White Americans have the chance to develop a greater fluency around race, including their own. Business leaders are also quietly having these discussions, recognizing that years of diversity efforts that focus on and are run primarily by people of color have failed in addressing issues rooted in the at-present minority culture or among racial and ethnic groups outside the White-Black binary. When we do work in colleges and corporate spaces, the conversation has shifted from "Should we think about getting our White team members involved?" to "How do we make sure White team members aren't left out?"

· · ·

You may notice that racial identifiers like Black and White are capitalized throughout the pages of this book, something that is in keeping with the style now adopted by the newsrooms where my work primarily appears. It's a change I applaud.

Many organizations decided to follow the lead of Black media organizations such as *Essence*, TheGrio, and the National Association of Black Journalists by capitalizing the B in the word *Black* after the death of George Floyd. It was a matter of respect and a recognition that a group long denied power deserved that designation to reflect their role and contribution to American life. And several journalists and academics strongly argued that the W in *White* should also be capitalized, as well, to reflect that population's place within the life and legacy of race in America—for good and for bad.

A statement issued by the Center for the Study of Social Policy in 2020 declared, "We believe that it is important to call attention to White as a race as a way to understand and give voice to how Whiteness functions in our social and political institutions and our communities. Moreover, the detachment of 'White' as a proper noun allows White people to sit out of conversations about race and removes accountability from White people's and White institutions' involvement in racism."

That raises a legitimate question. Why should White people get to stay on the sidelines holding VIP tickets to a space designated as "normal"? On the path toward racial healing, shouldn't everyone have skin in the game? As you will see in the stories throughout these pages, and as you have probably heard in the discussions and debates that make their way into the news cycle, White Americans are increasingly talking about themselves and their place in a period of rapid change.

Ten to fifteen years ago, I used to repeatedly hear White people talk about how they never really thought about their own race. I heard that claim over and over again in workshops, in my reporting, during informal conversations with neighbors or parents at my kids' schools. It wasn't an assertion that people were proud about. They were just honest about their ability to move through the world, buy homes and raise their children, apply for jobs, plan vacations, or decide what restaurant to visit on a Friday night without thinking about how the color of their skin would impact that experience. And often they were surprised to learn that people of color make constant calculations around identity. That has changed.

I rarely hear the "I just don't think about race" claims these days. I find both in my reporting and in my TRCP inbox that White people are more aware of their racial status, more willing to talk about it and explore issues tied to race, more motivated to vocally defend their racial identity, more inclined to see themselves as victims of reverse racism or agents of change through protests and activism of one kind or another . . . and more exhausted as a result.

Realizing that White is a race

Brian Steffen • Ankeny, IA

Five race family equals great dinners!!!!

Martin Clarke • Atlanta, GA

Sushi, fried chicken, and arroz con pollo. I'm African American, Asian, and Native American. My wife is Salvadoran, Mexican, and Italian. When you look at the statistical "Browning" of America, no one has really analyzed the great culinary benefits of all this mixing: great dinners. At my house, we have taken advantage of all the racial/ethnic/cultural mixes and laid them out on the dinner table. Different spices and ingredients mix to the great benefit of our palates. Our three daughters have grown up not knowing that their dinners are "blended"; it's just dinner to them. I think that the future of America will be the same. People will just take for granted the great benefits of a blended society; it will be just society. Cheerios ads with a mixed family won't spark outrage.

Other races resent us White people

Jeremy Andrews • Garland, TX

Why is that OK?

Finally noticing my own racial biases

Marilyn Sharp • San Francisco, CA

White and proud— doesn't mean racist

Jenna • USA

Every culture or race seems to have this deep interconnection with their skin color and culture and heritage. People seem to embrace their "uniqueness" and take pride in where they are from and who they are.

I am White. I am proud to be White. But why do those words sound so negative? If a person of color were to say those words, everyone would understand their pride and support it, but because I'm White, my pride is automatically discredited into racism or hate toward people of color. I'm White and proud—but that doesn't mean I am racist.

We the people = we White people

Sarah • Fridley, MN

White guilt misses the entire point

Gabrielle Durrett • Tucson, AZ

As a White person, I frequently feel White guilt whenever the topics of slavery and racism come up. For ages, I felt like I had to come up with excuses of why I shouldn't feel guilty, the most prominent of which was "Those were my ancestors, not me."

I still feel like I don't need to feel guilty, but not for the same reason. When I feel White guilt, I am making slavery/racism about me. "Oh, I'm so horrible. I'm White, and my ancestors were White, and they did appalling things to Black people. I feel so ashamed for what my ancestors did to them." What my ancestors did was horrible; there's no doubt about that. But by making my feelings about slavery/racism all about me feeling ashamed, I miss the point.

This isn't about me: it's about all the people who were and are treated cruelly because of what they look like. Instead of wallowing in self-pity, I should be getting angry on their behalf. I shouldn't feel like because I'm White, I can't possibly contribute anything to ending racism. The point I'm trying to make is that by spending all our time beating ourselves up, we White people give ourselves an excuse not to do anything. So, let's throw our White guilt out the window so that we can take action against slavery and racism in the world today. Let's make our White ancestors turn in their graves.

Born into implicit white privilege. Recovering.

Lois Knight • Centennial, CO

Owe you nothing, I'm not responsible

Tony • Concord, NC

I am tired of seeing White people feeling guilty or responsible for the misfortune of minorities.

So many racists look like me

Robert Goffeney • Pittsburgh, PA

It is okay to be White

Matthew • Felton, CA

Being White is not a crime

Sam Douglass • Australia

It is okay to be White

Deanna Pennewell • USA

I'm white but I hear you

Zoe Maag • Paragould, AR

Yes, it's OK to be White

J. F. Hathaway • Sacramento, CA

It is okay to be White

Sam • San Louis Obispo, CA

Ashamed that accomplished minorities surprise me

Dan • Seattle, WA

No matter how liberal and progressive I might claim to be, no matter how many workshops I've been to or essays I've read about privilege, I still hear my inner voice express pleasant surprise when I see a minority doing well at something. Whether I see a minority excelling in business, writing an editorial in the national press, or doing rounds in a hospital, inside I first say, "Wow, look at that!" I am not proud of this, and I don't know how to fix it.

White immigrant = not an immigrant

Linda M. Larsen • Hudson, WI

We are taught White is superior

Jen • Seattle, WA

Any White American who says they are not racist is either not honest with themselves or they have been locked in a basement since birth. No matter your generation, all White Americans have been persistently and intentionally drowned in messages that Black and Brown people are inferior. It is all our responsibility to really look at ourselves and the racial superiority we have internalized and admit to racism. We have to admit that we have a problem before we can be part of the solution. We had no choice but to hear constant White superiority messages all our lives, but we can see them for what they were and push back against those narratives.

Boomers and older Americans watched coverage of "race riots" and "inner-city crime waves" and heard their parents talk about the good old days when a Black man knew better than to look them in the eyes or address them as sir or ma'am. Every single day, Gen X heard about the "war on drugs" and "gang violence" and "welfare queens." You didn't have to hear anyone say, "We mean Black and Brown people are a problem," to know that's what they meant; the picture and implications were everywhere.

Today's youth are watching videos of angry Black protestors get in cops' faces, with much of the media implying they've no right to be disrespecting "law enforcement" who abuse Black bodies or stand by while their coworkers do so.

White folks, if you think you didn't internalize any of the messages that our body politic sent through the media about White superiority while keeping its foot on the neck of Black America, you fool yourselves. I have done years of work examining my biases, and I still cannot excise that White supremacy demon entirely.

We must admit that we have a problem and get to work fixing that problem—we *are* the problem that threatens Black and Brown lives in everyday ways (workplace discrimination, criminalization of poverty, gentrification, and so many more) as well as in violent ones.

Why can't we all just get along?

Steve Bennyhoff • Santa Fe, NM

As I've gotten older, I have become more compassionate about my fellow man. I now realize that any differences that we may have are only superficial and that if we got to know one another better as individuals, we would find that we are, in fact, from one big family.

White conservative.
Don't assume I'm racist

Quinn Meyer • Dubuque, IA

Growing up a White, conservative male in a suburban midwestern town automatically attaches labels to me. We all live with labels. Some are self-assigned, and some are assigned by society. More labels I'll add to my résumé include Catholic, private school educated, intact family unit with married parents and two brothers, healthy, and politically active, to name a few. You probably already have an image of who you think I am. That is how society works. We assign labels, and then we assume they are true. Aren't you sick and tired of labels? I am!

Labels and division between people were rampant and downright ugly (around the 2016 election cycle). As a conservative thinker, I found myself in a minority position on my college campus. People accused me of being unsympathetic toward Blacks and minorities because of my political ideology. Political views are complex. My political views are more fiscally conservative based and socially/morally conservative. I really don't believe I have any racism in my thoughts. I have friends of many races and colors. I am sick of people labeling me and assuming I'm racist because I'm White and conservative. People have got to stop making assumptions!

"White privilege" makes me feel invalid

Alice N. • TN

I want to feel like my achievements are because of me and not because of my race. However, I'm told that I've only gotten to where I am because I'm White. This makes me feel like years of studying into early morning and fighting to get myself noticed out of a sea of faces was for nothing. Being White automatically makes people think that I think I'm better than everyone, that I'm automatically racist, that I don't respect POC. I want to break free of those assumptions and just be me.

Because I'm White I'll never understand

Daisy Weeks • Colorado Springs, CO

Assumptions, with small grain of truth.

Don't hate me because I'm White

Julie Kendall • OK

What's this term *privileged* that I keep seeing posted everywhere in conjunction with being White? That's kind of offensive. Do you know my story? Have you walked in my shoes? Do you know me as a person? Do you know my heart? Don't judge and for sure don't hate. I consider myself pretty selfless, empathetic, loving, giving, and kind. I strive to see *all* people as just . . . people. I want fairness. I'm against racial injustice. I want peace and love for America. How can I help? How can we get there?

Not thinking about race, my privilege

Kevin Bess • Lubbock, TX

My privilege is that race simply is not part of my thought process. I have never wondered if that police officer behind me is going to pull me over because I'm White. I have never seen a person cross the street as they approached me and thought to myself, "Did they just cross because I am White?" When I don't get an interview for a job, I never wonder if it's because my name sounds too White. There is a problem in this country, and if you don't see it, your privilege is blinding you.

No one wants to hear your heritage

Macy Willett • Knoxville, TN

Yes, I do have a heritage. Yes, I am also White. While I celebrate the unique backgrounds of my friends and coworkers, I often feel as though I have no identity or culture to grasp onto. No one wants to hear your "percentages" if the end result is that you are simply Caucasian. But I am the daughter of a German immigrant who moved to the States as a single mom. I have stories, traditions, and culture. I am proud of my heritage, even if that looks like a percentage number to some people.

Stop acting like Blacks are saints

Jimmy • New York, NY

Black people don't want to have dialogues in this country; they want monologues, where White people sit there, listen, then do everything that was told to them to do to "make things right." Reparations in the hundreds of thousands, if not millions. They hate police yet tell us how awful it is to be Black because of all the violence. All the violence is within the community, not coming from the outside, and the only way to solve it is from education and policing. Yet so few Black people I know take education seriously.

I guess what I'm saying is that yeah, White people would be in that place and have those issues if they'd been oppressed, but liberal America needs to shut up and stop acting like Black people are the angels that they aren't. Poor Black people are just the same as poor White people . . . and like the poor White people in rural, downtrodden, crummy areas, they are undereducated, prone to violence and drugs, love disrespect and pissing off society, and hate the cops. And the Black people who were raised in privilege tend to be much higher caliber, just like White people of the same circumstance.

In other words, they're humans . . . mostly pretty shitty, some pretty good, a small percent really great, just like Whites and Chinese and Hispanics. But given they are where they are, they need to step it up and break the culture of promoting violence, dropping out of school, having babies as teenagers, fighting, drug dealing, and disrespecting women and gay people.

Thankful for parents who hated racism

Stephen Still • Birmingham, MI

I'm from a small town in the state of Washington. Didn't see a Black person until I was ten years old, but parents laid down the law early that I had to love everyone! Be like Jesus . . . "Red and yellow, Black and White, they are precious in his sight." My dad was transferred to Detroit in 1961. It was where I met racists. I'm not very religious now, but my parents drilled it into me. They were angry that Japanese friends were put in "concentration" camps during WWII. I grew up in Detroit, went to Wayne State, became a journalist, and lived a privileged life. Adopted daughter from China late in life. I believe you have to work hard to love.

My White guilt is all gone

Caren Boddie • Littleton, CO

I'm a good-hearted person who has always been extremely sensitive about people being treated unfairly. I've always stood up for people to be valued and respected, individual to individual. The renewed focus on race is very sad, and I'm done with caring. By the way, I wrote this: "Racism is garbage. *Do not* recycle. Just toss it." Please *stop recycling* old garbage. If you're focusing solely on race and seeing everything through it, you are just giving new life to an old evil.

I'm tired of being called evil

Jackson Bates • White Oak, TN

My children can be badly behaved

Erin Seaton • West Newbury, MA

I have two great kids. They are smart and kind and thoughtful, and sometimes they also fall apart. We are White, and one thing I am constantly conscious of is the fact that when my children do fall apart, in a doctor's office or library or restaurant, no one is judging them or me because of my race. I can fall apart or get frustrated or upset, too. And most of the time, people are often empathetic.

White privilege means that you have to walk through the world acutely aware that you are given such liberty and leniency because of the color of your skin. It's your responsibility to walk humbly when you carry this knowledge and to be very careful to grant others equal compassion.

They won't listen, they won't believe

Merritt Campbell Burton • Lewiston, ID

I considered myself color-blind until I learned that wasn't helping. I was one of those hippie-dippie people who would say, "We need to just move past it." We don't, not yet. We need to acknowledge and talk about it. Long conversations, uncomfortable conversations.

My first experience with racism was as a child. I can't remember distinguishing between "races" before then. My sister and I were being teased at the playground by a couple of Black children; they were calling us "vanilla ice cream." Finally, I said, "Oh yeah, well then, you're chocolate ice cream!" Their mother overheard me and was very angry, even more so when she discovered how it had all started.

Now I am forty-three years old. I've returned to college and am taking cultural anthropology and learning even more. I honestly didn't know that there are no genetic differences between "races" and that the term itself is completely inaccurate. I used to think Black people were genetically more athletic, for example.

I get so frustrated trying to communicate with other White people on the subject. They won't listen; they won't believe. They can watch a video of an unarmed Black man being killed by police and somehow justify it in their minds. They cannot, or willfully will not, see the advantages that our Whiteness has given us in our lifetimes, the doors that do not shut in our faces.

We still can't hold a real national conversation on racism. Too many people pretend it doesn't exist anymore.

There's only so much White guilt

Shannan Duisen • Highland, CA

White guilt is like oil; there's a lot of it, but it's not infinite, and people have been burning it at an unsustainable pace for decades. The race card has an expiration date, and that date is fast approaching.

I have benefited
from White privilege

Lise Dumont • Brisbane, CA

SHIFTING ALTITUDES

WHITE PEOPLE ARE NOT TRADITIONALLY in the foreground in this country's conversations about race, but this archive has become a place where hundreds of thousands have talked honestly about guilt, rage, privilege, displacement, power, romance, allegiance, frustration, or the world as seen through a White gaze.

"Yes, it's okay to be White." "You're nothing but poor White trash." "Hated for being a White cop." "Abuse was invisible because I'm White." "Not as White as I appear." "I'm White and not ashamed." "White privilege? More like White guilt." "We the people = we White people." "Other races resent us White people." "Most White people are not racists." "Black body language scares White people." "White people do not own racism." "I unpack my White privilege daily." "Only White people say we're colorblind." "Why are White people so afraid."

A man who asked that we withhold his name and location summed up the source of some of those fears in his 6-word essay: "These days I understand the WASPS." He explained why he chose those words in a lengthy backstory.

"I was born in the 1970s, to a family of mixed European origin—Jewish, Irish, Greek, German, Slovene, but definitely not British or Protestant. Growing up in the late twentieth century, I definitely felt that I was a White American, which I understood to mean just plain American. And I understood that in the earlier twentieth century my grandparents and great-grandparents—most of whom were not considered White when they came to this country—had triumphed over the prejudice of the WASPs to take their places as the American mainstream. People like us, what you might call 'twentieth-century White people,' didn't think much of the old WASPs who had run the place in the eighteenth and nineteenth centuries. In movies and TV, they were often ridiculed as Biffs and Muffys, with silly accents and old-fashioned tastes. We had taken over their colleges, their clubs, and even the White House. (It was only later, after 2008, that I understood why John F. Kennedy was so important to my grandparents' generation.)

"Well, now we're in their shoes. People of color are moving into the mainstream now; 'White' is no longer the default setting for 'American.' And though it's clear that this process is inevitable—it's just a matter of numbers and demographics—a lot of the time, to be honest, I'm sad about it. The country is changing in ways that aren't very good for me, and I've got no choice but to adapt. I'm not complaining; it's only fair that other people get the same opportunity we got. But now I find myself looking back at the WASPs with new respect. Though there were many notable exceptions, for the most part during their fall from power, they conducted themselves with quiet dignity. I'm sure it didn't feel good for them at the time, but for the most part, they just got on with their lives. We could learn from their example."

Part of the power of The Race Card Project is that it provides a way to peek in on conversations that people are having behind closed doors, in chat rooms online, in dorms on college campuses, in VFW halls and bowling alleys. Change is hard. Change is also inevitable. And it's harder to evolve past discomfort around change if the source of the anxiety is only discussed in hushed tones.

• • •

So, what happens when America crosses that milestone and becomes a majority-minority country? It's not like we should expect fireworks or flashing bells. There won't be a breaking news alert on our phones. That moment will arrive quietly in some maternity ward where the birth of one more brown-skinned child will tick the number toward a new and permanent reality. Demographers say that will likely happen sometime around 2045 but where these population shifts are concerned in the US, the future seems to keep arriving ahead of schedule. Just four years ago that projected date was 2047.

Even so, America's infrastructure around wealth, politics, education, and opportunity is so entrenched that White people, and White men in particular, will still likely hold the reins of power on Wall Street and Main Street for quite some time, with some exceptions. The evidence of change is likely to be more subtle. You will see it at the grocery store in the produce section and condiment aisle. You will see it in classrooms where the under-fifteen student population has already reached majority-minority status, according to the census. And unless you've been living under a rock, you've already seen it in a diverse array of movies and TV series and in multiracial advertisements from businesses that have figured out that the most important color to their bottom line is green.

When I first explored the coming majority-minority status in a *National Geographic* essay, I thought the demographic shifts would make for more uncomfortable race relations and possibly a moment when that tipping point would force America to face a central truth: that this country's Founding Fathers built White dominance into the fabric and laws of a nation that proclaims to love freedom and liberty. I held on to that belief in the months after George Floyd's murder, when street protests around the world stirred the public conscience and when corporations pledged more than $67 billion for racial justice. It looked like the country was going through, if not a reckoning, at least an awakening.

But just a few short years later, the backlash against so-called woke culture and the growing embrace of White nationalist ideologies have extinguished the myth of inevitable forward progress. America is thankfully more tolerant, more diverse, and more integrated based on changing laws and evolving attitudes, but that often means that our experiences, fears, and assumptions around race are more complicated as a result.

Progress and tumult are twin sides of the same coin.

It is not clear that America is more divided than it used to be (remember, this is a country that survived a bloody civil war), but there are a lot more ways for people to exploit the angst that fuels that division, especially on the Internet. We are sadly a country where people don't agree to a common set of *facts*. We are dangerously a country where surveys show that 46 percent of Americans believe the US is once again heading toward a civil war. We are ominously a country where disruptive fringe ideologies have gone mainstream. A poll released in early 2022 found that one-third of US adults say they think there is a coordinated effort to replace native-born US citizens with waves of immigrants. That same poll found that nearly half of Republicans embrace that ideology as an organizing truth in their politics and their lives. This is the fear that fuels the so-called great replacement theory, or GRT—until recently a fringe ideology that has worked its way into mainstream politics.

Most of the people who espouse and amplify the tenets of GRT are White and Republican, and that is why it's up to their fellow White Americans to counterprogram the toxic replacement narrative. Black and Brown people cannot dismantle an exploitive brand of fearmongering that is built around their very existence.

No matter how many chief diversity officers are hired or how many anti-racist workshops are scheduled, those efforts run hard up against a load-bearing wall of resistance from Americans who are clearly committed to or comfortable with maintaining the status quo. A lot of people at the centers of power—in Congress, in the corridors of high tech and finance, in the front offices at most professional sports franchises and hospitals—that serve an ever-diverse population are perfectly comfortable with leadership structures that in no way represent this country as a whole and often not their specific constituencies. They may talk about equity and commitments to change, but a lot of institutions that are successful across a broad array of metrics can't seem to make good on diversity efforts. It's not rocket science. It's a matter of will.

This is disappointing, but it should not be surprising. If you are part of a cohort that had held the reins of power for centuries, moral appeals alone won't incentivize individuals or institutions to step away from positions of prominence and let other cohorts have their shots. Reddit cofounder Alexis Ohanian, who is married to Serena Williams, stepped down from the company's board in June of 2020, urging that he be replaced by a Black person and indeed he was. He essentially used his platform to pass the mic to an extremely qualified candidate in tech entrepreneur Michael Seibel. Ohanian said he wanted to be able to answer to his daughter if she ever asked what he did in the wake of George Floyd's killing. Though widely applauded, his bold decision has not as yet sparked a stampede of similar door-opening moves.

Stepping away from power also means stepping beyond a zone of comfort. If you allowed yourself to fully understand the horrors of slavery, the brutal inequality of life under Jim Crow, the statistics and science and irrefutable evidence showing that Black people regardless of income or educational level have less access to the best-paying jobs, the most advantageous mortgages, and the pathways to leadership in almost every sector, then the decision to hold on to the status quo could appear to be either callous or calculated, or driven by the fear that Black people and other minorities might look for revenge if given any kind of authority or influence. We are not just battling one another.

These demographic trends will continue, and how that is explained—or, alternatively, exploited—will impact the safety and security of all Americans.

This is a challenge against the protective instincts of human nature. The psychology of loss aversion and a zero-sum mentality can so easily undermine efforts at fairness, unity, and justice, especially when dark forces can exploit people's fear by aerosolizing false information through social media. I have found that the fear of retribution is unfounded because the vast majority of people pushing for equality are interested in paychecks, not payback.

I try to be careful about generalizations, and I am not suggesting that everyone who embraces some part of that so-called great replacement theory is a White supremacist. But GRT is firmly rooted in White supremacist ideology. It comes from a fear of losing automatic status and entitlements if people of different races are allowed to stand as equals. Whiteness in the US has been socially engineered to be the organizing force in everything that is thought to be quintessentially American, from history to beauty standards. Majority status was the guarantee against that claim, and the tectonic demographic shifts underway have created a period of indigestion and vertigo for a growing number of people.

The overall population is becoming more diverse while the White population is aging and producing fewer children. The most common age for White people in the United States in 2018 was fifty-eight, according to the Pew Research Center. For the general population—including all non-White people—the most common age was twenty-seven.

The fanning of fears around those shifts is not just disruptive. It's dangerous.

We are now seeing, on a regular basis, just how incited and radicalized some maniacal Americans have become about these trends. We saw that tragically in Buffalo, where a young White gunman reportedly drove three hours specifically to target Black shoppers at a grocery store in the spring of 2022. We saw it in Charlottesville, where White nationalists spewing venom toward racial minorities and Jews carried torches and shouted, "You will not replace us." And we saw it in Charleston, South Carolina, where Dylann Roof murdered nine people at their African Methodist Episcopal church while they were attending Bible study.

GRT is like the fertilizer that feeds and sustains White fear when America's racial makeup is changing. These demographic trends will continue, and how that is explained—or alternatively exploited—will impact the safety and security of all Americans. But Black and Brown people cannot inoculate fears that Whiteness is no longer America's cultural default.

White Americans who care about democracy, who believe in the principles of fairness and equality, who believe that *we* is a more powerful word than *them,* need to step into this space armed with facts and righteous truths. White politicians, White business leaders, White clerics, White educators, White leaders, and White influencers need to denounce the supremacist agenda at the core of the great replacement theory.

White Americans who say they are repulsed by that agenda need to get used to talking about White supremacy and the way fears about Black and Brown people have historically been used to drive up gun sales and create a populist, vigilante agenda. The two words *White supremacy* make some people uncomfortable, exhausted, or defensive. Well, you can't solve a problem you are unwilling to name.

The fact that our diversity is part of our strength needs to be repeated, and more White folks are the ones who need to be saying that. The fact that so many families are already diverse is part of the story that needs to be told. The people who lead diverse communities in sports, religion, education, and the workplace need to speak up and demonstrate that Americans of various backgrounds can coexist and move together toward a common goal.

Not everyone who has drifted toward the alarmist tenets of the great replacement theory will let go of the false succor it provides. But GRT rose on the wind of fabricated rhetoric, and it will continue to flourish without a counternarrative based in truth. When so much is at stake, silence is no longer an option. Don't expect Black and Brown people to defuse the time bomb they did not create.

I'm glad my son is White

Franklin Oliver • USA

I'm glad my kids look White
Mark Mott • Hillsboro, OR

I'm glad my son is White
Rebecca Green Watson • Leesburg, VA

I'm ashamed to say that.

Glad my daughter is not White
Nice White Lady • San Francisco, CA

I'm a White mom to a Brown daughter who can't shake the shame and embarrassment that stems from a long history of White women instigating and being complicit in violence against Black people. When people see me, they see someone who is too fragile, too protected, too privileged, too clueless, and too annoying to be taken seriously. I know this because this is how I often feel about other White women I meet for the first time.

Designed to divide, conquer, oppress us
Teale Greylord • Madison, WI

I am an Armenian American descendant of genocide and diaspora; it's like living in the gray areas of identity, race, and recognition. Never forget.

I wish I had lighter skin
Anonymous • Malibu, CA

I wish I hadn't said that
Randy • Washington, DC

I wish I had learned Gujarati
Saheli Patel • Minneapolis, MN

I wish I reflected my heritage

Sage • Charlottesville, VA

I wish I had your tan

Colette Paul • Indianapolis, IN

I wish demographic questions didn't exist

Heather Holdridge • Dunwoody, GA

I wish my beauty was equal

Karla • Salem, OR

I wish we were all creamy-brown

Tony Cunningham • St. Cloud, MN

I was going to say "blue," but that would be a big adjustment. If we were all one race, we'd divide ourselves in other ways, but still, I'd like to make it a little harder to do so.

I wish we could ignore it

Noah Jacobs • Alton, IL

I wish racist Whites would chill

Sophia Adams • San Diego, CA

I wish we were all color-blind

Trey • Kansas City, MO

Race does not exist. The notion of race has been scientifically debunked many times before. Not only are genetic differences between races insignificant, but the vast majority of people have some degree of mixing, even if they don't know it. So few people are purely White, or Black, or any other race that identifying so strongly with one is pointless. We're all human. And yet, nobody can get past skin color. Life would be easier if we were all completely (seeing-the-world-in-black-and-white) color-blind.

I wish this didn't separate us

Scott McFarland • OH

Failed to befriend first black student

Lynn Scott Cochrane •
Los Angeles, CA

I grew up in a deeply segregated Charlotte, North Carolina, in the 1950s and '60s. When my high school, North Mecklenburg, was finally integrated in about 1963, there was one Black girl who always sat alone in the cafeteria. She may have been the only Black girl in the school that year. I *knew* I should befriend her, but I didn't have the courage to my everlasting regret and shame.

Not a victim, but a witness

Andrea Christine Torres • Riverside, CA

I have never been profiled or treated any differently based on my race before, which I am very thankful for. However, I have seen racism and discrimination right in front of me, and it broke my heart.

I work at a yogurt shop, and a nice old African American lady was making her yogurt, and she had parked right in front of the shop. I admit, her parking job was not the best, but it wasn't super busy or crowded, so it wasn't a big deal. But to this one White gentleman it was.

After she had paid and left, he walks in and uses the N-word when talking about this fine woman. He states how all people "like that" are dumb and that's what we get. I almost started crying because I had never experienced anything like this, and I was speechless.

To treat somebody with such hate and to have so much anger built up inside of you. The man didn't even know the woman and vice versa, and yet he treated her so badly. Nobody should have that happen to them ever; it's not an acceptable thing. I pray for those who have had something like that happen to them, and I wish it never did happen. I was not a victim, but a witness.

At the hospice, everyone is blue

Debbie Taylor • Ann Arbor, MI

My mother passed away on December 14, 2012, of liver cancer at the age of eighty, and she spent her last afternoon and night in [an] Ann Arbor Hospice. The staff was loving, kind, and professional. One nurse in particular examined my mother with such tenderness and care that I was moved beyond measure. It was such a contrast to the experience she'd had at the hands of another medical professional as a middle school child.

While playing with her brothers in a small town near Columbus, Ohio, she fell on a piece of glass and was carried by my uncles to a White doctor's house. He stitched up her wound *without* any anesthesia, leaving a scar to carry the rest of her life. She never shared that information herself—my uncle was the first to relate the story.

Progress in some areas of health disparities has surely been made, but I am concerned about others who have no access to the kind ministrations of a St. Joseph's Hospital or a fine hospice.

Sharing the words came easily and quickly because my mother raised us to have respect for *everyone*, including ourselves. All her children and grandchildren were taught that race was a strange, artificial construct and that "people are people." So, my six words were not the result of a personal revelation, but rather a sigh—one that I wished to share with others. I appreciated the opportunity to do so.

Every day she sees race matters

Carniesha Kwashie • Philadelphia, PA

This is in response to my White staffer and the racism she sees me endure as we work on an inauthentic project that states racial equity is a priority.

The ocean does not see race.

Mary Mills • Los Angeles, CA

I am a Black female surfer. (What stereotypes?)

Number of Black male colleagues: 0

Jason • Kansas City, MO

Justice for all requires White awakening.

Albert Marten • San Antonio, TX

I'm ashamed and embarrassed to admit how unaware I was as a White person about the hate, the daily indignities, and in many cases, the physical terror suffered by my fellow citizens because of the color of their skin. The failure of my country to live up to the ideals of equality and equal justice before the law is a source of constant pain. I want for all kids what I want for my own: a country making good on its promises.

Want to change
but do I?

Zach Wilson • St. Paul, MN

The energy we spend avoiding our history—
debating it, manipulating it—weaponizing it—
is a far higher price to pay than actually facing
it so we can finally move forward.

12

America: A Freight Train of a Word

IT'S ONE THING TO BE AMERICAN. The title officially applies to someone who was born in the US or is a citizen of the United States.

But to feel American? That is something entirely different.

An awful lot of people who are officially citizens of this country—people who are born here or have the papers or have raised their right hand to take the Oath of Allegiance—don't feel (and you can insert any number of descriptors here) American. They don't feel truly American or authentically American or fully accepted as an American in some traditionally narrow sense.

We are a country where legions of people qualify as some kind of hyphenated American because outside of Indigenous cultures—those people who are truly native to this land—most American citizens trace their ancestral origins to some other part of the world. We are a country of outsiders who made their way here and made a home here. But some of us have had an easier time claiming the demonym on the right side of that hyphen because over time it has come to essentially be the White side.

Toni Morrison made it plain when she said, "In this country, American means White. Everybody else has to hyphenate." Science tells us that there is no such thing in DNA or human biology as "White" . . . or Black, Asian, Latino, Indigenous, or Melungeon, for that matter. Racial categories are a configuration, an evolving architecture of social hierarchy that keeps some categories of people at the top and other cohorts mired on the lower rungs of this social scaffolding. People who arrived in America as a kind of lower-caste version of White, such as Italians, Slavs, Irish, or Greeks, evolved over generations into the full status of Whiteness with all the privileges and opportunities that club had to offer. The hyphen for these groups tends to exist more as a matter of cultural pride than a matter of social delineation. The hyphen, to the degree that it still exists at all, is situational. It comes and goes on holidays, bumper stickers, and kitchen magnets. But for other kinds of immigrants, newcomers and classes of people who are "otherized from Whiteness"—those from the southern hemisphere, those with darker skin, those who can move into wealth and status and power (the fruits of Whiteness) but cannot meld into the socially enforced optics of that racial category (the face of Whiteness)—the hyphen is often indelible, even if unspoken. It's a mark of pride, to be sure. But it's also a demarcation that separates the fringe from the perceived core.

The idea of a hyphenated American—a citizen with dual consciousness—has created controversy over time. As America was entering World War I, there were fears that a split identity would lead to fractured loyalties. Theodore Roosevelt railed against a tilt toward hyphenation in a 1915 speech at a Carnegie Hall Knights of Columbus gathering where the audience was filled with hundreds of Irish Catholics.

"There is no room in this country for hyphenated Americanism," Roosevelt said.

When I refer to hyphenated Americans, I do not refer to naturalized Americans. Some of the very best Americans I have ever known were naturalized Americans, Americans born abroad. But a hyphenated American is not an American at all.... The one absolutely certain way of bringing this nation to ruin, of preventing all possibility of its continuing to be a nation at all, would be to permit it to become a tangle of squabbling nationalities, an intricate knot of German-Americans, Irish-Americans, English-Americans, French-Americans, Scandinavian-Americans or Italian-Americans, each preserving its separate nationality, each at heart feeling more sympathy with Europeans of that nationality, than with the other citizens of the American Republic.... There is no such thing as a hyphenated American who is a good American. The only man who is a good American is the man who is an American and nothing else.

Roosevelt's utopian idea of being completely American with room for nothing else smacked hard up against how people were living their lives even as they rushed to assimilate into the American ideal. Americans who hailed from distant lands remained tethered to their root cultures in social clubs and cuisine, in traditions and travel, and in the way they decided to spend their time in worship (just look at the number of cities that have multitudes of Catholic church steeples that pierce the skyline so Italians, Poles, Germans, Lithuanians, Irish, or Germans could attend Sunday service alongside their own kind.)

And it's interesting that Roosevelt did not contemplate African, Latino, Caribbean, Arab, Asian, or Indigenous Americans in his screed. *American* was clearly understood to mean people of European origin. This narrow framing persists today, and it is not just about hurt feelings and the confusion around categorization. Words carry weight. Perceptions create boundaries that can be almost impenetrable. People not seen as fully American are also presumed to be not fully loyal to America and its ideals—perpetual foreigners in their own country.

• • •

The past few years, I have become deeply grateful to have been raised by parents who taught me to love a country even as I disdained its history and discovered its flaws. My father, a veteran and a Black man, had a special relationship to the flag that was perplexing to me as a teenager in the 1970s. He wore clothing emblazoned with red, white, and blue and placed little twelve-inch flags in the ground between the rosebushes alongside our house around Independence Day. He wore flag pins with pride decades before they became a performative staple of blowhard Fox News pundits. He was born in Birmingham, Alabama, and despite all he saw and experienced, he decided to love a country that did not love him back. My mother, someone who has always loved books, was also patriotic in her own way, surrounding herself with Americana and filling our house with books about American history—embodying the spirit of Langston Hughes and his poem that so beautifully asserts in its opening line, "I, too, sing America." I now see that they were practicing a special kind of patriotism, to see America for what it is with all its noxious disappointments and still believe in what it can and should be.

This has come in handy over the past few years as I try to explain to my own kids why it is worth fighting for and defending, and yes, even embracing a country that will most certainly break your heart.

• • •

The summer when I was working on the last stretch of this book, I encountered a dude at a gas station driving a big, dark pickup truck that had an American flag the size of a large roof tarp flapping in the breeze from a pole hoisted behind the driver's back window. It was a statement flag, huge and bright, trailing several feet behind him as he pulled into the bay of gas pumps. This was clearly a "This is my country" brand of patriotism. That was evident by the riot of MAGA bumper stickers emblazoned across his truck bed's door and by the way he glared at other patrons at the station—as if daring them to say something about the rock music blaring from speakers turned on blast.

I generally give folks like this a whole lot of leeway. So often they seem girded for a confrontation, but as I walked by him headed toward the kiosk that housed the cashier behind glass, I gave him a thumbs-up and said, "Right on. Go America."

I don't even know why I did it. *Right on* is such retrograde, stuck-in-the-seventies slang. Who even says that anymore? And *go America* is just not in my vernacular outside of rooting for Team USA at the Olympics. But in that moment, I wanted him to know that it's my friggin' flag, too. So yeah. "Go America!" I said it loud.

He was completely *fatootsed*. He literally whipped his head as if knocked back on his heels. Eyebrows up as if he'd just seen a spaceship fall from the sky. That flag was supposed to be his, not mine to claim. That flag was supposed to serve a gatekeeping function separating him . . . no, make that elevating him, above and beyond people who didn't meet his standards of what a true American is supposed to be.

In his poem "I, Too," Langston Hughes dreamed of the day when no one would dare tell Black (and Brown) Americans to "eat in the kitchen." He wrote elegantly of the imagined time when the majority culture would see how beautiful their Black and Brown brothers and sisters were and be ashamed of past bias. Sadly, that's not the way things work in America. The growth and prosperity of the at-present-minority population can seem just as likely to spark fear and resentment from some White Americans as calls for atonement or apologies for past sins.

Yet that flag and this country belong to all of us who are citizens of this land. The far right's aggressive flag waving is intended to make folks forget that fact. Getting people to concede their rightful claim to the centrality of what should be a collective symbol is a way to lessen the stakeholder status in the soil beneath our feet.

Don't fall for that. The flag is too powerful a symbol to concede. It carries our hopes and disappointments, our blood and our bounty, too. Our pain. Our plunder. Our promise. In her seminal book *The White Album*, Joan Didion said, "A place belongs forever to whoever claims it hardest, remembers it most obsessively, wrenches it from itself, shapes it, renders it, loves it so radically that he remakes it in his image."

She was talking about California. But I hear the song of America in those words. The song of a people who have refused to be broken by a country that kept them at the margins. The song of a people who lived in or swallowed anger and yet created a culture of joy that flaps like an unfurled flag, slapping against a twisted face of hate. The song of a people oppressed and overlooked who nonetheless created a sumptuous, crazy-sexy-cool culture in their dress, their music, dance, poetry, art, sports, street culture, and food.

From barbecue to hip-hop. From Jay-Z to J.Lo. From Beyoncé to Barack and Michelle Obama. From the music that gets people moving on the dance floor at the big family wedding and gets fans fired up in the biggest sports arenas, regardless of location or the color of the crowd. From the players who mesmerize us on the field and on the court. From the clothing and slang that kids emulate and amplify in every corner of the US from Appalachia to Alaska. From the K-pop bands whose slick dance moves are clearly inspired by or lifted wholesale from Black street culture, to the long line of White British music superstars who say their greatest inspiration came from Black blues or soul performers here in the US (Clapton, Jagger, Bowie, Cullum, Winehouse, Winwood, Burdon, Hucknall, Collins, Ronson, Stansfield, Michael, Sheeran, and Adele).

It's fair to say that a whole lot of thirteen-year-olds across this vast planet dream of acquiring even a glimmer of that crazy-sexy-cool magic of a people who created a thundering, definitional culture from the margins of American society—that fresh swagger, that fly strut, that calm under pressure, that ability to shine like the sun on one's own terms.

This is the delicious irony of twenty-first-century America. The rhythms and flavor of America's core culture are now defined by the people this country tried to disregard. Black culture is one of America's greatest exports and certainly one of its most profitable.

The people at the margins of a country that did not see them as fully human rendered the culture of that country beautifully and powerfully in their own image. It is just one of many reasons Black people should claim America's symbols for themselves. It's why any ethnic group that has come to this country should do the same because they all have added something of their rhythms, flavors, and traditions to our cultural gumbo.

America is a freight train of a word—a locomotive with many cars and many degrees of class, comfort, and service. But everyone on board, whether they are in first class or steerage, whether stoking coal or secretly scrambling inside a boxcar like a stowaway, are nonetheless fellow travelers.

America is yours. It's flags. It's anthems. It's tragedies. It's flaws. It's confounding complexities. The "me" in America includes us, and if we critique or complain, it does not invalidate our deed. As long as we are here, it is ours to claim . . . and yes, sometimes to cry over.

Taught all wrong,
now teaching others

Steve Jones • Durham, NC

I grew up in a segregated community and with the concept that African Americans (of course, not the word that was used) were inferior. It took a long time to get out of that mindset and even longer to acknowledge the privilege that comes with my White skin. It's a privilege to be able to teach about race in the US today as a way of undoing what I experienced.

American overseas and Black in America.

Kevin Simpson • Chicago, IL

I hope he'll look American enough

Katrina Nye • San Jose, CA

I am full Asian, and my husband is a quarter Japanese. Once our son was born, I asked my husband which one of us will have the responsibility to give him The Talk about dealing with racism. My husband replied that it had to be me because, even though he was proud of his Asian heritage, he looked "American enough" to not have to deal with racism growing up.

Mirrors remind me I am Asian

Mandy Padgett • Durham, NC

Never belonging. Puerto Rican or American?

Lorna Hagen • Brooklyn, NY

I am a Puerto Rico-born New Yorker that moved to the US [mainland] when I was twelve. Somewhere on the plane ride over, I lost something. I have no shared childhood experiences with my North American friends (lullabies, games, etc.) and no shared adolescent experiences with my Puerto Rican friends. It has always felt like a bubble that I'm in alone.

433

I'm just an American outside America!

Alma Gill • Columbia, MD

When I travel to other countries, I find it fascinating when asked, "Are you American?" I've never been asked or identified that way in my own country. I'm always flattered and proud to answer, "Why, yes, I am American."

As American as rice and beans

Jorge Valladares • Orlando, FL

My parents came to this country as undocumented immigrants from Honduras. Their three children provide public service of some kind—I work with students with disabilities at a public college, my sister is a high school Spanish teacher, and my brother is a former post-9/11 US Marine and current Brevard County, Florida, firefighter. We are today's American family—as American as rice and beans.

Becoming American, it is not easy

Sandra Casteñeda • Anaheim, CA

I have spent forty-two of my forty-four years in this country, and it doesn't make an ounce of difference. I'm still treated differently. My head says I'm American. My heart says I'm Colombian because that's where I'm accepted.

I'm just American. Not African American

Lottie • Saint Louis, MO

Born in L.A., raised in Compton, became an adult in Bay Area, relocated to Missouri. Loved by entrepreneur/homemaker grandparents. Raised by entrepreneur, GED, get-the-job-done, courageous, make-it-happen parents with fifty-plus years of marriage. I'm a well-balanced, contributing career woman, parent, wife, aunt, and daughter. My heritage is not African, nor Southern. I have no historical or cultural attachment to food. We have no field hand, gangbanging, slave, or integration stories. Now I live in a previous slave state, and most don't filter their opinions!

I'm just happy to be an American! By the way, I have beautiful brown skin.

David why don't you speak Spanish?
David Vargas • Perris, CA

As I have matured through age and experience, I know who I am and where my family comes from. In the end, I am David, with Mexican and American blood running through my veins. Nothing can change that; I am just as Mexican as Cesar Chavez and just as American as John Wayne.

Am always missing some of me
Yasmin Gill • Baltimore, MD

My mother is White American, and my father is Pakistani. Wherever I go, and whomever I am with, I rarely find someone who is at home with *all* of me. I am American, undeniably so, but there are pieces of me that are also uniquely Pakistani. Americans see or experience this as unusual, and interesting, but to me it just "is." And it sets me apart. Pakistanis see the American in me as mutually exclusive to their culture, and that sets me apart from them, as well. So, no matter where I go, a part of me has no voice. I am always missing some of me.

Muslim Americans are patriotic citizens too
Zaynab Malik • USA

¿Eres mexicana?, ¿por qué el disfraz?
Maria • Seattle, WA

You're Mexican? Then why the disguise? I was asked this by a viejito selling his wares in Tijuana, México, probably about twenty years ago. He had been shocked to hear me speak Spanish. I would have been in my early twenties, all rebellious with punked-out bleached-blond hair, red Converse, and ripped jeans. His comment pissed me off, but his question buried itself somewhere deep, and I still think about what he was asking me.

A proud American, unwanted in America…

Joseph A. Flores • Roswell, NM

The scion of pre-Chicano-era parents who believed assimilation into the American culture was the key to success. My English-only, college-graduate-led American lifestyle has been rejected by both the White "race" I was raised to engage with *and* the Hispanic ethnic group I "should" belong to . . . in very profound ways at every stage of my life.

Can only White people be American?

Nyssa Thongthai • Richmond, VA

Mom always said, "You're too American."

Ben Sian • Atlanta, GA

Born in the US to Filipino parents.

Map of Ireland on your face

Brigid • Milford, CT

Relax, gringo, we are American too

Juan Carlos Quevedo • Albuquerque, NM

Japanese and American, not Japanese-American

Aya Mimura • Ann Arbor, MI

Race by birth. American by choice

Richard Loper • Dayton, OH

America, we are your children too

Sheree Lewis • Fontana, CA

Remember Me As A Peaceful Earthling

Dominic Cox • Dania, FL

My thoughts on racial prejudice are that this state of mind present in humans must change someday, as all things do inevitably, and human consciousness will evolve or else we will destroy ourselves. Common interests ultimately form bonds between people, not race. That is what I've learned through the years observing myself and many others while living and working in different places, but you must seek out people who have transcended this notion that we are so different because of our outward appearances. That is the illusion when we are far more similar than different.

We each must want to live in harmony more than we want to seek conflict and division among ourselves regardless of our personal justification for it. For those of you that stand for peace, love, and harmony, let that be reflected in how you treat everyone. Use your life to set an example of how to treat people—that is the only way to change things, through one person's acts of love and respect for others at a time. Love is the only path to equality, unity, and peace. And yes, that includes love for those who have yet to learn that in truth humanity is the only race of people that matters. We can ill afford to fear, hate, or oppress our own kind in the vastness of the great cosmos that our tiny planet precariously floats in. Your skin color, religion, politics, finances that may differ from another are insignificant in the face of the truth—that our planet home can and will be whatever we make of it. It is the responsibility of every one of us to make it a place that we want to call home.

Epilogue

SO, LET ME TELL YOU one last story. It begins with a mystery.

What would you think if you saw a huge sign on the side of the road that had the word "THEM" sitting in the middle of a circle with the letters crossed out by a bright red slash?

Dr. Ted Loewenthal spotted that sign in a warehouse district while taking a shortcut on his way to the Bradley International Airport just outside Hartford, Connecticut, in November 2015. He was so troubled by what he saw that he looped back around to find it again and take a picture of what to him looked like a harsh anti-immigrant message. He had a flight to catch. His wife was fussing at him to stick to the schedule, but he needed to see that sign again with his own eyes and snap a picture as proof. The 2016 presidential campaign was just getting ramped up, and birtherism rhetoric was on the rise. In Ted's eyes, the sign was an obvious distillation of a nativist attitude: Us vs. Them.

The doctor knew the sign was not really directed at him, per se, but if they were coming for one group defined as *them* now, that group of undesirables could be extended over time to scoop up other people. Maybe even people like him. Ted is a retired gastroenterologist. His parents were active in the labor movement. He is descended from Ashkenazi Jews. He knows the danger of labels, and more than that, the danger of public pronouncements that shove people outside of social acceptance.

Two weeks later, I traveled to Hartford to lead a panel on race and racism. Ted came to see the panel, and at the reception, he introduced himself to me. "I'm so troubled by something I saw," he said, then pulled out his phone and showed me the photo of the sign. But where Ted had seen an obvious anti-immigrant message, I wasn't so sure. Wasn't it possible that there was another reading? Was the sign actually promoting the idea that there is no "them"? Instead, was it suggesting "Us" are in this thing called life together?

Ted emailed me his picture of that sign and I thought about it from time to time, particularly as divisive politicians stoked a hot gust of anti-"them" grievance. My mind

went to that sign when I heard a TEDx Talk from entrepreneur Dick Simon. Simon coined the term "them-ification," calling it "the root of the problems we deal with, both personally and geopolitically." He asserts that the word *them* is the "most dangerous four-letter word in the English language."

That may be an overstatement, but I couldn't get over that sign once I saw it. Seven years later I decided to do a little digging.

In July of 2022, I put Ted's photo on Twitter with the caption, "Good morning, Twitter people! I need help in solving a mystery. Does anyone in the Harford, CT, area remember seeing this sign on the way to Hartford Bradley airport in the fall of 2015? Anyone know who put it up and why? If you saw it, what went thru your mind?"

People started replying, and their responses were all over the map. "They're racist!" tweeted one, echoing Ted's suspicions. "Everyone is US!" wrote another, echoing mine. One person wondered if the sign was meant to be performance art. The renowned illustrator Joe McKendry said the picture "had the quality of the best street art, which raises more questions than it answers." One respondent gave it a distinct 2022 twist, suggesting it might be "an anti-they/them pronoun statement"—an interpretation that might not have been in the forefront of most people's minds in 2015.

To my surprise, someone reported that the sign was "still there. It's at the Walgreens distribution center. No one knows what it means." To which another person wrote, "I always figured it meant, 'we are not CVS.'"

Armed with this new information, I reached out to Steve Pemberton, who used to work as Walgreens vice president for diversity and inclusion. Here's what he told me:

FEEDBACK, PLEASE!

If you have any questions or concerns about your order please don't hesitate to get in touch with me. I'm easy to reach: lewis@bookrescue.com or the landline on my desk: 607-547-5187.

Assuming that you're happy with your book, *please leave good feedback* on the transaction.

Here are instructions on how to leave feedback:
Go to your Amazon Buyers Account.
Go to Your Orders, and then click Leave Seller Feedback.
Find this order, and then select the options that best reflect your experience.
Click Submit Feedback.
(Be sure to click on Leave Seller Feedback, not Write Product Review -- the latter is about the product, not the seller -- Amazon can be confusing.)

Thank you so much for helping!

Betsy
lewis@bookrescue.com   607-547-5187

Though I left Walgreens back in 2017, I can solve this mystery for you. Walgreens has a distribution center in Windsor, CT and that center (along with the one in Williamston, SC) employ a very high percentage of people with disabilities. (Employing this population has long been a focus of the company and during my time I oversaw this effort.) The sign you are describing is a company message to employees and the larger community—that we do not refer to people with disabilities as "them."

It was a daily reminder to all that there is no "them," only an "us," a message that the rest of society could benefit from . . .

It actually began inside the warehouse and then blossomed into the broader community because the message was so well-received. But this was before Donald Trump. His unapologetic anti-diversity message means that them with a slash through it now takes on a nativist connotation, even though the origin of that sign has the exact opposite meaning.

Talk about a sign of the times. A message of inclusion takes on the patina of exclusion because of debates taking place far from that industrial park next to the Bradley airport. America has indeed gone through a transformation of sorts when it comes to matters of race and identity.

After fourteen years of listening to Americans talk candidly about race, I've gone through a transformation myself. I no longer use the term *common ground*. It's not because I am a pessimist. It's because I am a realist. Americans don't agree on a lot of core principles, and that is not going to change anytime soon. Assuming that Americans can occupy a shared ideological space is folly. Studies find that 46 percent of Americans believe we are heading toward civil war. Civil war!

I applaud those who continue to bring people together to search for common ground, but I suggest we put more energy toward cultivating a generation of "bridge builders" who can help folks reach across differences to work toward better understanding and some framework for productivity while Americans remain in antagonistic political, ideological, racial, economic, social, or generational silos. I lean toward this concept of bridge building because people rarely cross a bridge in one direction. You usually travel to a different place and return to your home base informed and maybe even in some way enriched by your experience in another realm.

Think about a bridge you cross in your own life during your commute or a jaunt to the hardware store. Whether an interstate span across a mighty river or a covered walkway over a wooded ravine, some engineering heft went into building that bridge, and that work is an apt metaphor for the challenges we face in a moment when a lot of powerful people are invested in a divided America. Engineers must consider all the forces that could complicate their effort: jagged terrain, wind shear, payload, off-ramps, guardrails. They must understand the principles of tensile strength, the maximum stress that a wire or beam can withstand before it snaps. And before they can build a bridge linking one community with another, construction crews must precisely comprehend the distance that separates them. Imagine if we used those metrics to build a stronger America.

I wish we could find ways to promote this kind of work across several sectors. In our politics and our schools. In our communities and our churches. In our workplaces, where the bumper stickers in the parking lot often tell a story of the colliding anthems that sow our deep divisions.

Indeed, the business community may be most incentivized to embrace this thinking. Racial divisions can undermine productivity and drag down the bottom line, but racial diversity is not itself the answer. In her book *Biased*, Jennifer Eberhardt writes, "We've learned that diverse groups are more creative and reach better decisions, but they aren't always the happiest group of people." She asserts that more differences lead to more discord. Hierarchies shift. New cultures emerge. People have to learn how to share space both in terms of physical terrain and the assumed topography of leadership and privilege. Success, she says, depends on just how much people are willing to tolerate that discomfort and "make deeper efforts to sift the underlying cultures that lead to bias and exclusion."

It's time to reframe the way we talk about race and the reasons for doing it. Not about sensitivity training but more about acquiring skills. Not about finding common ground but learning to work effectively alongside someone you don't agree with. Not about a binary tension between Black and White Americans but an open-armed elastic dialogue that includes those who have too long been stuck at the fringe. Not as a political cudgel used to divide people by preying on their fears by keeping them afraid of a future that has already arrived. Not as a perspective that posits that those who wear the most red, white, and blue and fly the biggest flags and appropriate the term *patriot* can claim some sort of special status that appears on no government document or within no law (for now).

The generation in power rose in an era that introduced the popular maxim that diversity training and minority recruitment was the way forward. Some of it was ideological. Some of it was indemnification against lawsuits.

But the greatest challenge for the next generation of leaders is not just figuring out how to diversify the people in the room, it's trying to figure out how to get a team to row together in the same direction when they don't agree with each other. How do you keep a vessel afloat when it is full of people sending their energy in opposite directions? Whether it's a sports team, a hospital, a construction site, or managing the five people who work at the local gas station—this is the management challenge of the future.

Protecting kids from an examination of this country's dark chapters or uncomfortable conversations won't prepare them for that task. And make no mistake—that challenge awaits them.

Americans are always messaging that the next generation is going to lead us to some kind of racial nirvana. The idea is that because young people have inherited a more integrated world where they date across color lines, play sports together, listen to each other's music, and live more cross-pollinated lives, the path to fixing our racial brokenness will somehow be guaranteed.

What constitutes progress will not be universally embraced.

However, a dozen years of listening to people unburden themselves about race has left me with a clearer sense of the burden passed on to the next generation. The idea that the young people of today will collectively produce a magical balm that heals the nation is flawed. It will not be easy for successive generations to shed all the sticky, icky, coded, embedded, underlying racialized gunk they've inherited from us. We adults should know that because we are still choking on the racialized smog that has hung in the air since we ourselves were kids.

All this time doing a deep dive into a subject I thought no one wanted to talk about has not necessarily made me a pessimist, but I am more pragmatic now. I spent the first five decades of my life firmly believing that America was automatically destined to become a better, fairer, more egalitarian version of herself. Let me be clear. I still think that is possible. I pray fervently for that outcome. I believe in a better America. But I have removed a key adjective in that sentence. It won't happen *automatically*.

As former attorney general Eric Holder likes to say, "The arc of the moral universe is long, but it bends toward justice . . . only *if we reach out and grab it.*" He's right in amending that famous quote from the Rev. Dr. Martin Luther King Jr. with an additional eight words. Every successive generation needs to put in the effort to make sure the arc does not twist or torque in another, more menacing direction—a change in trajectory that, it must be said, would suit a certain sector of society just fine.

Instead of telling young people that racism is something that can be fixed or easily eradicated on their watch, perhaps we should be sending a different message. It is quite possible that some form of racism and bias will always be with us, that bias doesn't go away but instead mutates much like the Covid-19 virus that upended all our lives. It is quite likely that racism, bias, and prejudice will continue to present in different ways and different forms, on different platforms and with changing targets. With hard work and consistent vigilance, those forces will hopefully be less venomous over time. Maybe less common. Perhaps less consequential. More of a breeze than an upending hurricane. But believing that those forces will altogether disappear over some distant cliff is a bit like believing that the world is flat.

America has made commendable and incredible progress in matters of race. I never take that for granted, but continued progress will require collective and constant toil. What constitutes progress will not be universally embraced, and there will likely be backsliding and backlash. The endeavor will be complicated and exhausting, and it is worth every single bit of the effort. That should be the message rather than telling young folks to go forth and magically fix the fractured world we've left behind.

I am not suggesting that we weigh down our young people with worries or throw psychological speedbumps in their path. If you want your young ones to soar, you don't put rocks in their pockets. But a few pearls of wisdom about the complicated road that awaits them might keep them both grounded and girded for the journey ahead.

• • •

You've probably noticed that most of the stories people share at The Race Card Project are not related to screaming headlines about matters of race. They are generally about the small things in life.

Well, Understand this: when you examine the small stuff, you can begin to understand the big stuff.

It's how doctors interrogate disease.

It's how detectives solve crimes.

It's how historians make sense of the past.

It's how we can and should understand the role of race in our past and present lives.

I hope this book, and the mountain of stories that people share at The Race Card Project, will play some small role in helping future generations understand this complex world.

So, what are my six words on race? People naturally ask me that question all the time. When I began this project in 2010, the first thing that spilled onto the page was "Fooled them all. Not done yet." I'm a brown girl who grew up in Minnesota with a speech impediment as a very young child. A life working as a communicator in the highest perches of journalism was not something that was imagined for me. It's not that the initial six words no longer apply. Those two short sentences will always describe the arc of my life. But this journey has altered my answer to that question. What six words on race would I offer up today?

Still more work to be done.

It matters like it or not
Respect runs in a circular motion
Race does not exist BY ITSELF

· · ·

Race is everything but it's nothing
Today's soft segregation
still harms everyone
Black wears me wherever I go

· · ·

Does not define who I am
I admit to unconscious racial bias
Stereotype is a shackle—broke mine

· · ·

Suit. Degree. Still afraid of ME!
Still working harder than others are
I am fortunate to be caucasian

· · ·

The point of it all? Power
Git y'all's feet off our necks!!
Blacks complain constantly
despite obvious progress

But I voted for Barack Obama

Colors run together. Why can't people?

I hear my grandfather's hateful words

. . .

Think Dr. Seuss and the Sneetches

Pay no attention to my packaging

I am STILL not from Vietnam

. . .

Please stop saying I am articulate

Do articulate Whites also impress you?!

Diversity don't count, if it's White

. . .

Presumed understanding
is worse than ignorance

*What if classrooms
can't change racism?*

Not Chinese? You must be Japanese

. . .

I bet they're good at math

What do you mean, "you" people?

I am not like the rest

Easy to assume I am guilty

Terrified you assume I'm judging you

Hardest jails to escape are gateless

. . .

Pride or crutch? Please decide now

Sometimes I'm angry at White people

Am I failing my Latino son?

. . .

I am not like my parents

Talking about racism creates more racism

I really like a Black guy

. . .

I'm a girl. Not a fantasy

To you, always the exotic other

I am MORE than just WHITE

. . .

Didn't sound Chinese on the phone

Really, but you don't look Mexican

I thought you would be... Taller

Thank god it's a White woman
Every now and then, I remember
Grandparents passed.
New tree. No roots

. . .

White: whatever I do is wrong
Angry Black men are so scary
Embarrassed that I'm
frightened of Black boys

. . .

Minority obsession and majority guilt trip
Stop seeing my son as predator
I was taught fear of others

. . .

Everyone's racist in their own way
Always putting other people at ease
You don't have to whisper "Black"

. . .

There's nothing wrong with my hair
Got tired of straightening my hair
My natural hair isn't a statement

Yeah, but you're not BLACK-black
I'm light-skinned. My black is harder
Red hair gets the most stares

. . .

Black kid in my math class?!
People can hear the unspoken words
Just stop making everything about race

. . .

***Repeating proper pronunciation
hurts my feelings***
Can't pronounce my name? Try harder
Born in America. I am American

. . .

You don't know what I believe
Wouldn't have been White 100-years ago
So much depends on so little

. . .

Son upset. Called Whiteboy on bus
Why must our differences be wrong?
This old wound will never heal

No, i did not steal that
Only racist when I'm at Walmart
Never eat fried chicken in public

. . .

Underneath we all taste like chicken
It's hard being the "White friend"
You're Mexican? But we're so similar?

. . .

Not "illegal" human and
deserving compassion
Not all Mexicans can do landscaping
Please! Hispanic is not a race

. . .

You're White and you can dance?
The only Jew on Easter Sunday
I'm not just Caucasian, I'm CauCajun

. . .

You feel superior but you're not
Since when am I a racist?
Why'd you invite the White guy?

And you wonder why I'm mad
Worry I will say the wrong thing
We are all in this together

. . .

Native, no one knows I'm passing.
I feel uncomfortable with you here.
Nobody's a racist yet racism persists

. . .

Would all my ancestors love me?
Is that all your real hair?
You love God but not me?

. . .

You're here because of affirmative action
No, I am not the exception
I feel uncomfortable with you here.

. . .

Racism deniers are the worst racists
Stop thinking Black.
Start thinking human.
Can't be colorblind and see me

Yes, I am really her mom
Is Jewish a religion or a race?
I don't see you as Muslim

• • •

Equating "White" with "racist" is racism
Native Americans voiceless
in race conversation
Married, male, 65, grey, overweight, invisible

• • •

You've got to be carefully taught
Got to stop thinking this way
Sometimes stereotypes are true. Face it

• • •

Puerto Rican but everyone
thinks I'm Mexican
I am Polish. Not a joke
Race, a weapon of mass distraction

• • •

Progressives always gloss over the truth
Conservatives distort truth
to promote agenda
Spoke truth. Burned at the stake

White people continue to disappoint
Black people don't forget the past
Asked for equality. We got integration

. . .

You don't look Jewish to me
No, my name is not Maria
What is that on your head?

. . .

Don't try to understand.
Just accept.
I don't think I'll ever understand
Understand that you will never understand

. . .

Hispanic doctor is not an oxymoron
Yes, white skin and still Mexican
Henry is seen. Enrique is invisible

. . .

A clear head start for some
Insane how racists try so hard
White woman trying to do better

Why do Black people destroy neighborhoods?

My name doesn't predict my upbringing

Why is your baby so brown?

· · ·

I heard your dad is black

But like, where is your real dad?

Two communities. Neither one truly "mine."

· · ·

It is tough being a mutt

White immigrant—never asked where from

I have an accent, so what

So… I should just check other?

I'm sorry I'm staring at you

Silence, as I enter the room

· · ·

Stop pretending your racism is patriotism

Racism destroying America;
Putin, Xi laughing

We're all different and it's beautiful

The house I did not build

Quick to judge. Slow to understand

Let the past be the past

. . .

I will not ruin your bloodline

Can I love who I want?

Korean marries Italian in Chinese garden

. . .

Rebecca. Black maid. Taught me love

A terrible unnecessary barrier against love

Mommy, why can't we play together??

. . .

Beautiful differences made ugly by fear

His parents will never meet me

A smoldering volcano with Periodic Eruption

. . .

#1 don't talk about White club

Was he dot or feather Indian?

Native. No one knows I'm passing

Yet, still to America, you come
Blood is always the same color
Being comfortable is my unearned luxury

· · ·

I am not ignorant, just indifferent
I am white. I am listening
Race. America: deep scars. Tall fences

· · ·

Our untold stories keep us separate
Checked cosmic in the race box
Total non-issue when the aliens arrive

· · ·

There's only one race. Human race
One race matters, the human race
Race is only in the mind

· · ·

Human's DNA is 99% the same
Race is forever, prejudice is not
Not real. Still messes with us

ACKNOWLEDGMENTS

FOR ME IT ALL BEGINS with family, and that is the starting point for the cascade of gratitude I feel as I reach the finish line on this book. My husband, Broderick Johnson, understood both the power and potential of this project when most people were wondering why I was leaving a trail of little black-and-white postcards everywhere I went. Thanks, "Mr. Michigan," for being my rock and my refueling station on life's magnificent journey. Thanks to my kids, Aja, Norris, and Broddy. You are my greatest source of joy, pride, wonder, and awe. I watched you grow up and "glow up" while working on this project over so many years, and it has been so wonderful to see how you all have learned to walk confidently in your truth while making space for others to lift their voices. May you continue to use your intellect and curiosity to build bridges, and may your curiosity and compassion serve as a beacon for others. There's nothing quite like that big, loud circle of love and merriment that we call the NOJO crew. There were some funny times in the beginning when my younger kids thought their mommy ran something called The Race *CAR* Project and some challenging times for everyone in the family when keeping this project alive took a lot of my time, travel, energy, resources, and patience. Through it all, my family went out of their way to shower me with love, support, good humor, dance music, deep conversation, and the belief that I was building something bigger than all of us. Something that might help people understand the nuances and complexities around race in our current world years from now.

There are those little sayings our parents sprinkle over us when we are kids that wind up staying in our psyche deep into adulthood. My father used to remind me that everyone I meet in life could teach me something important, no matter their station. He led his own life as if trying to prove that point. He talked to everyone he encountered. It was more than just hellos. He struck up conversation and asked questions when he spoke to the grocery story clerk and the bus driver. When we traveled across Canada on vacation when I was around eleven, we wound up seeing bedraggled young men with big backpacks in several Canadian cities. Many of them were young Black men and perhaps that's how Dad knew they were part of that cohort of expats known as draft dodgers—people who had fled their home country to avoid going to war in Vietnam. Dad went out of his way to talk to them. In a few cases, he invited them to join us at a restaurant with the deal that he'd buy them a meal if they told him their story and explained why they fled. I was horrified by this. These dudes were dusty and unkempt. They were strangers. To my young mind, they were a bit scary. But all these years later, the message in those encounters stays with me. Listening is an act of courage and a measure of grace. Both my parents were postal workers, as was my maternal grandfather, so my mother has a special jolt of enthusiasm for this project that began with postcards drifting through the tentacles of America's mail delivery system. Thanks, Mom, for believing in me and teaching me how to be tenacious and tough without losing my "Minnesota Nice" veneer. Thanks for giving me a love of words (and of Wordle!), an appreciation for muscular storytelling, and for that little piece of paper you gave me when I left for college with a potent quote from Eleanor Roosevelt that read: " No one can make you feel inferior without your consent." Amen to that.

My two big sisters, Cindy and Marguerite, gave me an early love of books. Wish they were still here to hold this one in their hands. Special thanks to my "cousibs" (cousins who feel like siblings), Tracey and Rick Newberry and Christine Braziel, who help keep our family stable and strong, especially when I had my shoulder hard up against the wheel. Love and hugs to my extended family of nieces, nephews, in-laws, cousins, aunts, uncles, and loved ones. To the generation of young folks in our family, including Carlos, Carniesha, Dwight, Moon, Tamar, Jared, Marilena, Stephanie, Isa, Tetteh, Justin, Sophia, Spencer, Kayla Grace, Yaa-Fobi, Olivia, Bryn, and Carter, I hope your lights continue to shine bright.

If you have enjoyed what you have seen in these pages or at The Race Card Project website (www.theracecardproject.com), then join me in a praise song for Melissa Bear, my fourteen-year partner in this effort. Fate brought us together quite by accident but immediately we clicked, and Melissa has been the fuel, the steam, the heat, the heart, and the special sauce that has helped this effort grow into something that is bigger, stronger, richer, and more meaningful than we could have imagined. Fearless when the mountain is steep. Focused and even funny when it feels like chainsaws are raining down from the sky. I am forever grateful for your skills, stamina, vision, problem-solving abilities, potential-spotting efficiencies, good humor, and great friendship. Love you so very much. Thanks also to everyone who has worked on the tiny but mighty TRCP team over the past decade and a half, including design and web wizard Adrian Kinloch, who crafted our website and brought so much passion and compassion to our work; wordsmith and strategist Amrit Dhilon; producer extraordinaire Walter Ray Watson; Michael Goldberg, Peter Brown, and the team of wizards at QWF who keep our online presence humming; and David Walters, who gets an extra sprinkling of gratitude and confetti for his careful eye, outreach, research, editorial acumen, and the beautiful spirit he brings to every room he enters.

Gail Ross is so much more than my book agent. She is my friend, consigliere, and mentor who brings a fierce and delightful mama bear energy to all she does, and came to understand that where this book project was concerned, when it's right, it's right on time. Deep thanks for always being in my corner.

Thanks to my editor Mindy Marques. I loved working with you on this project. Your skills strengthened this work and helped it sparkle in a special way. Thanks also to Priscilla Painton, to Dawn Davis who championed this book from the beginning, to Jonathan Karp who believed in the vision, to Hana Park who kept her cool and remained amazingly efficient and focused even while reminding me that this was the second most complicated design and production process she had ever worked on. (I am still wondering about the book that topped that list . . .) Thanks to Jason Snyder who did beautiful, painstaking, delicious work in designing a book that jumps off the page and into the heart. Thanks also to Lewelin Polanco, Paul Dippolito, and to Jackie Seow for hanging in there while we found exactly the right notes to strike. Thanks also to Yvette Grant, Irene Kheradi, Julia Prosser, Anne Tate Pearce, Chonise Bass, Stephen Bedford, Tyanni Niles, Sienna Faris, Imany Seymour, and Elisa Rivlin.

A special thunder strike of gratitude and awe to Kadir Nelson, whose painting on the cover of this book is so beautiful that I have to catch my breath every time I see it. You are a genius in the way that you use your colorful brush strokes and your great big heart to help us see the best of ourselves in all of our splendid complexity. You also use your art to help us see and understand the knots in our history. Never has that been more important. You are a spectacular artist and an extraordinary human being. And to Jungmiwha Bullock, a note of appreciation for understanding the power and potential in this partnership.

Lisa Dickey provided skill and precision in helping me get organized and get my arms around the enormity of this work at a crucial moment. I kept hearing that you were one of the best in the biz and after working with you even for a brief time, I detect no lies.

Book writing is a team sport, and I am blessed to have worked with a great crew: fact-checker and researcher Brad Scriber, transcriber Deb Reeb, and researcher Karl Evanzz.

Michael Duffy is the best editor a columnist could ask for—always asking the right questions, pushing in the right directions, and pulling the best out of anyone lucky enough to work in his orbit. Thanks for your ear and your patience in helping me think through the most potent ways to tackle the hidden truths and hardened narratives of race.

Thanks to my colleagues in the opinion section of the *Washington Post* for always making me sharper and smarter and certainly better informed about our world. Thanks also to the team at National Geographic for supporting and spotlighting my work at The Race Card Project. I am so deeply honored to have been chosen as a National Geographic Storytelling Explorer at a key moment on my journey. Special thanks to Susan Goldberg, Debra Simmons, John Hoeffel, and Jean Case. A special shout-out and big dollop of gratitude to my former colleagues at NPR who created a home for TRCP on the radio almost a decade ago, especially Walter Ray Watson, Steve Inskeep, Madhulika Sikka, Chuck Holmes, Tracey Wahl, and Rhonda Ray.

I won the lottery when it comes to finding a strong and solid circle of fellow travelers on life's journey. Thanks to Sharon Malone and Eric Holder and Lisa and Kenny Jackson for holding me tight and holding me strong. Our village is indeed a thing of wonder. Thanks to Barack and Michelle Obama for friendship and a steady dose of wise counsel and deep laughter. Your candid thoughts at a key moment helped me find the right pathway forward and your constant encouragement always tops off my tank. Found family is such a beautiful thing. Thanks to my beloved posse of friends, Jose, Tichi, Richard, Paula, Van, Elizabeth, Kelly, Matrice, Ron, Denielle, Cornell, Valerie, Lisa, Kia, Demond, Debra, Toni, Dwight, Michelle, Harry, Marcia, Madhulika, Cheryl, Sheryll, Susan, Ian, Sonari, Heidi, Sherrilyn, Andy, Sarah, James, Kathleen, Andy, Dawn, Angela, A'Lelia, Athelia, Argelia, Dez, Asha, Cy, Ann, Ertharin, Scott B., Tia, Jamilah, Kevin, Sonya, Robert, Anthony, Melody, Heidi, Shaun, Ken, Eric, Cheryl, Laurie, and Joe. Abundant gratitude to my amazing circle of sister friends . . . the garden that sustains and supports me, makes me laugh, makes me strong, helps me find my best self always and in ALL ways.

To Gwen Ifill, thank you for imploring me to stick with this crazy project when few understood my obsession with the 6-word stories that were filling up my inbox. Miss you so very much. You would have been my first reader. Somehow, I know you are still looking over my shoulder.

Thanks to early supporters and cheerleaders who helped fertilize this project with partnerships, atta-girls, funding, expertise, advice, and elevation. Martha Jones, Mary Sue Coleman, and the University of Michigan. Rita Radostitz and the University of Oregon, Laysha Ward and the Target Foundation, Darren Walker, Elizabeth Alexander, Farai Chideya and The Ford Foundation, Jeff and Tricia Raikes, Bert Ifill, Gisele Becker, Sharon and John Hoffman, Bunny Copaken, Karol Mason, Katie Freeman, Heather Foster, David Seidman, Brad Meltzer, Tayari Jones, Sean Gibbons, Tom Kartsotis, Marjo Talbot and the community at Maret, Judge Claudia Rickert Isom, Kerri Miller at Minnesota Public Radio, Lonnie Bunch, Walter Isaacson, Kitty Boone, Eric Liu, Denielle Baussan, Elliot Gerson and The Aspen Institute, Jeff Goldberg, Brooke Anderson and Pivotal Ventures, the Shorenstein Center on Media, Politics and Public Policy at Harvard University, the Sine Institute of Policy & Politics at American University, St. James Episcopal Church and Zion Baptist Church in Marietta, Georgia (and Patricia Templeton and Cindy Brown for capturing that experience), Elizabeth Glidden, Andrea Jenkins, R.T. Rybak, and the One Minneapolis, One Read program. Thanks also to our corporate partners who put wind in our sails and allowed us to create spaces for courageous conversations, even, or especially, when people talked across different experiences and perspectives, including Apple, Accenture, Capital One, and the Tory Burch Foundation.

Special thanks to Mitch Kapor and Freada Kapor Klein, who are changing the world for the better every day by opening doors and creating equal access to opportunity. They live their values, and we are all the better for it. Thankful for your support and friendship.

A note of gratitude also goes to the academics, lawyers, and researchers who provided expertise, including Alondra Nelson, Thelma Golden, Susan Neiman, Angela Tucker, Clarence Jones, Arum Chung, Michelle Hughes, Ken Burns, Bijan Bayne, Kristin Pauker, Brian Nosek, Randall Kennedy, Nell Painter, Liz Raleigh, Diana Ramey Berry and the Minnesota Historical Society, the Minnesota Indian Affairs Council, and the Minnesota History Center.

I am still in awe of the hundreds of teachers, professors, instructors, and TAs who have used The Race Card Project in their classrooms, workshops, stage productions, and art studios. In some cases, I don't even know how you found The Race Card Project, but you did, and you introduced it to students and congregants and community members and used it to create networks of candor, vulnerability, and fellowship. I have a special place in my heart for the institutions that have used TRCP repeatedly—Ms. Sarah Tunik's classroom at Bishop O'Dowd High School in Oakland, American Canyon High School in Napa Valley's agricultural center, Anne Arundel Community College (with a shout-out to Gina Finelli), Corning Community College in New York's Finger Lakes region, Trinity Valley Community College in Athens, Texas, Spokane Falls Community College, Old Dominion College in Norfolk, Virginia, California Baptist University, Lehigh University, Monmouth University, Syracuse University, and the University of Richmond.

Special thanks also to the librarians who have shown so much love and support for TRCP, and have cooked up wonderful ways to use our work to engage their communities in places such as Salt Lake City, Duluth, Denver, and Nashville. And I am indebted to the museums that embraced this project and used it to find new ways to connect with the public, including the Hood Museum in Hanover, New Hampshire, the Brooklyn Museum, the Martha's Vineyard Museum, and the Carnegie Museums in Pittsburgh, with a special thanks to Cecille Shellman.

Big thanks to the all-star team at Keppler Speakers, including Francine Martineau, Theo Moll, and Chris Clifford.

Thanks to Brian Stauffer for his beautiful work as a graphic artist and Chris Rukan for his wisdom around visual storytelling elements.

Thanks to the team at the UPS store for collecting and protecting our postcards and to all those printers across the country that printed mountains of cards year over year.

Deep appreciation to James Bohan and Martin Oliva. Appreciate the friendship that has grown over years of working together. You keep the infrastructure running so the words can flow.

And a hat tip and a fountain of boundless regard to all of the people in my life who are there for me when I am standing in need of prayer, advice, a soothing shoulder, a hungry ear, or something good to eat.

Much love to all of you.

WITH GRATITUDE

THANK YOU to every single person who has contributed their 6-word story to The Race Card Project. I respect your time and your courage, and I cherish all the stories you have shared. They to me are like gems. I treasure them all and I have endeavored to make sure that my work honors your decision to give voice to your individual truths, even when your views or perspectives clash with my own.

Some of you wrote your words on postcards with pen, pencil, or crayon. Some of you sat in the glow of a computer with fingers dancing across a keyboard. There were those who wrote out letters in longhand and placed them in an envelope because the postcards just did not have enough space to hold the words that came spilling forth. And a torrent of people used their thumbs to tap out their stories on cell phones or BlackBerrys (that's how long we have been at this!).

I love diving into the inbox every day. We take the time to read your stories and, as time allows, reach out to learn more or collect oral histories. You have touched our hearts, tickled our curiosity, and expanded our minds. Your 6-word stories have stacked up over time like individual bricks, growing in scope and volume to build a bridge toward the greater understanding of other lives and other realms. Special thanks to all the people in this book who shared their stories, their photos, and a piece of themselves, often staring down painful memories or parts of their life that are not easy to digest. I regret that I could not share the entire archive in this book. It just simply was not possible to include the hundreds of thousands of stories we have collected over time. To those whose stories are not in these pages, know that your words and perspectives are prized and your willingness to share your candid thoughts on such a thorny issue might just influence or inform another person today, or maybe years from now, because the vast collection of stories in this archive will indeed help storytellers and cultural explorers of the future better understand the unique moment we live in right now.

· · ·

Just one more thing . . .

When Betty Reid Soskin was working as the oldest active park ranger for the National Park Service until the age of 100, she focused on telling the stories of people who were traditionally left out of the narratives around World War II. The woman known as "Ranger Betty" wanted to make sure that the people who visited the World War II Home Front National Historical Park in Richmond, California, learned about the experiences of Blacks, Hispanics, Latinos, Asians, and Native Americans who served in the armed forces, fighting for freedoms overseas that they themselves could not enjoy in a segregated America. She wanted visitors who had perhaps heard of Rosie the Riveter to know that there were also many women of color who worked in factories to support the war effort. She was sharing history but also sharing *her* story. Soskin was in the Boilermakers union during World War II, working as a shipyard clerk for an all-Black auxiliary.

Betty Reid Soskin is one of my sheroes, and my devotion to this project—and my deep gratitude for all those whose stories have fueled this effort—is captured in the words that Soskin cited as the mantra for her work:

"What gets remembered is a function of who's in the room doing the remembering." Soskin said.

I hope my role as a storyteller and story collector has created an entryway for more people to enter that proverbial room, so their vast river of stories is shared, studied, considered . . . and, yes, remembered.

Share your story because you never know who might need to hear it.

With endless gratitude,
Michele Norris

IMAGE CREDITS

Permissions for all of the photos that accompany 6-word stories were granted by individual authors of those submissions.

Find and explore source notes for essays and stories online at www.theracecardproject.com.